2/11/9

To all at Villiers Park,

You've witnessed the prolonged birth of this!

All Best Wishes,

Dominic (Shellard)

Harold Hobson: Witness and Judge

Harold Hobson: Witness and Judge

The Theatre Criticism of Harold Hobson

Dominic Shellard

KEELE UNIVERSITY PRESS

First published in 1995 by
Keele University Press
Keele, Staffordshire

© Dominic Shellard and
respective copyright owners
of quoted matter

Composed by
Keele University Press
Printed by Hartnolls
Bodmin, England

ISBN 1 85331 154 5

Contents

	Acknowledgements	6
	Introduction	7
1	The Apprenticeship: 1927–1939	9
2	The War Years: 1939–1945	37
3	The Accession: 1945–July 1947	57
4	The Foreign Revelation: July 1947–1954	73
5	The Watershed: 1955	107
6	The Dam Bursts: 1956–1958	133
7	The Dramatists Consolidate: 1959–1967	173
8	The Grand Old Man of the Theatre: 1968–1988	201
	Notes	217
	Bibliography	239
	Index	245

Acknowledgements

This book is dedicated to my father and mother, whose love and encouragement have made it possible.

Without the generous support of the following individuals and institutions, I would never have been able to embark upon, and then complete, this project. I am extremely grateful to: the Old Alleynian Endowment Fund; Bill Cater and *The Sunday Times*; my anonymous benefactor in the House of Lords; Charles Sanderson; St Peter's College; my tutor, Francis Warner; Gilbert McKay; the Worshipful Company of Leathersellers; Mary McGee and the *Christian Science Monitor*; Alan Ayckbourn; Michael Billington; Richard Jackson; Colin Chambers; Thelma Barratt; Liz Boyles; Jessica Shellard; Sonya Shellard; Jack Reading and the Society for Theatre Research; Keele University Press; Angus Easson; Matthew Gallon and Queen's Park Rangers Football Club.

The author acknowledges the kind co-operation of *The Sunday Times* in allowing many of its Theatre Reviews to be included in this work.

Introduction

Theatre critics have exerted a profound, but barely acknowledged, influence on the evolution of twentieth-century British theatre. Whilst accepted by most in the theatre profession as an inevitable presence and a necessary evil – necessary, in that they generate publicity, the lifeblood of a successful run; evil, because they are often perceived as failed and envious practitioners with unenlightened views to propagate – there have been no attempts to consider the complete *oeuvre* of a single critic during this period. This is all the more surprising given the unquestioning manner in which theatre historiographers utilize contemporary reviews to authenticate their opinions, with these reviews frequently being passed off as factual testimony. Historians working in any other field question the reliability of their source material before they begin to formulate academic judgements, but few drama specialists consider whether a theatre critic's views have been shaped by political, economic or editorial influences, let alone personal, religious or emotional sensibilities, or even the nature of the publication that they write for (daily, Sunday, weekly?) and the constrictions of the space that their editors permit them. These omissions are even more incredible when one considers how vibrant the British theatre has been in the last fifty years. Aside from Kathleen Tynan's biography of her husband, *The Life of Kenneth Tynan* (1988), which inevitably foregrounds this brilliant critic's flamboyant lifestyle, consideration of theatre criticism has rarely moved beyond jejune anthologies of disparate reviews, self-interested and star-struck 'insider' accounts about what it is *really* like to be a West End critic, or Vladimir and Estragon's estimation of the craft in *Waiting for Godot*, where the most wounding insult that they can hurl at each other is a grinding 'Crritic!'. Whilst a thoroughly researched and dispassionate account of post-war British theatre criticism as a whole still remains to be written, this book, by considering the career of the most important British theatre critic of the second half of the twentieth century, represents a small step in correcting the marginalization by academics of the practice of recording for posterity ephemeral dramatic performances.

Between 1947 and 1976 Harold Hobson was seated at the end of an aisle in the stalls at almost every first night of note in the London theatre. Unable to walk very far, even with the aid of his walking-stick, he rarely left his seat at the interval, preferring to enjoy the company and conversation of those friends and colleagues who were kind enough to come over. When he did struggle to his feet it was invariably for a highly important reason. During the Bay of Pigs crisis in 1962, when the world trembled on the brink of a nuclear conflagration, he astonished those around him by hobbling across the aisle to Kenneth Tynan, his protégé and great professional rival, and in measured and sonorous tones, addressing him thus: 'Kenneth, we may not be alive tomorrow, but before I depart this world I have one thing that I have to say to you.' He leant closer, the auditorium growing suddenly quieter, aware of the potential momentousness of this confrontation between the two critical titans. Would there be a public row about an unfavourable allusion, a misplaced phrase or a contentious opinion? Which publication would triumph in this particular battle, the older, venerable but occasionally reactionary *Sunday Times*, or the younger, more dynamic but sometimes erratic *Observer*? The metaphorical battle that took place every Sunday morning in the late 1950s and early 1960s and was eagerly digested by thousands of readers, stimulated by the atmosphere of intellectual debate and the invariably antithetical views of the two men, appeared to be about to be enacted for real. There was a pause, then Hobson spoke in a hushed, portentous voice: 'I never did much like Brecht.'

The comic bathos of this statement, gently parodying his own intense – and well-known – dislike of the German playwright whom Tynan inevitably heralded as the new dramatic saviour, is quintessential Hobson, both as a man and as a judicious and pertinent stylist. Witty, urbane and kind; fiercely proud of his Yorkshire roots and deeply respectful of Establishment values; severely restricted in movement and fiercely impressed by athletic prowess; sustained both by his faith in Christian Science and the devoted love of his first wife Elizabeth, the fascinating diversity of Hobson's personal life is mirrored by the eclecticism of his theatrical tastes. Crippled by polio at the age of 7, it is a remarkable testimony to his stoicism that he was able to leave the protection of his parents in Sheffield at all, let alone win a place at Oxford, be taken on to the staff of the *Christian Science Monitor* in the late 1920s, and then succeed James Agate in 1947 as the most powerful theatre critic in Britain. This study, by considering his entire written output from 1922 to 1988 as well as the significant events of his life, aims to explain how Hobson's critical views were formulated, to assess their significance in shaping the evolution of twentieth-century drama and to consider whether this critic, who for so long has been judged as the tortoise of theatre critics, can be judged by posterity to have outstripped the hares.

Chapter 1

The Apprenticeship: 1927–1939

One of Harold Hobson's earliest published articles, 'Impartial History?', written whilst still an undergraduate at Oriel College, Oxford and appearing on the educational page of the *Christian Science Monitor* on 13 December 1927, questioned the premise expressed in a recent British parliamentary debate that 'the teaching of history should be impartial and not propagandist'. With the self-confidence of the student convinced that his future lies in academic life (Hobson states in his autobiography, *Indirect Journey*, that his subsequent work as a drama critic was a second-choice career[1]), he proceeded to dispute the notion that a partisan approach to historical analysis is necessarily a dangerous attitude to adopt:

> … whatever may be the essential qualities of great history, impartiality is not one of them. But we might go even further, and say that not only is impartiality unnecessary, but is actually unattainable. In dealing with any complex event, it is impossible for the historian to act only like a truthful witness: since the size of books is limited he cannot give all the facts, but is bound to select those which seem to him relevant: and what will seem relevant to one man will inevitably, since opinions differ, appear irrelevant and misleading to another.[2]

This inescapable requirement of the historian to be selective, frequently reflecting his own interests, is then portrayed as a positive virtue – a belief that was greatly to influence Hobson's approach to theatre criticism – and it is with characteristic elegance that he rounds off this seminal article with the following defence of the informed, heartfelt opinion, since it will act as a beneficial catalyst in the development of a cultured society:

> Our conclusion then would appear to be this: Macaulay, Froude, Mommsen, Acton and Freeman wrote history as well as it is ever likely to be written; but they never reached even an approximate impartiality; from which it would seem that the British Parliament went somehow wrong in its consideration of this subject. Impartiality is, after all, only a negative virtue; and it is the positive and living virtues that are necessary in the writing of history as well as in the making of it. If we make sure that a historian is sincere, well informed and of an understanding mind, we can leave the question of impartiality

to take care of itself. His conclusions on any subject will be valuable even if we disagree with them: all the more valuable, perhaps, if we do disagree with them, for the study of history is cultural, and it is the mark of a cultured mind to be able to evaluate one theory against another, to compare one interpretation of things with a second, and to choose the better.[3]

If one were to substitute the word 'historian' with the phrase 'theatre critic' in this article, the piece would read as Hobson's manifesto on the art and purpose of theatre criticism. Hobson's second-class degree prevented him from becoming an academic, but his training as a historian inculcated certain values that are evident in this piece and which remained in his writing throughout his career as a theatre critic. The pedagogical slant of the article; the recognition that an informed appraisal of facts, intelligent selectivity, is necessary for the formation of intelligent opinion; the belief that the astute professional, be he a historian or a theatre critic, can enhance the development of the field which he closely observes; the conviction that impartiality is less important than the possession of a 'sincere, well-informed and ... understanding mind'; and, above all, the Hegelian belief that the positive clash of ideas and opinions will result in a progressive synthesis, are all traits that are evident in Hobson's fifty and more years of theatrical reviewing. Even in 1990 Hobson was as eager as ever to recognize the formative influence of his historical training:

> *HH*: ... My theory of the theatre was that on each visit to the theatre ... something happens. Something happens to the critic's mind and heart and the thing becomes a sort of historical event. Therefore my criticisms, I should say, are records of how I feel at a particular evening, at a particular play, that they are the foundation of a historical record more than the passing of a judgement. They're the narration of something that happened to me in the theatre rather than a judgement passed on the merits of the thing that I was seeing.
> *DMS*: Do you think that stems from your training as a historian?
> *HH*: I think it probably does, yes.
> *DMS*: How do you think your training helped you in your work as a critic?
> *HH*: Well, a historian recalls what happens to him when he considers certain events in history and writes them down. I regarded what was happening to me in the theatre as the basis for a historic record.[4]

Hobson's earliest journalistic writing did not immediately begin with the compilation of this 'historic record' of theatre criticisms. Whilst still at Oriel, Hobson had become friendly with a Rhodes Scholar by the name of Erwin Canham, who then occupied a subsidiary position on the Boston-based *Christian Science Monitor*. This paper, founded in 1908 to counter the sensationalism of other American dailies and intended less as a religious propaganda organ for Christian Science than as a serious-minded afternoon daily (although testimonies of healings brought about by Christian Science practitioners had featured in early editions),[5] had quickly grown in popularity in the United States between 1908 and 1918. By eschewing crime and disaster stories, it was able to devote more space to articles about Washington, foreign affairs and, in particular, literature, music, art and the theatre, and this cultured format attracted an initial readership of over 120,000. After a slight dip in readership at the beginning of the 1920s following a management dispute, the paper's fortunes were revived under the editorship of Willis J. Abbot, with the publication's finest editor eventually proving to be Hobson's great university friend, Erwin Canham. He joined the staff in 1925 and worked his way up from being Washington and foreign correspondent to becoming managing editor in 1940, editor in 1945 and eventually editor-in-chief in 1964. By the 1970s the paper had been voted one of the top six American dailies by 130 US publishers, and in 1971 it was able to boast of 275,000 readers in the US and 12,000 readers in the UK – its negatives being flown from Boston for printing in New Jersey, Chicago, Los Angeles and London.[6]

Circulation figures for the *Christian Science Monitor* in Britain in the 1920s are difficult to ascertain, but some indication can be gleaned from the fact that a *Report on the British Press* by the Political and Economic Planning group, published in 1946, gave details of a survey that it had conducted in four Oxfordshire and Gloucestershire villages in 1935 which revealed that, out of 214 households, only 1 had taken the *Christian Science Monitor*.[7] Even given that the paper was likely to be read by Christian Scientists at urban Christian Science reading-rooms, the publication clearly had a limited reach. Nevertheless, as a follower of the religion, Hobson would certainly have been aware of the paper's existence – it had, after all, been a policy of the paper's founders to build its worldwide distribution as quickly as possible. Its Thanksgiving issue in 1910, for example, carried seven tons of newsprint to London.[8] In 1927 Canham introduced Hobson to Willis J. Abbott, then one of the four members of the editorial board, who had travelled to Britain from America on a business trip. Hobson was invited to write what he later termed a 'speculative article',[9] presumably 'Impartial History?', and was then encouraged, on coming down from Oxford, to begin to submit articles as a freelance writer.

A year after 'Impartial History?', in January 1929, Hobson started to write short editorials that filled 'a gap in the English staff at the newspaper'[10] and whose content was left to his own discretion.[11] The subject-matter of the ninety-four editorials which he wrote in this first year (and which earned him two guineas apiece[12]) testifies to Hobson's eclectic tastes. His choice ranged from stained-glass windows to Scottish nationalism, public oratory to the promotion of judges, historical legends to the revival of waterways and from manual labour to the British water supply.

However, it is possible to identify, in the midst of this diverse mix, one field which particularly interested him – namely, that of the arts.

Every branch of the arts merited Hobson's attention as editorial subject-matter in his first year of journalism. On 30 March he writes that middle-class audiences will only learn to appreciate classical music when they are properly exposed to it,[13] and a similar sense of frustration at the lack of high-quality public outlets for the arts is evident on 30 July, when he discusses the projected closure of the Covent Garden Opera House in 1932[14] and the insipid theatrical fare exported from London to the provinces.[15] The movies are considered, too, in the light of the considerable public disquiet that had arisen after the introduction of sound to films in 1928. Although the problems of amplifying sound sufficiently for an audience and synchronizing it with the film image had almost been solved by the late 1920s, people were still worried about the effect that the 'talkies' were likely to have on language, grammar, dialect and the silent film industry. Hobson, however, was convinced that the 'talkies' would flourish after the initial setbacks and he was later to champion their merit in a debate with Erwin Canham in a 1932 article entitled 'Should the Movies Talk?'.[16]

Two other branches of the arts are covered in the editorials of 1929. Literature is a notable interest, given Hobson's championing of public libraries,[17] his defence of detective stories,[18] the comparison of the respective merits of Wordsworth and Browning,[19] his belief that the poet laureate has a right to refuse to produce verses to order on state occasions,[20] and his dismissal of the worth of the *Daily Telegraph*'s attempt to weigh up the respective merits of Goldsmith and Johnson[21] (since 'to laud one writer by depreciating another is but a poor method of giving praise'), yet it is the editorials on theatrical matters that, even at this early stage, bring forth the writing of the greatest conviction. 'Drama in the Schools',[22] for example, possessed the additional advantage of linking the theatre with Hobson's other prime interest, education. Having begun by terming drama 'an intellectual force of the first order', the writer proceeds to lament its absence from the schools of the day, since it can fulfil important academic functions. School drama encourages public speaking; 'it is an effective method of giving to young people an understanding of the most important and illustrious period of English Literature'; 'it is a remedy for the shyness and diffidence by which many people are handicapped'; 'it trains an appreciative audience for the Little Theatre movement, and it may set upon the path to future distinction the feet of a budding Irving.' Hobson was to retain this belief in the pedagogical value of the theatre throughout his career as a critic, its most visible manifestation being when he served as an adjudicator for the annual drama festival of the National Union of Students from 1956 to 1967.

Although he had had sufficient contact with the theatre to be able to evaluate the challenge to the stage that the improvement of film techniques would represent,[23] Hobson's first year as a journalist primarily produced editorials on a wide variety of topics. He did, however, review a radiocast that featured George Bernard Shaw[24] (the reverential tone of which was soon to give way to an intelligent scepticism on Hobson's part) and he witnessed the publication of five of his theatre criticisms. Of these, two are worthy of mention. Hobson's very first published criticism of a play in the *Christian Science Monitor* was a review of the production of Pirandello's new work, *Lazzaro*, at the Huddersfield Repertory Theatre, starring the doyen of provincial audiences, Donald Wolfit.[25] The article is typical of many of Hobson's early reviews in that it is short, precise, factual (the play was 'enthusiastically received') and unambitious (the work did not include 'too varied a lot of ideas'). Ashley Dukes's adaptation of Lion Feuchtwanger's novel, *Jew Süss*, at the Opera House, Manchester two months later, on the other hand, drew forth a more interesting reaction from the fledgling critic, in which one can see the first tentative steps towards the development of a critical style. The play is flawed, he claims, because the character of Naomi is introduced too late into the action and the characterization is not clearly delineated:

> It does not matter that the play fails to give the impression of profound mastery of the petty politics of a small German state that the book conveyed, but it is regrettable that it does not reveal more convincingly the transformation of Süss's character.[26]

But this structural flaw is redeemed somewhat by the 'beautiful interpretation' of the part of Naomi. Here Hobson not only recognizes the talent of the young Peggy Ashcroft, he demonstrates one of the most important facets of the critic's art – the ability to distinguish between the interpretation of a part by a performer and the script as written by the playwright. This review, therefore, is the first practicable demonstration of Hobson's desire to found a 'historic record' that emphasizes his own emotional reaction to the plays that he witnesses in addition to outlining the notable events of the evening.

Although the theatre criticism of Harold Hobson does not begin on a regular basis until 1931, when he was appointed the London drama critic of the *Christian Science Monitor*, these initial two years of journalistic activity formed an important apprenticeship. They helped to broaden the perspective of this remarkably stoical and courageous young man, whose childhood had been constricted both emotionally and physically. Born on 4 August 1904 at Thorpe Hedley, near Rotherham, the only child of Jacob and Minnie Hobson, Hobson's first seven years were dominated by his large number of relatives, his father's unpredictable temperament and his love of football. Jacob Hobson, an insurance agent, was one of eleven children and Hobson describes in his autobiography, *Indirect Journey*, some of the entertaining foibles of his uncles, in particular those of Uncle Tom, who delivered lectures for over forty years whilst pretending to be a D. Litt. and whose intellectual curiosity proved a constant source of inspiration. Hobson later stated that 'My father never read a book through in his life, but because of Tom he revered the idea of reading – this was vital to my childhood.'[27] As a young child, Hobson's relationship with his father was coloured by the parent's 'evil temper',[28] and it was from his mother that he received the most love and support:

> Without my mother's devotion, her ability, and her blind, uninstructed conviction (for which she had little tangible evidence) that I had one of the largest brains ever issued to a member of the human race, my career would have ended several years before it in fact began.[29]

Amusingly, the tenacious mother later sought to prove this conviction by taking Harold to visit a phrenologist, such was her belief in his genius. What was less incontrovertible was the young child's fascination with football. The proximity of the Hobson family's early residence in Warner Road, Sheffield to Hillsborough meant that 'some of the happiest days of my youth were spent in the Sheffield Wednesday football ground',[30] and even in his eighties Hobson was able to recall the matches that he had attended at this time.

This delight in physical exertion was shattered, however, for the seven-year-old Hobson in March 1912, when he awoke one morning to discover that he was paralysed on his right side, down, from, and including, the hip. He had been struck by polio. His parents, who were faithful adherents of the Church of England, could not comprehend why this had happened to them and, after a succession of conventional doctors had pronounced the case hopeless (one, a Doctor Birks, stating that Harold would be bedridden for the rest of his life and unable to earn his own living[31]), they turned in their desperation to the religion of Christian Science, after Jacob Hobson had discovered a Christian Science reading-room in Pinfold Street in the centre of Sheffield.[32]

At that time Christian Science was a recent but increasingly popular religion. Founded in 1879, when fifteen students of Mary Baker Eddy met with their teacher in Boston, Massachusetts to 'organize a church designed to commemorate the word and works of our Master which should reinstate primitive Christianity and its lost element of healing',[33] a distinctive – although not exclusive – part of Christian Science is its belief that physical disease as well as sin can be cured by spiritual means alone. In 1866 at Lynn, Massachusetts Mary Baker Eddy had recovered almost instantly from severe injury after reading the account of Jesus healing the man with palsy in the gospel of Matthew,[34] and the discovery of what she later termed 'Christian Science' ensued from this incident:

> I knew the Principle of all harmonious Mind-action to be God, and that cures were produced in primitive Christian healing by holy, uplifting faith; but I must know the science of this healing, and I won my way to absolute conclusions through divine revelation, reason and demonstration.[35]

Several years of study then followed before, in 1875, she published the Christian Science textbook, *Science and Health* (revised by her for the last time as *Science and Health, With Key to the Scriptures* in 1907), which is read in connection with the Bible in Christian Science services and can be found in all Christian Science reading-rooms. Initially, Baker Eddy hoped that her discovery would be accepted by the existing Churches, but by 1879 it had become clear that a distinct Church needed to be founded to counter scepticism and to maintain the purity of its teaching and practice. Therefore, The Church of Christ, Scientist was established in 1879 in Boston, becoming the Christian Science Mother Church, The First Church of Christ, Scientist in 1892 (other churches world-wide being regarded as branches) – such was the growth in the new creed's popularity. Indeed, by 1950 there were 3,006 branches of the Church world-wide, with 2,251 in the United States and 344 in the United Kingdom.[36] In the 1980s and 1990s, however, the credibility of the Church has been threatened both by well-publicized cases of children dying agonizing deaths after being deprived of conventional medical treatment by their Christian Science parents, and allegations of corruption amongst the board of directors, a body appointed to run the church by Baker Eddy after her death in 1910.

The central tenet of Christian Science is the distinction between what is real and what is apparent or seemingly real. Mary Baker Eddy explained this in the following way:

> All reality is in God and His creation, harmonious and eternal. That which he creates is good, and He makes all that is made. Therefore the only reality of sin, sickness or death is the awful fact that unrealities seem real to human, erring belief, until God strips off their disguise. They are not true, because they are not of God.[37]

A Christian Scientist consequently believes that, since man was created in God's image, sin and sickness are included within a range of mortal errors to be corrected and overcome by a scientific understanding of God, and it was to this 'scientific system of divine healing'[38] that Hobson's parents turned in 1912 in an attempt to help their son. Although no dramatic improvement occurred, Hobson always felt that he owed much to the discovery of this new spirituality, stating in 1978 that 'had not my parents discovered Christian Science ... my life would have been ruined'.[39] A Christian Science practitioner, Stanley Sydenham, came to talk to Hobson about the 'unreality' of the disease and each week asked him to learn a text from *Science and Health*. 'Gradually the miracle happened'[40] and within a month of Dr Birks giving up on the patient, the young boy was able to get out of bed. Friends rallied round. The son of his father's boss, a Mr Gibson, came to entertain him and impersonated the melodramatic actor, John Martin Harvey, whom he had seen performing the roles of Oedipus and Sydney Carton in London. Hobson was not to forget this. At the age of 10, Clara Richardson, an elementary schoolteacher who attended their local Christian Science church, came to teach him for an hour on Saturdays, encouraging him to read Scott; and the big breakthrough came with the passing of the test set by Sheffield Education Authority to ascertain whether he should be educated at home or attend a special school. Hobson passed by explaining the meaning of the word 'vehemently' and for the next eleven years the family resided in a new house in the centre of Sheffield.

Hobson's immersion in Christian Science during his early teens was to have a profound influence on his later criticism. He developed a taste for rich and profound oratory –

> I have great cause to be grateful that in Christian Science churches there is much public reading of the Bible. This reading of the Bible in the Authorized Version has been one of the formative influences of my taste, and has considerably moulded my professional career.[41]

– and he discovered, through the lessons of the First Reader, Arthur Allen, a touchstone that he would employ in his later critical writing:

> When he read Paul's admonition, 'If there be any virtue, and if there be any praise, think on these things,' he taught me the central lesson of criticism, a lesson appreciated by Balzac, and by me never forgotten. It is a good lesson, for what matters in a creative artist is not what he does wrong, but what he does right.[42]

But the intellectual stimulation that the services provided also emphasized the cosseted and over-protected environment that he had been compelled to endure on account of his disability, and therefore, at the age of 15, he left the house on crutches on his own for the first time in nine years to enquire of the headmaster of the Pupil Teaching Centre (later Sheffield Grammar School), Joseph Batey, whether he might attend his much-respected institution. Batey, clearly impressed by Hobson's intellectual capacity and mental fortitude, accepted him as a student, instructing the school doctor only to examine Hobson's chest, thereby permitting him to satisfy the health requirements of the school. Hobson's delayed educational career had now begun in earnest. In 1923, aged 18, he sat for the Northern Universities' Board matriculation, obtaining the necessary credits in English, History, Latin and French, and then proceeded to win a scholarship to Sheffield University. However, having read Matthew Arnold's *The Scholar Gypsy*, his thoughts turned to Oxford and he wrote to the Provost of Oriel College, Lancelot Ridley Phelps, enquiring whether there might be a place for him even though he was lame and could only expect to live on £20 a year. The provost, replying that they were full up for 1923, nevertheless encouraged him to apply for 1924. This Hobson did, and he was accepted for a 1924 entry. On arriving at Oriel in 1924, he was alone for the first time in his life and had already borne out Erwin Canham's much later judgement that 'His is a success story more typically associated with the New World.'[43]

Hobson's meeting with his fellow Christian Scientist Canham was perhaps the most important event in his career at Oxford, in that it was Canham's introduction to Willis J. Abbott that launched Hobson's career in journalism, but although 'Impartial History?' had been his first published article in the *Christian Science Monitor*, it did not represent Hobson's first appearance in print. Several letters in the *Sheffield Daily Telegraph* testify to his youthful support of the Labour party. The first, published on 18 October 1922, when he was just 18, attacked the newspaper's anti-Labour bias. The editor's belated response was magisterial: 'Mr Hobson's ... statements ... are a mixture of nonsense and loose phraseology with which we need not concern ourselves.'[44] Hobson's next salvo, compiled with a Sheffield friend, was more assured. Having been attacked by one H. W. Bowers-Broadbent for being Communists, Hobson replied:

> We were particularly pleased to note that 'the policy of the great Conservative Party is framed upon its desire and determination to obliterate such blots in our midst as still exist to be a cause of misery and distress.' As Mr Broadbent anticipated, this came somewhat as a surprise to us; but perhaps that was because we had hitherto judged the Party only by its actions. It had not occurred to us that it might have aspirations it is powerless to realise.[45]

An equally stylish but less leftish tone would suffuse some of Hobson's best criticisms in the years ahead.

Towards the end of his Oxford career, Hobson's eyes were focused not on journalism but on academic life. His failure to achieve a First in History and his rejection for a PhD at Sheffield deprived him of this option, however, and after a two-week visit to London with his mother, during which he visited the offices of the *Christian Science Monitor* in London, he returned home to begin compiling his editorials.

Although Hobson had been a frequent visitor as an undergraduate to the Oxford Playhouse, housed between 1923 and 1929 in the Big Game Museum in the Woodstock Road,[46] and was fortunate enough to have witnessed performances featuring John Gielgud, Flora Robson, Richard Goulden, Glen Byam Shaw, Alan Napier and Tyrone Guthrie, the tone of intellectual curiosity that marks the first two years of his writing for the *Christian Science Monitor* suggests that he wished to broaden the range of his artistic knowledge. Two examples of the type of article that helped to lay the foundations for his critical approach occur in 1931. In 'Happy Ending Realism'[47] he takes issue with the specifically Marxist belief that happy endings are no longer possible amidst the economic wreckage of capitalist societies by pointing out that man has an infinite capacity to make good of the most dismal situations:

> ... surely a realistic novel or ... a realistic film, should represent the gayety and happiness that abound in the world just as much as the

unhappiness and failure. An author is not being optimistically romantic, he is merely being prosaically realistic if he notes that sometimes the sun does shine, and observes that the grass is occasionally green. Realism is not less realism because it recognizes the common appropriateness of the happy ending.

The rejection of the view that optimistic and entertaining drama is necessarily simplistic and self-indulgent looks ahead to Hobson's dismissal of Brecht after the visit of the Berliner Ensemble to London in August 1956. In 'Art and the Soviet',[48] too, Hobson considers a related issue, reaches the same conclusion but utilizes the very dialectical approach that lies at the heart of all Marxist economic and social analysis, giving an early indication of the literary maturity that was to underpin his most effective theatre criticism. The article begins by returning to a constant preoccupation of Hobson's writing in 1930 and 1931, namely that of propaganda:

> No aspect of the Russian experiment is more interesting than its attitude to art. Russian painters, Russian dramatists and Russian sculptors are all being mobilized in an effort to make the Five Year Plan successful. A political battle has been organized between groups of Moscow theaters, in which marks of commendation are given to those houses that most effectively translate into terms of drama selected features of Communist philosophy. It is also reported that the Soviet pays regular salaries to about half the sculptors and artists in Russia, on condition that they produce a certain number of works of orthodox political tendency.

This factual opening paragraph is then followed by a gently subjective opinion; note that Hobson does not exclude the possibility that good art and propaganda are compatible:

> The days have probably gone by when it would have been maintained that good art cannot be propagandist in aim. It is true that many works of literature and painting that have had a moral or political purpose have been failures from the artistic point of view; but so have been many works of literature and painting that have had no purpose at all. On the other hand, the examples of successful propagandist art are legion. They include such diverse productions as 'Pygmalion', 'Richard II' and 'The Pilgrim's Progress'.

What Hobson objects to is not the intrinsically propagandist nature of works, but the compulsion on Soviet artists to espouse the party line. His measured expression of this view (given that he was writing for an American newspaper deeply hostile to Soviet totalitarianism), and in a style that takes over the literary approach utilized by many Marxist works of art (namely, the presentation of two points of view, with the reader expected to adopt the one that coincides with the 'correct' conclusion), reveals how Hobson's increasing contact with the larger issues of the world is having a beneficial effect on the touch and depth of his writing:

> But in spite of this, one looks on the Soviet plan in regard to art with none too robust a confidence. If a man wishes to use his art for propagating some idea or maintaining some thesis, the result may very possibly justify him from every point of view, including the artistic; but if he is compelled by an outside force to use his art in this way, whether he wishes to or not, the upshot is not likely to be very successful. The difference between a man doing what he wants and what he is forced to do is the difference between the Falstaff of 'Henry IV' and the Falstaff of 'The Merry Wives of Windsor'. It is conceivable that many Russian artists are not in enthusiastic sympathy with Bolshevist aims; it is certain that many of those who are in sympathy with them would prefer to direct their activities into other channels than political propaganda. In such cases it is improbable that either Russian propaganda will receive notable reinforcement, or the artistic world much enrichment, from the Soviet enthusiasm for making everyone a politician.

The tendency to make everyone a politician is something for which Hobson was soon to upbraid George Bernard Shaw, not because the introduction of politics into the theatre was dramatically unacceptable, but because Shaw's treatment of political issues in his plays was theatrically unfulfilling.

As with so many events in Hobson's life, it was through a fortuitous circumstance that he was to embark upon a career in theatre criticism. In an article in *Plays and Players*, published in 1976, he explains how he had become the London drama critic of the *Christian Science Monitor* in 1931 – a move which he describes as unforeseen, but for which, as the topics he had selected for his editorials reveal, he was unwittingly being trained. In 1930 Hobson and his parents had resettled in Warrington Crescent, Maida Vale, London – presumably to facilitate his career – and throughout the following year the young journalist was:

> ... a regular theatregoer, but never an ecstatic or devoted one. And I certainly had no idea of ever becoming a drama critic. The fact that I did so was entirely accidental. I used to write editorial leaders for the 'Christian Science Monitor' and, one day, I casually let slip to the London editor that I was going to see Jack Buchanan in 'Stand Up and Sing'. He said that if I wrote a piece about it that was printed, then he would pay for my seats. This seemed to me to be an extremely generous offer and, thereafter, they paid for my seats whenever I went to the theatre and wrote about it.[49]

Hobson began reviewing plays as a profession at a time when the London theatre was facing the twin external threats of the new media (the 'talkies', radio and later television), coupled with the world economic down-turn and the internal challenge of a realignment of the power balance between the actor, dramatist and director. The British film industry, which had been in decline during the 1920s, had been revived by two events: the stipulation of the 1927 Cinematograph Films Act that 5 per cent of screen time should be filled by British films (rising to 20 per cent in 1936), and, more significantly, by the advent of sound pictures in 1929. *The Jazz Singer*, the first sound film to be shown in Britain (September 1928), was quickly followed by Alfred Hitchcock's *Blackmail*, which, although originally silent, was reworked to become the first British sound film in 1930, pointing the way forward for such films as Korda's *The Private Life of Henry VIII* (1933), starring Charles Laughton and Robert Donat – the first British-made international success. The increase in the popularity of the cinema that these developments generated quickly affected the viability of the old theatrical touring companies and inevitably reduced theatre revenue – in 1930 two stalls tickets in the theatre cost 29 shillings, against 5 shillings for two cinema tickets. The radio also threatened to encroach upon the traditional territory of the theatre. Richard Hughes's *Danger* was the first play written for broadcasting in 1924, and with the two million licences taken out in 1927 rising to nine million by 1939, this represented a further threat to the financial viability of the theatre. As if these immediate problems were not serious enough, the transmission of the first television broadcast of a play in 1930, Pirandello's *The Man with the Flower in his Mouth*, together with the technically primitive productions transmitted directly from theatres (started by J. B. Priestley's *When We Are Married* in November 1938), adumbrated the challenge that this medium would pose in the 1950s.[50]

The London theatre (which Hobson focused on) responded to these dangers in a number of ways. Some productions, such as *Cavalcade*, *White Horse Inn*, *Late Night Final* and *Elizabeth of England* (all 1931), utilized cinematic techniques of intricate stage machinery and composite scenes in an attempt to match the dynamism of their cinematic rivals.[51] These grandly conceived shows were visually impressive but expensive to mount – Noël Coward's *Cavalcade* required a total company of over 250[52] – and four other types of more flexible productions were presented during the 1930s which found favour with the London play-goer. The first was the revival of old classics. The controversial creations of the producer/designer Theodore Komisarjevsky, such as his *Macbeth* at the Shakespeare Memorial Theatre in Stratford (1933), which stressed the universality of the play through scenery and costume that suggested episodes in the First World War;[53] innovative and reinvigorating Shakespearean productions, including Michael Macowan's *Troilus and Cressida* in 1938, which emphasized the futility of war; the work done at London's 'Old Vic' by a succession of directors – Harcourt Williams (1929–33), Tyrone Guthrie (1933–4) and Henry Cass (1934–6), all under the careful observation of Lilian Baylis;[54] and the performances of Laurence Olivier,

Ralph Richardson, Donald Wolfit and, in particular, John Gielgud (who was so popular that Dodie Smith, in her play *Call It a Day* (1935), has 15-year-old Ann Hilton place a photograph of him above her pillow[55]), all created a reawakening of interest in Shakespeare, the Greek dramatists and the popular English comic playwrights, such as Congreve, Sheridan and Goldsmith.

The second type of commercially successful play was the newly written work that attempted to continue the tradition of Sheridan and Goldsmith by gently satirizing conventional behaviour. Relentlessly upper middle-class, it either mocked new modes of thinking and new fads in social behaviour or sent up, amidst much comic banter, the anachronistic reluctance of the older generation to recognize that the advent of the 'Bright Young Things' necessitated a reconsideration of long-held values. This debate was never held at anything above a superficial level, however, with a work more likely to be witty, fast, and well constructed than profound or philosophical. The climax of Allan Monkhouse's *Cecilia*, where the timid Guy Daunt is punished by his father for being indolent, illustrates that, for new English comedy at least, the dramatic subject-matter remained as resolutely confined to the concerns of the upper classes in the 1930s as it had been during the previous decade:

Cecilia:	Well, did the anxious parent cut up rough?
Guy:	No. No need for him to be rough.
Cecilia:	Why?
Guy:	Because he's inflexible.
Dan:	He's given you marching orders?
Guy:	Thereabouts.
Cecilia:	What does it amount to?
Guy:	Back to Oxford – work up for a degree – then look round for a job.[56]

Whilst finding *Cecilia*'s unreality amusing,[57] Hobson was nevertheless able to perceive the derivative nature of this narrow brand of comedy, writing in 1934 that the cast of a similar work, Laurence Miller's *Head On Crash*: 'have to make remarks of stupendous silliness, and the dialogue is full of echoes of Shakespeare, Brooke, Yeats, Landor and Shaw',[58] and identifying, in 'On Contradicting Oneself', the limited achievements of some of the plays of this genre, as well as the pitfalls that they must avoid at all costs to ensure a palatable evening. Note in particular the deliberate way that the tone of the piece changes from weary tolerance of an uninspired plot, through exasperation at the attempt to imbue the work with a moral that it cannot support, to indignation at the myopia of the dramatist, Max Catto, who complacently ignores the chronic unemployment of the early 1930s. This is the start of Hobson's frustration at formulaic writing that would not be relieved until the appearance of the avant-garde in the 1950s:

'French Salad', at the Royalty Theater, is one of those plays that contradict themselves. It presents a shiftless, feckless, upper middle-class family, in which the son fancies himself as an actor, the daughters go in for art and the mother dithers expensively through it all while the bill is footed by a weary father out of the proceeds of something in the City to which no one pays any attention till it goes smash. Then follow complications with the least plausible stage diamond sharper we have ever seen which land the unhappy set of incompetents into ever deeper and deeper trouble.

All this is amusing enough. We have seen the family in the theater many times before, and there is no real reason why we should ever see it again, because it does not react to circumstances in any way possessing significance; but its futility and inability to face up to hard knocks pass the evening not unpleasantly. It is when it tries to be profound that the play tumbles to pieces. The daughter-in-law ... is supposed to be made of sterner stuff than the others, and at the end, in a set piece of rhetoric, she points the moral of the play. Her relatives, she announces, must stop looking for 'cushy' artistic jobs, and take up hard work; they must push trucks and invoice ledgers ... This is presented as the voice of stern common sense, but it is, of course, mere romantic moonshine. For the difficulty of the world today is that there are no trucks to push and very few ledgers to invoice. It is all very well for Mr Catto to expose the folly of those who think that they can without effort drop into attractive posts at £1000 a year. Unhappily, it is equally Micawberish to suppose that there is an unlimited supply of jobs at £250.[59]

Hobson allows an awareness of social conditions to intrude into his criticism twenty years before Kenneth Tynan made it a fashionable and commonplace practice to do so.

In addition to the revival of the classics and regular productions of the modern comedy of bad manners, London witnessed a proliferation of light entertainment during the 1930s, ranging from C. B. Cochran revues and Ivor Novello musicals to Ben Travers' farces and popular detective plays by playwrights such as Anthony Armstrong (*Ten Minute Alibi*, 1933) and Emlyn Williams (*Night Must Fall*, 1935).[60] A fourth type of play that was often performed in the decade prior to the Second World War was the drama with pretensions to social realism which highlighted a contemporary evil and permitted an examination of social problems. Into this category fell the works of Ibsen, Chekhov, Pirandello and Shaw. From the very start of his critical career, Hobson, whilst not unable to enjoy a specifically didactic work, was suspicious of the view that the intellectual dimension of a play should outweigh all its other components. A production of *Iphigenia in Tauris*, given by the English Verse Speaking Association at the Theatre Royal, Haymarket in December 1932, drew the following response:

> Just now a drama like 'Iphigenia' is of special significance in London. It shows that a solution of the cardinal problem of the British theater is possible. It is possible, because 'Iphigenia' itself solves it. Forty years ago in London plays were being brilliantly acted by such compelling players as Sir Henry Irving and Sir Johnston Forbes-Robertson. In the main, these plays had tolerably exciting and gripping plots. Their only fault was that they were utterly out of touch with the culture and intellectual and spiritual questions of the day. Since then the drama has changed. An intelligent discussion of any major problem of the age is as likely to be found in the theater today as anywhere else. Unfortunately, even the best examples of this kind of drama too often remain discussion only. They have little characterization, and no story. They give small scope for the most impressive kind of acting. But here is 'Iphigenia', which unites the chief virtues of the theater of Irving and the theater of Shaw, proving that a play may be intellectually respectable without being undramatic, and that though it is built on an exciting plot it need not be mentally beneath contempt.[61]

The Greek models should be utilized, he argues, since they present a unified experience that combines the virtues of a strong plot, convincing characterization and parts that permit actors to exploit the whole range of their abilities. They display, quite simply, a greater theatricality than the works of the theatre of discussion. These touchstones for effective drama run as leitmotifs throughout not just Hobson's writing in this decade, but the whole body of his work. In 'Toward a New Tragedy' (May 1933), an article of length that allows the critic to develop his ideas, Hobson wonders whether great tragedies will ever be written again:

> The cardinal difficulty of modern tragedy is to originate characters of the requisite magnitude. The task of the writers of ancient drama was considerably easier than that of their modern successors. Think whom they took for their protagonists. Oedipus was a king, Iphigenia a princess, Clytemnestra a queen ... These people breathe an atmosphere of grandeur very different from that of the clerks and school teachers whom realism compels the modern dramatist to take as his subject matter. In spite of the spread of democratic feeling, a twentieth-century audience still instinctively feels that kingly behaviour is more likely to be the mark of a king than of a shopkeeper. Whether this is or is not a justifiable feeling does not, in this connection, matter; the point is that it exists, and, existing, it affects the operation of the dramatist. Still, this is not an insuperable difficulty. Greatness of character, which is what tragedy demands, can be found in the lowly and obscure as well as in the exalted. A more serious handicap to the modern poet is found in the methods by which he is permitted to convey this impression of grandeur to his audience. He cannot today, as Shakespeare could, use verse.[62]

Two points should be noted here. Firstly, Hobson does not object to realism in itself (nor deny that it is capable of producing great works), he merely feels that its dominance inhibits the exploration of other legitimate avenues of dramatic invention. And, secondly, he strongly believes that plays written in verse have the greatest potential to achieve a cathartic effect. The problem in the 1930s, he argues, is that realism has removed the willingness to accept verse in a modern play and, after quoting some of Shakespeare's most mellifluous lines, he continues: 'It is not sufficient nor fair to say that the modern dramatist does not write lines like these because he cannot; he would not be allowed to if he could; for the convention of today is that he must write in prose.'[63] This insistence on a catholicity of theatrical genres, if the London stage is to be vibrant, foreshadows his championing both of the avant-garde in the 1950s and of such unfashionable exponents of upper-class comedy in the 1960s as William Douglas Home, whilst his defence of verse drama adumbrates his delight in the poetic style of Christopher Fry and the poetic resonance of Beckett, Pinter and Osborne.

Throughout this period Hobson frequently returns to the insipid nature of contemporary stage language:

> Three hundred years ago, any average play had numerous detachable jewels of speech sewn on to its fabric; but since then there has been a gradual movement away from this kind of dramatic writing, until the typical play of today has all its speeches woven into the warp and woof of its texture until they are inseparable from their context … The modern drama deliberately deals, not in big moments, however obtained, but in total impressions. It tries to make the garment of its prose seamless and indivisible. Its style is that of the Parthenon, in which the value of every stone lies in its relation to the sum of all the rest. It indulges neither in fine writing, nor in the effects of fine writing achieved by other means.[64]

This criticism of the well-made play is aimed at the numerous imitators of the work of such playwrights as Dodie Smith, Somerset Maugham and Laurence Miller, but the dismissal of the worth of works that concentrate on delivering a 'total impression' undoubtedly alludes to the plays of the most renowned figure of the English stage at that time, George Bernard Shaw.

Hobson's attitude to Shaw remained consistent throughout his career in that he felt that although Shaw possessed the greatest talent of all his contemporaries, he continually squandered this potential with an obsessive concentration on the discursive play of ideas. His first specific review of a Shavian production (in 1933) reflects this ambivalence. Revealingly entitled 'Magnificent Bungling',[65] Hobson begins his consideration of *On the Rocks* (which Shaw himself reported had received 'a unanimously good press (for once)'[66] with a blunt statement of the ultimate Shavian paradox:

> The trouble with Mr Shaw, of course, is that he is lazy. He has now been writing plays for upward of 40 years, and he has not even yet begun to pick up the elements of his job. It is commonly said of him that he is a master of theatrical craftmanship, but cannot invent good plots. As a matter of fact, as 'On the Rocks' makes abundantly clear, he can invent superb plots, and has not enough theatrical craftmanship to run a successful charade.

The lack of a sense of the theatrical is one of the biggest faults that a playwright can exhibit, in Hobson's view, and Shaw not only permits his actors insufficient opportunity to express themselves – he utilizes them as mouthpieces – but fails to exploit the dramatic possibilities of moments of potential tension:

> Mr Shaw lets them slide past as though they were completely unaware of their dramatic significance, or at least quite uninterested in them. After nearly half a century's experience he comes to the writing of plays with an equipment comparable to that of the orator who is ignorant of the rudiments of grammar and pronunciation.

Nevertheless, Hobson feels that Shaw is able to compensate in this work with his sparkling rhetoric:

> But everybody knows that an orator who is ignorant of grammar and pronunciation can often make a far more eloquent speech than one who is fully primed with the intricacies of syntax. In the same way, Mr Shaw, though he bungles his play, bungles it magnificently. He goes wrong with finer effect than most dramatists go right. He talks away all the dramatic potentiality of his story; but the talk itself is superb.[67]

One can only speculate as to whether Hobson was influenced in his views by the knowledge that a pivotal character, Lady Oracle, who is both a messenger of death and a healer, had been modelled by the playwright on Mary Baker Eddy.[68] What is certain, though, is that Hobson felt that Shaw's didacticism was all too often put across at the expense of dramatic effect. *Major Barbara* was a particular disappointment:

> Perhaps its chief defect is what Mr Shaw himself considers its principal merit – that it says so precisely and vividly what it means. Really great prose or poetry always says more, and it is this overplus that gives it its value.[69] Is it not the overtones and suggestions, rather than the literal significance of the words, that give so memorable an echo to a phrase like 'Time, which antiquates antiquitie'? Mr Shaw's prose is never so haunting as that, and so it misses the heights.[70]

But it is not just the language of Shaw's plays that makes them unsatisfactory; the one-dimensional nature of their characters is anti-dramatic, a point he makes explicitly in 'The Edwardians':

> It would be absurd to say of Mr Shaw, whose intellectual fertility is one of the greater marvels of the twentieth century, that his characters are people of one idea. But they are, far too often, people of one idea at a time. They act from a motive. That is perhaps why we so rarely believe in their actions. For people in real life act not on a motive, but on a complex of motives. Into even the most elementary action there enters a world of confused, conflicting impulses and ideas. By isolating a single one of these ideas, and exposing it with a brilliant lucidity, Mr Shaw adds to the intellectual clarity of his plays, but detracts from their dramatic veracity.[71]

He is, in effect, 'too often a debater instead of a dramatist' who makes his characters 'discuss systems of thought instead of showing how these systems of thought worked themselves out in their lives in definite incidents and effects'.[72]

Hobson's quarrel with Shaw stems primarily from a sense of frustration at the inability of a brilliant mind to recognize that effective propaganda on the stage can only come about when one perceives the difference between a tract and a living work of art. Whilst quite prepared to concede that at times Shaw's rhetorical brilliance can ensure a successful evening at the theatre, the critic often voiced the concern during the 1930s that Shaw's disciples were flooding the English stage with inferior copies of flawed masterpieces. Lesley Storm's *Dark Horizon*, a pacifist play that, in Hobson's view, could be seen to advocate war, was one example of this.[73] More ominously, the legacy of Shaw was such that, too often, critics and the public condemned as trivial any work, be it a musical comedy, pantomime or verse drama, that did not deal more or less directly with an urgent social question. Critical insight was being blurred by an amorphous mass of socially relevant plays, the public was less likely to investigate works that broke new ground and the theatre was becoming a place of instruction rather than a place of entertainment. It is important to recognize, though, that Hobson did not wish to see social problems excluded from the theatre, merely that, as with the greatest dramatists, they should be treated in a *dramatic* manner. 'Right and Left of the Stage' sums up his views on the overly discursive work of social realism at this time:

> A well-balanced view of life seeks to get out of every experience, not merely pleasure, but an appropriate pleasure. Economic and political science is a fascinating high one. But to appraise the theater, which is essentially a poetic art, by the rigid standards of political economy is to offer it more than the show of violence by applying a radically

inappropriate standard of judgement. It is like going to a football match so that the flight of the ball may give information concerning the nature of the parabola. To regard football as a commentary on mathematics is no more foolish than to demand of the theater that it be a gloss on the social situation.[74]

Another critical maxim had been established.

Hobson's approach to criticism was formed against the background of his historical training, which convinced him of the need to create a historical record of what he witnessed. It was a task that he began at a time of supreme dominance for the playwright and the producer (nowadays termed the director), which he felt neglected the potential of the actor. This belief is cogently expressed in the 1933 article 'The Actor as Artist'[75] and holds important implications for Hobson's post-war writing. He begins by warning against the tendency of some directors to assume responsibility for every aspect of production:

> It is Mr Gordon Craig who has brought the producer into the foreground of the picture. It is Mr Craig's conviction that both authors and actors are interlopers in the world of the theater, and that this world of the theater would be a better place, truer to its essential function, if the Shakespeares and O'Neills, the Irvings and the Cornells took themselves off to some other occupation than writing and mouthing theatrical libretti. For authors he would substitute stage directors, for the actors übermarionettes.

Whilst Reinhardt has succeeded in creating some magnificent stage effects, the truly creative, all-encompassing director should remember that the eye soon tires of splendid visual backdrops which overwhelm the stage and that a more suitable medium has recently been discovered for the ambitious director:

> If a man who finds that he is peculiarly fitted to the profession of producer in addition feels that he has an individual outlook on the universe which he would like to communicate by means of his art, there is another, and a better field of activity in which to accomplish his aims. The realm in which the producer holds undisputed sway is the cinema.

Having summarily dispensed with the claims of the director for pre-eminence, Hobson now turns to the playwright. He readily agrees that the modern theatre, 'in which producer and player are subordinated to author', has proved itself capable of 'affording the highest kind of theatrical experience', citing the existence of *A Doll's House, Candida, After All, Journey's End* and *St Joan*. Yet the ascendancy of the author at the expense of all else is doubly regrettable, not simply because it is stifling new approaches but, as with the director, the author, eager to convey a didactic message, has other forms of expression outside of the theatre:

> If every copy of every play of Mr Shaw's were to be instantly destroyed, the world would lose none of his essential message, because all that he has said in his dramas he has said in his prefaces as well.

The actor, however, has no alternative means of expression, and Hobson's fear that the performer's worth is in danger of neglect marks the start of a career-long recognition of the actor's contribution to the theatrical triumvirate:

> Where the actor is confined to embodying merely the ideas of the author, there is something lost to the world, namely, the ideas and vision of the actor himself. But in a theater, where the actor is allowed and indeed expected to use the written drama purely as a kind of musical instrument on which he plays any sort of tune that best harmonizes with his own outlook, the world loses nothing.

Thus far, this article is of the greatest significance to Hobson's criticism, in that it demonstrates a belief that the loss of theatricality that didactic theatre entails reflects an inability to appreciate that the most satisfying theatrical experience depends as much upon the ingenuity of the actor as it does upon the creativity of the author. Just as 'Impartial History?'[76] had implied that a clash of differing critical ideas and opinions can result in a progressive synthesis, Hobson claims that the ultimate expression of dramatic art will stem from the combination of two unique but complementary authorial and performing contributions.[77] To Allan Monkhouse's objection (author of *Cecilia*) that 'the actor is inferior to the dramatist because the actor's work perishes with his performance, whilst that of the dramatist remains', Hobson counters with passion:

> Coleridge once remarked that he rated poetry greater than painting or sculpture because, whilst it is inconceivable that, for example, 'Paradise Lost' should ever disappear from the earth, the Prophets of Michelangelo might easily be destroyed in some civil war. To me this seems one of the most amazing judgements that even Coleridge ever delivered. If there were only one copy of Milton's poem left in the world, and that copy were on the point of being burnt, surely the greatness of its poetry would be unaffected?

For the critic, the merit in a work of art does not depend upon its durability, and cannot be valued in a utilitarian fashion:

> The value of an experience in any art depends on the character and intensity of that experience, not on the possibility of its being repeated for other people an indefinite number of times …

– a phrase that was to underpin his subsequent critical practice, since it helps to explain the rationale behind the duty of the theatre critic to record and relate.

Hobson concludes 'The Actor as Artist' by developing this belief that the true role of the critic is to give permanence to the accomplished, yet ephemeral, performance, for this will not only establish a historical record, but will have a catalytic effect by stimulating interest in good theatre. Having further disputed Monkhouse's notion that the work of the dramatist remains immutable (pointing out that Sophocles' *Oedipus Rex* has lost much of its validity because 'the ways of thought that once gave it significance have now entirely vanished'), Hobson returns to dispute the argument that an actor, unlike the author, is unable to leave a record of his achievements for posterity:

> ... the transience of the actor's art is commonly exaggerated. Kean's performances, in the descriptions of Hazlitt, have actually enjoyed greater permanence than the works of any contemporary playwright. This reveals the real function of the dramatic critic. His most valuable business is not with the appraisement of plays, but with the preservation of the otherwise transient effects obtained by the great actor.[78]

Although Hobson was to modify this view in the light of the arrival of Beckett and the 'New Wave' dramatists, adding the discovery of new writing talent to the duty of the responsible critic, this belief in the ability of the critic to immortalize accomplished stage performances was expressed over twenty years before Kenneth Tynan delivered his more famous definition of the role of the critic – to 'give permanence to something impermanent'.[79]

For someone who possessed no direct experience of the theatre in either a performing or directorial sense, Hobson always revealed an intuitive understanding of the techniques that an actor employs to create a convincing representation of a character. The first major actor that Hobson had seen perform was Sir John Martin-Harvey as Sydney Carton in the stage adaptation of Dickens's *A Tale of Two Cities*, called *The Only Way*, and such was the cathartic effect that Sir John had achieved on the occasion of Hobson's schoolboy visit[80] (and subsequent performances) that the critic was to refer to it again and again as a demonstration of the sublime effect that the great stage interpretation can achieve.[81] By 1933 Sir John had performed the part over four thousand times in Britain, Canada and America, yet Hobson was still able to subdivide his performance in 'Retrospect'[82] into a brief checklist that could illustrate the technique of the greatest actors. Firstly, he demonstrated 'the extraordinary beauty of which the human voice is capable':

> Sir John treats the script of this part almost as though it were the libretto of a piece of music, so exquisitely are all the modulations of his voice calculated and controlled so as to produce an effect of aural loveliness not to be rivalled by any actor of the realistic school.

He considers the text to be a starting-point and not a definitive set of instructions:

> He enters so thoroughly into the spirit of his part ... that in places where the printed play affords no indication of what the actor should do, or what feelings he should express, he goes on acting without loosening his grip upon the part in the slightest degree.

The actor demonstrates how body posture and facial expression can be as effective as speech in conveying emotion:

> When Carton has substituted himself for Darnay, on the day before the latter's intended execution on the guillotine, and Darnay has been carried out of the prison cell, Carton has nothing to do but sit down at a small table while the curtain falls. But that is not how Sir John Martin Harvey treats the situation. Half a dozen emotions are clearly revealed in his face, during the few seconds that elapse between the speaking of the last word and the end of the scene – anxiety that his friend should escape, relief as each successive clang of the prison doors shows that Darney is drawing nearer to liberty, a deep thoughtfulness as he contemplates his own fate on the morrow – all these feelings, without a word or a single extravagant gesture, are made as clear as noonday by Sir John's luminous performance whilst sitting at his small table. Only the greatest actors can carry their performance beyond the point at which their part stops

By avoiding the 'obvious opportunity for heroics in the spectacle of a man going to the guillotine in Revolutionary Paris, in order to save the life of his friend', he displays one of the most difficult facets of the actor's art, namely restraint, a trait which all of Hobson's most-admired performers – Edwige Feuillère, Ralph Richardson and Peggy Ashcroft – were to exhibit.

By the mid-1930s it is evident that Hobson judges a play less on its realism or literary effect than on its theatricality. What he remembers 'is not so much any single play as a whole, as isolated moments in many different dramas'.[83] He firmly believes that Shakespeare is better seen than read.[84] He can identify with Ralph Richardson's frustration at the lack of opportunity that the Shavian type of drama affords the actor: 'It was inevitable that Irving should prefer "The Bells" to the work of Shaw, because in "The Bells" he could be a creative, while in Shaw, he could only be an interpretive, artist.'[85] He takes the view that poor plays can be transformed by good acting – 'Published plays that are ridiculous, and poverty stricken in imagination, may be intolerably dull to watch upon the stage; on the other hand, they may furnish an actor of genius with the very instrument best suited to his hand'[86] – and he can derive as much pleasure from the observance of a tiny gesture deliberately made by a minor character as he can from the grandiloquent rhetoric of a household name. This final point was to become a notable feature of Hobson's critical style – and one for which he was later much parodied – and is well demonstrated in an early article, 'Miss Hindle Takes a Bow'.[87] Miss Hindle had taken the role of Millie Venn, a dairymaid in

Eden Phillpotts's comedy, *A Cup of Happiness*. Having endured a life of drudgery, she receives an unexpected offer of marriage from the slow-witted second son of her employer. Hobson's concentration on Millie's reaction to this offer, his attention to details of body movement and facial expression and his pertinent interpretation of her emotional turmoil, all reveal a critic finely attuned to the nuances that an actor is capable of conveying in a single gesture or brief appearance:

> [The marriage offer] is the first compliment that Millie has received … in her life. But she takes it in a very calm and matter-of-fact, almost in an unflattering, manner. She shows no excitement, no elation, nearly, in fact, leaving the audience in doubt whether she will accept or refuse. Only at the very end of the scene, after her last word has been spoken, does she reveal the tremendous difference that Adam's proposal has made to her self-confidence and self-esteem. With her arms straight down by her side, and her palms stretched outwards, rather in the serene manner of some two-dimensional frescoed Egyptian divinity, she gives the impression of gliding, instead of prosaically walking, off the stage.

This ability to translate his power of observation into passionate, memorable prose was the basis of Hobson's most evocative reviews of stage performances.

In 1934, after five years of increasingly eloquent despair at the low standing of the English actor, Hobson was delighted to be able to announce in 'The Theater "Comes Back" In Europe'[88] that there were signs that the balance was beginning to alter. Whereas Russia and Germany had instituted a theatrical renaissance as an instrument of national propaganda, the revival in the fortunes of the English theatre appeared to be actor-led:

> Mr Ralph Richardson, for example, whose portrayal of a simple spirituality and goodness in Somerset Maugham's 'Sheppey' last year made an uneven play memorable, is an actor of richest promise. So is Mr John Gielgud, who is unrivaled in his sympathetic comprehension of human weakness, and of how victory may be snatched out of the jaws of defeat. So again is Mr Charles Laughton, a player of a darker cast than these two, and perhaps the only person serving in any capacity in the English theater who can drive at Aristotelian terror. And so is Miss Flora Robson, who has a Rembrandtesque faculty for discovering beauty in the most drab and unlikely places.

Hobson concludes the article by claiming that 'the actors of the current London theater give indications of richer future achievement than do its dramatists' and this was to prove a prophetic statement in describing the rest of the pre-war period. The paucity of works of high quality had a two-fold effect on the type of article that Hobson wrote in the second half of the 1930s. Firstly, he broadened the range of his writing by considering wider theatrical issues than mere reviews and character profiles. In 'Musical Comedy and the Aesthete'[89] he claims that only musical comedies now offer a substitute for the melodious feeling of Elizabethan and Caroline drama (albeit a poor one); in 'British Drama's Revival'[90] he champions the work of the repertory theatres; he was not afraid to condemn the disappointing fare being offered to the public – 'During 1937 there were several long arid stretches in which nothing worth seeing was put on in London theaters';[91] he began to examine the economics of producing plays;[92] and, as the international situation worsened towards the end of the decade, Hobson questioned the merit of plays that derived their success from too close an identification with world affairs, such as Robert Sherwood's *Idiot's Delight*,[93] and claimed that it was 'when the crisis is past that a vital theater will begin to reflect and interpret it, and use it for the purpose of art'.[94] The second effect of Hobson's dismay at the absence of new writing of quality was that those few plays that he did welcome enthusiastically are distinguished by the passion of his commendation.

One of the most thought-provoking plays of the 1930s is Ronald Gow and Walter Greenwood's stage adaptation of the latter's novel, *Love on the Dole*. Unashamedly tragic, the play differed markedly from the normal West End fare by attempting to portray the poverty trap that many northern families mistakenly believed they could escape. Its surprising success in London led Ronald Gow to comment later that he 'certainly didn't write a play about unemployment with any idea of a West End production, no one in their senses would do that'.[95] The authors avoid the flaw of most socially realistic plays by depicting characteristics of their protagonists that make them appear three-dimensional and independent of their creators. Thus, the action takes place in Hanky Park, a convincingly drawn area of deprivation, the dialogue is in a realistic Lancastrian dialect and care is taken to convey the conflict between human pride, not wishing to recognize one's poverty, and human need, where the stopping of one's dole means that the only alternative to starvation is the workhouse. A good example of the authors' sensitivity to this conflict can be found in the very first stage direction, describing Mr Hardcastle's dwelling: 'It is important to remember that this is not slum property, but the house of a respectable working man, whose incorrigible snobbery would be aroused if you suggested that North Street was a slum.'[96] In their relation of the Hardcastles' plight the authors express the belief, striking at the very root of the well-made play and the comedy of bad manners, that modern life has become so complex that it cannot be resolved either by a swift economic panacea or an authorial *Deus ex machina* – a view of humanity that was always to appeal to Hobson. This unwillingness to offer a direct solution to a social problem, preferring to let the audience draw its own conclusions from the events of the work, coupled with its novel subject-matter (northern poverty) accounted for the play's great success following its opening in

Manchester (26 February 1934) and its subsequent transfer to London's Garrick Theatre (1 February 1935), where it ran for 391 performances. The lack of omniscience that the authors readily display also differentiates the play from the sentimental work of Monkhouse, Smith and Coward, which posed no questions, and the didactic work of Shaw, which offered incontrovertible answers.

Hobson's appreciation of *Love on the Dole*, which he reviewed on 9 March 1935, focuses less on the call to political arms than on the tragedy of the Hardcastles' poverty. The play satisfies the most important criteria of effective social drama for Hobson, because it both moves and instructs, and he is therefore able to write that it was: 'the most boisterously and bitingly humorous, the most poignantly heroic play that has been seen in London since Mr Louis Golding's "Magnolia Street"'. The most perceptive passage of the review reveals the play's finest achievement, the celebration of human resourcefulness mixed with indignation at the squandering of human potential:

> In spite of its story and ending, 'Love on the Dole', is not a depressing, but an exhilarating as well as a touching experience. Over and over again, in little incidents wonderfully true and effective, a splendor of temper and fineness of courage are revealed in several characters of the play such as cause one to doubt whether one should be proud of belonging to a country that can produce such people, or ashamed because it treats them so wretchedly. These incidents are the more moving because written with a magnificent economy ...[97]

The play became the one work that dealt directly with social deprivation in the 1930s about which Hobson could be genuinely enthusiastic.

If *Love on the Dole* was the only British play of this era to handle successfully a social theme with strong didactic implications, W. H. Auden, in collaboration with Christopher Isherwood, was the one playwright whom Hobson felt was capable of redirecting English drama away from its obsession with upper-class manners and social behaviour, of moving beyond the stale, contemporary forms of expression and of exploring new, more ambitious dramatic structures. Quite simply, he saw Auden as a theatrical trail-blazer, and he began the 1935 review of *The Dance of Death*[98] with the following eulogy:

> 'The Dance of Death', Mr W. H. Auden's brilliant, and, in my opinion, entirely successful attempt to work out for the theater a new, significant art-form, may, in the strictest sense of the term, prove epoch-making. This, however, depends far less upon its intrinsic merits than on what is to be done in the same line in the future by Mr Auden and his followers. At the moment Mr Auden belongs more to the pioneers than to the masters of drama. His achievement consists rather in pointing out a fresh road than in travelling down it very far himself.

> The development of the theater is made up, on the one hand, of the discovery of original methods of expression, and, on the other, of the using of these means of expression to communicate a new content.

Hobson had spotted that the work (which had been influenced by the Reichstag fire of 1933[99]) was a technical experiment, in that it sought to update the medieval tradition of the *danse macabre* by means of an expressionist approach to poetic drama that bears witness to the 'the hell of bourgeois society in its late decline',[100] but he objected neither to its experimentation nor the critique of capitalism with which the play ends:

> Chorus: O Mr Marx, you've gathered
> All the material facts
> You know the economic
> Reasons for our acts.
>
> *[Enter Karl Marx (with two young communists)]*
>
> Karl Marx: The instruments of production have been too much for him. He is liquidated.
>
> *[Exeunt to a Dead March* [101]

This specifically didactic lamination is one of the cruder aspects of the play, but, to appreciate the drama as a role model, Hobson pointed out that one did not need to see the decline and fall of the middle classes as an essential prerequisite for the advance of society:

> To enjoy Mr Auden's play, and to perceive its importance in the development of the theater, one need not agree with the thesis which he uses it to expound ... No – it is not what Mr Auden says, but the way he says it, that is supremely interesting. He takes that most frivolous of entertainments, the musical comedy, and transforms it so that it becomes an instrument for the serious drama of which the potentialities, in his skilful handling, seem illimitable. It is an extraordinary achievement.[102]

By 1937, however, it was apparent that *The Dance of Death*'s example had not been followed and Hobson was beginning to despair that the London stage was ever going to act as a vehicle for effective works of intellectual stimulation. 'Wanted – Dramatists'[103] expresses his frustration most directly, dismissing A. A. Milne's *Sarah Simple* for its triviality –

> His story is his usual slight matrimonial misadventure that finishes with bells mildly ringing, and the bunting, figuratively, hung out; but it is more trivial than usual, and his dialogue is not quite up to his customary high standard ...

– and lamenting the unambitious nature of current play-writing:

34

Nothing that has been said should lead the reader to suppose that the British theater, even at the moment, is lacking in ability of certain kinds. But from the writing point of view, this ability seems to run almost exclusively in the direction of fabricating police plays, which are exercises in ingenious plot making, and touch the heart and mind about as much as a crossword puzzle.

There was only one recent play that Hobson felt 'might possibly be called a work of genius' in 1937, and that was a further expressionist drama by Auden and Isherwood, *The Ascent of F6*, which represented Auden's bold attempt 'to bring poetry back into the theater'.[104]

Hobson was to review one further work of Auden's prior to the outbreak of the Second World War – *On the Frontier*, in March 1939, which he found too discursive.[105] This led him to conclude in the same article that the 'gates of realism, though shaken, still stand' and he clearly looked to Auden to rediscover his experimental zest and challenge Shaw. The stasis in the theatrical world, briefly lifted for Hobson by Ralph Richardson's performance in J. B. Priestley's quasi-religious *Johnson Over Jordan*,[106] was not, however, to be paralleled in Hobson's own professional career. He had achieved his greatest ambition on 13 July 1935 when he married Elizabeth, whom he had met at a rehearsal of amateur dramatics a year earlier. The ceremony had been conducted by the Provost of Oriel in the church of St Mary the Virgin, Oxford and their wedding breakfast was held in the Senior Common Room of his old college. Their joint income – he had been taken on to the staff of the *Christian Science Monitor* shortly afterwards at a salary of £400 per annum and she was a schoolteacher – allowed them to take a small flat in Wanstead, and in April 1936 Elizabeth gave birth to a daughter, Margaret. Hobson had travelled a tremendous way since succumbing to polio over twenty years beforehand, but the end of the decade was to provide possibly the biggest break of all. Worried that Elizabeth was on the verge of being evacuated from London along with her school, Hobson telephoned the Board of Education and was astounded to be informed by a civil servant not only of her destination, but of the general plans for evacuation. Realizing that this was a scoop of the first order, Hobson wrote up the information and submitted the article in May 1939 to *The Sunday Times*. The story, entitled 'Families Who Will Make Their Own Evacuation Plans',[107] duly appeared on the front page the following Sunday and Hobson's fifty-year connection with the newspaper had begun.

Chapter 2

The War Years: 1939–1945

The declaration of war on 3 September 1939 was greeted in Britain with a mixture of fear at what the future was to hold and relief that the period of political uncertainty that had characterized the first half of 1939 was now giving way to a more decisive phase. Writing about the propaganda film *The Lion Has Wings* in December 1939 at Godalming, Surrey (where he and his family had been evacuated, along with the rest of the *Monitor* staff), Hobson reveals how warmly the end to the specious diplomacy was welcomed:

> It has some touches of astonishing veracity, as when Mr Ralph Richardson, as an air force officer, heaves a sigh of relief at the declaration of war and murmurs, 'Now we know where we are.' When the Prime Minister broadcast on the first Sunday of the war, I was sitting with an old farmer in a stone floor kitchen on the edge of the Cotswolds, and those were the very words with which he broke the silence, after the Prime Minister had finished his speech.[108]

The radio bulletin that carried Chamberlain's announcement of war also contained the news that all places of entertainment were to be closed by government order. The country's preoccupation with the international crisis had already resulted in a slump in theatre-going in the summer of 1939, as people preferred to frequent pubs and hotels to discuss the threatening situation,[109] but this new state of affairs posed the clearest threat yet to the theatrical health of the nation. Within days, however, many began to feel that this move had been an over-reaction – not least financially affected managers such as Binkie Beaumont, who organized a deputation from the Theatre Managers' Association to Downing Street[110] – and Lord Wigram, the king's former secretary, used his influence to have the order rescinded.[111] Those theatres and cinemas some distance from London and major industrial centres were allowed after a week to open freely, while from 14 September those in the cities could open until 10.00pm and those in the West End until 6.00pm.[112] Hobson's position as a British journalist, based in London, writing for the *Christian Science Monitor* – and hence for an American audience – means that much of his writing on the theatre is more informative and explicatory about the condition of the London stage than if he had been tailoring his articles for a domestic audience, well aware of the effect of bombing and rationing. Whilst his intention as a theatre critic was always to remain the creation of a historical record of the productions that he had witnessed, his output during the war, when the number of productions was necessarily curtailed, broadens to consider wider issues, such as the implications of the war for new play-writing, the importance of the arts in maintaining morale on the home front, the changed working conditions of actors, the social effects of the blackout on the business of theatre-going and the desirability or otherwise of the dominance of light entertainment. Hobson also kept a day-by-day record of the events of the war and conditions at home from September 1939 to September 1942 which was originally projected to appear in Leonard Russell's *Saturday Book* series, a series that had been founded in 1941 and included contributions from William Shirer and Alexander Werth (foreign correspondents); Sean O'Casey and James Agate (drama, music, art); H. E. Bates, John Steinbeck and Dilys Powell (fiction); and Cecil Beaton (photography). The eventual length of the diary, however – 100,000 words – meant that it was large enough to be published by Hutchinson as the first *Saturday Book* special volume, under the title *The First Three Years of the War*, in 1943. Consequently the years 1939–45 gave rise to a body of work that is historical and documentary not merely in the sense that it records Hobson's personal reaction to plays, but in that it provides an evolving, first-hand social history of the theatre during this unique time.

As the London theatres began tentatively to reopen, Hobson outlined for his largely American readership some of the difficulties that places of entertainment and audiences alike were having to encounter. In 'On Not Seeing "Stagecoach"'[113] he wittily relates how he was refused entry to a Guildford cinema because he was not carrying his gas mask, and in 'Farewell to the Gaiety'[114] he reports that the Gaiety has become the first theatre to be destroyed in the war – not through enemy action, but because of municipal street-widening. At this early stage of the conflict, however, it was the theatrical profession itself and not the theatres that was most likely to suffer from structural damage. Although there was to be a progressive recovery from September's nadir, with the Little Theatre (providing a revue that was performed three times a day) and the Westminster (giving the first night-time production – of J. B. Priestley's *Music at Night*) being the first theatres to reopen,[115] the total number of productions on offer had been catastrophically reduced, and by mid-November only around 800 out of a total of 8,000 Equity-registered actors were still working.[116] The work of bodies such as the Entertainments National Service Association (ENSA), which was based at Drury Lane under the leadership of Basil Dean and provided the bulk of the organized entertainment for the armed forces, went some way towards alleviating unemployment amongst actors and production teams (even if it did come to be referred to by some as purveying 'Every Night Something Awful'[117]), but with only sixteen theatres open by mid-December, the salaries of the leading players reduced from £80 to a uniform £5 a week[118] and a corresponding economizing on the scale and variety of productions, the first three months of the war were a dismal time professionally for the majority of theatre workers. This did not mean, however, that the public ceased to go to the theatre. On the contrary, Rex Harrison has described the nation in 1939 as 'starving for entertainment';[119] by the time that the first wartime Christmas had arrived, Hobson was able to report, in 'Laughter Rules in British Theaters',[120] that the practice of theatre-going was more popular than ever. What had changed was the type of production on offer.

In November Hobson had wondered, in 'Great Actors and Bad Plays',[121] whether the London theatre would become more frivolous and less fashionable when the playhouses reopened fully, obviously having in mind the experience of the First World War. Two weeks later he made this link explicit when he wrote that it 'was shown in the last war that there is a great theatrical public for musical comedies and revues in times of national peril'[122] and in 'Laughter Rules in British Theaters', his customary end-of-year report, it is interesting to note the voracious public appetite for revues. In the first three weeks of its run at the Palladium George Black's revue had been seen by a phenomenal 32,000 people and Herbert Farjeon's at the Little was now grossing £200 per week more than for the equivalent period a year ago. Indeed, anything that might divert audiences from the threatening reality of war was eagerly devoured, to the extent that song and dance, broad comedies and energetic farces dominated the London theatres – of which, remarkably, there were more by the year-end than there had been on the eve of the war. Hobson was well aware of how the altered sensibility of the public might work to the theatre's financial advantage:

> In a sense, war makes the business of entertainment easier. Even before the curtain goes up, the audience is in a state of potential emotion far keener than in peace times. The smallest hints only are needed to prompt response ... there has only to be an officer in uniform, a girl in tears, with the cold light of dawn stealing in through the ballroom curtains, and a band playing softly off-stage, for the handkerchiefs to come out at once. But as yet this mood has been sounded surprisingly little, though Miss Carole Lynne touches it to fine and delicate issue at the Ambassadors, in the 'Gate Theater Revue', when, sitting at a table, and gazing at a photograph she holds in her hands, she sings, in a tiny, but beautifully pure voice, 'My heart is marching'.[123]

This naked appeal to the sentiments was a rare event, as was the desire to see patriotism exhibited on the stage, a fact that can be attributed both to the nature of the 'phoney war', where nothing directly happened to Britain until the summer of 1940, and to the desire to escape from a consideration of the crisis. Thus, as the nights (and, to an extent, optimism about the course of the war) darkened, entertainment lightened.

The inevitable corollary of this demand for light entertainment was the demise of the serious drama. Hobson moves on in the same article

('Laughter Rules in British Theaters') to quote Leslie Banks's view that, in times of crisis, theatre-goers demand only the lightest kind of amusement and that it is not until the crisis is over that works of serious art arise out of it. While not, as yet, lamenting this state of affairs, Hobson does point out that at least Priestley's experimental *Music at Night* had a reasonable run at the start of the war at the Westminster – and behind the quotation of this example of a worthy intellectual drama is the dissenting voice that was occasionally to resurface to question the notion that the war had destroyed the need for the modern serious play. In any event, it is significant that Hobson ends 1939 with a careful analysis and objective discussion of Rice's *Judgement Day* in 'A Timely Revival',[124] where he boldly and correctly states that, for all the excitement of the trial scene, where the falsely accused defendants arraign their accusers (the Nazis), if:

> Mr Rice [had] taken Lord Acton's advice to his historical students that they should always do their best for the other side, it would have been something even better. Mr Rice does not do his best for the other side in this play. He forgets that no one is to himself an unadulterated villain. There are always excuses and explanations. Mr Rice gives none of them. In consequence his play misses the height of tragedy.

At this early stage of the war it was still possible for a critic to ignore the demands of propaganda, which would have required a ringing endorsement of this anti-German play, in favour of the need for objective analysis.

The foundation of the Council for the Encouragement of Music and the Arts (the forerunner of the Arts Council) on 19 January 1940 provided a welcome boost to repertory theatre in Britain, since it was created to 'endow theatreless areas (South Wales, the North East) with dramatic diversion',[125] and Hobson noted in his diary the following month that light entertainment in the capital was experiencing a similar blossoming: 'London theatres are very prosperous. Light shows are especial favourites. A revue at the Prince's, "Shepherd's Pie", with Sydney Howard and Arthur Riscoe in the cast, is taking £3,500 a week.'[126] The steady recovery in the fortunes of the London theatre that had begun in November 1939 continued during the first six months of 1940 and was mirrored by a proliferation of Hobson's published articles. Whilst continuing to write book reviews, occasional editorials, profiles of actors and pieces on the effect of the war on British life for the *Christian Science Monitor*, he began to increase his output of book reviews for *The Sunday Times*, contributed the odd review to the *Spectator* and made his first radio broadcast for the BBC in May 1940. This came about after Hobson had heard a talk given by the literary critic John Middleton Murry during the first winter of the war, which he considered to be of a poor standard. He wrote to the producer of the programme, primarily because he wished to increase his precarious income, stating that he could deliver a much better piece, and was subsequently invited to prove this at a salary of £8 per programme. The title of his first broadcast was 'Talking to the Stars' and it marked the beginning of an erratic wartime radio career. After this first talk, Hobson was commissioned to deliver further pieces on the theatre and, later, on cricket. His passion for cricket had first manifested itself in print with an article on Lord Frederick Beauclerk in the famous *Saturday Book* series in *The Sunday Times*, and the BBC, impressed by this article, commissioned a programme on the same subject. The Corporation was even more impressed by the surge of complimentary letters that flooded into its offices after the talk was given, and immediately commissioned a series. They were less impressed, however, when it became apparent that all the fan mail had, unbeknown to Hobson, been faked by a neighbour, and the series was cancelled.[127] A similar blow to Hobson's pride – and to his financial prospects – occurred when a contract to deliver thirteen talks for the BBC's American Service was also cancelled, because his Oxford accent was considered to be 'too offensively English' and beyond what the Americans could accept. This objection vanished, however, in July 1944, when an American company decided that they could, after all, utilize his services – as Hobson himself relates:

> The *Christian Science Monitor* had two war correspondents who came over to London, and they fled back to America when the flying bombs came. My accent was then forgiven, it was regarded as quaint and heroic, so I broadcast on every Tuesday and Friday at two o'clock in the morning until the end of the war.[128]

In the winter of 1940 the continued lack of direct enemy activity to interfere with the life of the capital meant that the Hobson family decided to return to London in April. It was now possible for Hobson to report both on artistic issues that interested him, thereby developing his critical style, as well as on the crucial influence that the war was exerting on the future direction of the theatre in Britain. To the former category belong several articles that have clear implications for his future criticism.

When Hobson first started to contribute to *The Sunday Times* in 1939, the paper's resident drama critic was the colourful James Agate. Witty, opinionated, endearingly pompous and promiscuously homosexual, Agate was a well-known figure both within and without the London theatrical scene, not just through his weekly reviews but because of the publication, since 1935, of his diaries, *Ego*. Perhaps with a view to the future, but certainly with a diplomatic touch that was rarely to desert him, Hobson began a book review of Agate's published criticisms from June 1937 to July 1939, entitled 'The Amazing Critic',[129] with a piece of unbridled sycophancy:

> There is no English twentieth-century writer more certain of literary immortality than James Agate. The vagaries of taste may sweep into

oblivion work more immediately celebrated than his. The damp of many winters may put a rust upon the Shavian wit; and time, on which Mr Priestley has speculated so devotedly, may consign those speculations to forgetfulness. But, whatever the fate of particular dramatists, people will always be interested in the theater. They will inquire what was the traffic of the stage between the two world wars, and they will find their answers in Agate, the only London dramatic critic who has regularly reprinted his views since 1920.

If one manages to stumble past this self-interested beginning, however, it is illuminating to discover that, aside from his understanding of human nature, Hobson also admires both Agate's knowledge of French literature, an interest that was to be developed during Hobson's own time as drama critic for *The Sunday Times* (and which was to lead to an acclaimed book on the subject, *French Theatre Since 1830*[130]), and his ability to achieve the difficult feat of describing distinctive moments of acting, a trait of Hobson's best work. Indeed, this early period of the war provides an example, from Ashley Dukes's adaptation of Machiavelli's *Mandragola*, of how Hobson, too, could encapsulate in a succinct passage the essential gestus of an actor:

> Mr John Laurie gives to Nicia, the deceived husband, a performance of extraordinary industry. The number of carefully composed and nicely differentiated facial expressions that Mr Laurie has invented for this part must run into hundreds. He is an inexhaustible armory of nods and grins and smirks and becks and wreathed smiles. They do not flow across his countenance with the easy motion of a moving picture. Instead, each one is jerked into place with the staccato movement of a magic lantern, left there for a moment, and then arbitrarily deposed for its successor. This is a performance that has all the apparatus of humor, except the faculty of being humorous. It is compact of intelligent hard work. But one is reminded by it of the problem whether it is worth while to go so far to learn so little, as the small boy said when he got to the end of the alphabet.[131]

This description of an actor's movements, with its pertinent observations, built around a line of poetry (line 28 of Milton's *L'Allegro*[132]) – its challenging imagery, its wry humour and its gentle irony – contains many of the traits that were to appear in Hobson's most accomplished criticisms. The one disagreement that Hobson permits himself here with his current superior is significant, too. At the end of the review he wonders why Agate is so lukewarm in his appreciation of Ralph Richardson. Even at this stage Hobson is full of admiration for the sophisticated actor, about whom he was to write a monograph in 1958.[133]

It has already been seen that the dominant theatrical figure of Hobson's first ten years as a writer on the theatre had been George Bernard Shaw, and Hobson retains his fascination with this theatrical giant at the beginning of the new decade. A *Radio Times* synopsis of a programme that Hobson had made, entitled 'What I'm Reading Now', even suggests that Hobson was planning a book on the playwright,[134] and during 1940 there seems to be a hardening of Hobson's position, as if the impending publication necessitates a greater clarity of thought and firmness of conviction. This is particularly apparent in the review of Shaw's latest play, *In Good King Charles's Golden Days*, that appeared under the title, 'Half a Century of Plays'.[135] Gone is the reverential tone with which the critic had addressed Shaw in the early 1930s; this is because Hobson firmly believes that Shaw has 'misconceived the true nature of the theatre', a view borne out by his most recent work. Shaw considers that the theatre is 'a place for intellectual exercise, and therefore he has no regrets for merely tickling the ribs, and brushing up the brains of his audiences, instead of touching their hearts'. Such is Hobson's belief that Shaw lacks an understanding of the theatricality that is essential to the business of drama – a belief that was rapidly becoming a creed for the critic[136] – that, ironically, the work is not even praised as a suitable counterbalance to the predominance of revues and musical comedies about which Hobson was manifestly uneasy. 'If truth were to be apprehended solely by the intellect,' Hobson states:

> the drama would have to take a low place in the hierarchy of the arts. But happily there are other modes of apprehension more congenial to the theater. Shakespeare knew of them: Mr Shaw does not. It is this which robs his work of supreme greatness.

The prematurely announced book did not, in fact, materialize, but this surely had less to do with Hobson's workload than with his inability to reconcile his grudging admiration of Shaw for his intention of investing English drama with an intellectual content that was so patently absent in the work of his popular contemporaries with his belief that Shaw's immense reputation was now having a deleterious effect on some aspects of serious drama, in that Shaw's imitators were copying not well-conceived intentions, but a poorly executed, overly discursive and anti-theatrical practice. Two further articles neatly illustrate this irreconcilable dichotomy. In the first, 'Romance and Mr Shaw',[137] Hobson claims that the playwright's abhorrence of an excessive romantic content in plays, passed on to many contemporary film actors through their own direct experience of his work, has meant that 'the most mawkish aspects of sentimentality are not often presented in British films'. But against this beneficial consequence of Shaw's dramaturgy must be set the harmful legacy that his phenomenal influence has left the theatre, and the second article states this plainly. Hobson argues, in 'A New Play by James Bridie',[138] that, whilst Shaw is unable to create an emotional dimension for his characters, he is at least able to treat them even-handedly, which is more than can be said for his disciples:

> If you really want to appreciate the genius of Mr Bernard Shaw, the best thing to do is to see a play written by one of his imitators. That is why James Bridie's 'Holy Isle' ... is a salutary and instructive experience.

This back-handed compliment to Shaw is really no compliment at all and symbolizes Hobson's continuing ambivalence toward the Irish playwright.

Up to this point in his career Hobson has been strangely quiet in his consideration of the Irish movement, with Shaw the only Irishman whose work he has considered in detail. 'Prejudice Defeated' partially explains this. Having begun by stating that not one mainstream theatre has produced a play by Yeats recently, Hobson concedes that he himself possesses an 'arrogant Philistinism':

> A mere Englishman, I freely admit that in the Scottish speech I recognise the voice of a superior race; broad Yorkshire fills me with joy; even the Oxford accent I find not unpleasant. But there is something in the sing-song tones of the fairy isle, the curious habit of bringing the opposition of a downward emphasis and a rising inflection to bear upon the last word of every sentence, creating a feeling of irresolution, a sort of linguistic facing-both-ways, that bangs, locks, bolts every door of appreciation within my rebellious breast.[139]

Given all this, and the fact that when he heard the first words of Yeats's *The Unicorn from the Stars* he felt 'like a slack piece of string, like an exhausted motor engine on a cold morning, like a wet day in Wigan', it seems a little surprising that the article is entitled 'Prejudice Defeated' and not 'Prejudices Reinforced'. Perhaps, however, this open confession of a dislike provoked a cathartic re-examination of his opinions, for Hobson was certainly able to overcome such superficial intransigence in his later critiques of the work of Beckett.

Such are some of the artistic issues that interested Hobson in the first six months of 1940, but they were clearly not discussed in a vacuum, for interspersed amongst them are numerous pieces that relate to the war's direct effect upon the theatre. Although no bombs had fallen yet, the black-out was having a more democratizing effect on the business of theatre-going than the most committed of egalitarian playwrights could have hoped. 'For several weeks entertainment seekers refused to grope through pitch-dark streets in the full panoply of evening clothes', Hobson reported in 'A Principal Joy',[140] and this sartorial decline was hastened by the switch to more matinée performances, earlier evening shows and the arrival in force of the Luftwaffe in August 1940. Hobson was not alarmed by this dropping of social standards, but he was concerned by the fall in the standard of new plays. Although the theatre had now proved that it had survived the opening of the Second World War rather better than the start of the First, with twenty-nine productions still on the boards at the beginning of 1940,[141] the theatre-goer was being offered a restricted choice of fare, in that most theatres were presenting revues with music-hall stars such as Stanley Lupino, Bobby Howes, Jack Hulbert and Leslie Henson to the exclusion of serious, modern drama. Hobson greets Alec Coppel's new work with enthusiasm simply because it offers a greater diversity, but he is honest enough to analyse and explain the reason for his approbation: 'it is above the average level of a stage whose standards have been regrettably lowered by war, whatever might be thought of it in normal times'.[142] Even the Lord Chamberlain, Lord Clarendon, had lowered his 'standards'. In the same article Hobson reveals that Terence Rattigan's *Follow My Leader*, which was censored in 1938 on the advice of the Foreign Office because two of its characters are obviously modelled on Hitler and Goering and might have given offence to a foreign power,[143] is now able to play unhindered.

However, before he was to plunge into unmitigated gloom at the inability of playwrights to produce works of originality and worth (the failure of five straight plays in a row – *Punch Without Judy*, *The Bare Idea*, *Follow My Leader*, *Believe It or Not* and *You, Of All People* – appearing an ominous sign), Emlyn Williams, the actor/producer and newly pre-eminent theatrical figure, put on *The Light of Heart*, about the regeneration of a failed actor, which proved to Hobson that there was a demand for new work of quality and that it could hold its own against such revivals as John Gielgud's production of *The Importance of Being Earnest* at the Globe, Elmer Rice's *Judgement Day* (Phoenix) and T. S. Eliot's *Murder in the Cathedral* (Mercury).[144] It was a theme to which Hobson returned in 'The Theater Meets Competition'[145] the very next month. Musical comedies and revues predominated not simply because of public demand, but because of specific managerial policy – the implication being that, whilst revues clearly had their place, room should also be made for alternative forms of theatre, since 'when put to the test, the public has in general responded, as is proved by the record of the Westminster Theater, which has succeeded in attracting the public to plays of the utmost seriousness of purpose'. The success of Robert Ardrey's intellectual work, *Thunder Rock*, whose optimism earned it, according to its leading actor Michael Redgrave, praise as 'a sort of national asset',[146] was also proof of this.[147]

In the same article the critic was able to claim that the war had already wrought one change to the English theatre which could be applauded as a great success, namely the eradication of the trivial comedy of bad manners, with its superficial love interest, obligatory inheritance and tedious conflict between Bright Young Thing and out-of-touch parent:

> ... the tremendous issues at stake in Europe make the content of the average peace-time West End play seem unbearably trivial. This consists usually of a boisterous charade of middle-class family life, or of fashionable repartee in a Mayfair salon. For years the critics have

been denouncing this kind of entertainment, but with no success. But what the critics have failed to do, Hitler has accomplished; for once the sword has taken precedence of the pen. The stage has been swept clear of these things.

In other words, the sterility of the drama of the 1930s had been exposed for all to see, which was another reason why there were few adequate competitors to the revues, farces and long-running sentimental musicals such as *Me and My Girl* by Arthur Rose and Douglas Furber, which in June 1940 had passed its 1,467th performance.[148] The serious drama was in a poor position to compete, because there was such a sickly legacy to build upon. By the end of June, however, the war clouds were gathering and more important battles were about to be fought. Hitler's destructive power was beginning to look less metaphorical by the day and the gaze began to be switched away from the stage and across the Channel – and finally up to the skies.

Between 27 May and 4 June 1940, after the capitulation of the Belgian Army in the north and the thrust of the German tank forces in the south had cut off the British Expeditionary Force and the French First Army, over 200,000 British troops and 120,000 French were evacuated from Dunkirk. The mood in Britain was again similar to the curious ambivalence with which many had greeted the declaration of war the previous September. People were naturally afraid of the imminence of invasion but they were also strangely exultant at the prospect of being in the front line at last.[149] The capture of the Channel ports by the Germans inevitably affected theatrical activity and promptly curtailed the recovery in the fortunes of the London theatre that had begun in October 1939. New productions, such as A. J. Cronin's *Jupiter Laughs* and Dame Marie Tempest's proposed revival of Dodie Smith's *Dear Octopus*, were postponed; *The Light of Heart* was taken on tour to the provinces for a month, thereby initiating what was to become a common policy when conditions in the capital became too uncomfortable; and the New Theatre in Oxford was booked by a London management for its summer production of half a dozen plays. All this was related by Hobson in an article entitled 'The Theater Watches'[150] – such was the gravity of the situation that the theatre had switched its introspective gaze away from its own artifice to the real-life drama now enveloping the country. Against this sombre backdrop, it may appear somewhat bizarre that in June and July Hobson could still write about the social implications of the war for the theatre, stating in an editorial, 'London Carries On',[151] that the old practice of wearing evening dress to the theatre had ceased, and claiming, in 'First Nights, Farewell', that the demise of the dress code and the imposition of a standard Equity wage for actors could have long-term, beneficial consequences:

> These changes may in time not be without effect for good. Though they detract from the superficial attractiveness of the theater, they

tend to stabilize its economic foundations, and to preserve it from becoming a mere appanage of social frivolity.[152]

Any criticism of Hobson for irrelevance, however, ignores the fact that it was partly this refusal to allow the threatening situation completely to disrupt their way of life that helped the inhabitants of Britain and, in particular, London to withstand the trauma of the Battle of Britain – a view that John Gielgud confirms in a theatrical context when he speaks of wartime audiences' 'feeling of grim determination'.[153] And, taking a wider view, Hobson's speculation about the impact of the changes to theatrical practice was prescient. Although the theatre partially lapsed back into its pre-war ways immediately after 1945, it is doubtful that the growth of repertory movement funded by the Arts Council and the revolution heralded by the arrival of the French dramatists and Beckett and secured by the playwrights of the 1950s and early 1960s could have taken place without the upheavals of the early 1940s.[154]

By the end of July it was apparent that the public, and even the profession itself, had lost its taste for the theatre, since, as Hobson wrote in 'The Touch of the Dramatist', 'the only theater which in these times interests even actors is the theater of war'.[155] At the beginning of August, as France fell and Britain prepared for invasion, Hobson penned a status report under the heading 'Actors Help in War Effort'.[156] Out of the sixty or so theatres in London, only one, the Queen's, was performing a play – Daphne du Maurier's *Rebecca*. Many theatres had been taken over for war service. The Strand, for example, was now providing a canteen and information service for Australian soldiers. Theatres that had remained open were admitting service personnel in uniform to the 10s. 6d. seats in the stalls for 3s. 6d. Children from the actors' orphanage were being sent to Los Angeles. The work that ENSA had done since the start of the war had had a great effect on morale and had provided much-needed employment for actors, yet the situation was greatly altered now. A dozen or more revues and musicals were still being performed, for 'popular entertainment is running strongly in the direction of the light and the frivolous', but the unasked question of the article is clearly: how long will they be able to survive? A week later, on 10 August, Hobson praised the forty or so American actors who had remained in Britain, focusing in particular – partly for propaganda purposes – on the comedian Vic Oliver, who happened to be Winston Churchill's son-in-law.[157] Five days after this article appeared, the Battle of Britain began.

On the day of the feared invasion of Britain, 7 September, when the signal 'Cromwell' for 'invasion imminent' was sent out in Britain,[158] Hobson's most unrealistic article of the war was published in the *Christian Science Monitor*. 'Theater Boom in London' may have been designed to convince the American readership of the unflappability of the British, but its list of burgeoning theatrical productions – Leslie Henson's *Up and Doing,* Geoffrey Kerr's *Cottage to Let, Shepherd's Pie* and *Black Velvet* (the proceeds of which would be donated the following month to the fund for the purchase of a Spitfire) – was less a sign of phenomenal commercial success than of courageous professional stoicism. This stoicism was something that Londoners exhibited in abundance at this time and perhaps accounts for the irritation evident in Hobson's next published article, where he criticizes Clare Boothe's new play at the Apollo, the insensitive *Margin for Error*. Although a huge success in America, it appears from a modern perspective to have been amazingly inappropriate for London in the Blitz, making jokes about barbed wire and falling bombs not within the context of a revue, but under the auspices of a serious play. Hobson wonders aloud why an audience can laugh at a comedian talking of these issues, but not at an actor:

> Why is it that [the comedians] amuse, whilst Miss Boothe's story of the Jewish policeman set to guard the German consulate in New York offends? The answer, I think, is that 'Margin for Error' changes its course half-way through. In the first act it gets to grips with urgent problems of society and war; in the second it becomes merely an ordinary detective story. London audiences in their present mood do not mind being flippant about serious things; but it is unwise to show them first the seriousness of the things about which you later ask them to be flippant.[159]

Entertainment now clearly had a duty to maintain morale as well as provide enjoyment.

Hobson's mood was not improved by his next visit to the theatre, discussed in 'From the Back of the Pit',[160] to see Vernon Sylvaine's farce, *Women Aren't Angels*. Just as with 'First Nights, Farewell', Hobson defines his personal attitude to an aspect of the theatre in the middle of a period of national crisis:

> I am not really very fond of farce. I take little pleasure in the spectacle of people chasing each other in and out of rooms, underneath and over tables, forcibly depriving each other of their clothing on the pretext that secret documents must be found, tripping each other up. However hard the players knock each other about, they do not bowl me over.

Whether this prim dismissal of farce is a result of the predominant mood of national seriousness or an innate dislike of the genre remained to be seen.

Hobson wrote very few reviews between the climax of the Battle of Britain and the end of the year because there were very few plays being produced. He was able to draw breath in October 1940, however, and take stock of the situation in 'Raids and Dictator Plays'.[161] The pattern of the war thus far in its relation to the theatre was now apparent. On the outbreak of war, the theatres closed; they staged a steady recovery during the period of the phoney war, to the point that they were overflowing and enjoying unparalleled prosperity; the threat of invasion diminished their success and the Blitz and subsequent enemy raids had rendered them empty again. The frequent air raids were now posing inevitable problems:

> From the beginning of the war [the places of entertainment] announced that, should a warning be given, they would stop the performance to allow those members of the audience wishing to leave to do so, and then continue for the benefit of the rest. That seemed fairly simple. But the matter has been complicated in that the period of warning has in several cases extended from dusk till dawn, and no play will last as long as that. Audiences in consequence have been themselves asked to give exhibitions of their talent, and so many people who never expected to have the chance of appearing on a West End stage have achieved this particular aspect of a heart's desire. Another difficulty has been provided by the natural wish of people caught out on the streets to dash into the nearest cinema on the warning of a raid, and managers have been much perplexed whether to admit them or not.

Given these practical difficulties, in addition to the scarcity of money and materials, the understandable reluctance of audiences to travel during the black-out and the physical destruction of such playhouses as the Queen's and the Saville, the theatre in London at the end of 1940 had again reached its lowest point since its enforced closure after the English Civil War.

As in 1939, the recovery from this nadir in 1941 was actor-led, something that was acknowledged at the time by an unnamed BBC official in the article 'The Theater Fights Back':

> I admire more than anything else the courage with which actors and actresses are tackling the difficulties that surround and impede them. They don't merely sit down and moan. They try first this, then that, until they get something that really works.[162]

After all, in spite of evacuation, there were still six million Londoners to entertain and 33 entertainment licences were taken out at the beginning of 1941, not too great a drop from the 50 of the previous year.[163] At this point, the nascent recovery was certainly not dramatist-led. Indeed, articulating the considerable anger felt in Britain at those artists and professionals who, in Sir Seymour Hicks' phrase, had 'Gone with the Wind Up',[164] Hobson questioned, in 'Before the Nightingales Sang', why there were so few modern playwrights left in Britain:

> ... where are the dramatists? Noël Coward, of course, is in Australia; or is it Japan? J. B. Priestley is telling America over the short waves what to be at war feels like. W. H. Auden and Christopher Isherwood are, it is rumoured, in Hollywood. But where are the others?[165]

In fact, Noël Coward, an indefatigable entertainer of the troops, was to return later in the year with his phenomenal success, *Blithe Spirit*, and J. B. Priestley was also to prove that he had not taken flight, but W. H. Auden, whose prophetic pre-war *The Dance of Death* and *The Ascent of F6* had convinced Hobson that he was to be the standard-bearer of the much-desired vibrant, intellectual drama, was not to be forgiven for his desertion of both the theatrical and the military battle. Indeed, some forty years later, in an article regretting the collapse of serious British drama entitled 'Has Our Theatre Lost Its Nerve?',[166] Hobson draws a parallel between the 'failure of nerve' in 1940 and the lack of conviction in the 1980s – defined as 'the spirit of the despairing and frightened Auden' – and in his personal retrospective on twentieth-century theatre, *Theatre in Britain*, published in 1984, Hobson makes explicit the charge that he had levelled against Auden ever since his departure:

> If there were in the Thirties any writers on whom we felt that in time of trial and crisis we could absolutely rely for strength and support, those writers were W. H. Auden and Christopher Isherwood ... Their departure had profound effects upon the intellectual world. It was so controversial that it prevented for years that taking over of the theatre by intellectuals which was effected after the war by Christopher Fry and T. S. Eliot.[167]

If 1940 had had little to offer theatrically other than the two British offerings, *Suspense* and *Diversion*, the American *Thunder Rock* and a song, the famous 'A Nightingale Sang in Berkeley Square' sung by Judy Campbell – prompting Hobson to write in February that the bird 'has dominated Britain for the last nine months ... What with nightingales through all the hours of the day, and bombers through the night, Britain in 1940 was a whirr of wings'[168] – it took 1941 a considerable time to offer some worthwhile home-grown talent. Hobson's writing until the summer provides a testimony to the gradual increase in theatrical activity, underpinned by a personal desire to see some sign of rebirth in the modern, British play – a wartime (and immediate post-war) leitmotif. In March, a month of professional difficulty for him because the damage that the Blitz had caused to the publishing industry had meant that there were no books for him to review for *The Sunday Times*, he reports that 'The war may have stopped most theatrical entertainment in London, but it has not stopped pantomime', a state of affairs which he can only partially applaud:

> For all its obvious weaknesses, its vulgarity, and its total failure to demonstrate or even to offer the remotest hint that man is a rational being, pantomime has a charm from which even the greatest are not exempt.[169]

This sense of frustration at the predictability and, to a degree, triviality of the fare is reinforced by a succession of articles which on the one hand celebrate the fact that plays are again being performed and testify to the resilience of the profession, but on the other lament the lack of ambition given the pool of existing talent. Hence, J. M. Barrie's *Dear Brutus*, a revival which had appeared during the last war, could boast a formidable cast list that included John Gielgud, Zena Dare, Margaret Rawlings, Ursula Jeans, Nora Swinburne, Mary Jerrold, Leon Quartermaine, Roger Livesey and Ronald Wood, whilst at the same time there were only two other serious plays on in London.[170] Eleven playhouses were open by April, but of the five straight plays being performed – *Dear Brutus*, *Once a Crook*, *Thunder Rock*, *When We Are Married* and *The Blue Goose* – only the last was not a revival.[171] George Black's supplanting of C. B. Cochran as the principal provider of light musical entertainment meant that London was now awash with 'low comedians' such as Nervo and Knox, Naughton and Gold and Flanagan and Allen,[172] and although S. N. Behrman's new play, *No Time for Comedy*, was occasionally 'topical and serious in theme', in its 'characters and story it is reminiscent of most of the brittle drawing-room comedies that have been written since Noël Coward first showed how profitable it is to present people doing worthless things'.[173] It is easy to see why Hobson was later to write of this period that the serious theatre had suffered from a shameful 'failure of nerve'.[174]

Noël Coward is not a playwright who ever found critical favour with Hobson. Whereas with Shaw he deplored the Irishman's loquaciousness at the expense of theatricality, with Coward he was unable to see the subtle irony beneath the crisp dialogue and brittle emotions of the Bright Young Things who featured in his works. Whilst the element of parody, even satire, in plays such as *Hay Fever*, *Private Lives* and *The Vortex* is now widely appreciated, Hobson was too constrained by his, generally correct, belief that new drama should reject the subject-matter of the middle-class family to concede that Coward's handling of this familiar theme was often challenging and refreshing. The arrival of *Blithe Spirit* in the summer of 1941 was the most notable theatrical event of the war to date, but Hobson's review of it, possibly influenced by his religious convictions, displayed a priggish inflexibility that seems out of character. Although he concedes that the play is constructed 'with astonishing technical skill', Hobson states that he found the work 'heartless, shallow and worthless' and his explanation of Coward's intentions contains one of his most excessive condemnations:

> [Mr Coward] has no feelings of any kind about immortality, or the sense of loss, or the enigmas of human existence. If he had felt impelled by an inner compulsion to write a play about life after death, I should probably have thought him unwise, because of the necessary limitations of the stage. But it would have been a compulsion that one could respect. Mr Coward has, however, no such compulsion. He is anxious

only to make a joke, and, in order to do so, he makes his characters behave with a callousness unparalleled in my playgoing experience.[175]

Why is Hobson so contemptuous of Coward? An answer may be gleaned from a review of Coward's next success, *Present Laughter*, in 1943. Hobson is quite clearly offended by what he perceives to be Coward's *Weltanschauung*: '"Present Laughter" is one of its author's greatest popular successes, but the picture it draws of human nature is almost wholly contemptuous', and, what is worse, Coward manages in this play to offend Hobson's personal religious sensibilities:

> One of Mr Coward's characters, who begins as a whimpering, grumbling sort of woman, becomes a Christian Scientist. Mr Coward's hero treats it as a personal affront that anyone should assume an air of superiority or satisfaction arising from spiritual experience. The woman in question is sufficiently awakened to show her mutual independence of conditions that are dragging her companions down, but it is unfortunate that Mr Coward treats this part of his play as a means of getting facile laughs.[176]

Hobson clearly protests too much here and has encountered his first critical blind spot. It is as if his frustration at the vapid nature of much of the London scene, a frustration that is compounded by the fact that he cannot condemn it, because it performs the crucial function of maintaining public morale (something which he acknowledges in *Theatre in Britain*, when he speaks of the wartime 'courage of the frivolous and the cowardice of the serious theatre'[177]), has boiled over at the sight of a talented and hugely successful playwright seemingly squandering his potential on irreverent and faintly offensive writing. Such is the shock that one feels at this lapse in Hobson's customary tone of measured objectivity that it provides an important reminder of how coolly informative and scrupulously fair the majority of his reviews have been up to this point.

The appearance of *Blithe Spirit* and the audiences that it attracted (it ran for 1,977 performances after its première on 2 July 1941[178]) constituted the most visible sign of the extraordinary recovery that the London theatre had made once again. Slowly, directors began to regain their confidence and significant productions were mounted, notably Tyrone Guthrie's *King John* at the New Theatre, starring Ernest Milton as the monarch. The launch of Operation Barbarossa on 22 June 1941, in which German tanks and troops poured into the Soviet Union, meant that Britain discovered that it had a new ally and before the year was out Hobson had already been to see two Russian plays, *Distant Point* by Afinogenov[179] and *Squaring the Circle* by Kataev, which he was amused to find was very much like an English comedy by Frederick Lonsdale.[180] The scarcity of new serious plays of quality persisted, however, a theme that was now beginning to dominate Hobson's rather less frequent articles on the theatre (the bulk of his output in 1942 was book reviews for *The Sunday Times* and *London Calling*, the overseas journal of the BBC, longer articles about life on the home front for the *Christian Science Monitor* and broadcasts for the BBC). Robert Morley told Hobson in an article that appeared in *London Calling* under the sub-title, 'London's Scarcity of Serious Plays', that the present situation had its origins in the malaise that had existed before the outbreak of war:

> The trouble is that ever since Hitler got into power our dramatists have been living in a dream world of the 1920s, when an epigram counted for more than a machine gun, the Bright Young Things loomed larger than the New Order.[181]

Readily concurring with this point of view, Hobson quickly moved on to dismiss the relevance of John Van Druten's comedy, *Old Acquaintance*, because its 'concern with the dubious activities of trivial people seems, in [the] face of the enormous happenings in the world today, to be old fashioned and lacking in perspective'.[182]

But it is in the piece entitled 'Revues Dominate London Stage'[183] that Hobson provides his clearest manifesto for the return of challenging theatre, cogently expressing his unease at the commercially successful but dramatically spurious light entertainment and demanding that old-fashioned, dismissive attitudes must be dispensed with if the theatre is to begin to reflect the enormity of the times. He starts by readily acknowledging the sense of prosperity that the theatre is enjoying as pleasure-starved Londoners flock to its performances. Entertainments like Leslie Henson's *Up and Doing* and the Prince's show, *Fun and Games*, had now been taking more than £3,000 for several months. Yet whereas one might expect this state of affairs to result in unbridled joy amongst members of the profession, the true mood is actually rather different. Hobson continues:

> The fact is that nobody really thinks that the British theater is at the moment measuring up to the tremendous challenge of world events. It is making a lot of money, but it is making it principally with revues in which the quality of wit is certainly not the element mainly responsible for their popularity.

Hobson obviously feels that they merely provide a diversion from the sombre world outside, yet he also believes that one should not scoff at them, for they are a symptom and not the cause of the problem. Their merit is that they 'help to keep those who like them cheerful and lighthearted, which is an important factor in preserving war morale. But they do not illuminate the problems of today. They spectacularly avoid them.' Hobson looks towards the serious playwrights to begin the examination of these problems, but none appear capable of the task, for 'most British, and to a certain extent, American, dramatists are still living in a dreamworld of the nineteen twenties, when a smart cynicism seemed to them an adequate substitution for any deeper philosophy'.

Although Hobson was to enjoy certain new modern plays in isolation during the rest of the war, such as Hugh Burden's *The Young and Lovely* (reviewed in 'A New English Dramatist'), which he greatly admired for its portrait of contented, married love,[184] and always felt obliged to encourage writers who submitted original material, even if he could not appreciate the end product (e.g. J. B. Priestley's *They Came to a City*: 'His statement of ideals ... lacks balance, and what he has to say he often says unfairly. But, in the London theatre of today, the fact that there is a dramatist who has anything to say at all is enormously refreshing'[185]), it remained a fact that nobody rose to his challenge. This period of constructive criticism, however, played a crucial part in the formation of his critical style. By espousing a wish for a drama that was unobtainable during the war, he honed his appreciation of the original and provocative work which left him well prepared to champion the innovative, the avant-garde and the theatrically ground-breaking. The origin of Hobson's pertinent comments that heralded the arrival of Beckett and ensured the acceptance of Pinter are patently evident in the frustration that characterizes his writing during the war.

If Hobson was ultimately to be disappointed in his hope for serious wartime drama, the second half of 1942 did at least bear witness to a new artistic development, namely the film and play that dealt with the war itself. The critic had wondered, after seeing the propaganda film *Next of Kin* – which reinforced the message that 'Careless Talk Costs Lives' by dramatizing the casualties involved in an Allied mission in France that had been betrayed to the Germans – whether subsequent films would now abjure the normal 'boy meets girl' plot.[186] Terence Rattigan's *Flare Path*, about the work of a fighter squadron, adhered to the old recipe, and drew an amusing comment from Hobson: 'many English airmen face many grave dangers by day and by night; but the number of those whose wives are on the point of running away with a film star is fortunately limited'.[187] A more convincing entertainment was Emlyn Williams's *The Morning Star*, which, instead of focusing on the action in the air and therefore relying to a large degree on complicated scenery and sound effects, concentrated on the experiences of those being bombed. The issue of the propriety of plays that dealt so closely with wartime experience was something that was raised as soon as these plays appeared, but Hobson was dismissive of the dissent that had been aroused:

> If Leslie Henson or Jack Hulbert puts on an enormously successful light musical show, the theater is rebuked for avoiding issues in a time of national peril; and if it deals with serious issues it is suspected of being heartless. But from the theater's point of view there is a mitigating circumstance in the fact that the general public does not appear to pay the slightest attention to anything dramatic critics say.[188]

Nevertheless, war plays were all the rage in the autumn of 1942, with the most notable being *The Morning Star* (which had already clocked up over 300 performances at the Globe by September 1942), *Flare Path*, *Lifeline* (which boasted an all-male cast for this navy drama by Norman Armstrong) and *Escort*. *Escort* was notable in the sense that it was universally panned: 'I have heard wittier conversation come from a perambulator', Hobson wrote,[189] and the play survived a mere twenty-four performances.

There is one aspect of the wartime theatre about which Hobson, not yet a full-time theatre critic for an English newspaper, regrettably wrote little. From the ending of the Blitz on 10 May 1941 to the arrival of the first V1 rockets in June 1944, the London theatre staged a remarkable recovery in popularity. In November 1943 over thirty theatres were open, with the two English princesses, Elizabeth and Margaret, providing confirmation of this by going to see *Arsenic and Old Lace* and the critic claiming that he was now witnessing the 'greatest popularity the theatre has enjoyed since the middle of the last war'.[190] Hobson bears witness to the absence of new writing of quality during this period, but seldom remarks on the excellence of the revival of the classics, stimulated by the country's very best stage actors. By the end of 1942 John Gielgud, who had made a wartime commitment to produce and act only in classics,[191] had already staged *The Importance of Being Earnest, Three Sisters, The School for Scandal, Richard II* and *The Merchant of Venice*[192] and it was apparent that the artistic quality of the Second World War was much higher than it had been in the First. But Hobson's role for the *Christian Science Monitor* demanded that he dwelt less on individual plays than supply a mixture of reviews and articles which provided an overall view of theatrical activity in Britain. The unfortunate aspect of this is that, instead of being able to read Hobson's opinions on the great acting performances of the war – for example, Olivier's Richard III at the New Theatre – he merely records the number of spectators who attended the play, 37,000 by November 1944.[193] A consideration of the artistic merits of a play had often to be sacrificed to a statistical approach. In addition to this, the increasing demands on his time from *The Sunday Times* – from 1943 his main employer – meant that he had even less opportunity to visit the theatre every night during the last three years of the war. Ironically, this enforced absence proved to have a beneficial influence on his chances of becoming a full-time critic, for such was the quality and regularity of his book reviewing that when Dilys Powell, the film critic, fell ill in September 1943, Hobson was the person chosen to deputize.

If the entry of the Soviet Union into the war in 1941 had provoked a flood of Russian plays to London, the arrival of the Americans for the invasion of Europe provoked the introduction of a number of articles in the British press articulating amazement and sometimes shock at what were perceived to be their lax moral standards. In November 1944 Hobson, writing one of his last articles of the war directly about the theatre, bears witness to the delicacy of British feeling. In 'A Difference of Manners'[194] he reports that two plays have recently caused uproar in the London theatre. The first, the farce *Felicity Jasmine* by Gordon Sherry, about a scent which rendered English girls attractive to American soldiers, survived four performances before the Lord Chamberlain withdrew its licence on the grounds that it was an immoral entertainment.[195] The second, *Daughter Janie*, was booed for its portrayal of American soldiers entertaining 16-year-old high school girls who were brash and abrasive, held 'necking parties' and behaved with 'extreme freedom'. Hobson himself was less shocked, possibly because it would have been injudicious to express outrage in an American paper. Whilst he recognized that the audiences felt that they were protesting about a matter of morals, they were, he claims diplomatically, in reality upset by a difference of manners.

From November 1944 to the end of the war Hobson was chiefly occupied with writing editorials on the Allies' thrust into Europe which were syndicated to other newspapers owned by the proprietor of *The Sunday Times*, Lord Kemsley, including the *Sheffield Daily Telegraph* (his sparring partner of old), the *Newcastle Journal and North Mail* and the *Daily Dispatch*. One editorial, however, reveals how the student socialist had now, at the age of 40, apparently embraced the ideals of Conservatism[196] and was beginning to consider the state of a post-war Britain. Having welcomed the Birmingham speech of Oliver Lyttleton, in which he had outlined seven principles of Conservative philosophy, Hobson goes on to agree with Lyttleton's analysis of Tory attributes: 'Conservatism is a political philosophy that is forward looking. It aims at keeping what is good from the past and earning what is better from the future. In short, it is a policy of deserving and preserving.'[197] In many ways, this political epigram (crushingly rejected by the British electorate of 1945) was less relevant to the political scene than to the progress of Hobson's own career. The diversity of his publications, the stringent demands of wartime conditions, his experience of other media, such as radio, the need to maintain morale without sacrificing objectivity, his function as a British journalist writing for a remote American audience and his passionate belief in the need for worthwhile, intellectual drama had all given his writing a clarity and incisiveness over the past six years that left him well prepared and suitably qualified for the post of chief drama critic of *The Sunday Times* which was to be unexpectedly bestowed upon him in 1947. By keeping what was good from the past in his writing and striving for something better in the future, Hobson was shortly to embark upon the path that was to lead to his becoming the twentieth century's most influential theatre critic.

Chapter 3

The Accession: 1945–July 1947

The inter-war period in Britain was the era of the press barons. By the end of the 1930s four men – Max Aitken (Lord Beaverbrook), Lord Rothermere, William Berry (Lord Camrose) and Gomer Berry (later Lord Kemsley) – owned half the national and provincial dailies and had a joint circulation of thirteen million readers.[198] The two Berry brothers had bought *The Sunday Times* in 1915, before its sole ownership (together with that of the *Sunday Graphic*, *Daily Sketch* and several provincial publications) passed into the hands of Kemsley in 1937, when the family firm, Allied Newspapers, was split into three. The division resulted in Kemsley becoming the largest newspaper proprietor in the country.

Described in the history of the newspaper, *The Pearl of Days*, as 'a philistine with a respect for the arts but no knowledge of them and only the sketchiest idea of world affairs',[199] Kemsley's vigorous support of Neville Chamberlain's pre-war policy of appeasement had damaged his favourite newspaper's reputation. He had even travelled to meet Adolf Hitler, as late as 27 July 1939, to assure the Führer that his newspapers stood unswervingly behind Chamberlain's position, that Churchill was an irrelevance and that the Prime Minister attached tremendous importance to the documents that had been signed between them at Munich.[200] No wonder Kemsley was the only newspaper proprietor whom Chamberlain trusted. But Kemsley's political naivety was matched by his business acumen and although his empathy with the arts and wider culture issues was limited, he recognized that a post-war readership would eagerly devour articles devoted to these issues. By continuing to enhance this aspect of the paper, featuring in-depth studies of well-known personalities (for example, Field Marshal Montgomery) and, above all, employing the astute editor W. W. Hadley, Kemsley helped *The Sunday Times* grow in readership from 330,135 in 1939 to 885,000 in 1959, when he sold it to Roy Thomson. One of the journalists concerned with the arts world, who had been connected with *The Sunday Times* for almost as long as Kemsley himself, was to play an inadvertent and crucial role in the advancement of Harold Hobson.

At the end of the Second World War the drama critic of *The Sunday Times* was the 67-year-old James Evershed Agate. He had occupied the post since 1923, having begun to write for the Manchester *Guardian* in 1907, but in 1945 he was as well known for his *Ego* diaries (eventually totalling nine volumes, covering 1932 to 1948), as he was for his criticism.

These diaries, which record his experience of London theatrical, literary and artistic life and which frequently encounter the distinctive personalities of the time, are noteworthy for the style, wit and dynamism of the diarist. They reveal a critic aware of the literary tradition in which he is writing; one who is confident that his readers will trust his intuition in judging the theatrical temper of a piece; who is suspicious of too intellectual and theoretical an approach to criticism, preferring to refer to acknowledged models of theatrical excellence, such as Irving for acting, and who has a keen appreciation of French literature – all traits that Hobson was to inherit in varying degrees. They also demonstrate a Wildean delight in the pithy phrase or sentence that presents a point with clarity and brilliance whilst simultaneously highlighting the pertinacity of the raconteur. An example of this occurs in *Ego 8*, where Agate relates a visit to the second Sixth Form Conference of the Schools of King Edward's Foundation, to which he had been invited by the schoolboy Kenneth Tynan – the future critic of the *Observer*. On being asked to define the number of rules for good dramatic criticism, Agate replied that there were only two that mattered: 'One. Decide what the playwright was trying to do, and pronounce how well or ill he has done it. Two. Determine whether the well-done thing was worth doing at all.'[201]

Although this ostentatious clarity was sometimes compromised in his journalistic criticism by a predilection for the grandiloquent phrase which often said more about the observer than the observed, Agate cut a noteworthy figure in the 1930s and early 1940s with his love of champagne and an Epicurean lifestyle, his flamboyant behaviour and devoted readership, and he was someone whom *The Sunday Times* could be proud to count amongst its staff. There was one fact about Agate, though, of which the proprietor of the newspaper, the autocratic Lord Kemsley, was remarkably unaware, given that it was an open secret throughout theatrical London – Agate was an energetic homosexual. In her biography of her husband, Kathleen Tynan relates how, on the same visit to King Edward's, the elderly critic broached the topic with the 18-year-old Tynan:

> On 19 July 1945, at the station in Birmingham, Ken met the sixty-eight-year-old critic,[202] who was wearing a tropical suit and a Panama hat. Into a taxi they climbed and, after a short exchange on the matter of the conference, the critic placed a hand on his host's knee and asked, 'Are you a homosexual, my boy?' 'I'm af-f-fraid not,' said Ken. 'Ah well,' Agate replied, 'I thought we'd get that out of the way.'[203]

Such equanimity, necessary in an era of strong disapproval of homosexuality, was to desert Agate in 1945.

The end of the war saw Harold Hobson depressed about his finances, in spite of having been appointed assistant literary editor of *The Sunday Times* in 1944. The cancellation by the BBC of his projected series on cricket and theatre had dealt a severe blow to his self-esteem and it seemed that, for the first time in his life, he construed himself as a failure, for not being able to provide as he would like financially for his beloved wife Elizabeth.[204] He sought and received permission from the editor, W. W. Hadley, to increase the number of book reviews he was writing and he even began work on a novel which he had conceived jointly with Leonard Russell[205] – colleague, friend and husband of Dilys Powell – at the beginning of the war. It was published by Longmans, Green and Company on 24 June 1946, for the price of 8s. 6d., under the title of *The Devil in Woodford Wells*. This plodding pot-boiler contained several elements that related to the Hobson family. The narrator, John Mallard, has a wife and an 8-year-old daughter called Patricia (Margaret Hobson was born in 1936). He went to an Oxford college, St Ambrose (Oriel), and is now the London drama critic of an American newspaper, the *Courier* (*Christian Science Monitor*). He drives a Morris 8, lives in Woodford Wells (in 1935 the Hobsons moved into a flat in Woodford Green, and in 1938 a house) and had at one time considered writing a novel with Boswell Smith, the manager of the Talks department at the BBC (presumably Leonard Russell) about the nineteenth-century cricketer, Lord Frederick Beauclerk. A similar lack of imagination surrounds the unravelling of the plot, which centres on Hobson's passion, cricket. Enoch Soames, having sold his soul to the Devil, returns to earth after his death to examine the British Museum catalogue. He wishes to determine whether posterity, unlike his contemporaries, will recognize his genius. Mallard, who meets Soames in the library during the war, enlists his help in deciphering the mystery of a cricket score-card for a game played during the Napoleonic War. Having met one of the players – Beauclerk – in the underworld, Soames is able to reveal that the erratic nature of the scores resulted from the fact that one of the participants had used the score-card to transmit coded secrets to Napoleon's forces. Things become even more preposterous when Soames, having explained, with characteristically bathetic humour, that Hell is based on the college system – 'Think of Oxford. You won't be far off the mark then'[206] – returns from the underworld not with Beauclerk, but with another player, one Marshall Strange. The nadir is reached when we learn that a contemporary report had mentioned the unusual shape of Strange's feet; it is revealed that Soames is not as human as he appears; and the two 'devils' are seen departing at the end of the book for the Russian front. Sparse of plot, continually arrested by incidental details that dominate and distract rather than enhance and illuminate and prone to verbose speculation about books, *The Devil in Woodford Wells* demonstrates how Hobson required the compressed form of the critical notice – which focused ideas and precluded irrelevant digression – for the expression of his literary talent.

Much more encouraging professionally for Hobson was his appointment in 1947 to the post of television critic of the *Listener*, for whom he wrote from May of that year to September 1951. With the simple brief of informing the reader in his monthly column, 'Critic on the Hearth', about what had been shown on this recent technical innovation during the previous four weeks, Hobson's approach varied little from the directness of his first article, 'A Month of Viewing'. In it he divides the television audience of 1947 into five categories. Firstly, 'there are the people who never like to keep their minds on one thing for more than a few seconds at a time'. Then, 'for those in search of light entertainment, there are brief revues and variety turns, with fast-stepping dancers and broad comedians'. Television also provides for 'that worthy and industrious section of the community that longs for instruction', 'the lazy, the lethargic (of whom I am one), the armchair athletes who want to see the big sporting events', as well as for 'a few deserters from the Third Programme who want to see plays'. Interestingly, Hobson is not left with an entirely satisfactory feeling after a month's viewing, and he puts this down to the inevitable primitiveness of the infant medium:

> ... for the moment an ordinary radio programme certainly seems to me to be rather stale and flat after the brightness and liveliness of television. Perhaps this feeling will wear off. I hope it will. For, unless television develops aesthetically far beyond anything suggested during the past month it is not going adequately to substitute.[207]

Two months after writing this article, the dramatic rise in Hobson's fortunes was completed when he was offered the post of the most powerful theatre critic in the land, something for which he could barely have hoped two years earlier. The basis of this remarkable accession lay in what he was later to term 'an irrelevant accident of social morality"[208] which had occurred in 1945.

One of James Agate's closest friends was the Scotsman Alan 'Jock' Dent, who had been the critic of the Manchester *Guardian* from 1935 to 1943, as well as Agate's secretary from 1926 to 1941.[209] For many years Dent was considered to be Agate's prospective successor at *The Sunday Times*, a view to which Agate himself certainly subscribed.[210] However, this possibility disappeared in the middle of July 1945, as Hobson himself relates:

> ... one day, as I was walking down the corridor of *The Sunday Times*, the editor, W. W. Hadley ... came very perturbed out of his room and said to me, 'You've written reviews for the *Christian Science Monitor* about the theatre. Well, you write instead of Agate on Sunday because Jimmy is ill.' He continued, 'Jimmy has written to me saying that he had asked Alan Dent to write this article ... I've told him that he can have time off because he's ill, but I shall choose who shall substitute.' Now, he had never done this before, but I didn't ask him why he said this, but wrote the article, I substituted for Agate.[211]

The reason for Dent's ill luck and Hobson's good fortune was that, shortly before this meeting, Agate had had to escape from a male brothel in his nightshirt, something so shocking to Lord Kemsley that, when he was informed, he had wanted to sack the critic there and then.[212] Hadley, however, had pointed out that this would bring a considerable amount of bad publicity given Agate's fame, and Kemsley relented reluctantly. Nevertheless, Dent was banned from the paper on account of his intimacy with Agate[213] and was then cruelly disowned by Agate, who, possibly in a vain attempt to rescue his reputation with Lord Kemsley, wrote to his friend Sydney Carroll – an influential adviser to the magnate – to recommend that he be succeeded by Hobson.[214] Thwarted in his ambition to take over Agate's position, Dent became the drama critic of the *News Chronicle* instead (holding the post from 1945 to 1960), wrote the screenplay for Olivier's film version of *Hamlet* and became respected for his solid theatrical knowledge. Indeed, in a 1948 article in the *Christian Science Monitor* on Olivier's film Hobson himself described Dent as 'one of the wittiest and subtlest of London's practising dramatic critics'.[215]

Relations between Agate and Hobson, who from now on was regarded as his permanent substitute, must have been strained. Although Hobson records that, having recovered, Agate was always very polite to him (perhaps out of a misplaced fear of blackmail) and they were to lunch every week at the Ivy restaurant in West Street, agreeing to pay for each other's drinks – 'I paid for his bottle of champagne, he paid for my bottle of lemonade'[216] – Agate was likely to have been unhappy with the state of affairs. This did not, however, prevent him from regaling the younger man with stories about his testicles, which he alleged had, over recent years, become as large as billiard balls and a brilliant orange colour, or from continually expressing his ardent desire to become the first drama critic to be awarded a knighthood (an honour that, ironically, was to fall to Hobson).[217]

For Hobson, though, the situation was a marvellous opportunity. Whilst not yet confirmed as Agate's successor, he was given the chance to serve an apprenticeship during which he could develop a critical style to suit a quality Sunday newspaper; reach a wider audience than he had ever addressed before (an audience, moreover, that possessed a tremendous appetite for discussion about the arts after the disrupted war years and was guaranteed to engage him in critical debate); try out new ideas and reassess old themes (the need for a revival of serious drama, for example); and reach the higher echelons of the theatrical world denied to him as a minor drama critic working for an American newspaper. Set against this was the need to shine in his own right when permitted the opportunity to substitute for the increasingly ailing Agate, without either duplicating the famous critic's views or, worse, stealing his thunder. The critical and professional tensions of this two-year apprenticeship were invaluable for Hobson's literary development.

The article that Hadley had wished Hobson to submit during Agate's first absence, 'Hazlitt Said No', duly appeared on 29 July 1945. Its very title (chosen by a sub-editor) implied continuity by echoing Agate's trait of referring to an acknowledged authority (Hazlitt had felt that *A Midsummer Night's Dream* was unactable), and some of the language employed also feels a little derivative, but Hobson's own mark was made by concentrating on a tiny but significant moment in the performance of Peggy Ashcroft (always a much-admired actress) which seemed to encapsulate the spirit of the production:

> ... if the Haymarket has few fairies it has the great glory of Miss Ashcroft's Titania; and in Miss Ashcroft there is more enchantment than in a whole wilderness of elves and sprites. Lovely at all times, both in grace of movement and in caressing beauty of speech, Miss Ashcroft's performance at one point touches the very crown of delight. I mean that speech in which Titania talks of the parentage of the little black boy who is the cause of her dispute with Oberon. Her first words, about 'the spiced Indian air' and 'Neptune's yellow sands' and 'the wanton wind', are a lovely device of elaborate decoration; but it is the sudden change to real and deep emotion on the line, 'But she, being mortal, of that boy did die,' which melts the heart and takes the reason captive.

Hobson is conscious that his critical style may be idiosyncratic, but he proceeds to defend his unfashionable practice of formulating a critical judgement with reference to the depth of emotion stirred by a significant moment:

> The method of judging performances by the impact of one charged moment is not, perhaps, well reputed. Nowadays plays win their victories by piling up points, not by the knock-out.[218]

Far from being an unfashionable, inappropriate irrelevancy, this device was the first of many that Hobson was to use to invest his best criticism with sincerity and plausibility, since it requires a close attention to detail, committed writing and personal involvement. In his autobiography, *Indirect Journey*, Hobson uses an incident while he was at Oxford to explain why he was always to pay close attention to tiny details. Returning to his rooms one evening, he found his way barred by a drunken hearty slumped across the path. Unsure as to how he was to get around him, given the very restricted movements of which he was capable after his attack of polio, he was so amazed and gratified when the drunk deliberately shifted his position to let him pass that the memory remained with him for the rest of his life. This was why he had 'frequently given a long and enthusiastic review to an actor or actress for what to most people seemed no more than a sudden change of inflection or a casual movement of the hands'.[219] As with much of the autobiography, this over-simplifies matters through deliberate self-effacement, but it does highlight the fact that Hobson was a disabled critic, which necessarily affected the discharge of his professional duties.[220] The supreme example of this detailed observation came two years later in 1947, when Hobson was watching a performance of Webster's *The White Devil*:

Flamineo has murdered his brother, and his mother, repenting her sudden anger, offers to the assembled lords and ruffians who compose the play's cast an explanation that lets him out. Then, treading on silence, a page whom I had not noticed, and was not to notice again, quietly says these five words: 'This is not true madam.' That is all. As this play counts noise, it is hardly more than a whisper. Am I right in thinking that the name of the actor who plays the page is not even mentioned on the programme? Yet for me it was the most striking moment in a performance in which such moments are not few.[221]

Such is Hobson's admiration at a minor task well performed that he sought out and printed the name of the actor, Patrick Macnee, two weeks later. He also refers to the moment in *Theatre 1* (a book of selected *Sunday Times* criticisms from September 1946 to December 1947) by publishing the actor's delighted reaction to this unexpected fame – thereby holding out the prospect of critical recognition to any future bit actor:

Dear Mr Harold Hobson,

As you wrote of the most striking moment in 'The White Devil' being the few words that I spoke at the time, I was very thrilled to read your entertaining and just notice. I've yet to find whether one's name is or is not on the programme, but whether or not, I assure you, as one who has few chances to do more than dash about stage and alter his clothes to fit in, what you said about those few words was more than welcome to

Yours very sincerely,
Patrick Macnee.[222]

The prosperity that the London theatre had enjoyed during the latter part of the war continued into the first two years of the post-war period. First nights became rarer because of the firmly established success of long-running shows – by July 1945 *Blithe Spirit* had notched up 1,716 performances at the Duchess, the longest London run ever experienced by a non-musical[223] – and in November 1945 the Embassy Theatre tried an experiment of presenting two different plays on the same day – *Skipper Next to God* at 6.15pm and *Worm's Eye View* at 8.45pm – to try to break the log-jam.[224] Hobson, however, was not prepared to compromise his belief, often expressed in the *Christian Science Monitor*, that 'the artistic value of an institution is not to be confused with the economic well-being of its workers',[225] and he utilized the occasional opportunity granted to him by Agate's absences in the second half of 1945 to stress the paucity of quality plays. In 'Faster, Faster'[226] he makes a simple, convincing plea (with reference to *Tomorrow's Eden*) for more realistic plots which predated by ten years the protests of the 'Kitchen Sink' dramatists at the unreality of the middle-class play:

If you write a study of the typical problems of an adolescent girl, it is foolish to make her so lovely that all the wealthiest men of her acquaintance fall in love with her. If you write a study on the typical problems of an East End parson, it is foolish to give him character and abilities so outstanding that he is bound to become Archbishop of Canterbury. And if you write a study of ordinary men and women facing the post-war future, it is foolish to provide them with a friend rich enough and willing to buy them an expensive farm in South Africa. The point is not that such a group of people could not exist; it is that, if they did exist, they would not be typical.

Hobson's dislike of escapism disguised as social comment had begun.

The characteristic combination of humour and irony with which this plea is presented is also echoed in 'Private Judgement',[227] where Hobson expresses gentle exasperation at the appetite of the London audience:

The main situation in 'Kiss and Tell' is the spectacle of a sixteen-year old-girl, Corliss Archer, being suspected by her friends, parents and neighbours of having an illegitimate baby. It is mildly odd that a play with a theme like this should emerge from a country whose delicacy of taste is so fragile that it cannot permit the speeches of the Duke of Bourbon in 'Henry V' to be heard in their entirety. It is odder still that a joke of this nature should be relied on to set a London theatre in a roar; and oddest of all, perhaps, that it should succeed in doing so.

Succeed it does. On the first night I sat, a small island of gloom and despondency, amidst a sea of riotous laughter, certainly uncontrolled and probably uncontrollable. A miraculous union of the talents of Mr Bernard Shaw and Mr Leslie Henson could not have produced a wilder merriment. Men who would have kept a straight face before Grimaldi rolled in the aisles. Women who would have found Grock dull screamed in an ecstasy of delight. I cheerfully admit that a crowded house appeared wholly to dissent from my judgement. It is no part of my purpose to defend the taste or the intelligence of a London audience.

This is fine, ironic writing, avoiding an unpalatable preaching, but refusing to compromise a heartfelt opinion in the face of a dissenting majority. A similar forthrightness that went against not just the views of the audience but the majority of critics was Hobson's opinion of one of the immediate post-war successes, Eileen Herlie's performance in Jean Cocteau's play, *The Eagle Has Two Heads*. 'A Unique Feat' is the first in a series of three articles that Hobson was to write during September 1946 while Agate was attending the Cannes Film Festival, and they illustrate the difficulty that Hobson encountered in trying to create his own distinctive voice without being unduly influenced by Agate's shadow. The past year's output for the *Christian Science Monitor* had consisted of articles on post-war conditions, theatrical news, politics,[228] and book and film reviews, with only rare opportunities to shine in *The Sunday Times*.

Agate's propitious absence meant that Hobson was able to write on one of the most talked-about plays of the year, which was to be awarded the Embassy prize for being the best new work of 1946 and for containing the best performance, in Herlie's queen.

The Eagle Has Two Heads was almost universally hailed and particular praise was accorded to Herlie for her stamina as the queen who wished to die painlessly at the hands of a revolutionary poet. Like other critics, Hobson marvels at the speech that Herlie delivers when the poet tumbles through her window during a storm. He had it timed at twenty-one minutes (by his friend Nora Taylor at the second performance[229]) and has even counted the total number of words, 2,882. This mechanical approach to evaluation is clearly designed to imply that Herlie's performance is similarly pedantic:

> It is a tremendous feat. I think of the music-hall artist handcuffed in the tank of water: I think of the triple-century Test-match innings: I think of this speech: and henceforth my symbols of endurance more than human are Houdini, Hutton and Herlie.[230]

Only once does Herlie move him and that is when she screams at the entrance of the assassin, thereby defining her performance as impressive rather than great – a conclusion that alarmed the news editor, Valentine Heywood, given the consensus of the other London critics.[231] This disapproval by one of his peers might explain why Hobson's article the following Sunday trod the seemingly safer rhetorical path followed by Agate for the past twenty years – to much poorer effect. Dispensing with the measured, incisive style that he had been developing at the *Christian Science Monitor*, Hobson resorts to a more showy, grandiloquent mode of expression in the face of a disappointing week for plays which has left him searching for inspiration:

> But here I interrupt myself [having objected to the triviality of Ralph Lynn's curtain speech after *The Love Lottery*]. For I can feel a sense of impatience rising among my readers. Instead of chattering on, I can hear them asking, why doesn't he tell us something about the play? Why doesn't he cut the cackle and get to the 'osses? But ah, my friends, what if the 'osses are spavined? What if, like Petruchio's steed, they are troubled with the lampass? Suppose they are stark spoiled with the staggers and swayed in the back? In such circumstances it is surely only human, it is even kind hearted, to procrastinate a little. For I cannot deny that 'The Love Lottery' is a lottery that has no prizes.[232]

This attempt to ape Agate's style fails because Hobson is not comfortable with the type of dazzling prose that presupposes a long-built-up and intimate relationship with a readership. It also illustrates that, in his eagerness to shine, he had temporarily ignored Leonard Russell's reminder, delivered at the end of the war, that the '*Sunday Times* pays you to say what you think, not to make fine phrases'.[233] He now had one article left to atone for this and re-establish his own credibility before Agate returned from France. With a stroke of good fortune that gives credence to the view that Hobson was now destined to inherit Agate's mantle, the next production he was called upon to review was the return of the Old Vic to the New Theatre, with Laurence Olivier as King Lear.

Laurence Olivier's Lear, like his 1944 Oedipus and Richard III, is generally acknowledged to be one of the most masterful theatrical performances of the twentieth century. The contemporary acclaim for the entire company was instantaneous and Olivier himself was greeted with adulation – Alan Dent claimed that 'Olivier's Lear is nothing short of a tremendous achievement' (*News Chronicle*), Peter Fleming wrote of 'a superb performance of which London has every right to be proud' (the *Spectator*) and Philip Hope-Wallace commended the 'great ease and mastery' with which Olivier both acted and directed.[234] It is perhaps Hobson's article, 'Mr Olivier's Lear',[235] however, in the wake of his flabby offering the previous week, that most evocatively conveys the actor's achievement. In true 'touchstone' style, he begins by relating how Irving started the play 'in noise and tumult and barbaric war' but doubts that this impressive opening could have been finer than Olivier's, for the production team and actor have solved the problem of making Lear's division of his kingdom appear plausible. They make the preliminary conversation between Kent and Gloucester 'a thing of easy and supple comedy', so that when the king himself appears:

> white-haired, white-bearded, yet swift and eager and active, we recognise him at once for what he is, a humourist, a man of infinite fecundity of wit, choleric maybe, but resilient and alert, ready in sheer intellectual energy and physical well-being for any jest or experimental escapade …

Hobson conveys the unpredictability of Lear at the start, as well as the coiled energy with which Olivier wanted to invest the part, by marrying a relation of the scene to an interpretation of the actor's intent:

> [Lear] is bursting with overflux of vital forces: from his brain at any moment may spring some plan, some scheme, half joke, half earnest, which, born on the inspiration of a moment, may, in sudden change of mood, have consequences to wreck kingdoms and ruin lives.

The brilliance of this review lies in the fact that it exploits rather than capitulates to the restrictions of space. The dynamic energy of the prose exactly parallels the suppressed energy of Lear which Hobson feels is an integral part of Olivier's performance. Hobson maintained that the most dramatic work that he had ever read was Thucydides' *History of the Peloponnesian War*, and he was to return to it throughout his career.[236] Noted for its balance between compression and breadth, its maintenance of pace, its scientific method, its elegant style and its analysis of the causal link between events, it has clearly influenced Hobson in accomplished reviews such as this, where personal observation, theatrical evaluation, historical information and the depiction of atmosphere are all blended into a distinctive and perfectly balanced whole. Even by this stage of the review, Hobson has referred to a historical precedent, considered a question of academic interpretation, conveyed a sense of occasion (so often lost in reviews of famous performances), mentioned the production team by name, described Olivier's physical presence, emotional depth and dramatic intent and alluded to Dr Johnson's confusion about the work – all with no loss of pace, no irrelevant digression and no discordant phrase. The perfection of Olivier's depiction is honoured by the craftmanship of Hobson's prose.

Having dealt with the play's opening, Hobson dispenses with the artificially elevated tone he had adopted just a week before and proceeds to compliment the actor on avoiding a well-laid trap:

> Mr Olivier's Lear is very old: he is also strong. There is about him none of that senility which many great actors have affected. In poetic truth undoubtedly this is right. Under one aspect this play presents man as the plaything of the gods: they kill us for their sport. Where the quarry is lame or feeble or impotent, surely the sport is poor? It was said of the great Duke of Marlborough that he could be bought, but that he was worth buying. Mr Olivier's Lear is a man who by temperament is capable of being tortured: but he is worth torturing. The cries and the lamentations, the curses and the threats that are torn out of his breast are like the crash of thunder and the stab of lightning. They are not the whimpering of a weak old man: they are the groaning and the weeping of the universe. This is a cosmic grief.

Indeed, Olivier's utterance of:

> ... I will do such things, –
> What they are yet I know not, but they shall be
> The terrors of the earth ...

when confronted by Regan, reminds Hobson of Olivier's anguished cry as Oedipus, 'which rang round the rafters of the New Theatre like the echo of the crack of doom'.

The penultimate paragraph of the review hints that this Lear is the result of the distillation of the very best elements of Olivier's previous roles:

> There was once a time when Mr Olivier was all violence, all extreme passion; like Kean, he was constantly upon the rack. But, as his passion has strengthened and his expression of it ripened, so has it grown more controlled. There are moments in his performance of Lear that are of utter stillness and of quiet pathos. The same power that can set the storm in motion can now calm it by the lifting of a hand.[237]

And so, after the effusive rhythm of the previous four paragraphs, the review also comes to a full close by highlighting two other noteworthy performances, Alec Guinness as the Fool and Peter Copley as Edmund, and then authoritatively proclaiming that 'there is no weakness anywhere'. The genius of Olivier's performance has inspired and suffused Hobson's own writing to the extent that the reader is convinced of the validity of the momentous last phrase, that 'the central performance must stand among the very greatest things ever accomplished upon the English stage.' Only the truly inspired critic can give substance to the insubstantial.

Conditions outside the theatre were particularly harsh in Britain during the first six months of 1947. On 9 January a strike by road-haulage workers ushered in a period of industrial strife in the transport, shipbuilding and engineering industries. The Cripps plan to counter coal shortages by rationing the fuel, announced on 13 January, coincided with the coldest weather for sixty-six years, which in turn was followed by floods. As Britain began to suffer from a major fuel shortage in February, Emmanuel Shinwell, the Minister of Fuel and Power, forecast complete disaster within ten days and announced the cessation of electricity supply for industrial consumers in London and parts of England; three days later (10 February) he went further and ordered the complete cessation of electricity to industry, resulting in the laying off of 1,800,000 workers. One crisis gave way to another. As fuel supplies began to increase at the beginning of March, Hugh Dalton was forced to raise indirect taxes in his budget in April and expressed concern at the deteriorating balance of payments situation. This fear was realized in June with a full-blown exchange crisis, requiring drastic cuts in imports such as tobacco, petrol and newsprint, continuing the circle of crisis and crisis measures, new crisis and new measures.[238] Inevitably, little of this permeated the theatre. People entered the auditorium for escapism and distraction and no West End managers (and few suburban theatre administrators) were prepared to take the commercial risk of altering the balance of the traditional – and highly popular – middle-class fare of revues, revivals, occasional foreign imports and simplistic comedies of bad manners, revolving around minor indiscretions on lounge sofas. With James Agate's health becoming increasingly precarious, Hobson was called upon more frequently to deputize for him, and when he encountered a play that attempted to introduce a new and challenging contemporary subject-matter to the London stage, Hobson was keen to champion it.

William Douglas Home was to become one of Hobson's favourite dramatists, and his early play *Now Barabbas* ..., produced at the Boltons in February 1947, was later to be described by him as the first 'new wave play'[239] and as the precursor of the English Stage Company, since it was 'the first play after the war that seriously questioned the assumptions on which society is based'.[240] Its setting was a model prison and much of its appeal lay in the fact that it alluded to contemporary social reality, superficially eschewed the mannered conversation topics of the drawing-room and provided a welcome contrast to a theatre which, at the time, was 'more or less satisfied with itself'.[241] Hobson's review, 'Is this Barabbas?', was aware of the play's technical deficiencies:

> Mr Douglas Home finds in his murderers, shoplifters, erring schoolmasters, bigamists, perverts and swindlers more virtue than you would get in a normal bunch of bishops: these ragged edges and sorry mountebanks of society show a truer love of literature, a more delicate appreciation of beauty and rhythm than you would run into at a combined meeting of the Book of the Month Club and the Poetry Society.

But the critic does not 'believe a word of it'. He also found its pace too breathless and the montage effect of its short scenes too cinematic, but these faults are much less important than the fact that Douglas Home writes with conviction, communicates the splendour of the human spirit and is capable of creating scenes that are deeply moving. This particularly applies, in Hobson's view:

> [to] the scene in which young Tufnell, condemned to death for the murder of a policeman waits for news of the result of his appeal. Hope rises high in his breast, and, for a few moments of extraordinary lyric beauty ... all the glory of the years he is snatching from the grave descends on him. Mr Douglas Home draws Tufnell's portrait with a great, and, I think, mistaken tenderness; the dead policeman is too easily forgotten; but, despite, this, I found it a beautiful and moving thing.

Hobson's review – centring on a moment of emotional intensity – demonstrates a concern for the theatrical health of the country which was to remain with him for the rest of his career. Douglas Home's play has notable faults, but the critic prefers to highlight the promising elements within it, recognizing that, in the precarious world of the theatre, promising playwrights need cherishing, the cornerstone of his mature criticism. He ends his review with an eye to the billboards: '"Now Barabbas ..." is a play that, though it excuses too much, understands a great deal; it is amusing and profoundly touching. I beg you to see it.'[242]

This desire to emphasize the positive, rather than dwell on the negative, highlights the philosophical basis – stemming from the Philippians quotation – that lies behind his criticism. St Paul's admonition to the Colossians had been lodged in his mind since childhood and came to encapsulate the very essence of what the outlook of a drama critic should be:

> Finally, brethren, whatsoever things are true, whatsoever things are just, whatsoever things are pure, whatsoever things are lovely, whatsoever things are of good report: if there be any virtue, and if there be any praise, think on these things.[243]

In accordance with the spirit of this passage, Hobson's general habit when writing reviews was to begin by emphasizing something that had given him particular pleasure, eschewing the practice of damaging a potential career in the pursuit of personal acknowledgement, since he believed that 'the way to success is not through destruction, but through perceiving ahead of other people where true and lasting talent lies'.[244] He was never a critic who wrote according to a personal political theory or who made a scientific application of the rules of Aristotle, for he considered that a review was:

> the outcome of what happens to a temperament when it meets a particular theatrical experience. It is the record of an experience vécu; and what that experience will be depends more on what [the critic's] family, his friends, and his life have made of him than upon his familiarity with certain theoretical treatises.[245]

Motivated by the desire to preserve a historical record of what he had witnessed in the body of his work, he firmly believed that: 'Any opinion on a play expressed by a critic is not a final judgement, but a rationalization of the emotion which that play has aroused in him.'[246] Ironically, this refusal to be dogmatic, allied to the simple stress on the primacy of his emotional response, is why he was to develop a subsequent reputation for unpredictability – a refreshing trait according to admirers, a sign of confusion according to detractors – because few understood at the time the basis on which he was working.

Hobson had often considered Shakespeare's *Othello* in his *Christian Science Monitor* articles. As recently as April 1946, in a discussion with an unnamed actor, but presumably John Gielgud, he had written that one of the four stage performances he would most have liked to have witnessed had been Kean's Othello,[247] and a week later he reported why Gielgud did not feel that he would make an effective Moor: 'he considers his voice to be wholly of tenor quality, while he maintains that Othello's speeches should have running through them a bass undertone that suggests the warrior and statesman'.[248] *The Sunday Times* column gave Hobson a chance to move beyond stage gossip and consider matters of analysis – the readership was intelligent and expected more than reportage – so on 6 April 1947 Hobson decided to consider whether the role of Othello 'was beyond the compass of an actor'.

The article, entitled 'Iago's Fault?',[249] is not an academic treatise, but raises an interesting point with regard to the principal character. Having seen Jack Hawkins's adequate but unexceptional performance in the title role at the Piccadilly a week before, Hobson wonders – in spite of Hazlitt's delight in Kean's portrayal – whether the part is capable of being played. He himself has 'never seen an Othello who affrighted and dominated the eye', and he agrees with one actor to whom he had spoken (again the unnamed Gielgud) that the character demands an actor of giant physical stature and a booming voice, qualities which are rare in great contemporary performers. A second anonymous actor, however, suggests that the difficulty in playing Othello lies not in the physical demands of the role, but in his overshadowing by Iago. It is this which intrigues Hobson and he concludes that it is Iago 'who sets the plot in motion, and controls the action', with Othello only enjoying two significant moments: 'when he delivers his speech to the Senate about his wooing of Desdemona, and when he stills the brawl in the streets with the astounding "Keep up your bright swords, for the dew will rust them".' The article then ends with three rhetorical questions:

> Would our Othellos then be better if our Iagos were worse? Has Shakespeare here written a play of which the effect is greatest when one of the chief characters is less than perfectly played? And if so, is this a defect in craftmanship?

The Sunday Times received a deluge of letters in response to this piece, mostly listing recent praiseworthy Othellos, including Matheson Lang, Paul Robeson, Baliol Holloway, Louis Calvert, Lewis Waller, Giovanni Grasso and Godfrey Tearle.[250] Hobson had discovered his audience.

One person who took a particularly strong objection to Hobson's supposition was James Agate. In *Theatre 1*, published in 1948, Hobson hints for the only time at the suppressed antipathy that Agate held for him:

> Jimmie didn't like my views on Iago at all. Always very generous in praise, he had given me a great deal of encouragement in the past: but this time his patience was worn out. I never discovered why. I only know that they irritated him so much that when he was questioned about them, beyond saying that in his opinion they were unbelievably wrong, he lapsed into gloomy silence, a most unusual condition for one so chatty as Jimmie.[251]

Six weeks after Hobson's article on Iago, Agate was to write his last piece as the drama critic of *The Sunday Times*, and there is a fitting irony in the way in which 'Catching Up – II'[252] finishes. His last theatre notice focuses on the St James's production of *The Play's the Thing* and the final ten lines relate the coincidence of his three-word verdict on the work – 'No, it isn't' – being an exact version of an earlier contradiction by Hobson. Agate's last sentence reads: 'Well, well, great minds ...', thereby unwittingly preparing the way for Hobson's imminent succession. Agate died, whilst correcting some proofs, of a heart attack on Friday 6 June 1947 and Hobson's appreciation, in which he described Agate as 'being as brilliant as Hazlitt' and 'as kind, as generous, as courageous and as gay as Hazlitt's contemporary, Lamb', is characteristically noble. He wrote that Agate possessed 'that fundamental seriousness of outlook without which all solid and durable writing is impossible' – a trait that Hobson shared – and he had always read Agate 'with admiration and envious despair'. Of particular interest, given the continuing dearth of new plays that Hobson was to encounter, is his regard for Agate's attitude to actors:

> ... any competent critic can discuss a play, but Agate could perpetuate a player. That is a far harder thing to do. The one can be accomplished by any skilful scholar: to do the other requires the creative artist.²⁵³

This again emphasizes the importance to Hobson of creating a permanent historical record of ephemeral stage performances through writing of literary merit.

After the embarrassment of Agate's sexual proclivities, the prejudiced Lord Kemsley wanted to ensure that there was no similar mistake in the appointment of the new critic. Many years later, during the research for a book on the history of the paper, *The Pearl of Days*, Hobson was to learn that Kemsley had obdurately exclaimed in 1945: 'Hobson's all right. Hobson has a daughter. Let's have Hobson.'²⁵⁴ This discovery caused Hobson some pain – 'I thought I'd been asked to deputise and to be their drama critic because of my brilliance as a craftsman, but I found ... well, I say that my life was full of accidents, but this was the humiliating reason'²⁵⁵ – but he had clearly earned the chance to succeed Agate by 1947, and on 11 July, the editor, W. W. Hadley, invited him to lunch at the Reform Club and offered him the post of drama critic to *The Sunday Times*.²⁵⁶

Chapter 4

The Foreign Revelation: July 1947–1954

Harold Hobson's accession to the post of drama critic of *The Sunday Times* coincided with the first decline in London theatre attendance for several years.[257] Whilst popular, lavishly staged musicals such as *Oklahoma!*, *Annie Get Your Gun* and *Bless the Bride* retained their appeal, many new works seemed derivative and faintly ridiculous – a fact that Hobson noted in 'They're All the Same', an article written for the *Christian Science Monitor* (whose London bureau chief, Saville Davis, had recently trebled Hobson's salary in the light of his promotion at *The Sunday Times*[258]):

> the plays that have not been seen before on any stage … give the impression of repeating things that have been produced earlier. 'Now Barabbas …' was about men in a model prison; 'Boys in Brown' … is about boys in a reformatory. 'Miranda' told the adventures of a mermaid. 'A Fish in the Family' … tells the adventures of another mermaid. 'Dark Emmanuel' … showed the world after it had been devastated by an atomic rocket. 'Calcutta in the Morning' showed the world after it had been devastated by an atomic bomb. 'Birthmark' … gave us a hue and cry after Eva Braun: and now 'Spanish Incident' gives a hue and cry after another woman alleged to be high in the hierarchy of the Nazis.[259]

Faced with a disappointing and unstimulating West End, Hobson started his career by writing about the work of the club theatres in the suburbs, theatres that avoided the licensing requirements of the Lord Chamberlain by only admitting members of the theatre club as audience. On 14 September 1947 he discusses the Torch's production of Sudermann's *The Witches Ride*; on 21 September he reports on the Mercury's *Happy as Larry*; and a week later he devotes part of his column to Tennyson's *Queen Mary* at the Gateway. This willingness to explore and appreciate the work of the fringe theatres was made in a spirit of frustration rather than exploration – a point he makes in an intelligent diagnosis of the ills of the West End. Hobson had been asked by a friend whether he has not, in the last three weeks, exaggerated the importance of the little theatres at the expense of the West End. His answer is blunt:

> If I have written little lately about the West End, it is because in the West End there has been little to write about. There has been a great

lack of first nights. Moreover, the small suburban theatres – the coterie theatres – have been producing works of interest and significance. They have given us 'The Witches Ride', 'Happy as Larry', 'Queen Mary': and if two of these plays are not new, they are at least new to contemporary London.[260]

In this article, 'The West End', the new critic is setting out his stall and he proceeds to illustrate how he considers that one of his critical functions is to differentiate between the short-term popularity of a play and its long-term value:

> There are more than thirty theatres open in the West End, but it would be hard to match this short list from among them. In plays like 'Edward, My Son', 'Present Laughter', 'The Chiltern Hundreds', 'Dr Angelus', 'Off the Record', and some others, there is excellent entertainment; there are also some first-class musicals. But is there any piece that seventy years hence, will be played even by a coterie theatre, even in an attic?

One of the greatest virtues of Hobson's writing is that the clarity and gracefulness of his style allow him to make intelligent points with a succinctness that compliments the constriction of the newspaper article. Such is the case here, where Hobson now calls upon both his sense of historical overview and upon his belief that the term 'theatre' embraces many components to explain his thesis. The paucity of quality drama, he continues:

> is not in itself a condemnation of the commercial theatre, which is far too often criticised. The theatre, it should be remembered, is a wider thing than the drama: theatrical art can flourish when the contemporary drama flags. The great ages of the English theatre are the Elizabethan, the Restoration, the age of Garrick, the age of Kean, the age of Irving and the first years of the present century. Three of these halcyon periods were made by dramatists: and three by actors, by actors, moreover, who did practically nothing to assist worthwhile contemporary writers.

But this does not mean that actors should be blamed for this neglect, since they have a distinctive and valuable input of their own, a view first expressed by Hobson as long ago as 1933 in 'The Actor as Artist',[261] and reiterated here:

> Art is the expression of a vision of life. In the theatre, if the vision be a high one, it does not matter whether it is the actor's vision, or the dramatist's. Irving was right to play in 'The Bells'; Martin-Harvey was right to play in 'The Only Way'. Their contribution to the living theatre was valid, just as, in a different way, Mr Shaw's or Mr Priestley's is valid. The theatre can live if it has great plays; and it can live if it has poorish plays, but great acting.

The problem at the moment, however, is that the acting in the West End, although very good, 'falls short of greatness' and thus cannot compensate for the drama. Gielgud is in America, whilst Richardson and Olivier are both away filming, leaving nobody to supply an 'illumination of the mind, an opening of windows on new experience', which Hobson considers to be the hallmark of great acting.

The absence of the star actors and the drabness of the London stage reflected the fatigue of the country as a whole. The economic legacy of the war had been severe debt, an exhausted workforce, antiquated industrial practices and an urgent need to find work for the five million people who had left their usual occupations to join the armed forces.[262] Morale was further weakened by the speedy realization that Britain now occupied a less influential role on the world stage, caught between the political demands of America and the territorial ambitions of Russia. Unsurprisingly, Hobson found little to enthuse about in the next six months. He enjoyed Alec Guinness as Richard II (the latest in a long line of recent performances of this part which included Gielgud, Maurice Evans, George Hayes and Robert Harris,[263] although John of Gaunt's patriotic paean must have had a very different resonance for a post-war austerity audience); he hailed Paul Scofield as 'one of the most promising of our younger players'[264] after seeing him play Tybalt in *Romeo and Juliet*; and he also, uncharacteristically, urged young dramatists to follow the example of Shaw, having witnessed a revival of *St Joan*, because he always obeys the advice of Acton, the historian, to 'Do what you can for the other side' – essential for convincing 'drama of controversy'.[265] But the tone of irritation that he strikes when defending Christianity against the cynicism of the contemporary world – 'I am tired of hearing that the religion whose central doctrine is love is the world's chief source of hate: of listening to politicians (whose own brilliant success the earth's present condition so strikingly illustrates) explaining that the churches have failed'[266] – is a more accurate reflection of Hobson's attitude to what he was to term 'one of the dimmest autumn seasons the London theater has ever known'.[267] He is similarly brusque with the average theatre-goer: when he commends Bridget Boland's *Cockpit* for its depiction of the confusion in post-war Europe caused by the number of displaced refugees, he simultaneously laments its poor chance of success, fearing 'London isn't half intelligent enough for it'.[268] It was to take a work that briefly promised to initiate a school of drama which would transcend the dominance that realism had exerted over the English stage in the last fifty years – but which was later recognized as having been a false start for post-war drama – that was to make Hobson more optimistic that the West End could recover from this trough.

There had been stirrings of twentieth-century poetic drama long before Christopher Fry's *The Lady's Not for Burning* was premièred at the Arts Theatre on 10 March 1948. Yeats at the Abbey Theatre, Auden and Isherwood at the Group Theatre, and T. S. Eliot at religious festivals had all produced verse drama that reacted against the conventional realism of current commercial theatre. E. Martin Browne had achieved a considerable success by directing the first performance of T. S. Eliot's *Murder in the Cathedral* in 1935, and his Pilgrim Players theatre group travelled throughout the country during the war, presenting Eliot's and others' verse plays in theatres and schools. Hobson agreed with Browne that the dominance of realism in late nineteenth- and early twentieth-century drama was becoming a suffocating influence and he applauded his attempt to re-establish a poetic drama in Britain, but he was unsure whether the plays that Browne had championed made the best use of the form, outlining his doubts in a *Christian Science Monitor* article of March 1947:[269]

> The sort of poetic drama that he has inspired has certain definite characteristics. It is intensely serious. It is intensely intellectual. It is sometimes difficult … The chief lack of the plays he has evolved that I have seen is, I think, their comparative want of sensuous beauty. They have often the intellectual ingenuity of Donne, sometimes the wit of Pope, and but rarely the stabbing loveliness, the overwhelming excitement that are the essence of poetry.

Put bluntly, the poetry must 'intoxicate, or it is nothing'.[270] Hobson perceived a similar lack of theatricality in *Murder in the Cathedral*:

> Mr T. S. Eliot's verse play has been much admired, and I can't deny that it is full of ideological ingenuities and nice turns of theological thought. No poetic drama of our time is more worthy of our respect. And as far as I am concerned, that finishes it. The very last quality for which I look in a poem is respectability: passion, music, abandon, magic, the divine afflatus, what you will: but respectability? No. Either poetry intoxicates, or it is nothing. In all this elaborate ritual I found not a dram, a drain, a fluid ounce of aesthetic inebriety. It is as sober as a judge, about as inspired as the Woolsack.[271]

Hobson was thus not an instinctive devotee of verse drama, but when he visited the Arts Theatre to see *The Lady's Not for Burning*, he was struck by the invigorating language of the playwright, whose earlier verse play, *A Phoenix Too Frequent*, produced in November 1946, he had found unexpectedly amusing.[272] This language (which now appears fastidiously ornate) differentiated Fry's medieval poetic fantastication from other plays of the time, and Hobson appreciated its linguistic novelty:

> For thirty years much of even the best English drama has been written in brilliant banalities. Is there a single memorable phrase in all Coward? The words of our best reputed modern plays are stripped of overtones and associations. Therefore I welcome Mr Fry, who is bemused with the glory of words, who scorneth tea-cups, and is not interested in little misdemeanours on drawing room sofas.[273]

As yet, though, Hobson can only welcome Fry as 'a possible influence rather than as a dramatist', because although 'Rich evocative speeches are excellent things ... the structure of drama is situation and character.' Nevertheless Fry, who, along with W. P. Templeton, had been appointed a dramatist in residence at the Arts by its director, Alec Clunes, represented the prospect of a change of direction, by consolidating what had been worthwhile from the recent past and moving it on to a higher plane in the future.

In spite of its box-office success – its West End transfer to the Globe Theatre ran for 294 performances[274] – the theatrical movement that was launched by *The Lady's Not for Burning* was abruptly superseded by the revolution of the Kitchen Sink dramatists a mere nine years later. The success of *Look Back in Anger* has been seen by many as the crucial event determining the reorientation of British theatre in the late 1950s,[275] but there had been other, less visible, milestones on the journey from stilted drawing-room drama to more diverse theatrical genres. The opening-up of the London stage to creative contact with New York and Paris, for example, was an event every bit as important for the evolution of twentieth-century English drama as the advent of Osborne, Wesker and the other New Wave dramatists. This fresh artistic contact introduced new techniques in acting through the example of Jean-Louis Barrault and the Comédie Française, who illustrated how English actors performed primarily with their voice, whilst their French counterparts utilized their entire body. Brecht's stress on the 'Gestus' of a performer, with body movement unlocking textual meaning, was to prove similarly illuminating. New ideas about acting and directing were absorbed through the work of Elia Kazan and the 'method' technique developed by Lee Strasberg. The brash, glittering, technically perfect American musicals, symbolized by Rodgers and Hammerstein's smash hit *Oklahoma!*, provoked English producers to consider new ideas in stagecraft. Exposure to new types of play – by Sartre, Genet, Anouilh and Ionesco on the one hand and Arthur Miller and Tennessee Williams on the other – provided a creative impulse that could not have been envisaged during the war, and contact with new dramatic theories, such as French existentialism and, later, Brecht's 'epic theatre', led a number of playwrights to apply these new theatrical approaches to their own work. Although it is true to state that there was little new *English* writing between 1945 and 1955, it is disingenuous to conclude from this that the London theatre was a cultural wasteland. In many ways, this ten-year period was crucial to the developments of the 1950s and 1960s which were to make the English stage the most vibrant in the world, and it formed an important period of apprenticeship for actors, directors, playwrights and critics alike.

In the summer of 1948 Hobson encountered one of the first of these new, significant foreign imports, in the form of Jean-Paul Sartre's *Crime Passionnel* at the Lyric, Hammersmith – a theatre that was to produce many French plays in the coming years. He considered it to be a great improvement on the earlier *Men Without Shadows*, which he had judged to have all the aesthetic merit of a 'street accident',[276] and decided that *Crime Passionnel* was a play that could be enjoyed in three ways: as a thriller, which made London's other thrillers 'seem material for the children's hour', as an ingenious exposition 'of two standard methods of attaining power' and as a 'philosophical' (i.e. existential) tragedy. He was also impressed with the 'tirade' (soliloquy) that Michael Gough delivered, since its length contrasted with the work of Coward and Rattigan, which was written in 'coughs, exclamations, and words of one syllable', whilst its ordinariness differentiated it from the 'Elizabethan richness' of Christopher Fry. As a religious man, Hobson was not inclined to appreciate the views of the existentialists – the idea of man being born into 'le néant', an abyss, being anathema to him – and it is likely that at this point he was not fully conversant with the implications of the philosophy, because he treats Sartre in a much gentler fashion than he was later inclined to do. Nevertheless, the play contained a credible theatricality and represented a new impulse, and was welcomed as such:

> *Crime Passionnel* goes further towards justifying Mr Jean-Paul Sartre's position as the most important – certainly the most publicised – force in the contemporary drama than any of his works we have seen in London.[277]

The work was certainly a more plausible attempt to relate concerns outside the theatre to the stage than the offerings of contemporary British playwrights. William Douglas Home's *Ambassador Extraordinary*, a bizarre allegorical plea for reconciliation between warring nations, appeared at a time of great international tension, with the beginning of the Soviet blockade of Berlin. The plot centres on a Martian visitor who tries to blackmail the world into submission by the threat of wholesale destruction and who is only appeased when the Foreign Secretary agrees to sell his daughter to the enraptured alien. Hobson concludes his review of the play, having condemned its doctrine as 'both ineffective and evil', with the understated comment: 'I do not believe that the road to international virtue leads through private immorality.' All he can applaud is the playwright's curtain speech amidst great booing at the end of the first night – 'the finest exhibition of casual courage' Hobson had ever seen.[278]

The second half of 1948 brought Hobson a further contact with the French that was to have a profound effect on his life. Whilst attending his first (and the event's second) Edinburgh Festival – staying with Elizabeth and 11-year-old Margaret at the Marine Hotel in North Berwick, his Festival base for the next thirty years – he witnessed a performance of *Hamlet* with Jean-Louis Barrault in the title role. He was intrigued by the way in which the Frenchman utilized the whole of his body to express himself in performance, in comparison with which English actors appeared locked in rigor mortis.[279] The restricted nature of English acting was further emphasized by the London visit of the Comédie Française in the following month, October. Performing *Le Misanthrope* at the Cambridge Theatre, the whole company 'in its lighthearted exploitation of every note and inflection of which the human voice is capable, shows us within how limited a vocal range our English actors work'.[280] Hobson then saw Barrault again in Paris; having travelled to see Noël Coward in *Present Laughter*, the show had been cancelled because Coward had laryngitis (ironic, given Hobson's frequent complaints about inaudibility on the London stage), and Hobson had decided instead to watch Camus's *L'Etat de Siège*.[281] This exposure to French acting sparked a love of French theatre which was recognized by the award of the Légion d'honneur by the French government in 1960.

It was a nominal French theme that had provided Terence Rattigan with his first West End success in 1936, *French Without Tears*. *Flare Path* (1942), *While the Sun Shines* (1943) and *The Winslow Boy* (1946) had also achieved great popularity before Rattigan wrote *The Browning Version* (1948), a fine work that can be held up against the charge that his plays are vapid depictions of trivial, irrelevant scenes, designed for unquestioning consumption by middle-class audiences. Tightly constructed and movingly drawn, the play is a brilliant psychological depiction of the academic and personal failure of a deeply disliked schoolmaster, Andrew Crocker-Harris. The masterly control of language and sentiment, the universality of the characters, the poignant depiction of Crocker-Harris's inadequacy, and the faint optimism of the ending lifted Rattigan's work on to a new and unrecognizable plane and Hobson was swift to acknowledge this in his reviews for *The Sunday Times* and the *Christian Science Monitor*, 'Two Plays' and 'London Sees Two 1-Acters By Rattigan' respectively. In the former piece the critic focused on the language of the finely crafted and quietly written play:

> As one listens wearily night after night to the banal, clipped, naturalistic dialogue of the modern drama, one's heart cries out for writing of courage and colour, for the evocative word and the bannered phrase. But Mr Rattigan makes one doubt the necessity of that cry.

Hobson found the performance of Eric Portman as Andrew Crocker-Harris particularly fine, and the 'breakdown after he has asked for a dose of medicine … almost unbearably moving. I do not hesitate to say that Mr Portman's is the most complete and touching performance to be seen in London today.'[282] Both the play and the playing 'one encounters only once in a thousand nights', and Hobson was more affected the second time that he saw it – a significant indication of success and an early testimony of his willingness to re-visit productions. The *Christian Science Monitor* article that appeared a month later sets the work in the context of Rattigan's oeuvre. Referring specifically to *French Without Tears* and *While the Sun Shines*, Hobson states:

Great as Mr Rattigan's success has been, it has had sharply defined limits. He can draw a portrait of a debonair young earl serving as an able seaman, not to the life perhaps, but as we should like such people to be if they really existed. His touch could not be defter, nor his pretence of belief in such amiable nonsense more engaging. He can be hilariously amusing – oh, but in such a nice, well-bred way – about a crammer where wealthy young Englishmen go to learn French and remain to flirt. These have been Rattigan triumphs. Life has been for him roses, roses all the way, and his plays cockleshells and gilliflowers.[283]

Perhaps the view that Rattigan is a trivial playwright is somewhat self-inflicted – 'no one hitherto has taken Mr Rattigan's talent as a dramatist very seriously, not even Mr Rattigan himself' – but *The Browning Version* may change this perception, since 'If Mr Rattigan goes on writing like this, he is the man the English theater is looking for.'

Unfortunately, Rattigan's later demise resulted from a combination of being a victim of his own success, emphasizing the absence of alternative forms of drama – Hobson was ironically to write, in connection with *The Deep Blue See* (1952), that the middle-aged playwright 'has been the leading young British dramatist now for many years ...';[284] of rapidly changing theatrical priorities that necessitated the denigration of his oeuvre, highlighting his weakest plays and ignoring his more accomplished ones; and of an unfortunate propensity on the playwright's part to invite misconception. When Rattigan's *Collected Plays* were published in 1953, he wrote a preface to the second volume in which he created the character of 'Aunt Edna', 'a nice, respectable, middle-class, middle-aged, maiden lady'[285] – the average middle-brow matinée attender – whom playwrights must take into account. Critics were later to use this light-hearted invention as a focus for their complaints about the insipidity of his plays,[286] and the Kitchen Sink dramatists (notably Shelagh Delaney, who was provoked into writing *A Taste of Honey* after seeing Rattigan's *Variation on a Theme*[287]) reacted passionately against him. It was a reaction that Hobson was to come to deplore, commenting in the 1970s that the bitterness and discontent of the attack on the conventional drama of the day was something that 'surprised and distressed'[288] him. Even Kenneth Tynan, in a pertinent and sympathetic parody of *Separate Tables*[289] in 1954, demonstrated an appreciation of Rattigan's finer drama.

The most significant British theatrical event of 1948 came at the very end of the year, when the governors of the Old Vic decided not to renew the contracts of Laurence Olivier and Ralph Richardson on their expiry the following summer. Before the war the Old Vic was considered to be a cultural theatre of the lower middle classes, the intellectuals and the intelligent. It offered low-price, basic productions of a generally high standard, with the resident company expected to form the nucleus of an eventual National Theatre. This impression of artistic excellence was cemented in 1944 with the renowned productions of *Peer Gynt*, *King Lear*, *Richard III* and *Oedipus Rex*, starring Olivier and Richardson, but the company then began to encounter problems as a result of its popularity; whilst its policy was to pay leading actors a modest £60 a week, the wages that they could command in the commercial theatre rose to £300, and on the screen to an astronomical £1,000. Unsurprisingly, the leading players chose to exploit their market worth, resulting in ever rarer appearances at the Old Vic, a decline from the high standards that they had created for the company, an increase in the burden of administrative duties for the third director/manager, John Burrell,[290] and a tailing-off in audience numbers. No official statement about what most perceived to be the firing of the stars was given by the board, but it was generally felt that the governors had wished to remove the financially crippling sense of anti-climax that arose whenever the stars were not appearing.[291] The previous season without Olivier and Richardson, 1947–8, had proved an inevitable anti-climax and led to losses of £9,000.[292] Hobson postponed making any detailed comment on the affair in *The Sunday Times* for ten months, perhaps wishing to see how the new regime, under the direction of the former director of the Bristol Old Vic, Hugh Hunt, prospered, but when he did address the issue in October 1949, he openly regretted the decision of the governors in the article, 'The Old Vic and the National Theatre'.[293]

The phrasing of the first National Theatre Bill, passed in February 1949, had been deliberately cautious – the sum of £1 million would be given, 'subject to such conditions as the Treasury may think fit'[294] – and the problem for the two administrators of the Old Vic, Llewellyn Rees and Hugh Hunt, was this continuing evasiveness not just about funding but the kind of company that the authorities wished to create. Hobson concedes that the government's attitude is an unnecessary impediment – 'until the Government decides how much money it is to spend on the National Theatre any question of drawing up binding contracts is absurd' – yet he is dubious about the chances of success of a team of young actors without any star names and he advances three reasons why stars should be engaged. Firstly, many dramatists require great actors in leading roles, with 'nearly all Shakespeare … designed for the star actor or actress'. Secondly, to avoid merely being a 'good provincial stock company', the National Theatre must have 'a national repute', and, thirdly, the employment of stars would not necessarily dispense with the need for good team work, especially if the actors and actresses are committed to three-year contracts.[295] The selection of readers' letters that appeared in *The Sunday Times* in response to this article reflects the keenness of the theatrical public's interest in the issue,[296] but whatever the merits or otherwise of the decision to terminate the contracts, the 'dismissals' – a public relations fiasco – did little to halt the decline in the Old Vic's fortunes.

Hobson's first full calendar year as the drama critic of *The Sunday Times* had brought him into contact with a disappointingly limited range of plays, and this absence of stimulating, new British works was to continue into 1949. This was the year, however, which marked the consolidation of what Hobson later termed the 'Foreign Revelation',[297] which had taken place in the aftermath of the war and which was to introduce to the London stage two American plays that aroused great interest as well as an important work by Anouilh. There was also another memorable Shakespearean performance by Olivier and a significant verse drama by Eliot.

At the beginning of 1949 Hobson had encountered a young man who was to become his chief professional rival during the upheaval of the 1950s. Kenneth Tynan was now an undergraduate at Oxford, more renowned for his bohemian lifestyle than for his drama, and towards the end of January Hobson witnessed a performance by the Oxford University Dramatic Society (OUDS) in the Rudolf Steiner Hall, London of the First Quarto *Hamlet*, a production which bore the flamboyant student's unmistakable stamp. The play, Hobson wrote, was:

> under the direction of Ken Tynan of Magdalen, a long, lean, dialectically brilliant young man who seems to occupy in the contemporary University a position pretty similar to that of Harold Acton when I was up.
>
> In other words, Mr Tynan appears to be the mascot of, as well as the driving force behind, those cultural experiments of which Oxford, when at its best, is usually full. Undoubtedly he is a man of ideas, several of which he has crammed into this production of a 'Hamlet' which, travestied as it is by its own text, he does not hesitate high-spiritedly to travesty still further by the lively pranks of his direction.[298]

These 'pranks' included an eighteenth-century setting, a king dressed in a coloured waistcoat and a queen wearing a green riding-cloak, and Hobson concludes that the evening, in which Tynan took the role of the Second Player, was 'memorable, irreverent, and highly interesting' – adjectives which could all be applied to the best of Tynan's subsequent criticism.

They might equally have been used to describe the decision of the Old Vic governors to dispense with the services of Laurence Olivier at the end of the summer. An early opportunity to assess what the governors had rejected arose with productions of *The School for Scandal*, *Richard III* and Anouilh's *Antigone*, all at the New Theatre. Hobson felt that the first production suffered from a lack of style, a virtue which he succinctly defined as 'that quality which gives to a man distinction even when he is doing or saying something of no consequence'.[299] There was no such distraction in *Richard III*, however, with Hobson's article, 'The Theatre Justified',[300] providing further support for the view that the immediate post-war era was notable for the occasional outstanding acting performance. As with Olivier's 1946 performance of King Lear, the presence of genius is exquisitely captured in Hobson's heightened prose:

> From the moment when Sir Laurence's malign hunchback first hobbles across the stage, after entering through a door whose lock he avariciously fingers as if to see that decency and generosity have been shut out, this performance amuses, delights and astonishes. Mark how, in that opening soliloquy, by a waving of the arms, and a swaying of his crooked body, a mad nodding of his monstrously-nosed head, and a rapid quickening of his speech, he creates a choking, snaring forest: and mark, too, the effect, at once pitiful and revolting, when he drops on his knee to court the Lady Anne, and falls to one side in his deformity. These things prepare one for the greater achievements to come.

This ability to capture the hypnotic atmosphere of a great performance is a notable feature of Hobson's writing and it serves him well when he proceeds to describe the two haunting stage pictures that Olivier has created:

> The first is after he has accepted the invitation of Buckingham and half a dozen seedy citizens to be king. He has been reading a prayer book in a window, and Buckingham thinks that he is a man whom he can manage. But when the last citizen has departed, Richard flings the book of devotion aside, leaps from the window, gains the centre of the stage, and extends his hand for Buckingham to kiss in a gesture of royalty horrible, evil, twisted and grotesque, but sickeningly powerful. The relationship between the two men changes on the instant without a word being spoken. With one astounded look Buckingham realises that what he thought was a lizard is a rattlesnake.

The second picture occurs at the very end of the play 'on a note just as striking':

> [Olivier] leaves the fighting to Kean, but after Richmond, foot planted on his breast, has spiked him on his sword, he is tremendous. Convulsively freeing himself from his enemy, but still lying on his back, he performs what, with its shooting out of the legs like the darting tongue of a viper, can only be described as a horizontal dance. It is an amazing end to a memorable evening.[301]

This sickening dance of death, a feat of athleticism as well as imagination, was one of Olivier's most remarkable stage effects.

The final play in this 1949 trilogy of Olivier Old Vic productions was Anouilh's *Antigone*. Although Hobson claims that his review 'partakes on the nature of an exposition' of existentialism, its flippant tone intimates both that Hobson has grappled none too successfully with the tenets of the philosophy and that he has instinctively disliked what he has gleaned. Whilst he recognizes that 'Existentialist drama is a drama of situations in which choice is imperative', his amplification of this idea, comparing the inscription on a friend's Somersetshire mug – 'Do zummat: do good if you can, but do zummat' – to the moral imperative under which Antigone labours, is a poor substitute for a better-informed discussion of the play's philosophical background and related theatricality. Not only does Hobson fail to raise the pertinent question (much discussed in France at the time) of whether the work is an apologia for, or a call to arms against, the Nazis,[302] but he fails even to touch upon the existentialist beliefs that the 'existence' of man must precede his 'essence'; that man is therefore condemned to an absolute freedom; and that he is thus obliged to make choices (since even the refusal to choose is in itself a choice). This idea that man cannot be defined other than by the sum of his actions is important for an understanding of *Antigone* and Hobson sadly passes over this background, preferring to compliment the tragic necessity conveyed by Olivier as the Chorus, since this diverts from what he (falsely) perceives to be the purely expository nature of the action: 'It is as though, instead of being taken for a drive in the country, we were treated to an extremely interesting discourse on the internal combustion engine.'[303]

One of the limitations of Hobson's critical approach is that his subjective desire to create a historical record of personal reaction sometimes leaves him ill-prepared for discussion of a new and detailed theatrical theory which he instinctively finds alien – although he was to correct his initial misconception of *Antigone* in his book, *French Theatre since 1830*, when he referred to the undeniable 'theatrical vitality' of the work.[304] This same flaw is also apparent in his encounters with Brecht's theory of epic theatre and partially explains why he was to write so erratically about the German playwright in the next decade.

A more palatable way of approaching a play that has not given pleasure is to couch the review in ironic and amusing language, something at which Hobson is a master and which he demonstrates in an article on *Caligula* by Albert Camus:

Three Hours of it
Caligula throttled his mistress, rammed poison down the throat of an old man who shot round the stage like a terrified mouse, seduced a middle-aged lady before the eyes of her husband and the guests at a dinner party, and still yelled and shrieked for fresh experiences. Caligula yearned, I yawned, the more fortunate among us went to sleep, and a few brave souls left the theatre. The evening went on and on, until at the end of three hours the stage lights were lowered while a band of singularly leisurely conspirators stabbed Caligula to death in the darkness. After this there came a moment of supreme horror, for the lights went up, and Caligula was seen clinging, with bleeding mouth, to a mirror from which the glass had been thoughtfully removed. He then uttered the electrifying threat, 'I'm still alive', and I dare say that not a man in the audience did not turn pale, fearing that there was more to come. The alarm proved groundless, but I doubt if my nerves will ever be the same again.[305]

There have been few reviews that have so accurately conveyed the desperation that envelops an audience when confronted by a long and tedious drama.

In the first six months of 1949 the commercial success of *September Tide*, *Oklahoma!* (celebrating its second birthday), *Bless the Bride*, *Annie Get Your Gun*, Danny Kaye's appearances at the Palladium,[306] and *The Heiress* by Ruth and Augustus Goetz (Peggy Ashcroft's biggest success thus far) emphasized the total dominance of lighter entertainment and the absence of works that paid any attention to the contemporary world. A series of plays, *The Way Back*, *Twice Upon a Time* and Lesley Storm's *Black Chiffon*, centred on a new theatrical fad, psychiatry; *Shooting Star* dealt with an issue that was of interest to millions, namely football transfer fees and the question of a footballer's minimum wage of £12 per week; Commander Stephen King-Hall's *Number 10, Downing Street* was a story about the British Prime Minister absconding to Washington during the next war and selling the United Kingdom to the United States; but, on the whole, most new drama was as effervescent and insubstantial as Ronald Millar's matrimonial comedy, *Champagne for Delilah*. Hobson was keen to stress that the mere decision to write about contemporary issues would not guarantee a playwright literary acclaim – 'what matters about a play is not whether it has social significance, but whether the author's imagination has been dramatically excited'[307] – though he would clearly welcome the opportunity to view a work that broke with the fashion for revue and light comedy. Such an opportunity was granted to him in the summer of 1949.

Recognizing, in Hobson's words, 'as was rarely done at that time, the great importance of foreign drama in its relationship to the English stage, and to Western culture',[308] or, to put it less charitably, having espied a gap in the market, Lord Kemsley suggested that Hobson should travel to New York to report on the theatrical activity of Broadway. It was a rewarding trip, since Hobson was to obtain an early viewing of the socially critical *Death of a Salesman* by Arthur Miller, a play whose maturity and seriousness provided the flabby London stage with something to aspire to. Hobson's opinion of the play's message differed from the majority of American critics, who saw the work as a parable about the American dream which implicitly criticizes the economic system through which that dream is to be attained. Writing from New York, in 'Broadway Misses The Point',[309] Hobson explains the divergence of view:

> Where I really differ from everybody here is that I cannot see that 'Death of a Salesman' is an exposure of the supposedly American superstition that the object of life is to make more and more money, sell more and more goods, not keep up with, but out-distance, the Joneses. What killed Loman was not the American determination to get rich at all costs, but his own failure to get rich at all. It was not ambition, but ambition disappointed, that did for him. You do not

show an ambition to be worthless by revealing the misery of someone who fails to achieve it: nor prove that a mountain does not repay climbing by concentrating on someone who is winded by the first half-mile scramble.

Hobson is guilty of unusually muddled thinking here, for the point of *Death of a Salesman* is that the pressures that a success-orientated, hugely materialistic society exert on the majority of people far outweigh the rarer examples of the achievement of personal wealth. The value of the play lies in the fact that its poignant domestic tragedy, centring on Willy Loman, complements the larger indictment of a society gone wrong, with both strands drawing on each other to maintain momentum – and not appearing mutually exclusive. Hobson's arguable interpretation may have stemmed from a reluctance to convey a socialist interpretation of the work at a sensitive time in British politics (*The Sunday Times* opposed the faltering Attlee government) and from a dissatisfaction with the leading actor, for when the play arrived in London in July, he describes it as a work of 'enormous distinction',[310] with the Willy Loman of Paul Muni being more moving than the depiction on Broadway by Lee J. Cobb and bringing the audience to tears on at least five occasions. He also now recognized the innovative nature of the play, in that the way in which its multitude of episodes melt imperceptibly into each other represented 'a complete break with the realistic dramatic formulae that have been current in Britain for the last half century'.[311] To be fair to Hobson, other British critics also felt that the play's focus was on the inadequacy of Willy rather than of American society, with the *Daily Telegraph*'s critic, W. A. Darlington, encapsulating the view of many in seeing the play as the 'tragedy of a little man who will not accept the fact of his littleness'.[312]

The American trip also granted Hobson the opportunity to see *Mister Roberts*, *South Pacific* and *A Streetcar Named Desire*, an experience he put to use when he was called upon to defend the latter against a powerful moral outcry in Britain four months later. Hobson had not been endeared to Tennessee Williams's first play to appear in London, *The Glass Menagerie*, in the summer of 1948. He had concluded that not even John Gielgud's direction could conceal the author's desire to have it both ways, by depicting 'the pathos of a girl too unattractive to have a chance of getting proposals' and 'demonstrating this unattractiveness by making the first young man who meets her fall in love'.[313] This dramatic implausibility is then mercilessly exposed:

> If you write a play about a crippled half wit, surely it is fundamental that your heroine should be half witted and crippled. But to do such a thing would be undeniably painful, and Mr Williams cannot bring himself to do it.

Hobson's second London encounter with the American's work, *A Streetcar Named Desire* in October 1949, was initially less important to him than the humorous, cathartic relation of a particularly miserable evening watching *Love's Labour's Lost*:

> There were moments on Tuesday night, whilst Berowne and his companions were pouring out their intricate coruscations of barren verbal jewels, when I slumped into my stall in despair, longing for one of the players to faint, for somebody to start a row in the gallery, for an atom bomb to blow up the theatre, for something, anything, to stop the unbearable torture of the brain, the tormenting of the ears, by the incomprehensible references, irresistible, remorseless sweep of elaborate puns and unrewarding obscurities that make up three-quarters of this artificial play.[314]

A Streetcar Named Desire, on this occasion, receives only a brief mention, in which Hobson relates that a poignant moment in the American production, when the newspaper boy touches Blanche's heart, is lost in the London transfer. The next week, however, Hobson atones for this brevity by making a notable and spirited rebuttal of the vocal charge that the play was vulgar and appealed only to those in search of the salacious.

Public anticipation for the opening of *A Streetcar Named Desire* had been enormous. There had been over ten thousand postal applications[315] to witness the appearance of Vivien Leigh in a modern American play directed by her husband, Laurence Olivier, and fights had broken out amongst members of the eager and impatient queue. After the first performance had finally been given, the critical reaction in the press was sharply – and antagonistically – divided. Some critics were attracted to the poignancy of Vivien Leigh as the abused Blanche – *The Times*, for example, spoke of Vivien Leigh's performance being 'impressive … for its delicately insistent suggestion of a mind with a slowly loosening hold on reason'.[316] They also admired the frankness of the acting demanded by the director, which, whilst it was not according to the 'method' style, nevertheless dispensed with the poise and good breeding more associated with British acting for the sake of emotionally committed performances. Others, however, were outraged by what they chose to see as an indecent, lavatorial work. Anthony Cookman's half-hearted assertion in the *Tatler* that it was 'a vigorous piece of melodrama'[317] suggests disconcertion at the frank depiction of Blanche's sordid past and demise into madness. J. C. Trewin's description in the *Observer* went further, characterizing it as 'a tedious and squalid anecdote'.[318] Baroness Ravensdale of the Public Morality Council spluttered that the 'play is thoroughly indecent and we should be ashamed that children and servants are allowed to sit in the theatre and see it',[319] Princess Alice cancelled a visit, stating that it was not the 'kind of entertainment she would enjoy',[320] whilst simple disgust was expressed in the parish notes of the Reverend Colin Cuttell, priest-vicar of Southwark:

Is there no statesman in high places who will speak out from other than political and economic motives and tell the United States to keep the sewage? A pathological obsession with sex is a mark of this age, as it has been the mark of any dying civilisation from Babylon to Rome. Peradventure the Lord Chamberlain (chief licensee of all theatres) is on a journey or sleepeth ...[321]

Any discomfort that the increasingly beleaguered Attlee government might have felt as a result of such attacks on its alleged moral laxity was exacerbated by the row that developed over the decision to grant tax exemption to the play on the grounds that it was partly cultural and partly educational. To offset the high cost of production (£10,000), the management, Tennent Productions Limited, had turned itself into a non-profit-making registered charity to avoid incurring entertainment tax, an action that was challenged by MPs in the House of Commons. When the financial secretary, Glenvil Hall, sought to explain that it was perfectly in order for the management to claim exemption on educational grounds, the Conservative Member for Brighton, A. Marlowe, asked whether the minister was aware 'that this particular play is only educational to those who are ignorant of the facts of life?'[322]

In many ways, Hobson's response to this *brouhaha*, the article 'Miss Vivien Leigh', marked a new level of critical maturity. He had already demonstrated his ability to capture atmosphere, to describe great acting and to maintain a historical overview: now he was called upon to rectify the erroneous interpretation of a play that was engendered in an atmosphere of moral hysteria. He begins with a spirited defence of Tennessee Williams, by directly rebutting the charge of immorality. On the contrary, the play:

> ... is strictly, and even puritanically, moral. It is the story of a woman, not otherwise questionable, whose sexual nature is, against the striving of better things in her, rendered so uncontrollable by circumstances that she ends in madness. It is no good saying that this kind of character is never portrayed on the stage. What we really mean is that it is never portrayed honestly. In musical comedies and farces girls who behave like Blanche du Bois are common enough; and they end not in an asylum, but in sables and Park Lane.

The charge of moral hypocrisy on the part of the work's detractors is maintained when he claims that it is impossible to be shocked by *Streetcar* yet amused by *Oklahoma!*, for the latter contains a song that is provocatively entitled 'I can't say no'. In any case, Williams's moral is actually that 'the wages of sin is spiritual death', and he concludes his defence of the dramatist by writing that the play is 'a distinguished work', and that 'in its reiterated insistence upon the need for kindness, noble'.[323]

Hobson then opens a second flank by switching to consider the leading lady. Vivien Leigh, in his view, is finer than Uta Hagen, who had appeared in New York, with a particular highlight of her performance being her 'pathetic nervous brightening at the merest suggestion of a compliment'. Hobson had returned to see the play a second time and was prepared to reconsider his earlier impression:

> I saw it again on Wednesday afternoon, and found it almost unbearably poignant. I said a month ago that this performance casts out pity with terror. I was wrong. The terror is there, and the struggle with the woman medical attendant chills the spine. But the pity is overwhelming.

The conclusion of this finely written piece is not content with looking back – re-viewing – but wishes to look forward, by encouraging Leigh to withstand the storm of publicity, strengthened by the knowledge that her performance is one of integrity and achievement:

> I do not know which to admire the more, the power, the emotion of this performance, or the courage that enables Miss Leigh to go on giving it, with undiminished lustre, amidst these foolish suggestions that her play is a public indecency.[324]

This is Hobson's writing at its best – intelligent, bold, committed and stylish, with the intention of encouraging examples of fine theatre, whether this accords with the prevailing view or not. The play was to run at the Aldwych Theatre for 333 performances.[325]

The one new British play that provoked great interest in 1949 was actually written by an American, T. S. Eliot. *The Cocktail Party*, premièred at the Lyceum, Edinburgh during the Festival and brought to London the following May, seemed initially as if it would add to the growing momentum of the verse dramatists. Hobson, in 'A Festival Triumph', described the drama as 'a distinguished, a profound, and an absorbing play'[326] and *The Times* admired the way that it 'endows everyday speech with a delicate precision and a strictly occasional poetic intensity'.[327] But there were already signs that the poetic drama movement would be thwarted in its infancy. For one thing, the new, vibrant theatre from America, with its emphasis on raw emotion and elemental acting, was hastening the demise of society drama. Although written in verse, *The Cocktail Party* was in many ways highly conventional. Its action took place in one room and was populated by characters from the upper middle classes. It utilized favourite dramatic scenarios from previous drawing-room dramas – cocktail parties, adulterous couples, mysterious upper-class characters – and even exploited a recent theatrical fad, an interest in psychiatry. Although the shocking (but implausible) death of Celia Coplestone and the moral implications of Sir Henry Harcourt-Reilly's logical questioning alter the template, the work was not sufficiently original to maintain the cause of verse drama on its own. A second reason why the poetic movement had insufficiently strong roots to withstand a change in theatrical fashion was that the other creative impulse, Christopher Fry, was admired for the intellectual curiosity of his mind and the eclectic content of his plays rather than for his contemporary relevance or exciting theatricality. His works were construed as being demanding, and were therefore unlikely to command a sufficiently large band of devotees once the initial novelty had worn off. Even as it was premièred, the vibrant energy of foreign drama was rendering *The Cocktail Party* obsolete, and it is perhaps most notable now for providing Alec Guinness with a role (Sir Henry) that helped him to challenge the acting triumvirate of Gielgud, Olivier and Richardson.

By way of a coda to Hobson's writing in 1949, October saw another example of the remarkable intertwining of his career with that of Kenneth Tynan's. Whilst at a party to celebrate the 225th anniversary of his publishers, Longmans, Hobson had met the precocious young man once again, since Longmans had just accepted the manuscript of Tynan's collection of criticisms, *He Who Plays the King* – on the advice of Hobson. In an article entitled 'Interest in U.S. Theater' the older critic intriguingly reveals his fascination with the young pretender:

> I first became acquainted with Mr Tynan about a year ago when I received a letter from him asking if I would use any influence I might have to secure him a job of dramatic critic on a certain famous London paper. Since the dramatic critic of this paper happened to be myself, I concluded the writer to be an enterprising young man possessed of whimsical humour. Both enterprising and humorous, Mr Tynan certainly is, and very able, too.[328]

As was the practice of all enterprising, young theatrical men at the time, Tynan was directing the British début of an American work – Eugene O'Neill's *The Iceman Cometh* – at Camden. His directing ambitions frustrated, he was eventually to become the drama critic of the *Evening Standard* in 1952.

If 1949 had been the year of the American play on the London stage, 1950 was to prove the year of the French. At the beginning of the new decade the most popular domestic dramatist was Christopher Fry. In January 1950 he was enjoying unparalleled success, with three of his plays running simultaneously in the West End – *Venus Observed* (starring Laurence Olivier as the Duke of Altair), *The Lady's Not for Burning* (concluding an eight-month run at the Globe) and an early religious work, *The Boy with a Cart* (at the Lyric). The appetite for what he termed his 'sliced prose' (which Hobson amended to 'spiced sliced prose',[329] to emphasize the linguistic dexterity of the works) seemed unquenchable. A fourth Fry work, appearing in February at the Globe, marked a new departure, in that it was not only in prose but was also a translation of Jean Anouilh's *L'Invitation au Château*, entitled *Ring Round the Moon*. Although Hobson had earlier been captivated by Fry's language, 'All his characters talk like an Oscar Wilde stuffed with the picturesque learning, the astronomical divagations, the love philtres, and the Latin echoes of a Robert Burton'[330] (rather belying his claim in

Theatre in Britain that 'Fry was the last of the writers ... who spoke to the entire theatre audience from the very start'[331]), he required further convincing that there was much of substance beneath the glittering exterior, yet it is hard to escape the overall conclusion that what enchanted Hobson and the other devotees of Fry was less his intrinsic *dramatic* merit than his utilization of an unusual and innovative idiom, a point implicit in Hobson's comment three months later that: 'Fry gives ... almost a pentecostal feeling that he is speaking a new and inexhaustible tongue. It is like being released from a verbal prison.'[332]

What is undeniable is that *Ring Round the Moon* convinced many that, as well as being intellectually stimulating, French drama could be entertaining in a less uncompromising manner. The play, coupled with the appetite for travel engendered by his trip to America and the sterility of new plays in London, certainly influenced Hobson in his decision to devote much of his critical work over the next three years to considering the respective merits of London, Paris and New York. As far as French drama was concerned, this resulted as much from his enjoyment of French literature as from the increasing proliferation of French works on the London stage and his belief that a possible solution to London's stasis would be to take selective lessons from the French experience. Hobson admired not just the diversity of new drama in France since the war, but the French belief that culture was a civilizing influence on human behaviour – which is why the French government supported its theatrical profession in a way unimaginable in Britain, given that the London stage was too class-bound and the British government too penurious. Many of his articles in 1950 read like envious bulletins on the greater robustness of the French stage. In 'The Theatre in Paris and London'[333] he gives vent to the obvious: since the war, the English theatre has flourished commercially rather than artistically, whereas the French has passed through a great financial crisis to the flourishing of admirable, new works. In 'Frenchmen Take the Arts Seriously'[334] the fact that a French government minister met the Barraults at the airport on their return from a South American tour in August 1950, the proliferation of theatre bookshops in Paris and the number of French theatrical commentaries are all cited as evidence of a proper respect for the arts. 'A Fine Play' considers that Jean Anouilh's *Ardèle* should not be missed by any respectable theatre-goer, because it is written by 'one of the most considerable of contemporary dramatists',[335] and 'Jean Anouilh' marvels at the Renaud/Barrault company's production of *La Répétition* and explains that Anouilh's *Eurydice* (playing as *Point of Departure* at the Lyric, Hammersmith) justifies 'one's feeling that M. Anouilh is the most exciting dramatist working in the contemporary theatre'.[336]

In 'Drama's Capital'[337] the European critic draws together the observations that he has made on his travels in the last eighteen months and concludes that the small number of theatres in New York (36, compared with London's 40+ and 60+ in Paris) is indicative of an underlying weakness in the American theatre: 'If the drama must prosper as an industry so that it can flourish as an art, the world in the immediate future will look for its significant theatre in Paris and London rather than New York.' Yet each artistic centre is suffering from the same debilitating malaise, for 'none of them is served by a sufficient number of authors capable of inventing original plots'. Paris falls back on classical myths, New York over-uses fresh story lines (as with *Gentlemen Prefer Blondes*, where a novel spawned a film, a play and then a musical), whereas London's 'dependence on revivals and importations causes exasperation to many unacted and aspiring dramatists'. On a more positive note, Hobson considers that New York is unrivalled when it comes to production and musicals; London excels in 'acting on the big scale, in which vitality and power are informed by intelligence and taste' (principally Gielgud, Guinness, Olivier and Richardson); and Paris boasts by far the finest list of dramatists, including Jean Anouilh, Armand Salacrou, Paul Claudel, François Mauriac, Marcel Achard, Michel de Ghelderode, André Gide, Albert Camus and Jacques Deval. Against this 'dazzling list', which is mostly populated by new writers, Britain can offer only Fry and Eliot, leading to the inescapable conclusion that 'the most significant drama in the world today is being written in Paris'. To his historical overview, Hobson had now added a European perspective and a passionate belief in the importance of new writing.

'On the most private lives today public matters impinge', Hobson wrote in February 1951,[338] against a background of East–West tension, the escalating arms race, the Korean War, an increase in world prices (British retail prices rose by 10 per cent in 1951[339]) and political uncertainty at home (the Labour Government was to fall in October 1951), but one would be hard pushed to perceive this from a study of the theatrical fare on offer in London at the time. For pithier drama, one would have to travel to France: 'In Paris plays on such subjects are produced at the rate of more than one a month, as often as not followed by a riot. In England, even if they are written, they are hardly produced at all.'[340] This regrettable state of affairs was particularly unfortunate in the year of the Festival of Britain, which had been conceived as a centenary celebration of the Great Exhibition of 1851 to illustrate the best of the country's talent in art and design, since the works chosen to illustrate the depth of British dramatic achievement merely emphasized the extent to which the stage was being forced to rely upon the glories of the past. The Festival was dominated by a mixture of Shakespeare and Shaw. The Old Vic, having produced *Man and Superman*, put on *Captain Brassbound's Conversion*. The Arts and St Martin's Theatres contributed three Shaw plays each. The players at Stratford performed *Richard II* (again – the living embodiment of stasis), *Henry IV, Part One* and *Two*, and *Henry V* (starring the young Richard Burton as the king), whilst Laurence Olivier appeared in alternate-night productions of *Antony and Cleopatra* and *Caesar and Cleopatra*. This apotheosis of Shaw, who had died the previous year, was not something that Hobson greatly welcomed. In his retrospect on Shaw's career, which he wrote for the *Christian Science Monitor* under the title 'Shaw Pitted Ideas Against ... Ideas',[341] Hobson summarized his attitude to the playwright's works, developed from the days when he had first read Shaw's plays in a drama group at Oriel. Hobson felt that Shaw's greatest achievement was that he had 'applied the classic fundamentals of drama to the theater of ideas'. He did not 'oppose character to character, for he could not create characters and had no desire to do so. What he did was to oppose ideas to each other.' This may not be enough, however, to ensure continued popularity:

> He made his plays the most exciting and exhilarating entertainments of their day, though whether they will survive into an age that is unable to put them into their intellectual and social context is a matter that can, and no doubt will, be argued.

Hobson was also disappointed that the finest acting talent in the Festival was often squandered on undeserving plays, a notable example being Dame Edith Evans and Dame Sybil Thorndike's appearance in N. C. Hunter's *Waters of the Moon*,[342] and he felt that, although the Festival had seen acting 'unrivalled in the modern world'[343] (citing Gielgud's Leontes in *The Winter's Tale*, Richardson's Vershinin in *Three Sisters*, Olivier's Caesar in *Caesar and Cleopatra* and Guinness's Hamlet[344]), only one new play of note had been premièred, Christopher Fry's *A Sleep of Prisoners* (which proved to be the ultimate Christian verse drama). Paris, of course, could point to three during the same period: Sartre's *Le Diable et le Bon Dieu* and Anouilh's *La Répétition* and *Colombe*.

Even the one brand of entertainment that could usually be relied upon to divert attention from the meagre fare, the musical, began to irritate Hobson in the first half of 1951. Although he had enjoyed Ivor Novello's *Gay's the Word* in February, because Novello possessed 'the prime necessity of all artists, a view of life, and his technical skill in expressing this view is such that we can enjoy its theatrical statement even when disagreeing with its philosophical substance',[345] the derivative nature of the latest American import, *Kiss Me, Kate*, seemed to symbolize all the very worst features of American cultural imperialism, sending the normally mild critic into near apoplexy:

> the most remarkable phenomenon in today's international theatre is the acknowledged failure of creative imagination. I do not think there has ever been a time when so many able talents in so many countries have tacitly admitted their inability to invent an original plot.

Hobson then turns on the creators of the musical's book:

> Porter and Spewack ... fly so well on other people's wings that one regrets they attempt a few flights of their own. The jokes in the play are humiliatingly naive, and the central incident of the public spanking

of the leading actress by the leading actor, referred to again and again (King Charles's head is simply not in it compared with another part of Miss Patricia Morison's anatomy) is grotesquely inadequate as the foundation of an intelligent story.

But there is nothing much wrong with the show as a whole. If ninety-nine per cent of the references to this episode were deleted, and a good joke was introduced every half hour, and the long, mocking speech about theatrical glamour was drastically reduced or, better still, cut, and asides about 'angels' and an organisation that sounded like the Federation of British Industries but was something quite different were either explained to British audiences or omitted, and Miss Morison and Mr Bill Johnson put more realism into their assaults and batteries (at present they have the fury of a badly frightened sheep), and the second act was improved all through, then 'Kiss Me, Kate' would thoroughly deserve the two-year run which it is bound to have.[346]

Hobson was equally dismissive of *South Pacific*, claiming in November that its 'humour is based on the venerable formula of thinking of something in bad taste and repeating it three times'.[347]

The degree of frustration evident in Hobson's writing of 1951 stemmed from his belief that the great reserves of acting talent of which Britain could now boast were not being given any new works of note in which to shine. This did not mean, though, that Hobson was unable to appreciate the skill apparent in the many revivals of classic works, or the development of a younger generation of actors. Pre-eminent amongst this latter group was Richard Burton, who had first come to Hobson's notice as the shy Richard in the 1949 production of Fry's *The Lady's Not for Burning*. The quizzical, faintly bemused tone of Hobson's review of Burton's Henry IV suggests a performance notable for its thought-provoking originality and rare in its fresh interpretation of a familiar text:

> This production of the first half of 'Henry IV' offers what must be one of the rarest of theatrical experiences: namely, a performance in a principal part which, in the light of the text and the received notions of the author's intentions, cannot be accorded even the moderate praise of being called good, yet which gives the deep and ordered emotional release that is among the actual marks of greatness. Moreover, this suggestion of greatness is not a thing of flashes merely, coming only at the crises of the play, though that in itself would be sufficiently memorable. It is in the bone and sinew of the performance, and is as evident in the actor's stillness when other players are speaking as when he is sailing the full flood of his mistaken inspiration.

The originality of Burton's interpretation lay in his depiction of Prince Henry not as a gay libertine, but as 'a man who had had a private vision of the Holy Grail, and was as determined to say nothing about it as he was incapable of forgetting it'. Hobson, demonstrating his unique understanding of the actor's craft – remarkable even in someone who has had practical experience of the stage – and with a perfect use of metaphor that is reminiscent of Hazlitt at his most incisive, maintains that, although this interpretation is hard to justify textually, it is permissible given the new dimension that it gives to the work:

> An actor, it cannot be too often said, is not merely an embodiment of other men's ideas. He has a flame of his own to light, and to get it going he sometimes burns the paper his author has written on. Instead of a light-hearted rapscallion Mr Burton offers a young knight keeping a long vigil in the cathedral of his own mind. The knighthood is authentic, the vigil upheld by interior exaltation.

If Burton has gone wrong, Hobson is claiming, then he has gone wrong magnificently. He ends his notice with a neat utilization of his diminishing newspaper space: 'But, like Mr Burton himself, I am short of inches, and the catalogue of praise must end long before it is exhausted'[348] – a notice that has reiterated Hobson's high regard for the actor's contribution to drama.

Another interpretation that challenged the familiar conception of a classic theatrical text – but with a less happy outcome – was Alec Guinness's eagerly awaited Hamlet at the New Theatre in May 1951. Hobson's review was one of the few that he completed immediately after the fall of the curtain[349] (his usual practice being to consider other critical views before putting pen to paper[350]), and this may partly explain why he is so forthright about such a respected actor, beginning his review, provocatively entitled 'Disaster'[351] by the sub-editor, in the following way:

> Dickens had his 'Hard Times', Shakespeare his 'Titus Andronicus', Napoleon his Waterloo, Wellington his premiership, and now Mr Alec Guinness has acted Hamlet. It is the custom of genius to do things in a big way, and the cropper that Mr Guinness came on Thursday night was truly monumental.

Guinness's mistake, in Hobson's view, was to attempt a Freudian portrayal of Hamlet – exploring 'the dark underside of the Prince's mind' – and there is a clear sense that Hobson is shocked more by the decisiveness with which the actor has broken with the nineteenth-century tradition of portraying the prince as shy and retiring than by the components of his performance, about which Hobson says regrettably little. The critic does point out that Guinness was not helped by the erratic nature of the production, with lights being switched on and off at the wrong time, Rosencrantz's distracting black eye-patch and a very poor level of supporting acting, but Hobson has been so distracted by these technical flaws that he neglects to justify the harshness of his judgement. Although 'Disaster' represents one of Hobson's weakest reviews, he was not alone in condemning Guinness – T. C. Worsley felt that the whole thing had been 'a complete misfire',[352] Ivor Brown viewed it as 'a lullaby performance',[353] and Anthony Cookman termed it 'very odd'.[354] Only W. A. Darlington recognized Guinness's performance as 'intelligent and sardonic', if marred by production problems.[355]

A month later Hobson revisited the New Theatre and wrote a second notice, fully aware that the adverse publicity that surrounded its opening had meant that the production was being withdrawn at the end of June, with the producer, Henry Sherek, eventually losing £15,000. This willingness to take a further look at a production, to consider that he may have reached a false conclusion and to be prepared to correct his initial impression is one of Hobson's finest critical attributes.[356] The review, '"Hamlet" Revisited',[357] is a much finer one than the first. It notes the damage that criticisms such as his had done and regards the early closure as 'regrettable'; it acknowledges that the faults of the first night constituted a distraction and have now been ironed out – the supporting cast 'proves itself worthy of its leading actor', the lighting has improved and Guinness has dispensed with his unusual beard; whilst emphasizing this prince's coarseness, it describes in detail two aspects of Guinness's portrayal – his highlighting of the weakness of Hamlet and a moving rendition of the 'paragon of animals' speech – to help convey some of the actor's dramatic intention; and it completes the retraction with the verdict that the performance is 'memorable in its originality, integrity, courage, and pathos' and urges the reader to make a visit: 'if the New Theatre is not thronged at every one of the last sixteen performances I shall lose all hope of the British public'. Fine as this second article is in its recording of an original and profound piece of acting (now regarded as an innovative approach to the role), it must have brought only limited comfort to the leading actor. Hobson is to be admired for his eagerness to confirm a first opinion by revisiting a show and then honestly recognizing and correcting its unfairness, but the injustice of the original piece had a lasting effect – and demonstrates the importance for a critic of separating an individual performance from its surrounding cast, just as a good critic will differentiate between a good production and a good script.

There was no such unevenness in the performances that Jean-Louis Barrault's company gave on its visit to Britain in the autumn of 1951, a visit that was to supply Hobson with one of his touchstones for acting, to be added to John Martin-Harvey in *The Only Way*, Irving in *The Bells* (assimilated through contemporary reports) and Peggy Ashcroft at her moments of greatest calm. In 'Visitors'[358] the French theatre's most devoted admirer in England wrote of Madeleine Renaud's role in Marivaux's *Les Fausses Confidences* that: 'I have never seen the dawn of love so beautifully, so delicately portrayed as in her performance of Araminte', yet even this rhapsodic praise was surpassed after Hobson had seen Edwige Feuillère in Claudel's *Partage de Midi* at the St James's Theatre:

> ... when in twenty years time or so, one comes to consider the theatre since 1930, this performance of 'Partage de Midi' will be reckoned, along with John Gielgud's 'Richard of Bordeaux', Laurence Olivier's 'Richard III', and Ralph Richardson's 'Johnson Over Jordan', as one of the half-dozen greatest, most exciting experiences the stage has given us.[359]

Part of the credit, Hobson reluctantly concedes, must be due to Claudel, but it is primarily down to the mesmerizing Feuillière, praised in the most rapturous manner that Hobson had ever devised for a piece of acting:

> The part of Ysé brings to London Mme. Edwige Feuillière, an actress too resplendent in her own right to be fobbed off on us as a mere reincarnation of some star of the past. Her voice is miraculously soft, and comforting and caressing; she wears her Edwardian costumes with supple grace; has apparently the gift of being able to make her eyes swim with tears at will; at every moment is in complete control of her performance; can utter words as simple as 'Qu'il fait chaud' with such languor, such a sense of voluptuous suffocation, that the air of the theatre seems heavy with heat; and she has a gaiety that is interesting to compare with Mme. Madeleine Renaud's. Into both pain can enter. But whereas with Mme Renaud one knows the pain will soon pass and sunshine return, with Mme. Feuillière the pain is always there, though the rippling laughter often hides it. Hers is a great performance.

So great was it, 'combining physical allure with a mastery of theatrical art to a degree I have not encountered in any other actress in thirty years of playgoing',[360] that Hobson was to retain the memory of it as his image of perfection in acting for the rest of his career. When he writes in *The Theatre Now* that Feuillière is 'the only actress I know who unites absolute mastery of her art with utter physical beauty and radiance',[361] he accords her the highest compliment he was ever to make.

In spite of his love of all things French, Hobson did not let this blind him to the continuing problems of the London stage at the end of 1951, unhappily lamenting that Anouilh, with *Traveller Without Luggage*, his seventh play on the London stage in the last four years,[362] was now 'the most popular postwar British dramatist'.[363] Hobson was always of the belief that foreign works should show British works the way forward in a time of sterility – not replace them.[364] A further trip to Paris – always a cathartic experience – finally convinced Hobson that he needed to speak out in protest at the vacuous nature of the British theatre. 'London Survey', published on 30 March 1952, represents the first 'Angry Young Man' criticism to appear in a Sunday newspaper – penned by a 48-year-old critic, four years before such a movement was born.[365]

On his return from Paris, Hobson had noticed the marked differences between the two capitals. The most striking aspect of the London stage was 'its extraordinary detachment' and 'its indifference to the world in which it is living'. This remoteness appeared deliberate and unremitting:

> I came back to a country whose newspapers are mainly filled with tidings of war, insurrection, industrial unrest, political controversy, and parliamentary misbehaviour; and to a theatre from which it seems to me, in the first shock of re-acquaintance, that all echo of these things is shut off as by sound-proof walls.

The list of entertainments to which he has been invited that week – comedians at the Palladium, 'a persuasively restful' production of *Uncle Vanya*, a dramatization of Jane Austen's *Lady Susan* and a revival of the Stratford *Tempest* – verifies this impression. The crux of the article then adumbrates the premise behind much of Kenneth Tynan's later criticism:

> That the human race is passionate, pathological, physical, poetic, paradoxical, and even philosophical is recognised in the West End: the first in 'The Deep Blue Sea'; the second in 'Third Person', 'The Same Sky' and 'Women of Twilight'; the third in 'Bet Your Life' and 'The Vortex'; the fourth in 'Much Ado About Nothing', though scarcely in the Old Vic's 'King Lear', a doubly staggering production that astonishes no less than it totters; the fifth in 'White Sheep of the Family'; and the sixth in 'Nightmare Abbey' and 'The Love of Four Colonels', both extremely diverting. But, except in the way of fantasy in the last-named play, that the human race is also political the contemporary English theatre by implication and neglect absolutely denies.[366]

Hobson goes on to add that, while much in contemporary politics is worth ignoring and French drama does possess the advantage of being able to utilize such searing topics as collaboration, the treatment of broader issues might be rewarding in Britain, too. Eight months later just how extensive that range of topics had become was to be seen in the content of Genet's *Les Bonnes*, which Hobson described as an 'unsavoury nightmare of Lesbianism, flagellation, masochism, and incest, over which the author can, I should think, be heard smacking his lips as far away as the red-light district of Marseilles'.[367]

What differentiates Hobson from later drama critics and playwrights, fiercely indignant at the sterility evident in Britain, is that he has no political manifesto to which to adhere and is interested merely in the general *theatrical* health of the nation. The occasional political colour that has intruded into his criticism thus far seems less a result of personal conviction than a willingness to echo editorial policy (Kemsley's loyalty to the Conservatives being predicated on a personal devotion to Churchill[368]). Hobson's diagnosis is measured and heartfelt; he takes pains to record that he speaks 'as a witness and not as a judge',[369] and he never loses sight of the fact that plays must be credible theatrically before they can convey any message. The gentle persuasiveness of his argument was bound to be overshadowed by more passionate outbursts, better aping the language and temper of a newly indignant generation, yet the legitimacy of what he writes is not effaced by the words of his more vibrant colleagues. Many wrote for more radical publications and, not running the risk of being unfairly associated with the views of a right-wing owner, were never in danger of being misinterpreted by people who were not regular readers of their columns. In fact, Hobson seems to be rediscovering some of the socialist principles of his student days. Writing in the *Christian Science Monitor* on the need to ease the tax burden on artists, he stresses that they should be seen as a special case:

> I am not in this matter protesting against high taxation as such. In England a man with a regular income of £3000 pays £1000 in income tax. Strong arguments can be brought to justify this. Socialism in Britain, aided by high taxation, has produced many exasperations, but it has also largely eliminated poverty and given a higher average strength and well-being to the nation than it has known before.[370]

This is a somewhat different point of view from the one he expressed in the 1945 general election in the editorials of the provincial newspapers owned by Lord Kemsley. What is a matter of record is that Hobson was the first weekly critic to recognize that some reorientation was necessary, and his vision is an impressive virtue.

Hobson was a positive critic, always seeking out fresh sources of pleasure during even the most unpropitious period. Thus the indignation expressed in 'London Survey' did not develop into an unremitting pessimism. Two months later, aware that fresh writing would not appear immediately, he pointed out that, because of the lack of good plays, the actor was entrusted with a great responsibility as well as being granted a great opportunity, since he is now 'called upon to supply a creative vision of his own':

> To them we look for the creative vision generally lacking in the modern playwrights. This vision can only come from rich and profound personalities; and if it comes, as I hope it will, it may not always obviously accord with the intention of the author in association with whom it is displayed. Richard Burton's Prince Hal at Stratford last year had none of the roistering gaiety that some of that young gentleman's speeches suggest; but it had a splendid spiritual calm I cannot forget, a calm superbly existing in its own right. It was a performance, I am persuaded, infinitely higher in value than many others which keep more obediently to the text.[371]

Talented actors can not only take liberties with the text, but can also deliver bad performances that are worth viewing. This conundrum is explained in 'A Great Actor'[372] with reference to Ralph Richardson's much-debated Stratford Macbeth. There are two reasons why a great actor may give a poor performance, Hobson argues. The first is that he may simply be lacking inspiration, a fault common to all actors at times, but the second is one that is peculiar to the great actor, in that 'the thing that gives him his value as a creative artist, his individual view of life, is at odds with the play in which he exhibits it'. This is the difficulty that Richardson encounters as Macbeth, 'a difficulty that could not arise if Richardson were not a great actor'. Richardson's talent lies in the 'sane, quiet, and undemonstrative English way' in which he looks at life and 'finds it incomprehensible' – the keynote to his performances being 'a puzzled perplexity'. At the beginning of *Macbeth* this causes him problems – he depicts the soldier as being 'caught up in a murder he does not understand' and the result is unsatisfactory. In the middle of the work, however, the inspiration of the author and the actor meet, and Richardson movingly presents the baffled pathos on Macbeth's part when he realizes that it is Duncan and not himself who has found peace. The play gets 'better and better' (something Hobson had never experienced in *Macbeth* before):

> until at the end I am bound to record that Sir Ralph's performance, though it begins by being at war with the text, gave me stronger and deeper delight than the Macbeths either of Mr Michael Redgrave or Sir Godfrey Tearle, of Mr Alec Clunes or Mr Gielgud.

By attempting to understand the actor's intention by employing the historian's technique of measuring present action against past precedent and subscribing to the view that criticism should be constructive rather than destructive, Hobson was often able to find merit in a performance which others found simply incomprehensible. This does not mean that a partiality to a particular actor whom he has enjoyed in the past will blind him to genuine defects. Richardson's second critical disaster at Stratford in 1952 was as Volpone, which Hobson was unable to defend. Since 'he knows the simple goodness of the human heart as does no other player in the British theatre', he was too placid to be Volpone. The regret expressed in 'Why Volpone?'[373] is palpable.

The first five years of Hobson's tenure at *The Sunday Times* had established him as one of the most famous critics in London, alongside Ivor Brown of the *Observer*. A sense of his fame – and upper middle-class readership – can be gauged by a competition which the *Spectator* ran in February 1953, inviting readers to submit excerpts of Hobson or Brown reviewing Laurence Olivier and Vivien Leigh in 'Macbeth on Ice'. The winning extracts all parodied recognizable traits of Hobson's criticism – his references to France, his belief in propriety, his elegant turn of phrase and his sense of comedy – but they were humorously ironic rather than bitingly satirical:

> … It disturbed me, however, to see the aged Duncan skating blithely to the Castle gates. How shall old age be served? Doubtless we shall see when it comes to the turn of King Lear (M. E. Fossey).

> I confess I expected my reactions to *Macbeth* on ice to be glacial. Granted the unlooked-for success of *Hamlet* on skates, the brilliant glissades of Barrault in Paris (where *Phèdre Gelée* is playing to packed houses). I still frowned on the prospect of a refrigerated Dunsinane … (Nancy Smith).
>
> … Only a very slight hesitation here and there in his speeches betrayed the fact that any feet but metrical were his concern … (P.M.).[374]

Since 1947 Hobson had captured the sense of occasion in a number of great individual performances, lamented the vacuousness of British playwriting, welcomed efforts to change the direction of the British theatre and suggested that foreign examples might aid the process of reorientation. Above all, his cultured and elegant prose had begun to establish an eyewitness account of the evolution of post-war British drama, a task whose importance he outlines in his 1952 book, *Verdict at Midnight*:

> The dramatic critic is not merely a judge, placing authors and actors in classes like a School Certificate examiner, still less a tipster guessing how long a play will run, he is a historian recording memorable experience.[375]

Hobson the historian is very much in evidence in *Verdict at Midnight*, his most accomplished publication in book form. In it, he takes thirty-seven of the most important theatrical productions of the last sixty years and considers how the opinions of the first-night critics have stood up to the judgement of posterity. The book thereby becomes a history of recent English theatre from the perspective of critics who have not had the benefit of leisured, academic consideration. Their work, Hobson feels, should be considered as 'a despatch from the battlefield, not a memorandum issued after the peace treaty'[376] – an intelligent analogy to differentiate between academic and journalistic critics. What is interesting to observe, in the light of the theatre's plight in the early 1950s, is how often the process of regeneration over the previous sixty years had been begun by foreign influences (a point that is implicit rather than explicit in Hobson's narrative), the most obvious example being the way in which Ibsen's arrival killed the taste (without ever becoming popular himself) for conventional comedy and melodrama in the 1890s. Other notable imports were the American musical in the 1890s (*The Belle of New York*) and the 1940s (*Oklahoma!*), which proved to be the salvation of musical comedy; the Russian works of Chekhov, which brought a new awareness of nuance in dialogue and character; the catalytic plays of Yeats and Shaw; and the French and American serious drama of the immediate post-war period. The critics that Hobson cites were predictably erratic in their recognition of the importance of these arrivals. William Archer's call in 1882 for plays that dispense with a violent and superficial realism is matched by Clement Scott's aversion in his *Daily Telegraph* columns to the plays of Ibsen; and Agate's championing of *The Cherry Orchard* is similarly offset by his vilification of Wilde after his trial and the initial hostility to Shaw. The conclusion that Hobson draws from these opinions is that it is vital for a critic to distinguish between the welcome that a play receives and the recognition of its merit – something which he did to impressive effect in his notice of *A Streetcar Named Desire*. He also concludes that the criticism of the past sixty years had, on the whole, been cultured and tolerant but lacking in burning convictions and a passionate faith – a criticism that was to be levelled again in the late 1950s. One conclusion which Hobson did not deduce from his detailed, readable and thoroughly researched historical survey was that a similar shift, after exposure to foreign invigoration, was again on the horizon. The signs were beginning to become apparent.

The year 1953 did nothing to disrupt the continuity of revivals and uninspiring comedies and in 'Welcome Daring' Hobson further developed his leitmotif that actors had a part to play in the process of regeneration by supporting new writing. After complimenting Ralph Richardson for taking on a role in a new play, R. C. Sherriff's *The White Carnation*, the critic upbraids some other actors for a lack of similar courage:

> Mr Gielgud and Mr Wolfit are having a high old time somewhere in the suburbs in plays done hundreds of times before, Miss Ashcroft and Mr Redgrave (also in familiar pieces) have withdrawn into the provinces, Sir Laurence Olivier's plans have fluctuated disconcertingly, and Mr Guinness (I must say I sympathise with him) intends to place 3000 miles of ocean between himself and the London public before he tries Hamlet again. In contrast with all this dithering and playing safe, Sir Ralph's courage is a shining thing.[377]

This is clearly overstating the case, particularly given that Peggy Ashcroft and Michael Redgrave's stay in the provinces was to produce a memorable production of *Antony and Cleopatra*, saluted by Hobson in the article 'Mutual Knock Out'.[378] It is also hardly the fault of the best actors if they are not out actively espying new works of quality. Unsurprisingly, reaction was swift, with Alec Guinness, in a letter to *The Sunday Times*,[379] defending himself against the charge of playing safe and revealing barely concealed irritation at the critic who had reviewed his Hamlet under the headline 'Disaster':

> I do not consider that accepting an invitation to go to Canada to play in a theatre-in-the-round, not yet built, in a town with a population of only 18,000, a programme which would be quite impossible to present commercially in the West End ('Richard III' and 'All's Well That Ends Well') is entirely unadventurous. The possibilities of disasters are quite formidable.

He also points out that it is difficult for actors to hunt out what simply does not exist. Hobson then decided to clarify his views in 'Dear Mr Guinness ...', the second time that he had been provoked by the actor to reconsider his views:

> Mr Guinness implies that good new plays do not exist, and therefore that he and those of comparable quality with him cannot be blamed for not appearing in them. He is on strong but not impregnable ground here. Good new plays are few, but on that account such as do exist deserve the most careful tending.[380]

This view is more acceptable: both critics and actors must take care to nurture shoots of potential.

The American musical had needed little outside encouragement to ensure its flourishing in post-war Britain. *Oklahoma!*, *Annie Get your Gun*, *Pal Joey*, *Kiss Me, Kate*, *Call Me Madam*, *Porgy and Bess* and now in May 1953, *Guys and Dolls* all enjoyed considerable success. Hobson greeted this latest musical, however, with the same irritated tones that he had employed to greet *Kiss Me, Kate*. It was as if, unable to express his frustration at the emptiness of home-grown drama in his customary elegant style, unwilling to embrace a more vituperative form of language, and lacking a political philosophy through which he could criticize the malaise in society and in drama, he found his only outlet in indignantly lacerating shows which contained evidence of alleged and unintelligent impropriety:

> Is America really peopled with brutalised half-wits, as this picturisation of Damon Runyon's stories implies? Is it really witty to bring a Salvation Army girl to the edge of fornication by the not very original trick of putting intoxicants into her milk shake? Is it clever to quote words of Jesus in the melancholy hope of raising a laugh? Let me make it clear that I am not protesting against either irreverence or impropriety as such. I only ask that they should attain a certain level of intelligence. I see no reason why religion should not be attacked or even traduced in the theatre. It is, I am sure, quite strong enough to defend itself. But let the attack have some intellectual basis. Otherwise it becomes a bore. That, alas, is what 'Guys and Dolls' is, despite its numerous striking incidental merits; an interminable, an overwhelming, and in the end intolerable bore.[381]

Other critics found the musical similarly dull – 'One reaches the interval ... bludgeoned with boredom'[382] (T. C. Worsley) – but the mood in British society was changing. People were beginning to long for emancipation from the old taboos. The gradual ending of rationing had initiated a reconsideration on the part of young and educated people of the values to which their parents adhered. Rock 'n Roll burst on to the scene in 1954 and a youth culture began to emerge. The war generation, the moral pronouncements of the Church and the conservatism of society (in spite of a post-war socialist government) were now regarded as an anachronism by many and the digestibility of prim, jejune views such as these was rapidly diminishing. Kenneth Tynan, in the *Evening Standard*, applauded the pace, music and humour of the show, particularly enjoying the prayer meeting to which Hobson objects. He significantly termed the work 'a *young* masterpiece'[383] (my italics). Anthony Cookman in the *Tatler* found it 'fascinating in its exoticism, in its originality and in its verve'[384] and John Elsom was also bowled over by the freshness of the musicals, neatly encapsulating their liberating atmosphere in his retrospective work, *Post-War British Theatre Criticism*:

> ... when I first started to go to the theatre regularly, in the early 1950s, an evening at an American musical was usually one of sheer delight, not unmixed with a sense of guilty awareness that I went to see Shakespeare or Eliot at the Old Vic in a spirit of dutiful respect.[385]

Hobson's writing at this time – 1953 and 1954 – was temporarily superseded by critics who more adequately expressed the temper of this dissatisfaction, and his impatience with sub-standard material led him to pen several sub-standard articles, which made him appear less a prophet for the new (which he was) than a defender of the old. This perception was reinforced by articles such as 'As Others See Us', 'A Survey' and 'There and Back'. In the first piece, published on 31 January 1954, Hobson devotes the whole of the article to a consideration of the French critics' verdict on the Redgrave and Ashcroft production of *Antony and Cleopatra*, recently seen in Paris. The reviews seem overwhelmingly negative and Hobson uses this to highlight the difference of approach to performance by the two countries. This type of analysis, which appeared fresh and thought-provoking just two years ago, now had a self-indulgent and distant air to it. Those English theatre-goers and critics who were demanding a more intelligent West End play were becoming less inclined to read highbrow articles that focused on the experiences of a foreign country (especially if they were as insipid as this one) than those by young, energetic critics willing to relate the demise of the theatre to contemporary issues. An article such as this, with little reference to the common experience of his readership (hardly any could have seen the production discussed) meant that Hobson's concern with France was now in danger of appearing an obsession.[386]

Hobson suffered, too, for his optimism. Never willing to concede that there was nothing from which pleasure could be gained in the London theatre, even in a period as depressing as this, his optimistic disposition was not what the younger generation wanted to hear. They preferred a more negative, bitingly ironic tone. Looking back over the 1953/4 season in 'A Survey',[387] Hobson accurately describes the battlefield – 'As for the London year, it is as we have seen it, a few successes dogged by boredom, fatuity and incompetence' – but his highlighting of certain rays of hope – N. C. Hunter's *A Day by the Sea*, Rattigan's *The Sleeping Prince*, the acting of Gielgud, Richardson, Thorndike, Olivier and Leigh – allowed some to depict him unfairly as an apologist for the status quo:

> Let it be granted then that at the moment the Western theatre is languishing. The reflection, however, is not entirely depressing. For the theatre must be a vital institution indeed if, even in its present condition, it can give us so many and so varied pleasures as it is putting before us.

Hobson's elegant language and delicate nuance of meaning invited misinterpretation by those interested in broad generalizations, provocative outbursts and banner headlines.

A third article, 'There and Back', is a good example of how Hobson's worst pieces of this period, those which give too much rein to his middle-class predilections, would soon come to appear tired and outdated. The leisured tone of the opening, describing a mannered existence that symbolized everything that the 'Angry Young Men' opposed, conveys the flavour of the article:

> After travelling more than a thousand miles in four days to see Aeschylus's 'Prométhée Enchaîné' at the Festival of Lyon-Charbonnières, and back again to London for 'Six Characters in Search of an Author', my memories at the moment are rich but confused. I remember fast trains, marathon meals, a wooden dog being taken for a stroll in the Boulevard St. Germain, the helpfulness of the employees of British Railways, the Pullman Company, and the S.N.C.F., and the unmitigated sun beating down on the statue of Louis XIV in the Place Bellecour (the sun in Lyons leaps on one like a tiger, as Alexander Smith said it did, most improbably, on Edinburgh in 1866).[388]

Hobson, who by now had moved into a flat in the highly desirable Dolphin Square complex in London, appeared dangerously ill-prepared for the coming earthquake.

The tremors of this approaching upheaval could be felt throughout 1954 and Hobson reported many of them, implicitly stressing the dichotomy between the new and the old. He recognized that the new topicality introduced by John Whiting's *Marching Song* extended 'the boundaries of English drama'.[389] Having been troubled by verse drama's inability to deal with the 'ordinary and usual' after seeing Eliot's *The Confidential Clerk*,[390] he concluded that Christopher Fry's new play, *The Dark Is Light Enough*, produced a similar sense of frustration, for 'What Mr Fry is interested in is not the orderly progression of an exciting story, but the capture of a mood of wonder at the universe's infinite surprise'[391] – not an aim likely to imbue his work with greater relevance. 'Producer at Work'[392] concentrated entirely on how the success of the Stratford *Midsummer Night's Dream* – whose bandy-legged Puck, grating elves and cockney lovers Hobson found novel and disconcerting – was due more to the director, George Devine, than to the author, and he commends the even-handedness of Arthur Miller's *The Crucible*, claiming that, although this appeared to give a better case to Senator McCarthy's contemporary witch-hunts than reports suggested he deserved, this was crucial to the dramatic success of the work.[393] It is clear, then, that Hobson had not lost his perceptive, critical faculty, but it had become blurred in the face of a confused theatrical scene. Kenneth Tynan, the new *Observer* critic and the protégé-turned-competitor, was better placed to evince the need for radical revolution in suitably accessible language, as the brilliant 'West-End Apathy', lamenting the sterility of London drama, proved:

> ... If you seek a tombstone, look about you; survey the peculiar nullity of our drama's prevalent genre, the Loamshire play. Its setting is a country house in what used to be called Loamshire but is now, as a heroic tribute to realism, sometimes called Berkshire. Except when someone must sneeze, or be murdered, the sun invariably shines. The inhabitants belong to a social class derived partly from romantic novels and partly from the playwright's vision of the leisured life he will lead after the play is a success – this being the only effort of imagination he is called on to make. Joys and sorrows are giggles and whimpers: the crash of denunciation dwindles into 'Oh, stuff, Mummy!' and 'Oh, really, Daddy!' And so grim is the continuity of these things that the foregoing paragraph might have been written at any time during the last thirty years ... Some of us need no miracles to keep our faith; we feed it on memories and imaginings. But many more – people of passionate intellectual appetites – are losing heart, falling away, joining the queues outside the Curzon Cinema. To lure them home, the theatre must widen its scope, broaden its horizon so the Loamshire appears merely as the play-pen, not as the whole palace of drama. We need plays about cabmen and demi-gods, plays about warriors, politicians, and grocers – I care not, so Loamshire be invaded and subdued. I counsel aggression because, as a critic, I had rather be a war correspondent than a necrologist.[394]

This was an increasingly familiar call, couched in a new, dynamic language. Modern, witty, irreverent, provocative, intelligent and passionate, Tynan's prose captured the feeling of frustration on the part of the younger generation at what they felt was the myopia and inadequacy of the older one. His diagnosis was suitably propagandistic, and his demolishing of totems acceptably radical. The problem for Hobson was simple – how could his writing evolve to meet the challenge of this new dynamic critic, and how should he adapt to the arrival of the new school of drama, so frequently longed for, but recently obscured, in his own writing?

Chapter 5

The Watershed: 1955

Two days after Sir Harold Hobson died, on Thursday 12 March 1992, a number of fulsome tributes appeared in the quality British press. A common leitmotif ran through them all. John Calder, writing in the *Independent*, described the critic's style as being 'always enthusiastic and extremely readable';[395] the *Daily Telegraph* felt that 'What made him such a vital critic was the force and conviction of his advocacy';[396] Michael Billington, the drama critic of the *Guardian*, admired the way in which Hobson 'was unafraid to invest theatre criticism with personal passion';[397] and *The Times* praised his all-embracing love for the theatre, claiming that: 'He had no intention of being a "safe" critic. He loved the theatre, he enjoyed talking about it. He wrote about it with passion and when he was strongly moved ... he could reach genuine eloquence.'[398]

This shared perception that Hobson's enthusiasm for drama was one of his greatest attributes was not a view politely distilled for a dignified obituary. On Monday 9 March 1992, unaware of Hobson's impending death, the playwright Alan Ayckbourn – a writer whose first seven plays Hobson had disliked – was speaking of Hobson's 'passion and ... commitment to the theatre', a trait which Ayckbourn was unable to perceive in any practising, contemporary critic.[399] It was this passion, this love of the process of theatre-going, which made Hobson so keen to protect the *future* health of the theatre. His unconcern with the challenging of political orthodoxies through the theatre may have made him seem temporarily anachronistic at the end of 1954, but an analysis of his output in 1955 reveals that his best writing in that watershed year possessed a durability and a prescience that is only now apparent. Hobson chose to fight Tynan and his less-talented disciples not on the younger critic's home ground – coruscating denunciations of entrenched and dated attitudes – but by capitalizing on his own strengths: a simple belief that theatre-going can be a thrilling and rewarding pursuit, allied to a personal, implicit fervour for drama which underpins his criticisms and inspires his reader. Thus, by re-emphasizing some of the enthusiasm that had been apparent in his belief in the educational value of BBC radio, his welcome of the new style of drama created by W. H. Auden and his admiration of the acting of Ralph Richardson in the 1930s; his fascination with Laurence Olivier, his interest in the experiments of Christopher Fry and his defence of Tennessee Williams in the 1940s; and his delight in the acting of Edwige Feuillère and Jean-Louis Barrault in the early 1950s, Hobson was able to transcend the self-indulgent tone that had spoilt several of the reviews of the last two years and to place himself in a much stronger position to maintain a distinctive critical identity by becoming a champion of the avant-garde.

This recovery in Hobson's writing is remarkable in that the body of work produced can be seen as representing not simply a resurrection of his talent, but as a microcosm of some of his greatest critical strengths. To some extent, this revival can be explained by the fact that 1955 was as important a year for the British theatre as a whole as the more lauded 1956. It provided the necessary stimulus after a decade of erratic artistic achievement. But it is also due to the tremendous resilience of Hobson, outwardly symbolized by his triumph over disability and apparent professionally by the way in which he adapted to the changing atmosphere of the British theatre and refused to capitulate to the new, more aggressive breed of critic. This reinvigoration of his approach was to culminate in Tynan and Hobson's fascinating weekly duel from 1954 to 1958, and from 1960 to 1962, which was to remain fresh in the memory for many years. Michael Billington, who was to become the critic of the *Guardian*, summarizes the sense of excitement that their critical clashes generated when he states that:

> The reason I started reading Harold was, first of all, that I had a growing appetite for the theatre and secondly that there was this extraordinary man who made the theatre every week in London sound very exciting, and you always felt momentous events were happening in London through his column ... There was also the fascination, which is very difficult to recreate now, of the weekly duel between these two figures, Tynan and Hobson, who were violently opposed in their tastes, but who both made the theatre sound glamorous, exciting, filled with large presences and personalities.[400]

Alan Ayckbourn was similarly enthralled as a young actor:

> ... one of the big theatre jokes used to be that when you opened *The Sunday Times* and the *Observer*, you used to read these two guys, and they were always totally, diametrically opposed. Tynan would say that this is the greatest show on earth, Hobson would hate it. If you had a play on and you opened it and Tynan gave you a good review, you knew that Harold was going to loathe it.[401]

There is little doubt that the general interest that these two committed and eloquent writers aroused in the state of the British theatre helped to create a climate in which ground-breaking new writing could be accepted more readily. Readers soon came to realize that, on the rare occasions when they did both agree in their praise, something momentous had occurred in the theatre. The two most notable examples of this were *Waiting for Godot* and *Look Back in Anger*.

hostility, rather than praise, is, in the case of young players, the best mark of future success.

Hobson, too, possessed a distinctive quality to his writing which would inevitably provoke hostility. The challenge for him now was whether he would be able to educate his readership into accepting that he was suitably qualified not only to reflect but to mould the taste of tomorrow.

It is at about this time in his career that Hobson began to attract the label of unpredictability (which ultimately led to the charge being concretely expressed by Penelope Gilliatt in 1959[403]), and a superficial examination of his articles in 1955 goes some way to revealing why this was so. How else could one explain a passionate enthusiasm for the linguistic decency of Christopher Fry ('He is the first serious poet to make Pegasus win his races by riding him for a fall'[404]) set alongside an admiration for the literature of the 'prison-haunted pervert', Genet?[405] Or reconcile a belief that Fry's *Tiger at the Gates* (an adaptation of an Anouilh work) is one of the most intellectually stimulating plays in London[406] to a respect for the methods and aims adopted by Joan Littlewood and her Theatre Workshop?[407] The problem with this approach to Hobson's work is that it fails to perceive that his criticism resolutely refuses to be dogmatic. His taste was undeniably eclectic, but the consistency of his writing is supplied by an insistence that his reviews are a historical record of his own personal, emotional reaction to an evening rather than the pre-considered rationalization of a play to comply with a theoretical statement (be it political, theatrical or academic). This does not mean that he is never idiosyncratic or that his views were never very wide of the mark; they were sometimes both. But, guided by his desire to enthuse his readership with a sense of the excitement that a visit to the theatre could generate, he offered an intuitive reaction to what he witnessed which was sometimes wrong, more often right and rarely uninteresting. The recovery that the events of 1955 instigated was also due to a strengthening of his desire to consider what audiences would be watching in ten years' time – the fundamental theoretical framework that Hobson applied to his criticisms.

Whenever Hobson visited Paris in the immediate post-war period, he would make a mental note of productions which he felt might merit a transfer from the acknowledged innovatory French theatre to the inspiration-starved London stage. One such work, Eugène Ionesco's *The Lesson*, came to mind again after he had seen a February 1955 production of Sartre's play, *Vicious Circle* (*Huis Clos*), at the Watergate:

> M. Sartre's 'Vicious Circle' was first acted in 1944. In 1951 another 'closed circle play', 'The Lesson', was presented at the Théâtre de Poche. It is by Eugène Ionesco, an author who I think is as yet unknown in this country. It is a very short play; so is 'Vicious Circle', and I cannot but believe that to see them both in the same evening would be a memorable experience. 'The Lesson' is grotesque and

Hobson's first *Sunday Times* article of 1955, 'Making a Name',[402] was provoked by the news that the promising stage actress, Mary Ure, had been awarded a film contract. Formerly this would have caused Hobson some distress, since: 'It has seemed to me unjust, and injurious to the drama, that the theatre should discover talent, and then lose it to a wealthier rival.' But he was no longer so pessimistic. Experience had shown that the cinema had not always been wise in its selection of stage stars. Often an actor had been offered a contract on the strength of an accomplished early performance but had lacked the basic training supplied by the theatre to develop and exploit his potential. Hobson points wryly to the muted stage arrivals of Olivier (for years lambasted for not being able to speak verse properly), Gielgud (little noticed on his London début in *The Cherry Orchard*), Richardson (reproached by James Agate for his performance in *Marriage is No Joke*) and Alec Guinness (ignored in his walk-on part in *Libel*) to illustrate the thesis that early success is no guarantee of sustained achievement. He continues:

> It is not an accident that the greatest players do not, as a rule, get the most praise on their first appearance. The player who provokes ecstasies the first time he puts greasepaint on his nose does so because he fits to a nicety the taste of the day; but the player who is going to make a lasting reputation is one who will fit the taste of many tomorrows. He will not only fit that taste, he will also help mould it.

The remarkable aspect of this extract is not its eminent good sense or its stylish simplicity, but that the situation it is describing adumbrates Hobson's own experience over the next ten years. Writing for the reactionary *Sunday Times* in the mid-1950s, Hobson's civilized, considered style did not accord to the 'taste of the day' for many in the theatre, and certainly not for the young and recently educated, yearning for the overthrow of conservative values. Hobson was unable and unwilling to match the crisp political vignettes that Tynan was able to produce. He preferred subjective impressions to Tynan's rational deductions, shafts of perception to insistent campaigning. He tried to look ahead by refusing to be tied to the significance of contemporary events, firmly believing his own words that, in criticism, too, 'the player who is going to make a lasting reputation is one who will fit the taste of many tomorrows.' Hobson ends the article by stressing the importance to performers of educating audiences in the business of their art, a belief that had particular resonance for the critic too:

> Who can doubt that Dame Edith Evans, Miss Margaret Leighton and Miss Kay Hammond have had to educate the public to recognise the magic of their unique and surprising voices, voices that are among the splendours of our stage? In the artist who will last down the years there is nearly always something unusual, something which, because it is unusual, will, on its first appearance, arouse hostility. This

excessive; it strains credulity; it is absolutely unforgettable. There is a moment in it when the stupid schoolgirl, having failed to subtract three from four, multiplies (apparently in her head) 3,755,998,251 by 5,162,303,508, which is comparable with the bursting open of the door in 'Vicious Circle'. There are several intelligent and enterprising managers in London. I think they would find it interesting to take a look at M. Ionesco. They might not like him, but I am sure they would find him – well, interesting.[408]

The uncertainty of Hobson as to how to classify Ionesco's drama reflects the fact that he had come across one of the leading exponents of what later came to be called the 'Theatre of the Absurd' at the earliest stage of the playwright's career (*La Leçon*, a highly disturbing vision of existence, where language is used as a lethal physical weapon, was written in 1951). What is significant here is that Hobson had stored away the experience of discovering the play in Paris, had responded to Sartre's play in such a way that it had unlocked the memory of Ionesco's, and was now actively recommending that conservative London managers consider producing the French/Romanian's work, since it represented a new departure for both the French and the English theatre.

One month later there was indeed a London production of Ionesco's play, directed by Peter Hall at the Arts Theatre, but Hobson was not inclined to be triumphant that his message had been absorbed. Rather, he sought to explain to his readership that this type of play demanded a different attitude on the part of an English audience accustomed to being able to glean meaning from a theatrical production. In other words, he undertook one of the earliest expositions in English of Absurdist drama.[409] He begins the appropriately titled 'Something New'[410] by stressing that the play is the story of a 'double reversal'. The first reversal, where a timid professor grows visibly stronger until his 18-year-old pupil becomes 'a whining, snivelling, terrified puppet', is judged by Hobson to be 'a magnificent piece of melodramatic theatre'. This is then followed by an episode of seeming illogicality:

> There is a moment in the play, about half way through, when the pupil, by an unexpected and indeed quite extraordinary mental recovery, almost destroys the professor. One may say that this recovery is brought about illogically, for it depends upon a stupendous feat of memory, and it has already been demonstrated that the girl has no memory at all: she cannot, for example, remember the names of the four seasons.

Yet this illogicality is quite unimportant, Hobson maintains, for: 'The theatre is not a school of logic: it is a place of passion, feeling, excitement, terror and exaltation. It has similarities to a madhouse, but none at all to Euclid.' The critic then proceeds to explain that new forms of drama require new modes of thinking:

> There are, however, theatregoers from whom this is hidden, and several of them came to the first night of 'The Lesson.' The theatre, with its heat and its crowds and its mass hysteria, is of all places that which is least suitable to rational thought; yet there are many playgoers who demand that the theatre should flatter them into thinking that they think.

Hobson's dismissal of the theatre as a place where rational thought is possible is extreme, and helps to explain why he was to write so poorly about the work of Brecht, but his insistence that plays do not necessarily require a consistency of thought and an easy comprehensibility to have a theatrical effect is both a powerful justification for Absurdist theatre and a refreshing call in the mid-1950s for English audiences to vary their desire for well-made plays with wrapped-up endings. Kenneth Tynan, too, shared a dislike of well-made, middle-class plays, but he was equally critical of playwrights who sought to avoid questions of social realism. Three years later, in the summer of 1958, whilst reviewing a Royal Court revival of *The Lesson* and *The Chairs*, Tynan attacked Ionesco for being 'a self-proclaimed advocate of *anti-theatre*: explicitly anti-realist and by implication anti-reality as well'.[411] The following week Ionesco defended himself in the same paper by differentiating between the work of the politician and the function of the playwright, claiming that:

> to deliver a message to the world, to wish to direct its course, to save it, is the business of the founders of religions, of the moralists or the politicians ... A playwright simply writes plays, in which he can offer only a testimony, not a didactic message.[412]

A comparison of the two critics' views on Ionesco is illuminating, since it reveals their most marked critical deficiencies. Hobson, mistrustful of logic in the theatre, is unable to concede that politically didactic drama such as Brecht's can succeed or be entertaining, since he believes that the theatre is unsuited to rational thought, whereas Tynan, obsessed with the importance of the theatre in shaping society, insists that drama that resolutely refuses to be didactic is therefore diversionary and self-indulgent.

At this point in the article Hobson returns to the idea of clear meaning, sacrosanct to the English play-goer:

> Such people are not content with the drive, the tension, the humour, the fear of 'The Lesson' ... They are not content to be excited, transported or even amused. They want to know what the play *means*. What does a sunset mean, or the victory of Samothrace?

In an Absurdist drama (a term which Hobson does not utilize in the criticism, since it became popular after the appearance of Martin Esslin's book, *The Theatre of the Absurd*, in 1961) the detection of meaning is not the principal task of the audience. Of much greater relevance to this type of play – a new theatrical phenomenon – is a consideration of the role of language, and the play's second reversal highlights this innovation:

> M. Ionesco and his friends complain that in conventional drama language expresses the characters' emotions, but does not act on or modify them. In plays man is the master of his instrument of speech, or at least the dramatist is, if he is a good dramatist. This gives the impression that, being the master of one instrument, man is the master of all. Now today this is simply not true ... So M. Ionesco shows the professor, as he gains domination over his pupil, becoming himself dominated by the wild, unstoppable excitement of his own language, which ceases to be a rational statement of thought and turns into a frenzied dance in whose compulsion the professor is as helpless as the pupil in the hands of the professor. Now, there is, of course, a trick here. The professor's speeches, from the moment he says, 'Mademoiselle, Spanish is the mother tongue of all the neo-Spanish languages,' take the whip hand of the professor, but they do not take the whip hand of the author ... On the contrary, they are never more strictly controlled than when they seem most uncontrollable. It is only the steadiest mind which can keep these speeches the same unvarying distance from rationality, giving without faltering the nightmare sense of having the hand always almost upon meaning, and yet never being able to grasp it.[413]

The final sentence here could equally serve as an encapsulation of the achievement of Ionesco, Beckett or Pinter and reveals why, of all the English critics, it was inevitable that Hobson would be the only one to possess enough knowledge of the practice of the Absurdist dramatists to rescue *The Birthday Party* from oblivion in 1958.

Reinvigorated by the new dramatic impulses with which he had come into contact, Hobson now sought to advance the avant-garde cause in his columns. At the end of May, in 'Avant-Garde Drama in Paris',[414] Hobson was to write, by way of an exposition for his American readership and with an informative style reminiscent of his best wartime reports for the *Christian Science Monitor*, that the nascent movement was beginning to take hold:

> For the first time since the end of the war there is a strong avant-garde movement developing in the western theater. In England its only representative is John Whiting, and Mr Whiting has been so bludgeoned by the critics, so misunderstood and maltreated by the general public that the movement of which in London he is both the vanguard and the rear cannot be said to be firmly established.

In Paris the situation was different, of course, but whereas at the beginning of the 1950s Hobson was lauding French plays that had been considerable commercial successes, the avant-garde writers whom he now admired in the French capital shared the same degree of public obscurity as John Whiting:

> The avant-garde writers are not darlings of the big theatrical public. They walk instead of ride, and they wear mackintoshes instead of overcoats. They are not played in the red plush theaters of the Right Bank. If they were, they would not be avant-garde. For the avant-garde comes into existence only when a group of dramatists present an aspect of the world so different from that of the conventional theater that the general public is bewildered or even repelled.

Before defining their vision, Hobson diagnoses the parochialism of much contemporary theatre, espousing similar sentiments to Tynan, but in a less declamatory style:

> The conventional realistic drama of today is still philosophically dominated by the nineteenth century. In light comedies one is presented with fashionable apartments that breathe of riches and security. There is no suggestion that they are poised on top of a bubble that may burst or be exploded at any moment.
>
> The characters are on the whole kindly and understanding. They wish, at least if the cost to themselves is not too great, to make everyone happy. The conventional drama is a comfortable drama. It flatters the sense of security and automatic prosperity.

The Absurdists, however, deal with a different world, a world which was not – as Tynan was later to claim – 'anti-reality',[415] but which was, on the contrary, starkly contemporary and which takes as its stimulus the inability of language in human society to convey meaning – the real condition of society in the 1950s, born out of Cold War tension:

> The world of Ionesco and Adamov is not the safe nineteenth century world of fashionable London and New York comedies, but the world of the political news of contemporary newspapers – a world in which nations distrust each other, plot each other's destruction, move in desperate terror of each other's inventions, and find it impossible, or nearly impossible, to discover any means of understanding each other ... Just as the world's statesmen seem to find it almost impossible to hit on any means of speech that will breed understanding and sympathy between them, so Adamov and Ionesco write plays in which, as in 'Le Ping-Pong' at the Théâtre des Noctambules, there is never any communication even between individuals ... Each character lives isolated in his own solitary world, whose walls are never broken. This isolation is emphasized by the fact that Ionesco and Adamov deliberately write dialogue that is made up of the flattest clichés, the least eloquent phrases that they can think of.[416]

Given the break with the theatrical past that this approach represented, it is not surprising that Hobson was to conclude this seminal exposition with the statement that 'the general public as yet is baffled by their work.' Crucially for the English theatre, however, this critic saw further than the transience of public taste.

As yet the tremors of the impending earthquake could only be vaguely felt in the English theatre. As the critic had pointed out, John Whiting had been pigeon-holed as perplexing – and thus largely ignored – and only readers of Hobson's Sunday columns would have gleaned a snapshot of burgeoning new ideas developing across the Channel. Nevertheless, Hobson's intuitive understanding of the methodology of the new movement is frequently apparent, and in the early summer of 1955 he felt passionately that the London stage was in danger of being atrophied:

> Aesthetically the weakness of the London theater is that it still tends to reflect the secure, well-bred world of the prewar period. It has devised no new techniques to deal with the insecurity and desperate searching for safety of contemporary mankind.[417]

Just as it was only a matter of time before another Absurdist drama crossed the Channel to the London stage, it was similarly inevitable that the critic who would write most intelligently about its immediate appearance would be the one who had been following the genesis of the movement to which it belonged with the most sympathetic and responsive eye.

Waiting for Godot received its English première on 3 August 1955 in a production at the Arts Theatre, directed by Peter Hall. The rehearsal period for the play had not been propitious, for the Lord Chamberlain had objected to the propriety of the work's language and requested several changes, only some of which the playwright was prepared to acquiesce to. The fall of Estragon's trousers and the exchange between the two tramps on the subject of erections had to remain, so it was necessary to stage a club performance to ensure that the play received a London airing at all.[418] Peter Bull, who played the part of Pozzo, describes the reaction of the first-night audience:

> Waves of hostility came whirling over the footlights, and the mass exodus, which was to form such a feature of the piece, started quite soon after the curtain had risen ... The curtain fell to mild applause, we took a scant three calls and a depression and sense of anti-climax descended on us all. Very few people came round, most of those who did were in a high state of intoxication and made even less sense than the play.[419]

The critical reaction in the daily newspapers the following day was one of blank incomprehension and no little irritation that a talented production team had been wasted on such unpromising material. Some critics barely sought to conceal their loathing. Milton Shulman in the *Evening Standard* claimed that 'the excellent work of the cast cannot obscure many deadly dull and pretentious passages';[420] Stephen Williams in the *Evening News*, picking up on the fact that Beckett had once been the secretary of James Joyce, summarized the work as 'an occasional faint flash of the genius that was James and long invertebrate stretches of tedium that was Joyce';[421] David Lewin in the *Daily Express*, under the memorable title 'Nothing happens, it's awful (it's life)', wrote that, although the play was well acted, 'there are passages when no one could carry the thought along. And I too became weary of waiting for Godot ... who never comes';[422] Colin Wilson in the *Daily Mail* struck a stridently chauvinistic note, announcing, under the banner headline 'The Left Bank Can Keep It', that: 'This play comes to us with a great reputation among the intelligentsia of Paris. And so far as I am concerned the intelligentsia of Paris may have it back as soon as they wish',[423] and W. A. Darlington, who maintained a career-long suspicion of plays without a beginning, a middle and an end, wrote in a *Daily Telegraph* article, 'An Evening of Funny Obscurity', that Beckett was the head boy of 'a school of dramatists at present whose pupils love obscurity for obscurity's sake'.[424] Darlington developed this theme the following month in 'The Story's the Thing',[425] when he wrote of *Waiting for Godot* as part of a wider (and unwelcome) reaction against good theatrical story-telling:

> It has no plot, no clearly defined purpose, and only a vaguely suggested meaning. It is superb as a serious frolic for highbrows; but in the regular workaday theatre it has no conceivable plan at all ... in its deliberate formlessness and obscurity it merely carries to its logical extreme a fashion which is bedevilling the work of a whole group of our younger dramatists.[426] They all love obscurity.

Other critics, whilst trying to credit the playwright with innovation, were forced to admit that they found his intentions baffling. One such reviewer was the anonymous contributor to *The Times* who, having hailed the production as 'brilliant', concluded that:

> The thoroughbred Irish intelligence of much of Mr Beckett's dialogue and his power of theatrical invention force one to take his fantasy seriously, but it remains a fantasy. His patently elemental personages are figments in whom we cannot ultimately believe since they lack universality.[427]

Only one of the daily reviewers, Philip Hope-Wallace, writing in the *Guardian*, was able to detect anything remotely stimulating about the play itself. He found that:

> ... at the end of it, for all its inexplicit and deliberately fatuous flatness, a curious sense of the passage of time and the wretchedness of man's uncertainty about his destiny has been communicated out of the very unpromising material.

He concluded with the refreshing assertion that: 'It is good to find that plays at once dubbed "incomprehensible and pretentious" can still get a staging. Where better than the Arts Theatre?'[428] The opening night of *Waiting for Godot* was a critical flop as far as the daily reviewers were concerned. Worse still, some of the reviews were so vituperative that a sensitive writer attempting to pioneer a new type of play might conclude that the effort was no longer worth it. What better situation for a writer such as Hobson, the self-confessed admirer of the avant-garde, to demonstrate his journalistic flair by swimming against the tide; to exhibit his own sense of drama (essential to his critical style) and to emphasize his passionate desire to defend work of merit, whatever the general critical opinion? Especially since he fervently believed that 'there is no more thrilling experience in dramatic criticism than to be absolutely certain that all the others are wrong'.[429]

The title chosen for Hobson's *Sunday Times* review of *Waiting for Godot*, which appeared on 7 August 1955, four days after the première of the play, was simply 'Tomorrow'. The article, one of Hobson's best known, represented not just the remarkable discovery of a remarkable play, but an opportunity to convince an English public that here at last was an Absurdist play that merited close and frequent attention, since it was not boring or baffling but 'insidiously exciting'. As so often when in the presence of genius, Hobson's critical faculties were at their most finely tuned. While the review implicitly maintained that the play pointed to the future direction of the theatre, Hobson's style simultaneously confirmed him as an adroit manipulator of language, a writer whose judicious depiction of rhetorical devices enabled him to derive inspiration from the necessary restrictions of newspaper space, and as a stylist, whose intuitive sense of the appropriate word or phrase intrigues, entertains and informs.

In the first four of the nine paragraphs of 'Tomorrow' Hobson adopts the highly unconventional (and dramatic) approach of listing the apparent deficiencies of the play, because he wishes to convey to the reader the importance of approaching a play of this type with a mind unshackled by previous habits of theatre-going. Hobson the educator is unwittingly adopting the Brechtian technique of 'Verfremdung' to inculcate new ways of thinking, by freeing the reader from his prejudices:

> The objections to Mr Samuel Beckett's play as a theatrical entertainment are many and obvious. Anyone keen-sighted enough to see a church at noonday can perceive what they are. 'Waiting for Godot' has nothing to seduce the senses. Its drab, bare scene is dominated by a withered tree and a garbage can, and for a large part of the evening this lugubrious setting, which makes the worst of both town and country, is inhabited only by a couple of tramps, verminous, decayed, their hats broken and their clothes soiled, with sweaty feet, inconstant bladders, and boils on the backside.

Notice already how the first sentence contains the intriguing hint that there may be a moment of peripeteia at the end of the narrative – the unstated 'but' hanging pregnantly over the rest of the criticism; how Hobson's diverse linguistic register – everyday clichés ('church at noonday'), trendy American vocabulary ('garbage can'), and deliberately indecorous nouns ('boils', 'bladders' and 'backsides') – creates an air of unpredictability; how he teases the reader, accustomed to brilliantly colourful American musicals and sumptuously furnished drawing-room sets, with the sheer desolation of the Godot stage; and how he has created all these effects in a paragraph notable for its clarity and compression. This toying with the reader, continuing to postpone a resolution (which both frustrates and intrigues, mirroring the play), proceeds into the second paragraph:

> This is not all. In the course of the play, nothing happens. Such dramatic progress as there is, is not towards a climax, but towards a perpetual postponement. Vladimir and Estragon are waiting for Godot, but this gentleman's appearance (*if* he is a gentleman, and not something of another species) is not prepared with any recognisable theatrical tension, for the audience knows well enough from the very beginning that Godot will never come. The dialogue is studded with words that have no meaning for normal ears; repeatedly the play announces that it has come to a stop, and will have to start again; never does it reconcile itself with reason.

The play appears, then, to follow none of the conventional rules of the theatre: it has no development, some of the dialogue is incomprehensible and the work frequently displays a consciousness of its own artifice, threatening to come to a halt. Hobson is skilfully leading the reader to the precipice of incomprehensibility before swiftly pulling him back from the edge. Only such shock treatment will permit an acceptance of the play on its own terms. The third paragraph now slyly addresses the scorn that the description thus far will have aroused, by parallelling this with the scorn of the first-night audience:

> It is hardly surprising that, English audiences notoriously disliking anything not immediately understandable, certain early lines in the play, such as 'I have had better entertainment elsewhere,' were received on the first night with ironical laughter; or that when one of the characters yawned, the yawn was echoed and amplified by a humourist in the stalls. Yet at the end the play was warmly applauded. There were even a few calls for 'Author!' But these were rather shame-faced cries, as if those who uttered them doubted whether it were seemly to make too much noise whilst turning their coats.

With the claim that English audiences rarely persist in their attempts to understand complex issues, Hobson aims to shame the reader who is threatening to lose patience with his own description of such a bizarre work – a common journalistic technique, utilized in this instance for the defence of art. Humour, too, is added to Hobson's armoury. The mention of the shamefaced cries and the desire not to make a public scene is the literary equivalent of the Pont cartoons of the 1930s, satirizing the inhibited behaviour of the British as a race.[430]

The fourth paragraph of 'Tomorrow' begins to prepare the reader for the crux of the criticism, with a consideration of a subject much discussed by Hobson of late, namely that of meaning in a play. Rather surprisingly, the critic claims to have identified one in *Waiting for Godot*:

> Strange as the play is, and curious as are its processes of thought, it has a meaning; and this meaning is untrue. To attempt to put this meaning into a paragraph is like trying to catch Leviathan in a butterfly net, but nevertheless the effort must be made. The upshot of 'Waiting for Godot' is that the two tramps are always waiting for the future, their ruinous consolation being that there is always tomorrow; they never realise that today is today. In this, says Mr Beckett, they are like all humanity, which dawdles and drivels its life, postponing action, eschewing enjoyment, waiting only for some far-off, divine event, the millennium, the Day of Judgement.

Hobson's attempt at deducing meaning, however, appears partly motivated by the realization that one review will not change the expectation of his reader for an explanation of what the play signifies. What is more surprising is Hobson's assertion in the next paragraph that, although the work's message is erroneous, this has no effect on the success of the work. In plays of this type, the message of a work is less important than the process of its delivery. Hobson's preparation for this revelation is one of characteristic subterfuge, holding back until the last minute to create the maximum effect:

> Mr Beckett has, of course, got it all wrong. Humanity worries very little over the Day of Judgement. It is far too busy hire-purchasing television sets, popping into three star restaurants, planting itself vineyards, building helicopters. *But he has got it wrong in a tremendous way. And this is what matters.* There is no need at all for a dramatist to philosophise rightly; he can leave that to the philosophers. But it is essential that if he philosophises wrongly, he should do so with swagger. Mr Beckett has any amount of swagger. A dusty, coarse, irreverent, pessimistic, violent swagger? Possibly. But the genuine thing, the real McCoy.

The moment of peripeteia, indicated by my highlights, is all the more effective because the reader can now see that he has been coaxed up to this point to consider Hobson's verdict in a way that relied not on the reader's past experience of the theatre, but on his future expectation of ground-breaking developments. The lack of contemporary theatrical accoutrements – a lavish, naturalistic set, well-bred, recognizable characters, a linear development of plot and the reassurance of a comprehensible meaning – is the very basis of the appeal of this new type of play. Hobson now seeks to secure the play's reputation by stressing its universal relevance, in direct contrast to the claim made by the critic of *The Times*:

> Vladimir and Estragon have each a kind of universality. They wear their rags with a difference. Vladimir is eternally hopeful; if Godot does not come this evening then he will certainly come tomorrow, or at the very latest the day after. Estragon, much troubled by his boots, is less confident. He thinks the game is not worth playing, and is ready to hang himself. Or so he says. But he does nothing. Like Vladimir he only talks. They both idly spin away the great top of their life in the vain expectation that some master whip will one day give it eternal vitality. Meanwhile their conversation often has the simplicity, in this case the delusive simplicity, of music hall cross-talk, now and again pierced with a shaft that seems for a second or so to touch the edge of truth's garment. It is bewildering. It is exasperating. It is insidiously exciting.

Hobson's conclusion to this review emphasizes his desire to create an audience for Absurdist drama. It also manages to trump the memorable claim that the play is 'insidiously exciting' by combining an enthusiastic adjuration to visit the Arts Theatre with a colourful and original lyricism:

> Go and see 'Waiting for Godot'. At the worst you will discover a curiosity, a four-leaved clover, a black tulip; at the best, something that will securely lodge in a corner of your mind for as long as you live.

It is the passionate nature of Hobson's advocacy, the deeply felt conviction that *Waiting for Godot* represented a new way forward for drama and must be defended from its exaggeratedly hostile detractors, and the literary skill with which he advances his argument that make this review so compelling a piece of writing. The sentiments are clearly overstated, but Hobson's achievement is that he recognized that, in certain circumstances, arguments need to be overstated in order to gain an audience. A grateful Beckett read the criticism with emotion and considered it to be courageous and touching.[431]

Whenever devotees of the British theatre think back to the gladiatorial struggle that was waged between Tynan and Hobson in the second half of the 1950s, a struggle that made the London theatre seem so vibrant and exciting in an era struggling to emerge from post-war austerity (rationing only ended in 1954), they distinctly remember the rarity and significance of agreement between these two critical titans. Sunday 7 August 1955 was one such occasion. Tynan opened his review of *Waiting for Godot*[432] with the sentence: 'A special virtue attaches to plays which remind the drama of how much it can do without and still exist', and the tenor of his review is that the work is not pretentious, as many of the first-night audience found, but ground-breaking:

It forced me to re-examine the rules which have hitherto governed the drama; and having done so, to pronounce them not elastic enough. It is validly new, and hence I declare myself, as the Spanish would say, *godoista*.

What differentiated Hobson's attitude from Tynan's, however, was that Hobson recognized the play as the latest example of European Absurdist drama and he was determined to champion it with a passionate intensity that verged upon magnificent obsession. For Hobson, the battle of the avant-garde had only just begun and he proceeded to occupy a position in the front line in several of his columns over the coming months. Six days after 'Tomorrow' had appeared, Hobson returned to the play in the *Christian Science Monitor*, claiming that Beckett's implicit message was about humanity:

> To him humanity never says, '*Now* is the accepted time, *now* is the day of salvation.' It is always saying there will be a tomorrow, and then we can enjoy ourselves. And so the years pass by in futility and waste, and nothing is ever done.[433]

More significantly, in his following Sunday's article, triumphantly entitled 'Samuel Beckett',[434] Hobson returns to a further consideration of the play. Believing that he had committed an omission the previous week by saying nothing about the play's humour, he now maintains that the work 'is one of the four funniest entertainments in London'. This humour is linguistic, 'based on a remarkable ear for repetition of sound, and the spaces between sounds'. Hobson also focuses on the religious dimension of the work, unsurprisingly (and arguably) choosing to espy a Christian dimension:

> The play is anti-religious but it is not irreverent. Rather the contrary; though the spirit is certainly not derided, but beautifully and musically questioned, the forms are exquisitely preserved; and when Vladimir is told by a young boy at the end of the play that Godot for whom he has been vainly waiting all his life has a white beard, his awed exclamation, 'Christ have mercy upon us,' is the most solemn thing heard in our comic theatre for many years. Much is due here to the actor, Mr Paul Daneman, whose momentary hesitation and sudden lifting of his battered hat when realisation dawns are gestures of extraordinary and moving delicacy …

On account of this simple (and inadvertent) action, Hobson chooses to see Godot as God. The critic is on more secure ground, though, when he claims in the concluding paragraph that: 'The best parts of "Waiting for Godot" are precisely those that cannot be precisely explained.' It is this perceptive identification of the stimulatingly elusive appeal of Beckett's work that is Hobson's most intelligent critical conclusion and leads

Beckett's biographer, Deirdre Bair, to describe him as 'one of Beckett's most perceptive commentators'.[435]

The critical furore that *Waiting for Godot* generated, the contradictory notices of similarly passionate intensity, ensured that the play was able to transfer into the West End's Criterion Theatre on 12 September, such was the public desire to witness this theatrical curiosity. It was to play to packed houses until May 1956. Hobson's continued championing of the work – he gave the transfer a short review on 18 September[436] – was matched by the disgust of a number of journalists. Collie Knox in the *Daily Mail* spoke for many in 'I've Been Led by the Nose Long Enough'.[437] Convinced that *Waiting for Godot* was dangerously pessimistic, he attacked it for being 'a conglomeration of tripe' which was 'harmful in that it glorifies defeatism and hopelessness'. In essence, it was 'the glorification of the gutless'. Hobson felt compelled to reply. Six days later (and seven weeks after the première at the Arts) he took it upon himself once again to defend the play, and unusually addressed himself directly to a journalistic colleague:

> At the Criterion is one of the most noble and moving plays of our generation, a threnody of hope deceived and deferred but never extinguished; a play suffused with tenderness of the whole human perplexity; with phrases that come like a sharp stab of beauty and pain; with strophes and antistrophes as exquisite as any imagined by Cranmer ... I grieve that Mr Collie Knox, a man whose wit and true gentleness of spirit I know and admire, has made himself the spokesman of [bat-blind abuse] ... Phrases like 'They are born astride a grave' – phrases beyond the compass of any English prose dramatist at present writing in England – are to Mr Knox incoherent, a 'conglomeration of tripe', a 'glorification of the gutless.' It is this complacent inability to recognise the highest when they see it, this apparently natural enmity towards exaltation of the spirit, which for a moment checks one's heart.[438]

Hobson's combination of polite praise and authoritative rebuke is devastatingly effective. Even Collie Knox, still resolutely adhering to his views one week later,[439] was forced to concede that he had been ticked off 'charmingly'. Of course, the publicity that disputes such as these generate was of immense value to the production. By continuing to engage on its behalf, Hobson played his part in ensuring that Beckett's play would come to be regarded as a seminal influence on twentieth-century British drama.

If Hobson's encounter with *Waiting for Godot* illustrated his unique reaction to stimulating new drama, his response to Laurence Olivier's Stratford Macbeth further demonstrated his talent for encapsulating the excitement of a memorable acting performance in print. The theatrical vibrancy of 1955 in England was enhanced by superb individual acting performances and these gave the critic an opportunity to reassert himself with stylish, probing performance portraits that sought to relate stage action to an elucidation of the text. *Macbeth* opened on 6 June and Hobson's review, triumphantly headed 'Nonpareil',[440] contains all the best facets of Hobson's style – a sense of the dramatic, an intimation of the unexpected, a momentum that invests the review with a mannered urgency and, above all, a feeling that something significant and exciting had occurred in the theatre at that performance. There is no attempt to delay the verdict in 'Nonpareil', the opening sentence relates that 'Sir Laurence Olivier's is the best Macbeth since – Macbeth's', but Hobson then proceeds indirectly to foreshadow the technique employed in 'Tomorrow' by boldly asserting that some aspects of Olivier's performance are nevertheless flawed, expressing this with an unusual, yet effective analogy:

> His performance reminds one of the insolent magnificence of that Sunderland football 'team of all talents' which, in the season before the first world war, stayed at the bottom of the League all through September, and the following April finished at the top with a record number of points. For, it must be admitted, the opening scenes of Sir Laurence's Macbeth are bad; bad with the confident badness of the master who knows that he has miracles to come.

Searching for a way of illustrating the magnificence of Olivier's recovery, the critic has chanced upon a childhood memory from 1912, when the north-eastern football team Sunderland lost a number of their opening games only to recover to win the Football League Championship. A clue as to why this memory had stuck in his mind appears in his autobiography, *Indirect Journey*:

> The concept of the slow starter who then streaks through the opposition like lightning is something that has always excited me, and this memory of Sunderland is one that I have carried with me throughout my life.[441]

Hobson always considered himself to have been a slow starter. Crippled with polio at 7, his accession to the post of theatre critic at *The Sunday Times* had in many ways been as remarkable as the championship run of Sunderland. The illness had resulted in a severe restriction of his physical movements and this meant that he had to be carried from his car to the theatre if the weather was sufficiently bad to risk him slipping.[442] An insight into his frailty is given in a fascinating letter written by Samuel Beckett in 1961. Hobson, who loved driving and the mobility that his car afforded him, had driven to Paris in July of that year to see productions of *Krapp's Last Tape* and *Waiting for Godot*. The playwright and the critic had become friends after discovering their mutual love of cricket, attending a match at Lords together the previous month. Following this social event, Hobson had published an article in *The Times* which gave details of their conversation at lunch – something which upset the publicity-shy Beckett, since he felt that it contained details about his private life as well as his work. Before he was able to tackle Hobson about this, however, he received a telephone call from an agitated Hobson requesting his help, since his car had broken down and his French was not up to the task of dealing with mechanics and supervising repairs. The playwright spent the whole day contacting garages and attending to Hobson's needs, for the critic seemed so frail and helpless in the face of this catastrophe. Once he was finally able to tackle the more composed critic about the interview, Hobson immediately apologized for unknowingly violating Beckett's private confidence and Beckett, in turn, reassured him that he had never questioned his integrity as a journalist, but simply wished to shun the public spotlight wherever possible.[443]

Whenever Hobson went to review a play, he generally sat in an aisle seat for easy access and was accompanied by someone to help him if necessary. These theatrical companions were most frequently his first wife (theatre managers would breathe a sigh of relief if they saw Elizabeth accompanying her husband, because this increased the chances of a favourable review[444]); Edward Sutro; and, particularly during the last ten years of Hobson's career, Richard Jackson, the theatrical agent. A further practical consideration that resulted from Hobson's disability was that he rarely left his seat at the interval and never went to the bar to fraternize with the other critics – the only way that he discovered the views of his colleagues, aside from a brief conversation at his seat, was by reading them when published.

Whilst the critic of *The Sunday Times*, Hobson was remarkably sanguine about the effect of his disability; as for any effect it had on his critical approach, it only increased his admiration for feats of athletic prowess and physical exertion.[445] As he moved from Sheffield to Oxford in the 1920s, his passion for football and Sheffield Wednesday was matched and exceeded by his interest in cricket. He followed it with the quiet fanaticism that only devotees of the game can manifest and not only based his one novel, *The Devil in Woodford Wells*, on the intricate details of a score-card, but became a member of the MCC and a repository of knowledge on batsmen, bowlers and averages. His first theatrical idol in the 1930s was Jack Buchanan, the epitome of the energetic, all-action performer (to whose show, *Stand Up and Sing*, he had been given free tickets by Roscoe Drummond of the *Christian Science Monitor* in 1931, launching him on his career as a critic[446]) and he was frequently to admire similarly slick performers. One actor who radiated a mesmerizing physicality on stage was Laurence Olivier, and it is an indication of the enormity of his performance as Macbeth that Hobson should attempt to convey a feature of his interpretation by means of an analogy that had great personal resonance for the critic. The famous 'Sunderland' analogy indicates both how Hobson's style owed much to his journalistic flair, sensing the dramatic effect of an original yet appropriate metaphor, and how, of all the twentieth-century theatre critics, Hobson is the most consistently autobiographical, always insisting that his subjective emotional response is conditioned by the shaping effects of his life. He is the High Romantic critic *par excellence*.

Having baldly stated that Olivier's opening scenes as Macbeth are bad, Hobson proceeds to explain that this is because the actor is simply not interested in the business of deposing Duncan. He throws away the 'Is this a dagger …' speech and appears to be bored during the actual murder. This was disconcerting for the audience, who felt that they were about to witness the humbling of a once-great actor into 'the Second Division'. However, the moment of peripeteia that normally occurs in the best of Hobson's reviews actually occurs in this instance on the Stratford stage, for then there 'almost immediately began that superb leap upwards into glory which confounded the wicked, and made the righteous cheer'. When Olivier utters the 'Methought I heard a voice cry, "Sleep no more"' speech, Hobson identifies the heart of the actor's interpretation of the role, namely 'not Macbeth's imagination of Duncan's murder, but his conscience after it' – and herein lay the basis of Olivier's great triumph:

> His 'multitudinous seas incarnadine' is tremendous; it is greasy and slippery with an immense revulsion. As distress and agony enter into him, the actor multiplies in stature before our eyes until he dominates this play, and Stratford, and, I would say, the whole English theatre. When, after the knocking on the door, he reappears in a black monkish gown tied with a rope, he looks like Judas, like a character in a greater drama than Macbeth's, a Judas who, in his dark brooding silence, has begun already to think of the potter's field and the gallows.

Having identified Olivier's approach to the part, Hobson now turns to the second act, an act that was 'full of unforgettable things'. This Macbeth 'briefs the murderers of Banquo with a contempt for their trade which is exceeded by his contempt for himself, a contempt the more arresting because it is tinged with a bitter amusement'. It was a moment of extreme tension and Donald Spoto, in his biography of Olivier, explains how the actor created this:

> In the scene with the murderers … there are three words often tossed aside and sometimes even cut – 'well, then, now' – but Olivier made sense of them. He stopped, eyed the two killers mockingly, pointed with both index fingers at them and said 'Well' enquiringly. After a pause he said 'Then' in a tone suggesting he wanted them to approach him. But they remained still and his 'Now', after a pause, was a terrifying imperative.[447]

Just as Olivier was able to invest single, unpromising lines with great significance, Hobson too could imbue simple stage events with a tremendous, almost overpowering relevance. This technique of exaggeration was later to invite ridicule when it was excessively applied, but in 'Nonpareil' it accords perfectly with Hobson's tone of unlimited enthusiasm. He marvels at the scene where the ghost of Banquo appears: 'At the feast Sir Laurence slides into the seeing of Banquo's ghost and a subsequent cry with a gradual ease that has not been equalled on the English stage since his sensational lamentation in "Oedipus Tyrannus"' – and he reserves his greatest admiration for a facet of Olivier's interpretation that complements Hobson's own Christian attitude to life. If his belief that *Waiting for Godot* contains a positive Christian dimension is debatable, his identification of the spiritual malaise of *Macbeth* as the source of the work's tragedy is entirely appropriate:

> ... the finest element in his performance here is that, in the midst of all this remorse and terror, he never forgets that despair is the greatest of sins. Macbeth's life has been such that he ought to despair; his fortune is such that he must despair; but despair he does not. In this refusal he discovers a terrible grandeur, so that when he reminds his wife that his enemies are still assailable, one's heart rises to him, both to the pathos of a man who will not recognise an inevitable destruction, and to a courage that may be evil but is certainly unquenchable.

This grandeur is maintained to the end of the work because, although Hobson feels that the play collapses after the feast, 'Sir Laurence remains astoundingly aloft':

> When he says that his way of life is fallen into the sere and yellow leaf, you would swear that Macbeth, for all his wickedness, has a right to feel that the universe has monstrously betrayed him. And nothing more beautiful than his speaking of 'She should have died hereafter' will be heard in England till the golden-crested wren becomes a nightingale.

Many elements of this production have concurred with the strongest personal and critical interests of Hobson – the emphasis upon an aspect of Christian theology, the sin of despair; a depiction of the beauty of marriage, ironically implicit in Olivier's tender delivery of the 'She should have died hereafter' line; the unexpected recovery of the main actor which permits an eventual victory for the slow starter and almost made Olivier support Sunderland instead of Chelsea;[448] and a gripping theatricality that would always appeal to a critic whose style was rooted in a subjective, emotional response. As in his 1946 review of Olivier's King Lear, Hobson's exposure to genius had again had a catalytic effect upon his writing, enabling him both to record Olivier's achievement and convey an impression of its substance – the goal of the finest critics. Hobson's success can be measured by the fact that, when he ends his review by stating that: 'Macbeth is notoriously one of the most treacherous parts in the entire realm of drama; but Sir Laurence's performance is such that I do not believe there is an actor in the world who can come near him' – we are inclined to consider his judgement plausible.

The summer of 1955 was a significant period for the British theatre, marred only by the customary lack of new British plays of talent. June saw Olivier's magnificent Macbeth; July the production that confirmed Brecht's arrival in Britain – Joan Littlewood's performance as Mother Courage; and August the première of *Waiting for Godot* and the appearance of Peter Brook's production of *Titus Andronicus* at Stratford. Hobson was much struck by this last play, which he felt was not the corpse-laden anachronism that it was generally considered to be. Indeed, this fine production, starring Olivier and Vivien Leigh again, might even stimulate new dramatists to produce more relevant work. According to Hobson, the horrors of *Titus Andronicus* would not be wasted 'if they wake up the British stage to a sense of reality', and it is significant, given his interest in the linguistic dexterity of Ionesco and Beckett, that it is the language and contemporary relevance of this sixteenth-century play that he finds most striking:

> There is absolutely nothing in the bleeding barbarity of 'Titus Andronicus' which would have astonished anyone at Buchenwald ... Even in its moments of curious verbal delicacy 'Titus Andronicus' parallels exactly our own age. The dismemberment of Lavinia is described as 'trimming', as one might talk of decorating a hat; just as today we speak of torment and torture by a hygienic term like 'brain washing', as though it were something similar to sending clothes to a laundry. The audience which thinks that its sensationalism makes 'Titus Andronicus' unreal and absurd is probably weak in the stomach; it is undoubtedly weak in the head.

But this does not mean that *Titus Andronicus* is an effective play, because 'something more than a vigorous picture of objective reality is needed to make great drama. Theatre must be a consistent point of view.' This implicit side-swipe at Brecht's epic theatre is made explicit when the critic writes:

> It is well known that Shakespeare was never quite sure how to write his own name. I should not be surprised if, about the time he was thinking of 'Titus Andronicus', he thought the proper spelling was Brecht.[449]

From this moment on, Brecht and the idea that plays should depict a sense of social reality was the topic that divided the two principal theatre critics in Britain most markedly.

The post-war rediscovery of Brecht in Britain owed much to the championing of the playwright by Hobson's rival, Kenneth Tynan. In one of his first reviews for the *Observer*, a general discussion of European theatre in December 1954, Tynan had rebuked the British theatre for its insularity, regretting that 'Of Brecht, whose plays have captured Central Europe, we know nothing at all.'[450] The next month he travelled to Paris to review a performance of *Mother Courage* by the Théâtre National Populaire and was sufficiently enthused to write of 'a glorious performance of a contemporary classic which has been acclaimed everywhere in Europe save in London'.[451] Although disappointed by Joan Littlewood's interpretation of *Mother Courage* in July 1955, feeling that her paring-down of the cast and her cutting of Mother Courage's principal song merely travestied the text,[452] his growing interest in Brechtian stage theory was undiminished and his conversion to the cause was completed by his exposure to the work of Brecht's own company, the Berliner Ensemble, at the second Paris Theatre Festival. Reviewing the Ensemble's production of *The Caucasian Chalk Circle* in June 1956, Tynan declared that: 'Once in a generation the world discovers a new way of telling a story; this generation's pathfinder is Brecht, both as playwright and director of the Berliner Ensemble',[453] and he proceeded to give a brief, sympathetic résumé of the much talked-about 'Verfremdungseffekt'. This belief was confirmed for Tynan by the German company's visit to London in August 1956.

Hobson's first contact with Brecht was at the disappointing Theatre Workshop performance of *Mother Courage* at the Queen's Hall, Barnstaple, a production mounted as part of the Devon Festival. The fact that both Tynan and Hobson were prepared to travel to the West Country is indicative of the interest that Brecht's considerable success on the Continent was arousing in British theatrical circles in the summer of 1955. At the outset of 'Try Again'[454] Hobson is swift to point out that Joan Littlewood's 'colourless, indecisive and often inaudible performance' does not provide a fair opportunity for assessing Brecht's merits:

[it] would indeed be a pity if its defects discouraged English interest in Brecht ... For even in the lamentable proceedings on Thursday it was intermittently evident that 'Mother Courage' is a work of some quality.

He is intrigued by some of Brecht's suggestive thoughts – 'It is only bad government ... that needs the moral virtues; the good general can win his victories without his men showing unexceptional bravery' – and he is particularly impressed by the 'excellent theatrical speech' (poorly delivered by Littlewood) 'on the theme that defeat for princes does not necessarily mean disaster for their subjects'. In Hobson's view, however, the problem with the play, which explains Joan Littlewood's relative failure, is that 'Mother Courage is the hardest role an English actress has been called upon to shoulder this century': 'The difficulty, colossal and intimidating, comes in Brecht's attitude to the theatre; for Brecht is revolutionary both in ideological content and in theatrical technique.'

Hobson correctly points out that only using props that are solidly naturalistic is not an original technique, citing the earlier practice of the Stage Society – what *is* 'new and potentially baffling' is the 'famous doctrine of alienation' ('Verfremdung'). Hobson's interpretation of the aims of Brecht here is particularly interesting because, even within the confines of a journalistic review, he is able to provide a cogent and even-handed explanation of the rationale behind epic practice:

Brecht wants Mother Courage to appeal, not to our emotions, but to our understanding; this is why the actress must put us at a distance. She must never raise the question, 'Do we like Mother Courage or despise her,' but only the questions 'How did Mother Courage happen? What were the social conditions that produced her?' We must comprehend the social process, not pity or condemn the individual. It is in loyally trying to convey this that Miss Littlewood comes a cropper, and one has for her a certain sympathy. Brecht requires the actress to do the almost impossible, and the simple truth is that Miss Littlewood has not come near it.

For a critic whose technique of assessment relies upon an emotional, autobiographical response, this form of theatre – rigorously opposed to illusion and catharsis – would inevitably provide difficulties. But Hobson is prepared to concede that Brecht requires an actress to do the *almost* impossible. In other words, not enough evidence has been gathered to reach a conclusive verdict. Compare this reasonable and measured assessment, however, with the opinions that Hobson was to venture on the same play, but this time to his American readership, in the *Christian Science Monitor* three weeks later:[455]

> The essence of Brecht's play is that we cannot say of any human being or any human action that it is good or bad until we know what is the process that has produced it. These things are not to be judged by the canons of humanity, Christianity, fair play, generosity, love, or any criteria like these; but only by whether they aid or hinder a certain social development. In judging events, we must beware of pity or contempt; and the massacre of political opponents is justified if it helps the establishment of the classless society, even though those opponents may be individually good and kindly men. This is the meaning of Brecht's theory. The western world will, of course, recoil from it in horror, and it is right to do so, for it is the negation of everything that is most valuable in humanity. But in its recoil the western world would do well not to be too self-righteous, for, in time of war at least, it is ready enough to adopt this doctrine itself. Between 1939 and 1945 all the western countries were ready to sacrifice, in mass bombing raids, the lives of worthy people, because this sacrifice contributed to a certain social process, the winning of the war. Brecht extends this principle to times of peace; he regards the setting up of a classless society as equally important as military victory. It is a terrible theory.

Far from following his own advice of waiting for further productions of plays by Brecht before assessing their merit, Hobson, in the space of three weeks, has reached the conclusion that epic theatre is not only antitheatrical, but implicitly dangerous. He is now convinced that it dismisses some of the attitudes that he holds most dear – Christianity, love and fair play – and is thus anathema to him. His tone is uncharacteristically dismissive and his analysis unappealingly imbalanced, and it appears to be influenced by some of the starkest rhetoric of the Cold War. How can this intemperate volte-face be explained? It may have resulted from a realization that a new, anti-emotional response in the theatre was now being called for. Hobson would certainly have disliked the nakedly political dimension to the theory of epic theatre and the physical frontality of Brecht's style. Michael Billington points out that Hobson 'loved things that were somehow slightly oblique, insidious and emotionally suggestive, rather than aggressive',[456] and there is little doubt that the starkness of Brecht's belief that man is the product of his environment and that the theatre is a forum for improving this environment ran against Hobson's love of the grandly theatrical and his delight in the implicitly suggestive. Just as he had tired of the predictability of the well-made play, Hobson reacted against the insistence that an audience should be provoked into some degree of social action. His dislike may also have stemmed from the fact that he was an instinctive admirer of the French and had never displayed a similar interest in the Teutonic, and that his, by now, fierce critical rival, the young pretender Tynan, was championing Brecht as a pathfinder and becoming the spokesman of the disaffected, instinctively leftish young in Britain – a group that Hobson was less able to address.

Hobson's adoration of the French theatre ironically reached its apotheosis shortly after this production of *Mother Courage*. Fresh from Brecht, Olivier and Beckett – all in the space of two months – Hobson was once again to encounter, at the 1955 Edinburgh Festival, the French actress whom he was to consider the greatest he had ever seen. His reaction to Edwige Feuillère's performance as Marguérite Gautier in *La Dame aux Camélias* at the Lyceum, Edinburgh[457] emphasizes the increasingly stark contrast between his critical style and Tynan's. Passages of lyrical, romantic prose – 'Her performance is not made up of discrete notes, like a firework piece on a piano. It has rather the unbroken beauty of a violin' – are interrupted by moments of rhapsodic praise – 'her death scene is … miraculously moving'; breathless, emotional reactions are listed alongside moments of revelatory insight gleaned from the tiniest gestures, such as the force of a 'Jamais' uttered by Feuillère; phrases in French are quoted to give an indication (to those familiar with the language) of the magnificence of touch, and Hobson freely acknowledges his deliberately impressionistic approach by concluding that: 'to detail the beauties of Mme Feuillère's performance is to give the wrong impression'. Removed from the event, Hobson's praise seems excessive (particularly given the deficiencies of his own spoken French), but the ridicule that this form of criticism provoked had more to do with the changing theatrical taste, the rejection of the Romantic in the desire for the Augustan, than any failing on the part of Hobson. Stephen Bagnall, in a letter to *The Sunday Times* the following Sunday, spoke for many when he objected to the critic's 'incomprehensible francomania'[458] – for against the sharp, socially perceptive comments of Tynan, prose such as this was regarded as self-indulgent and incorrigibly highbrow. This, of course, was a partisan view that chose to identify the cloying nature of the Feuillère review as the sum of Hobson's output rather than as a single component. Indeed, on the very Sunday that the letter was published Hobson provided a convincing manifesto for the type of criticism that he represented:

> The critic is not a legislator, nor does he apply a code. He is a historian, the historian of what happens to his own heart and mind when he is subjected to a certain artistic experience. He undergoes an emotion, and then searches for reasons to justify it. But the essential thing is that he has the emotion first. Thus the critic is on the one hand less, and on the other much more, arrogant than is generally supposed. He does not deliver a judgement from heaven. He merely describes the impact which a play or a performance makes on his own taste, which has been formed by a million influences during the whole of his life. And if other people do not register a similar impact he does not hesitate to conclude that their taste has been less happily formed than his. Conceited? Of course, but it is the only way in which enduring theatrical criticism – like Hazlitt's and Shaw's – can be made. Both men leapt to their conclusions, and found their reasons afterwards. It is the emotion that counts; the rest is shadow-boxing. If it were otherwise anybody with a passable skill in deduction could outshine Montague.[459]

The following week Hobson replied to Bagnall's charge of Francomania with a rigorous defence of his love of the French. The critical opprobrium that had greeted *Waiting for Godot* had merely reinforced his passion:

> It is this complacent inability to recognise the highest when they see it, this apparently natural enmity towards exaltation of the spirit, which for a moment checks one's heart. It is this attitude that is the reason why Olivier and Gielgud are playing Shakespeare, why Redgrave is playing Giraudoux, and Wolfit, Hochwälder. It is the reason why some of us are Francomaniacs. It has left *them* nothing else to do. It has left *us* little else to be.[460]

The infusion of invigorating foreign works in 1955 meant, paradoxically, that the following years would see plenty of home-grown plays for accomplished British actors to perform in and many more causes for stimulating critics to champion. Hobson's passionate support of the innovative dramatic work, irrespective of its country of origin, was as important in creating a receptive climate for new British work as the oft-repeated calls for more socially relevant drama.

Chapter 6

The Dam Bursts: 1956–1958

The 1950s constituted a contradictory period, when conflicting impulses for change and the preservation of the status quo were played out against a background of rapid technical advancement and deteriorating super-power relations. At the beginning of the decade the Cold War intensified with the revelation in January 1950 that Dr Klaus Fuchs, head of theoretical physics at the Harwell Atomic Research Establishment of the Atomic Energy Authority, had passed on information to the Russians, saving them ten years' work in their quest for an atomic bomb. The West's sense of invulnerability was immediately shattered and the Korean War seemed an ominous sign of even greater conflagration ahead. This international tension served to intensify the bleakness of a Britain still attempting to emerge from the economic consequences of the last war. In spite of official efforts to encourage the nation to look ahead, symbolized by the Festival of Britain in 1951 which was visited by eight million glamour-starved people, the country appeared curiously trapped between the future and the past. Post-war austerity continued to be felt, with the meat ration of 1s. 6d., set in 1945, being reduced to 8d. in 1951.[461] Indeed, rationing was not phased out in its entirety until 1954, when meat, bacon and butter were released on to the open market. Several British cities still bore the scars of bomb damage and many people began to cast envious glances across the Atlantic to a nation that was beginning to experience years of abundance. In the first half of the decade the phenomenon of consumerism was introduced from the United States, and it soon became fashionable to display in one's home the latest technological development exported from America – a refrigerator or a washing machine, perhaps. For the majority of Britons, however, these acquisitions did not become possible until the restrictions on hire purchase were lifted in 1958.

In the realm of social attitudes, Britain at the start of the decade remained a country where people were expected to know their place, display a suitable deference to their elders and betters and eschew demonstrations of excessive emotion or bad taste. Whilst it was generally recognized that television had come of age with Richard Dimbleby's commentary on the Coronation for the BBC in 1953, many regarded with horror the arrival of commercial television, launched as ITV on 22 September 1955, prompting the magazine *Plays and Players* to term the protracted discussion of its value the 'Most boring controversy of the year'.[462] Hobson records a fine example of prim indignation at the minimal excesses of a new ITV programme in an article for the *Christian Science Monitor*, mischievously entitled 'No Joke in Britain' by an American sub-editor, amused at the strait-laced attitudes of the Britons. The article relates how Sir Kenneth Clark, the chairman of the Independent Television Authority, had moved swiftly on the day of his election to the Athenaeum Club to reassure those who had been outraged by the programme 'People Are Funny' that he, too, disapproved of its tasteless excesses. Hobson's description of the offending programme reveals it as a primitive forerunner of 'Candid Camera' and 'Beadle's About':

> 'People Are Funny' is a programme in which men and women are made to do foolish things, for which they are rewarded with prizes like washing machines, radios and clocks. On one occasion a boy was sent out to squeeze toothpaste on someone else's furniture: on another, a woman, carrying suitcases, was told to knock on a stranger's door and say she had come to spend the night.[463]

He indicates his own amusement at Sir Kenneth's undue discomfort by considering his admonition to have been 'a very Athenaeumlike warning'.

It is precisely this unadventurous, conservative and 'sensible' outlook that the younger generation began to find increasingly frustrating. For the educated young, opportunity appeared rigidly class-based and meritocracy a foreign concept. The Butler Education Act of 1944 had meant that a new, intelligent generation was now emerging to demand a more equitable society, and by 1956 three-quarters of university students were dependent on state grants that had been subject to a means test.[464] They therefore had no vested interest in preserving the status quo. Young writers, such as Kingsley Amis with *Lucky Jim* (1954) and *That Uncertain Feeling* (1955) and John Wain with *Hurry On Down* (1953), encapsulated this discontent in novels that focused on the outsider struggling to find his feet in a society that he despises, and there was an increasing desire to question the values of their parents' generation, be it in the adherence to an uncontrovertible propriety or the prevailing conspiracy of silence over sex.

The first half of the decade marked the beginning of the transition in Britain from austerity to prosperity, and the shift away from the unquestioned acceptance of status to the more fluid consideration of image. There were signs in the theatre, too, that some unquestioned orthodoxies that had prevailed since before the war were about to come under increasing scrutiny. The pre-eminent theatrical manager in London during the post-war decade had been Hugh 'Binkie' Beaumont, the managing director of H. M. Tennent Ltd. A mysterious man and much feared in the theatrical profession, it was a common belief that any actor who had crossed him was placed on his infamous black list, virtually precluding the possibility of finding good parts in the West End again.

Richard Huggett, in his sympathetic biography of Binkie, points out that, whether or not the list actually existed, the belief that it did enabled Binkie to keep actors under his control even when they held a legitimate grievance. Amongst the many grievances of actors employed by him were the poverty wages paid to all but the stars, a cavalier disregard for regulations governing working conditions that had been negotiated and a legendary meanness. Ray Witch, the stage manager for *Irma la Douce* and an understudy on no less than eight occasions, relates a graphic example of this:

> The whole run was a nightmare because I had only one rehearsal a week and I was paid £16 which seemed to be standard in those days. I later took over the part of Jo-Jo, the company went on tour and I asked for a raise, to £30. I was asked to go and see Bernard Gordon: he was sitting at his desk and the top was covered in money, piles of notes and bags of silver. He was counting out the various salaries. 'I gather that you want £30 a week, Mr Witch. This production is not making money so I'm afraid that the answer will have to be "no".' I then asked if I could see Binkie but I later received a letter from him offering £25. I was advised by Frank Stevens, our stage director, to accept it. There was no point in making waves, he said, and if I tried to put pressure on Binkie I'd be black-listed. There was one week when my throat was so bad that I could hardly speak. My doctor said I must not go on but Binkie wouldn't let me miss a performance. He wasn't going to take my or my doctor's word that I wasn't well enough and he brought his own doctor, a Harley Street specialist, who examined my throat and gave me a pain-killing drug which allowed me to speak without pain. I had these injections for the rest of the week and then I was allowed to go to hospital for two weeks but when I was out and back at work I received a bill for £30 from the Harley Street specialist. Binkie called him but I had to pay him.[465]

Hardly the 'good, old fashioned paternalism' with which Huggett credits Binkie Beaumont.[466]

This accumulation of power was such that, in 1954, Binkie was presenting a monopolistic sixteen productions in the West End, which, given his notorious dislike of intelligent plays ('Who wants intelligence when they go to the theatre?'[467]), was a further stifling influence on the prospects of any new, home-grown writing. It is not surprising given this – and the fact that Kitty Black, Tennent's 'in-house dramaturge',[468] rejected the script for *Look Back in Anger* with the claim that the author might be 'put on a charge'[469] – that John Osborne was later to describe Binkie as the 'most powerful of the unacceptable faeces of theatrical capitalism'.[470] In 1954, however, a significant challenge to Binkie's hegemony was mounted by the Labour MP, Woodrow Wyatt, who introduced a bill into the House of Commons 'To control non-profit making theatrical companies'. Binkie had formed such a company in 1941,

Tennent Plays Ltd, to avoid paying entertainment tax, which then stood at 30 per cent. Receipts from this company were immediately ploughed back into the parent organization, H. M. Tennent's, to comply with the non-profit-making regulations, thus proving to be an extremely lucrative loophole. Even though the Inland Revenue ruled that he was obliged to pay £15,000 in income tax in 1946, after the company carelessly declared that it intended to present some productions in dance halls, which were not granted tax exemption, Binkie simply wound up Tennent Plays Ltd and re-formed it as Tennent Productions Ltd. His productions invariably earned huge sums of money, N. C. Hunter's *Waters of the Moon* grossing three-quarters of a million pounds over two years alone, but voices, in addition to those of envious fellow theatre managers, were openly beginning to question Binkie's exploitation of a loophole designed to permit drama of an educational value to survive in a commercial environment. The *Sunday Express* had objected strongly to the tax exemption that had been granted in 1949 to *A Streetcar Named Desire* – a Tennent production – and Binkie was subsequently summoned to a parliamentary sub-committee, which he managed to placate. Wyatt's 1954 bill, however, represented a far greater challenge and, although it failed to become law, it marked the beginning of a strident campaign to have the loophole closed. In 1957 the Conservative government, bowing to the pressure of opinion, decided that the swiftest way to resolve the problem was to abolish the tax entirely, a disastrous move for Binkie, who, as Richard Huggett claims, must have viewed the tax's demise with the same distress that Al Capone felt at the end of prohibition.[471] It is an eloquent testimony to the years of upheaval that were about to be ushered into the British theatre that Huggett's chronological evaluation of Binkie's career omits the period from 1954 to 1958 – the omnipotent theatrical impresario quickly became the symbol of a dated theatrical past.

In many ways, Hobson is the perfect critic to read to gain an insight into the era that gave birth to the much-trumpeted phenomenon of the Angry Young Man. As a critic whose self-proclaimed task was to act as a witness and not as a judge (although he was clearly both), he enjoyed writing as a social historian as well as an assessor of plays. At the beginning of 1956 he was clearly regarded by his chief employers, *The Sunday Times*, as one of their main assets and this was to lend a new confidence and authority to his writing. An advertisement for the paper that appeared in January 1956 posed the question in large type: 'What does Harold Hobson say about it?', and then explained that:

> Whenever and wherever the theatre is talked about, or thought about, Harold Hobson's critical views are a matter of great importance. His theatre notes in the 'Sunday Times' are one of the most widely appreciated features of this great newspaper. His witty and often scathing pen does justice to his great knowledge of the drama and his courage of opinion.[472]

Such was the interest that his literary dual with Tynan was now arousing, that their weekly sparring was regarded as good for sales. *The Sunday Times*, capitalizing on Hobson's growing renown, also initiated the first National Union of Students' Drama Festival, which took place in the Victoria Rooms, Clifton, Bristol from 31 December 1955 to 5 January 1956. Since the paper was awarding a cup for the best student production, it was appropriate that their noted drama critic should adjudicate. In awarding the first prize to a production of Thornton Wilder's *Our Town* by Regent Street Polytechnic, Hobson once again stressed the primacy of emotion for him in a successful theatrical performance, when he explained that: 'They had innumerable technical faults; but they were the only company which made me forget that they were acting, or trying to act; and at the end they made me want to cry out loud with sorrow.'[473] Hobson was also asked to be one of the six judges of the prestigious *Evening Standard* drama awards for 1955. Prior to the ceremony, the deliberation of the adjudicators appeared almost as exciting as the plays that they wished to commend. Three of the judges – the novelist Rosamond Lehmann, Sir Michael Balcon, the head of Ealing Film Studios, and Hobson, the implacable champion of the avant-garde – wished to award the title of best play to *Waiting for Godot*. The remaining three – John Fernald, the Principal of RADA, Sir Malcolm Sargent, the conductor, and Milton Shulman, the drama critic of the *Evening Standard* and scourge of Beckett – were resolutely opposed to this course of action. In the end, a clumsy compromise was agreed, whereby the Best Play Award for 1955 was given to Jean Giraudoux's *Tiger at the Gates*, with a special soubriquet of 'the most controversial play of 1955' being awarded to *Waiting for Godot*. Loyal to the last, Hobson was initially unprepared to venture a second choice – a fact gleefully related in the *Evening Standard*'s report of the proceedings, which could scarcely conceal the newspaper's joy at the extra publicity to be gained from this critical dissension.[474]

Many of Hobson's articles of this period testify to the forces of change that were now apparent in the mid-1950s. In 'At Command'[475] and 'Command Performance at Home'[476] Hobson admires the technological advances that have made it possible to listen to gramophone recordings of theatre performances in one's own home. 'On National Anthems'[477] applauds the decision of the Theatre Workshop to drop the practice of playing the National Anthem at the end of the evening, because this will bring Britain into line with other countries and avoid the unseemly race to escape from one's seat before the music begins. In April 'Transition in British Theater'[478] reports on 'a new organization called the English Stage Company, which is setting out to discover new authors', and in a series of twelve articles for the *Christian Science Monitor* Hobson relates his impressions of life in the Soviet capital whilst accompanying Peter Brook's *Hamlet* company on their tour in November 1955.

The death of Stalin in March 1953 had led temporarily to a more relaxed international atmosphere and stimulated curiosity in the West about the condition of life behind the Iron Curtain. These pieces by Hobson must have been of particular contemporary interest to an American readership familiar with the concept of Moscow as the headquarters of an enemy power, because he takes the trouble to record as rounded a view as possible of Moscow life. Inevitably, the majority of articles are concerned with theatre-related experiences, yet he also manages to convey an impression of the street atmosphere and the hotels,[479] the difficulty and expense of travelling to Moscow via Helsinki,[480] the differences between the Soviet Communists and their more aggressive western counterparts[481] and the scale, grandeur and lack of beauty of Soviet architecture.[482] Generally, Hobson avoids lapsing into Cold War rhetoric, although one article, 'Soviets Shun Fun to Pursue Culture',[483] is filled with strong criticisms of the Soviet ethos. At one point, Hobson directly tackles the philosophical basis of the Communist state:

> Is it not founded on one of the most attractive but also most disastrous mistakes in all history, the supposition that salvation can be imposed from above? We in the West believe that the individual must work out his own problems; the Soviet claim is that the state can prevent the individual's problems from arising. To this end it strives to protect him from temptation. It believes that this policy is morally right; but the end of that policy is tyranny.

The condemnatory tone of this article is as much a reflection of the political stance of the *Christian Science Monitor* as an indication of the continued seriousness of the international situation.

'The most striking memory I have brought back with me from Moscow in connection with the theater … is the Stanislavsky method … a splendid method of theatrical production.'[484] Given Hobson's admiration of this naturalistic technique of acting (whose influence was now at its height in the West, having been associated with the Group Theatre in the 1930s under Lee Strasberg, Cheryl Campbell and Harold Clurman, and with the Actors' Studio after the Second World War under Elia Kazan and then Strasberg), it comes as something of a surprise for Hobson to give the first West End production of Brecht's *The Threepenny Opera*, at the Royal Court (February 1956), an enthusiastic review. In the opening paragraph of 'Revolution'[485] he describes Sam Wanamaker's production as 'one of the most exciting things seen in London for some time' and maintains that, once it has got going, it 'provides a really thrilling experience to the playgoer who takes the art of the drama seriously'. He attempts once again to explain Brecht's theatrical technique, picking out passages of text that encapsulate the notion of 'Verfremdung', such as an actor stepping to the front of the stage and stating that 'robbing a bank is nothing like so great a crime as founding a bank', but, unlike Hobson's outspoken article of the previous summer, 'Brecht Drama in Britain',[486] 'Revolution' contains only the briefest, almost shamefaced criticism of the philosophy behind the theory, when the critic claims that: 'Brecht's theory is not revolutionary only aesthetically: it is revolutionary politically, in that it lends itself to subversion.' Two explanations may be offered for the less denunciatory tone of the whole article. Firstly, Hobson may be giving greater thought to his opinions in the light of the increasing interest in Brechtian practice in British theatrical circles – what could be dismissed last summer as an unappealing phenomenon primarily performed overseas now demanded greater respect. Secondly, Hobson would have been aware of Tynan's growing excitement at the emergence of Brecht and may have wished to learn more about the playwright before returning to the attack. Tynan's enthusiasm was plain to see on the very same Sunday that Hobson's article was published, an article that validates the claim by Ronald Hayman that Tynan was 'the critic who primed our theatre for Brechtian infiltration'.[487] Under the rallying headline, 'The Way Ahead',[488] Tynan stated in the *Observer* that the Berliner Ensemble was 'arguably the best [company] in the world' and that it promised to be a good year for a Brechtian:

> a person who believes that low drama with high principles is better than high principles with no audience; that the worst plays are those which depend wholly on suspense and the illusion of reality; and that the drama of the future will be a wedding of song and narrative in which neither partner marries beneath itself.

The political dimension of epic theatre which had so antagonized Hobson the previous summer – and which still rankled – was the very aspect of Brecht's oeuvre which Tynan found so invigorating. He commended the theme of *The Threepenny Opera* for being 'one of evergreen irony: the idea that unsanctioned crime, which we call anti-social, is merely a reflection in little of the greater, sanctioned crime which we call social justice', and he ended his review with a ringing endorsement of Brecht's compassion and humanity:

> I would forgive much in return for a musical show in which no word or note is coy, dainty or sugary. These qualities are lies; beguiling lies, perhaps, but denials of life. Brecht's honesty, tart though it tastes, is an affirmation. It says that whoever we are, and however vile, we are worth singing about.

It is here, in the very nature of *The Threepenny Opera*, that one can find the most plausible explanation for Hobson's reticence. Written in 1928, at a time when Brecht had just begun his systematic study of Marxism, the work does not yet exhibit the doctrinal approach of the works of the early 1930s, such as *The Measures Taken*, or the physical frontality of his best works, including *Mother Courage*, which the impressionistic Hobson found so disconcerting. Brecht wrote of the musical in *Versuche 3* that 'Die Dreigroschenoper ist ein Versuch im epischen Theater'[489] ('*The Threepenny Opera* is an experiment in epic theatre'), and it is the exploratory nature of the work, allowing elements of epic theatre (direct addresses to the audience, placards bearing revolutionary slogans) to blend with more conventional emotional techniques, which Hobson found intriguing. He was not to demonstrate a similar tolerance with Brecht's maturer works.

At the beginning of April 1956 Hobson detected a mood in the London theatre akin to a calm before a storm, a feeling he shared with his American readership when he stated that: 'In London there has been a lull before what is expected to be an outbreak of one of the most remarkable spring seasons for some years.'[490] This sense of expectation had been generated by the imminent arrival of Enid Bagnold's *The Chalk Garden* from Broadway, Peter Hall's production of Graham Greene's *The Power and the Glory*, adapted by Denis Cannan and Pierre Bost, and 'the first presentations of a new organization called the English Stage Company, which is vowed to the discovery of new dramatists'.[491] Initially, these eager expectations were unfulfilled. The much-heralded *The Chalk Garden* did not travel well; even with a quality cast that included Dame Edith Evans and Peggy Ashcroft, it proved to be a bitter disappointment for Hobson, who termed it 'pretentious, obvious, irritating'.[492] *The Power and the Glory*, too, in spite of a religious motif that Hobson felt deepened 'greatly the quality of the play', was only a partial success for him, with the work being likened to 'a long-distance runner who is determined not to exhaust his resources until the tape is well in sight',[493] and Angus Wilson's *The Mulberry Bush* was politely received merely as the first shot of an interesting campaign at the Royal Court, since 'its ideas and its wit are still stronger than its dramatic development'.[494] No one could have imagined that, out of this unpropitious environment, would emerge a play that would provoke a fundamental reorientation of British drama.

In an era when it was considered to be slightly daring to use garlic, travel abroad or wear a duffel coat, it was not surprising that many of *Look Back in Anger*'s innovations, innovations which admittedly appear tame and jejune thirty-five years on, provoked equal measures of admiration and disapproval. The opening curtain rose to an unfamiliar scene of cramped, suburban shabbiness, with Alison Porter performing the most mundane of tasks – the ironing. One contemporary witness, Bernice Coupe, remembered that the first shock of the evening was the depressing nature of the Porter's flat; she was particularly disconcerted by the sight of the ironing-board to which Alison seemed to be chained – an object which belonged in the home and certainly not in the theatre.[495] Another early surprise was the fact that the actors were not articulating in politely strangulated accents, but speaking in a variety of regional tones that had previously been the preserve of maids, bobbies and artisans. A recording of Kenneth Haigh playing the first Jimmy Porter still has the power to shock with the violent intensity of his delivery, the unmellifluous rasp of his accusations and the passion of his frequent outbursts. For many people in the 1950s, when well-formulated diction was proof positive of intelligence, Jimmy Porter's combination of volubility, accent and intellectual prowess was very hard to accept, and this challenge to contemporary assumptions was compounded by the sheer irreverence of many of Jimmy's attacks. Whether the target was Priestley, likened to Alison's daddy, 'still casting well-fed glances back to the Edwardian twilight from his comfortable, disenfranchised wilderness',[496] or senseless, upper-class ambition, symbolized by Alison's brother Nigel, variously described as 'the straight-backed, chinless wonder from Sandhurst' and 'the platitude from Outer Space',[497] it was difficult to perceive which aspect of Jimmy's critique should be construed as the more heterodox – the passionate and implicitly left-wing nature of the attack, or the confident and riveting new idiom in which it was formulated. To many, particularly the young and the university-educated, this depiction of a reinvigorated, eloquent, liberal conscience at work was the revelation for which they had been waiting. Frustrated at the mental atrophy that they discerned in British society, they were thrilled by Jimmy Porter's clarion call to rebellion, be it in his exasperation at British docility – 'Nobody thinks, nobody cares. No beliefs, no convictions and no enthusiasm'[498] – his dangerously radical toying with taboos –

> I've just about had enough of this 'expense of spirit' lark, as far as women are concerned. Honestly, it's enough to make you become a scoutmaster or something, isn't it? Sometimes I almost envy old Gide and the Greek Chorus boys. Oh, I'm not saying that it mustn't be hell for them a lot of the time. But, at least, they do seem to have a cause[499]

– or in his central complaint, that intelligent people such as himself had no opportunity to contribute to society:

> There aren't any good, brave causes left. If the big bang does come, and we all get killed off, it won't be in aid of the old-fashioned, grand design. It'll just be for the Brave-New-nothing-very-much-thank-you. About as pointless and inglorious as stepping in front of a bus. No, there's nothing left for it, me boy, but to let yourself be butchered by the women.[500]

The hyperbole of Jimmy's last sentence is typical of Osborne's technique: a serious point is pricked by exaggeration, raising the question of whether there is more to the work than a passionate denunciation of society's failings. This fine linguistic distinction was lost by many in the immediate critical reaction to a work that broke with the timidity of the recent British theatrical past. The journalist Edward Pearce, then a young student, remembers how disappointing the reality of post-war life had proved to be, compared with the excitement of the pre-war causes that he had read about in his textbooks. Everything had 'settled down into a blancmange-like existence of common sense, tolerance and half-a-grain change', and he, too, longed for a good, brave cause – 'preferably not to die for, but to get paid for' – as well as 'the therapy of conflict'.[501]

Look Back in Anger was a revelation because it represented such a break with the past, it suggested that the old world was now over. The conventionality of its form merely accentuated the revolutionary nature of its content and it was the generational conflict that the work seemed to desire which attracted the most interest after the première of the work on 8 May 1956. It would be left to Harold Hobson to point out in the heat of the battle that there was more to the work than a manifesto for revolution, and that the play possessed more dramatic merit than simply a piece of rhetoric.

The first-night reaction to *Look Back in Anger* in the daily newspapers was mixed. Patrick Gibbs in the *Daily Telegraph* claimed that Jimmy Porter was 'a character who should have gone to a psychiatrist rather than have come to a dramatist',[502] whereas John Barber of the *Daily Express* was attracted to the work because the hero was 'like thousands of young Londoners today' and the play itself was 'intense, angry, feverish, undisciplined. It is even crazy. But it is young, young, young.'[503] Colin Wilson voiced a common view when he wrote in the *Daily Mail* that Osborne was a good dramatist who had somehow written the wrong play,[504] and even Milton Shulman of the *Evening Standard*, who was unable to share John Barber's enthusiasm, feeling that the work was 'a self-pitying snivel' and a failure because of 'its inability to be coherent about its despair', conceded that: 'When he stops being angry – or when he lets us in on what he is being angry about – he may write a very good play.'[505] Good try, better luck next time, seemed to be the general consensus.

There is a peculiar irony to 'the desultory talk of being "saved by the Sundays"'[506] which, Osborne relates in the second volume of his autobiography, *Almost a Gentleman*, was passing round the Royal Court Company after the appearance of the daily reviews, since the play itself viewed the Sunday newspapers as symptoms of the prevailing intellectual paralysis. Osborne recalls that, at the time, he considered both *The Sunday Times* and the *Observer* to have been equally obsessed with anything French:

> For as long as I could remember the literary and academic classes seemed to have been tyrannized by the French. The 'posh papers' every Sunday blubbered with self-abasement in the face of the bombast of the French language and its absurd posture as the torch-bearer of Logic, which apparently was something to which no one in these islands had access.
>
> Certain writers gave the impression that it was downright indelicate to write in English at all, which is why *The Sunday Times* and the *Observer* were peppered with italics until they sometimes looked like linguistic lace curtains.[507]

Given this dim view of the intellectual judgement of the 'posh papers', it seems a rather desperate exercise in optimism to have expected the salvation of so English and contemporary a play from such devotees of the

French. Osborne may have been frustrated by the Francomania of these publications, but Jimmy Porter still retained a latent respect for their writing. Although he mocks the pretentious excesses of what are clearly *The Sunday Times* and the *Observer* – 'I've just read three whole columns on the English Novel. Half of it's in French. Do the Sunday newspapers make you feel ignorant?'[508] – both he and Cliff are first seen 'sprawled way out beyond the newspapers which hide the rest of them from sight', and Jimmy evidently recognizes the social implications of adhering to the religious ritual of working one's way through the Sundays:

Jimmy: Haven't you read the other posh paper yet?
Cliff: Which?
Jimmy: Well, there are only two posh papers on a Sunday – the one you're reading, and this one.[509]

Although there is no hint in the work of Jimmy Porter being interested in dramatic criticism, it is significant that even he considers it important to consider and compare the views of journalists from the two opposing camps. John Osborne himself was certainly interested in dramatic criticism when he made his way to a newsagent in Mortlake the following Sunday and sat reading their verdicts on 'a corporation bench in the bright May early morning sunshine'.[510] He was convinced before he had read them that the previous evening's performance of *Look Back in Anger* was destined to be its last.

'It is the best young play of its decade' (Kenneth Tynan, 'The Voice of the Young', *Observer*, 13 May 1956); 'he is a writer of outstanding promise' (Harold Hobson, 'A New Author', *Sunday Times*, 13 May 1956). Cheerfully brushing aside Jimmy Porter's critique of their publications – Hobson perceptively wrote that the hero possesses 'a sort of admiring hatred' of the 'posh papers' – the two most influential theatre critics were united in their admiration of the third production of the English Stage Company. The basis of their respective enthusiasm, however, was inevitably different and provides a fine illustration of their contrasting theatrical perspectives. For Tynan, *Look Back in Anger* was 'a minor miracle', in that it displayed qualities that:

one had despaired of ever seeing on the stage – the drift towards anarchy, the instinctive leftishness, the automatic rejection of 'official' attitudes, the surrealist sense of humour ... the casual promiscuity, the sense of lacking a crusade worth fighting for and, underlying all these, the determination that no one who dies shall go unmourned.

It challenged a status quo encapsulated in Somerset Maugham's verdict that state-aided university students were scum (Tynan memorably ends his first paragraph with the warning that *Look Back in Anger* 'is all scum and a mile wide'); it contained a hero who was not passive and acquiescent but 'simply and abundantly alive'; it broke with a sterile theatrical past and bore testimony to 'that rarest of dramatic phenomena, the act of original creation'; it dramatized the dilemma of the eloquent young – 'The Porters of our time deplore the tyranny of "good taste" and refuse to accept "emotional" as a term of abuse; they are classless, and they are also leaderless'; and it offered the prospect of a dramatist to lead this alienated class out of the wilderness – 'Mr Osborne is their first spokesman in the London theatre.' Quite simply, Tynan had discovered the antithesis of the much-loathed Loamshire play, and he overstates his case with a passion and plausibility that are reminiscent of Hobson's delight in discovering *Waiting for Godot*. Tynan's concluding comments are a deliberate challenge to all those who considered themselves to be modern and forward-looking:

> I agree that 'Look Back In Anger' is likely to remain a minority taste. What matters, however, is the size of the minority. I estimate it at roughly 6,733,000, which is the number of people in this country between the ages of twenty and thirty. And this figure will doubtlessly be swelled by refugees from other age-groups who are curious to know precisely what the contemporary young pup is thinking and feeling. I doubt if I could love anyone who did not wish to see 'Look Back In Anger'.

Such startlingly committed writing probably helped *Look Back in Anger* to secure the twenty-five-minute television showing on the BBC which produced an immediate effect at the box-office (takings went up from £900 to £1,700 per week[511]) and which enabled the production to transfer from the Royal Court Theatre to the Lyric, Hammersmith. Tynan, the politically committed critic, felt that he had come across the first post-war, political playwright to identify correctly the plight of the alienated young. And he was British.

Hobson, the Romantic critic, interested in theatricality and emotional power, naturally took a different line. Consequently his notice had less contemporary resonance but it can now be seen as a more accurate analysis of the play itself. In the introduction to the second *International Theatre Annual*, which appeared in 1957, a book devoted to providing a world-wide view of the theatre and which Hobson edited from 1956 to 1961, John Osborne explained what he thought was wrong with British society and how he felt the theatre could contribute to its recovery:

> I do not like the kind of society in which I find myself. I like it less and less. I love the theatre more than ever because I know that it is what I always dreamed it might be: a weapon. I am sure that it can be one of the decisive weapons of our time ... What is most disastrous about the British way of life is the British Way of Feeling, and this is something the theatre can attack. We need a new feeling as much as we need a new language. Out of the feeling will come the language.[512]

Tynan had correctly identified the aggressive, revolutionary tone in *Look Back in Anger*: indeed, the passion of the Angry Young Man, was the only tone he recognized, describing the final reconciliation scene as 'painful whimsy', but the second theatrical concern that Osborne reveals, a desire to rediscover a new way of feeling, is better explained by Hobson.

Just as Osborne's foreword had implied that, behind the rhetoric, there was more to his dramatic intentions than a didactic rant against society, Hobson's review of *Look Back in Anger*, 'A New Author',[513] sought to identify the two plays that are contained within the one work. The article begins with a characteristic piece of Hobson rhetoric, mixing seeming dismissal with vivid exaggeration and then enthusiastic encouragement:

> Mr John Osborne, the author of 'Look Back In Anger', is a writer who at present does not know what he is doing. He seems to think that he is crashing through the world with deadly right uppercuts, whereas all the time it is his unregarded left that is doing the damage. Though the blinkers still obscure his vision, he is a writer of outstanding promise, and the English Stage Company are to be congratulated on having discovered him.

For Hobson, Osborne's promise lay not in the first of the 'two plays in "Look Back In Anger"', which is 'ordinary and noisy ... with some wit but more prolixity', but in the second, which:

> is sketched into the margin of the first, and consists of hardly any words at all, but is controlled by a fine and sympathetic imagination, and is superbly played, in long passages of pain and silence, by Mary Ure.

To describe the immediacy of Jimmy Porter's language as ordinary is a mistake – it was, after all, a distinct change from the recent theatrical past – and Hobson undervalues the ground-breaking nature of the language employed. Whilst able to praise the 'flash of theatrical talent' on Osborne's part in the creation of Jimmy Porter, the use of the off-stage trumpet which the hero plays so jarringly and the brilliant opening of the third act, Hobson is not as enraptured as Tynan by the depiction of young talent frustrated by conservative attitudes. This may have been partly due to the age-difference between the two critics – Tynan was 29, Hobson 51. What to Tynan appeared an eloquent and understandable complaint against official attitudes seemed to Hobson more 'the inexhaustible outpouring of vicious self-pity' which came 'near to wearying the audience's patience'. This is not to say, however, that Hobson did not hold the work in as high an esteem as Tynan; he was simply temperamentally inclined to appreciate different aspects – in particular, the focus on the relationship between Jimmy and his wife.

The work's chief fault, Hobson feels, is that there 'are episodes of whimsy that might have made Barrie blush [he is thinking of the embarrassing squirrel and bear speech at the end of the play] and Jimmy's grievances are too rarely translated from words into concrete theatrical situations'. This is offset, however, by the poignant situation of Jimmy Porter's wife:

Alison Porter is a subsidiary in 'Look Back In Anger'; it is not she, but her husband, who throws into the past a maleficent gaze. But it is her endurance, her futile endeavour to escape, and her final breakdown which are the truly moving part of the play. The dramatist that is in Mr Osborne comes in the end to feel this himself, and it is to Alison, when at last she makes her heart-broken, grovelling, yet peace-securing submission, to whom the final big speech is given.

Hobson finds this attempt at marital reconciliation to be the fundamental moment in the play:

Here is in its way a kind of victory; and because it is a kind of victory, it releases instead of depressing the spirit. To know when to give up the struggle, to realise when the battle no longer counts, this also is a sort of triumph. There is a poignant moment during the second act when Alison desperately cries, 'I want a little peace.' It is peace that she gets at the end, as Raskolnikov gets it when he ceases to maintain himself innocent.

This concentration on a single moment of emotional power, the preference for insidious feeling as opposed to overt didacticism, and the delight in a portrayal of marital tenderness (no matter how oblique) is archetypal Hobson. He has spotted the underlying lyricism that underpins the work and it is this, as opposed to the political dimension, that gives the play its long-term value as a piece of theatrical art rather than as a mere historical curiosity.

The commercial success of *Look Back in Anger* stemmed from its novel and topical content – it 'appeared at precisely the right moment of time to meet [the] mood of disillusioned youth', as Hugh Hunt puts it [514] – and a combination of the publicity that was generated by Tynan and Hobson's support, the television excerpts and the widespread media discussion about the phenomenon of the Angry Young Man. Its long-term importance to the British theatre was equally as great as its immediate impact. For the first time since the war, commercial and repertory managements were able to see that plays by young, unknown British playwrights could return a profit. It encouraged other aspiring dramatists to tackle previously uncommercial themes, such as political commitment, contemporary social satire and broad issues of class. It ensured that the Royal Court came to be seen as a powerhouse of new, dynamic writers, nurtured by the benevolent George Devine, and it provided a second avenue of social protest to match the Absurdist approach of Beckett. Hobson's appreciation of this latter genre was further enhanced in the summer of 1956, when he travelled to Paris to view what he contentiously termed the 'definitive' version of *Waiting for Godot* – definitive, in that it had been approved by the author. This contact with the master, even through the second-hand medium of the play, is related in a suitably reverential criticism that attempts to chart the differences between the

Criterion production of 1955 and the author-approved French revival in 1956. Hobson states in 'A Revelation'[515] that, whilst the work 'is one of the great theatrical experiences of our time ... it is the nature of masterpieces to yield up different treasure to the various people who delve into them', and he explains that there are three notable differences in the French production. Firstly, the stage is emptier, emphasizing the total isolation of the tramps from comfort and distraction; secondly, Lucien Raimbourg plays Vladimir without the 'flicker of hope' which Hobson had controversially detected in Paul Daneman's portrayal, deepening the audience's sympathy for his predicament; and, thirdly, Hobson is enormously impressed by the performance of Jean Martin as Lucky, which 'reaches over the very edge of bearable':

> His shaking and quivering, which never cease, are a miracle of acting, and appalling to behold. They have the cosmic terror of an earthquake, and the private horror of St. Vitus's Dance. With incredible and frightening virtuosity, they continue throughout his celebrated speech, which pours from him like the agonized scream of a dumb man. It is in this terrifying figure, rather than in those of the tramps, that Mr Beckett's compassion for mankind reveals itself, a compassion unlimited, intensely dramatic, and almost unlit by any hope.

It is the quality of such clear and evocative observations – conveying the actor's achievement and relating this to a critical interpretation – that renders Hobson's magnificent obsession with *Waiting for Godot* so compelling. The uniquely personal revelation of Hobson's thrill at his discovery – '"Waiting For Godot" stays in the mind as an illumination, bizarre, lovely, and ribald, of the soul; "En Attendant Godot" is as unforgettable as a knife twisted in the ribs. It is only a few hours since I saw the performance, and the wound is still in my entrails' – is the reason why the review is so tremendously exciting to read, and his passionate enthusiasm for the play, together with his identification with Lucky's isolation, stimulates a similar act of empathy on the part of the reader for Hobson himself, creating a sense of curiosity and wonder at the work. This empathetic appeal lies at the root of Hobson's most powerful writing.

A second rallying-point for the new generation of theatre-goers was Joan Littlewood's production of Brendan Behan's *The Quare Fellow* at Stratford East, which received its first British performance on 24 May 1956. Behan's dramatic technique of centring the action around a character who never appears – the condemned man – was a highly effective way of creating an implicit condemnation of a hotly debated contemporary issue, capital punishment. This focus on an instinctively left-wing attitude, together with the absence of star roles, the need for ensemble playing, the Brechtian depiction of characters as types (Prisoner A, Prisoner B, The Other Fellow) and the interpolation of songs, required a very different company from that which had dominated the West End for the last ten years. Joan Littlewood's Theatre Workshop, with its emphasis on group acting, personal selflessness, hard work for little reward and a left-wing outlook on life, fitted the bill perfectly.

The Quare Fellow's tragicomic questioning of official attitudes and its contemporary relevance – the bill to end hanging, introduced by the Labour MP Sydney Silverman, obtained a majority in the House of Commons in July 1956 – struck a chord with many play-goers, and its opening run was so well received that it soon transferred from East to West, to the Comedy Theatre. Hobson had not reviewed the original Stratford production, but he sought to make amends with a notice of the opening night at the Comedy. In 'The Pity of It'[516] he relates the sense of deflation that this first-night audience experienced:

> On Tuesday night, at the Comedy theatre, it was obvious to ears even less sharp than mine that the audience had assembled to cheer; but as the performance went on, and expectations, pitched absurdly high, were disappointed, the determination gradually weakened, and at the end the dinner jackets and the bare shoulders in the stalls made only a moderate hullabaloo, while afterwards, in the warm air outside, the gallery openly discussed its disillusion.

That Hobson regards this as unfortunate is obvious from his sympathy for the playwright: 'I was sorry for this, and I was sorry for Mr Behan. Less should have been asked for him, but more, much more, ought to have been given.' What made the work so disappointing for the theatre-goers, who had hoped that the play would be relentlessly political – the absence of a direct denunciation of the inhumanity of hanging, peppered with critiques of the Establishment – was exactly what, for Hobson, made the work so theatrically effective. For him, it was another work whose suggestive, allusive quality ensured that it was infinitely superior to more obviously didactic pieces:

> 'The Quare Fellow' is not the story of the last moments of a condemned man. The condemned murderer never appears except in the conversation of his fellow-prisoner. It is not, dramatically, a plea for the abolition of capital punishment, whatever may be the private philosophy of the author. If, therefore, you expect a sensational tale of hanging, or a sharp argument for the shelving of the death penalty, you will be disappointed. What interests Mr Behan the dramatist about hanging, as distinct from what he may feel about it as a citizen, is its terrible, trivial, and impressive ritual.

Behan's detailing of this ritual – 'the digging of the grave, the holy oils with which are anointed the feet of a condemned Catholic, the bacon and eggs on the day before the execution' – creates, for the critic, 'a feeling of elegiac reverence', and it is this identification of the poetry behind the prose that helps the reader to spot the universality of *The Quare Fellow*. With this review, Hobson had started to demonstrate that the topical subject-matter of the New Wave drama would provide no barrier to his critical appreciation as long as the works conformed to his touchstone criteria – they must move him and they must always be theatrically effective. He is able to praise Behan's 'ritual elegy' with great conviction because the playwright has obeyed these edicts, and he was sufficiently moved to end his review with a rebuttal of those first-nighters who were offended that the work was not out of the ordinary, by stating that 'There is nothing quite like it in London.'

If the old certainties of society were beginning to be questioned in the theatre in 1956, through works such as *Look Back in Anger* and *The Quare Fellow*, then the old certainties of theatre practice were inevitably subjected to reassessment as well. One issue that had been debated periodically, from the time that the Lord Chamberlain was empowered to vet plays under Sir Robert Walpole's stage Licensing Act of 1737, was that of the censorship of the theatre. Hobson himself had considered the issue in one of his earliest pieces of journalism, an editorial written for the *Christian Science Monitor* in 1929 entitled 'The Freedom of the Press'. In this short article he puritanically claimed that 'the censorship of the stage, an institution readily lending itself to abuse, has frequently failed to work satisfactorily', whereas the law as it stood on the press functioned well because 'it is not so much important to be free to say what one likes, as to have something worth while to say'.[517] He had modified his opinion by 1932 – but only to the extent that he had come to feel, in 'Censorship and "The Green Pastures"',[518] that the system worked well because the Lord Chamberlain was often granted the opportunity to reassess his original decision, since banned works could sometimes be produced in private theatre clubs. This article had been written by the 25-year-old Hobson in response to the ban on *The Green Pastures* by Marc Connelly for representing the deity on stage.

This myopic view was no longer sustainable by the mid-1950s because a number of playwrights were now choosing to portray issues that were increasingly discussed in British society but which were still falling victim to the censor's pen. The tectonic plates of social values were beginning to shift and a confluence of altered moral attitudes was starting to make the Lord Chamberlain's position increasingly problematic. In 1953, for example, the Kinsey Report on *Sexual Behaviour in the Human Female* was published, and its findings, including the revelation that half of the 6,000 women questioned had admitted to having had sexual intercourse before marriage, shattered the taboo that sex should be confined to the marital bedroom.[519] In the same year Ian Fleming introduced James Bond to the world in *Casino Royale*, a character who made it fashionable for a man to be portrayed with a vigorous sexual appetite. Religious uncertainty, exacerbated by the Cold War; the questioning of official attitudes; the diminishing of respect for the Establishment; the rise of the scantily clad sex symbol (Monroe, Bardot, Dors); the emergence of a 'Rock 'n Roll' culture; and the dawning of a liberal conscience that demanded access to contraception and the loosening of the laws governing homosexuality all brought into question the value of an institution that failed to permit freedom of expression.

The play that highlighted the constriction of censorship in 1956 was not the product of a British playwright but of an American, Arthur Miller. Miller had already experienced official disapproval of a sinister kind when he was summoned before the House Un-American Activities Committee in June 1953 and requested to supply the names of alleged Communist sympathizers in the arts – a formative experience that led to the creation of *The Crucible* in the same year. In Britain, however, the cause of discomfort three years later was not any perceived political sympathy, but a readiness on Miller's part to refer to a moral issue that was moving closer to the centre stage of public discussion yet banned as a subject for drama. By touching on the theme of homosexuality, Miller was also introducing into the public domain a topic which had a peculiar resonance for a number in the theatrical profession. Many actors derived a sense of security from the close-knit nature of the acting community which permitted them to express their homosexuality, whilst at the same time many also fell victim to the repressive laws that frequently ensnared homosexuals. The most celebrated actor-victim of recent years had been Sir John Gielgud, who was arrested in October 1953 for a 'homosexual offence' in Chelsea, fined ten pounds by the magistrate, Mr E. R. Guest, and advised to pay a visit to his doctor.[520]

Arthur Miller's sixth play, *A View from the Bridge*, emphasizes the sexual confusion of the central character, the longshoreman Eddie Carbone. Initially it appears that Eddie's concern for the welfare of his niece Catherine, whilst over-protective, is understandable, given the tough quay-side environment in which they live. As the action progresses, Eddie's concern develops into a hint of sexual jealousy, yet when the blond Rodolpho, an illegal immigrant from Sicily whom Eddie agrees to shelter, arrives in the house, it becomes clear that Eddie's fury at Rodolpho's tenderness for Catherine stems less from disappointment at his own inability to possess his niece than from a repressed homosexual desire for her lover. This homosexual theme is more than the 'strand' to which Hobson refers in 'Censorship in the British Theater'[521] and which meant that the Lord Chamberlain refused to grant the play a public performance licence. It is an integral part of the action, with Eddie continually claiming that 'the guy ain't right', deprecating Rodolpho's handsome appearance and eventually delivering the startling kiss in Act Two – ostensibly to humiliate Rodolpho, but plainly with overtones of sexual desire. The Lord Chamberlain's intransigence meant that several London managers decided to re-form the defunct Watergate Club so as to arrange a series of club performances of this play at the Comedy Theatre to highlight the restrictive nature of censorship. The production was given some extra publicity when Miller's wife, Marilyn Monroe, became the first member of the New Watergate Theatre Club prior to the first night on 11 October.

Before the play's première in London, Hobson chose to use his *Sunday Times* column to discuss several questions to which the formation of the club (which also intended to present two other banned plays, Robert Anderson's *Tea and Sympathy* and Tennessee Williams's *Cat on a Hot Tin Roof*) had given rise. He had already stated in 'Censorship in the British Theater' in August that he did not feel that the power of the Lord Chamberlain would be reduced on account of the controversy – censorship had too strong a hold in Britain – and he similarly avoided the question of the merits of censorship itself in this article, 'Censor's Debate'.[522] Instead, he chose to consider two points of view that the renewed public interest in the issue had provoked:

> From the discussions I have heard and read on this subject, two convictions seem to be firmly planted in people's minds on both sides of the Atlantic. The first is that the present inferiority of British to American playwrighting is due to the shackles which the Lord Chamberlain places on English drama. The second is that, outside Britain, the theatre freely and boldly probes into questions of sexual perversion, the argument being that by doing so it brings itself into intelligent relation with an important contemporary social problem.
>
> I do not defend the censorship; nevertheless, neither of these convictions is true.

They are not true, he argues, because American dramatists, whilst not having to face a Lord Chamberlain, have 'to reckon with the censorship of American public opinion, which in its way, is just as rigid', and (citing the example of *The Crucible*) because: 'Any man who has a masterpiece, or anything like a masterpiece, in him, will get it out, no matter what rules of censorship, official or unofficial, exist.' That Hobson is too optimistic here, placing excessive reliance on the specious argument that works of quality will always find an audience, is incontestable. He underestimates the power of the Lord Chamberlain to dictate the environment in which new playwrights should work and is unable to perceive that the freedom of expression in a changing society was an integral part of the armoury of the New Wave dramatists. Consequently, his concluding statement – 'The reason that more good plays are being written in America than in England is not that America has no Lord Chamberlain. It is, quite simply, that America has more good dramatists' – is uncharacteristically simplistic.

Hobson's attitude to censorship thus far illustrates one of the dangers of a subjective approach to criticism. His personal antipathy to homosexuality – a 'sexual perversion' that represents the negation of his belief in the sanctity of marriage – has prevented him from considering the wider implications of the role of a professional censor in upholding the values of an Establishment which playwrights are now beginning to probe. His review of *A View from the Bridge* two weeks later admired the 'the skill and the maintained freshness of inspiration with which Mr Miller has changed a short one-act drama into a full evening's programme',[523] but lamented the fact that 'Things which brooded in the dark recesses of undefined feeling have been brought into the light and rendered explicit'. Yet the rewritten version of the play, which heightens the theme of marital sexual maladjustment, remains highly suggestive and undidactic. When the critic claims that: 'Mr Miller has tarnished his play's glory. As it stands, it is among the finest plays seen in London – not this year but for many years; as it stood, it was a masterpiece', the tone of the conclusion, both commending and criticizing, appears inconsistent with the general sentiments of the review and of the earlier article, 'A Censor's Debate'. This periphrastic thinking must surely stem from a discomfort with homosexuality, a theme which Hobson was often to treat erratically. His later review of Tennessee Williams's *Cat on a Hot Tin Roof*, for example, strikes a completely opposite note when he upbraids the playwright for writing 'as though Gide had never been':

> [Williams] blushes and stammers like a Sunday-school teacher. Just when it seems likely that the awful unmentionable word might pop out, someone cries, in an access of embarrassing prudery, 'You are naming it dirty.'
>
> 'You are naming it dirty.' Nothing could more vividly illustrate the lower-middle class inhibitions of the theatre than that, about homosexuality, Mr Williams, a dramatist of high talent, shall speak much less plainly than the Archbishop of Canterbury.[524]

Ironically, the absolute ban on homosexuality as a theatrical theme in Britain was abolished in 1958 by the Lord Chamberlain, Lord Scarborough, in the light of the Wolfenden Report on *Homosexuality and Prostitution*,[525] a decision that Hobson felt would not necessarily lessen the overall moral tone of British drama.[526]

One element of the theatre that Hobson did address with a fundamental consistency throughout his career was his conception of the actor as an artist. Sandwiched in between Behan's *The Quare Fellow* and the West End production of Brecht's *The Good Woman of Setzuan*, two works that rejected the notion of a play as a vehicle for the star player, was an Old Vic performance of *Timon of Athens* which featured Hobson's favourite actor, Sir Ralph Richardson. The review, 'Here's Glory',[527] took the form of a eulogy and, in its description of Richardson as a slow starter, bears a remarkable similarity to the 1955 notice of Olivier's Macbeth:

> Wednesday was one of London's golden evenings in the theatre. It restored to the stage one of our finest actors, one of the finest actors in the world. It restored him in triumph: and the triumph when it came, was all the sweeter in that for a long time the issue seemed doubtful.

As with Olivier, Richardson began poorly and had an uncomfortable first act. Then, in the second act, 'the transformation and the miracle occurred'

– not because he suddenly remembered Shakespeare's conception of Timon as a man brought to a bitter recognition of the selfishness of his friends, but because Richardson offered an interpretation of the role that was honest, heartfelt and accorded with his own personal philosophy. Not for Richardson the raging, cursing Timon that a reading of the text might imply:

> Sir Ralph cannot understand the wickedness and bitterness of men; of all our players, his is the eye that is most perceptive of goodness and nobility. And so, probably unconsciously, driven by the force of his compulsive personality, he plays Timon, in the later scenes, not as a screaming, lesser Lear, but as a resigned, misfortune-accepting Edward II. Each Shakespearean viciousness of phrase is transformed into a threnody, a lamentation. Borne along by the music of the verse, blandly kicking the meaning out of the window, he presents a Timon on whom there falls at last 'a silence luminous and serene, a shining peace.'

In Hobson's view, Richardson's idiosyncratic approach to the part was valid because it was an original act of creation that added a new perspective to the work. As if aware of the controversy that the production would create, Hobson sought to defend it with a similarly passionate intensity:

> This kind of acting may be, and is, hotly disputed. Let the academic and the narrow-minded call it a flagrant betrayal of the intentions of the author, or the product of slipshod reading. I don't care: neither, I imagine, does Sir Ralph. It is, quite simply, creative acting of the highest kind, in which the actor as artist presents to the world his own vision, and thereby enriches it.

To this Romantic critic, the actor as artist presenting the world with his own vision, a revelation of his own personality, represented the height of theatrical achievement for a performer. This opinion had not been formulated recently. It had first been stated in the article 'The Actor as Artist' as long ago as 1933,[528] was developed during the war and its aftermath, and was then reformulated in Hobson's book, *The Theatre Now* (1954), in which, borrowing Gilles Quéant's terms, Hobson had divided actors into *acteurs* (players who impose themselves on a part) and *comédiens* (players who become the part).[529] The finest performers were those who were capable of being *acteurs* as well as *comédiens*, since he states in *The Theatre Now* that:

> I once looked on Sir Ralph Richardson purely as an *acteur*, as a player who used to artistic ends his natural qualities of kindness and humanity. But his performance in Doctor Sloper in *The Heiress*, a performance of extraordinarily precise and clinical cruelty, showed him to be a *comédien* also.[530]

Victor Lazarow's claim that 'To Hobson, the true artist is the *acteur*'[531] is too sweeping, in that it ignores Hobson's belief that, while the philosophy of the *acteur* should predominate, the technique of the *comédien* can only enhance the achievement of the *acteur*. This is proved by the opening paragraphs of Hobson's description of Edwige Feuillère's return to London in March 1957:

> In a letter which he wrote to Jacques Rivière in 1910 Claudel observed that every artist comes into the world to make a personal statement, to 'say one single thing, one single little thing; it is this into which all his work is integrated.' His function is to establish, as eloquently, as profoundly, as dazzlingly, as poignantly as he can, whatever illumination may lie at the heart of his personality.
>
> This is the conception of greatness which I accept; on the necessarily rare occasions on which it is legitimate to talk of greatness in acting it is the test I apply. I am aware that there are many who think differently. They hold that the mark of greatness in a player is what Baudelaire found to be 'the incomparable privilege of the poet, who can at his wish be both himself and someone else. Like those wandering souls that seek a body ... the artist enters into whatever character he wills.' There, sharply opposed, are the two criteria of what makes a great actor or actress. On the one hand, in its highest degree, intensity; on the other, versatility. Much of the excitement of the past week at the Palace has lain in the fact that, not merely by one test or the other, but by both, Madame Edwige Feuillère has demonstrated her unchallengeable supremacy, a supremacy which in my opinion is absolute, unshakeable, and royal.[532]

Feuillère's achievement, which Hobson concludes makes her 'the greatest actress in the world', is derived from the fact that she is the archetypal *actrice* who is blessed with the technique of the *comédienne*.

Why was Hobson keen to stress the importance of the actor at this time? One answer may lie in the increasing interest in Brechtian techniques of collaboration, which necessarily provided limited scope for the *acteur*. In epic theatre individual actors were subordinate to the company ethos of dispelling an excessive emotional commitment on the part of the audience to ensure that it assessed objectively the events that occurred on stage. The emotions could only be engaged if this enhanced the activity of the brain. For a critic who felt that the theatre was a place for more than rational thought, this philosophy was now regarded with disdain.

The third rallying-point for new theatre-goers in 1956 was the visit to Britain of the Berliner Ensemble in August and the production of *The Good Woman of Setzuan* by the Royal Court in November, which permitted both Hobson and Kenneth Tynan to clarify their feelings about didactic theatre. Tynan had despised the Old Vic performance of *Timon of Athens*, terming it 'the ghastly norm' for London and ridiculing Richardson's highly eccentric interpretation:

> To the role of the scoutmaster Sir Ralph Richardson brings his familiar attributes: a vagrant eye, gestures so eccentric that their true significance could only be revealed by trepanning, and a mode of speech that democratically regards all symbols as equal.[533]

Conversely, the visit of the Berliner Ensemble had been a revelation for the *Observer* critic. Here was a succession of works (*Mother Courage*, *Trumpets and Drums*, and *Caucasian Chalk Circle*) that not only rejected the conventionality of the London stage, but allowed contemporary reality to intrude:

> As Eric Bentley said, 'Brecht does not believe in inner reality, a higher reality or a deeper reality, but simply in reality.' It is something for which we have lost the taste: raised on a diet of gin and goulash, we call Brecht naive when he gives us bread and wine. He wrote morality plays and directed them as such: and if we of the West End and Broadway find them as tiresome as religion, we are in a shrinking minority. There is a world elsewhere. 'I was bored to death,' said a bright Chelsea girl after 'Mother Courage'. 'Bored to life' would have been apter.

Part of the Chelsea girl's boredom would have stemmed from the fact that the play was delivered in German and Tynan's review is mainly concerned with visual descriptions and general theoretical discussion, but he leaves the reader in no doubt of his adherence to the cause and is able to give a comprehensible explanation of the 'Verfremdungseffekt':

> the clearest illustration of 'A-effect' comes in the national anthem, which the Berliner Ensemble have so arranged that it provokes, instead of patriotic ardour, laughter. The melody is backed by a trumpet *obbligato* so feeble and hopeless that it suggests a boy bugler on a rapidly-sinking ship. The orchestration is a criticism of the lyrics and a double flavour results, the ironic flavour which is 'A-effect' ...[534]

Hobson, too, understood the irreverent purpose of the orchestration, calling it, in his review 'A Doubt about Brecht',[535] 'deliberate carelessness', and he also identifies the dramatic intention that lies behind *Mother Courage* – 'We are not expected to sympathise with Mother Courage: we are intended rather to realise that in war human nature corrodes and putrefies' – but he finds the fundamental premise of epic theatre to run too directly against his love of the implicit, the suggestive and the revelatory moment to be able to accept it as theatrically effective:

> To claim that the theatre, where hundreds of people are crowded together in conditions of more or less discomfort, subject to all the influences of mass suggestion, is a suitable place for clear thinking seems to me childish ... The audience which thinks that it is thinking at these performances flatters and deceives itself.

The palpable note of irritation in this extract may have had as much to do with Tynan's dynamic championing of a brave, new cause, couched in a suitably accessible idiom, as with Hobson's clear discomfort at Brecht's dramatic theory. Although Hobson was able to write with some wit in the 1957 edition of the *International Theatre Annual* that the 'most engagingly volatile of my colleagues from time to time fills out his columns with what I have said the week before. So much so, in fact, that I have often thought of letting him have the proofs of my next Sunday's article in order that he may keep strictly up to date', and although he attempts to claim that: 'this regular suggestion that one's views are so influential that they must be almost systematically denied lest they corrupt the public is perhaps the next to the greatest compliment a dramatic critic can claim',[536] it seems likely that Tynan's eloquent obsession with a topic about which Hobson was uneasy proved galling to Hobson. In any event, Hobson decided to clarify his attitude to epic theatre three months later, after witnessing Peggy Ashcroft in the demanding role of Shen Te in *The Good Woman of Setzuan*.

Hobson's intention of setting the record straight is apparent from the tone of the opening paragraph of 'Bertolt Brecht',[537] written in November 1956: 'Now that a first-class company has brought Brecht in English to the West End it is time to speak out.' His central thesis is that Brecht was writing for 'an ignorant proletariat ... which had been brutalised by war, starvation, and oppression', and that this is the reason why epic theatre consists of broad gestures instead of subtle brush-strokes. Although he does not acknowledge this in his review, Hobson is disturbed by the direct and elemental nature of epic theatre and occasionally fails to prevent his analysis slipping from objectivity to condescension:

> An audience which goes to the Court Theatre and plays the game properly, which throws away its sophistication, abandons its irritation at being told the same thing over and over again, leaves its intelligence in the cloakroom, and is willing to introduce the mentality of six into the bodies of sixteen, twenty-six or sixty will have a tolerable time.

Significantly, what most disturbs the critic is that talented, young dramatists might be influenced by Brecht's example:

> There is an alarming rumour ... that John Osborne, who appears in 'The Good Woman of Setzuan' (not to much advantage, by the way), is likely to be influenced by Brecht in the new play he is writing to follow up the striking 'Look Back In Anger' ... I earnestly hope that this is not so, though Mr Osborne himself does not deny it. Mr Osborne has a decided theatrical talent for representing young people as morbid, cowardly, self-pitying, complaining and weak-willed. It is in this that his genius lies, not in devising techniques to suit the sort of people who have failed at eleven-plus. It will be a desolating day for his own

future, and, in a small way, for the future of the English theatre, if anyone persuades him that the case is otherwise.

Apart from the irony that the structure of *The Entertainer* (the new play in question) does indeed appear to have been influenced by epic theatre – and that Hobson was to marvel at the work – this review confirms that Hobson was as temperamentally disinclined to write effortlessly about Brecht as he was about homosexuality. Whatever validity his critical objections about Brechtian technique possessed was marred by an untypical churlishness which pervaded his considerations of the German playwright. That Tynan wrote about Brecht as if he were a prophet proclaiming the second coming – 'The production must not be missed by anyone interested in hearing the fundamental problems of human (as opposed to Western European) existence discussed in the theatre'[538] – merely emphasized the mediocrity of Hobson's own approach. Yet this was an aberration in a year notable for an intelligent analysis of groundbreaking new work. The very next week Hobson was urging play-goers to flock to the Arts Theatre 'in thousands' to witness 'the wildly funny ... and disturbing' *The Bald Prima Donna*, by Eugène Ionesco. Hobson felt that the French playwright's style was the antithesis of the German's, since 'Brecht believes that if society is perfect, man will be perfect, too; Ionesco believes that if society is perfect, man morally and aesthetically speaking will be annihilated.'[539] No clearer illustration of the dichotomy between Hobson's critical philosophy and Tynan's could be displayed.

Two external events at the end of 1956 added to the mood of collective uncertainty in Britain. The crushing of the insurrection in Hungary in November caused despondency amongst those on the left who had hoped that Khrushchev (who had visited London in April) might introduce a more humane version of Communism which could be adopted by the West; whilst on the right, the humiliation of the Suez débâcle precipitated the resignation of the very pinnacle of the Tory Establishment, the Prime Minister, Anthony Eden. The disaster in Egypt had the more profound effect on the British psyche and galvanized a number of authors and playwrights in a way that would have appeared unimaginable just one year before. It had long been rooted in British mythology that the Suez Canal was the umbilical chord that linked Britain to its empire, a line of communications that had to be protected at all cost, so when it was decided in July 1956 to teach the nationalist Nasser a lesson for refusing to join the Baghdad pact and for recognizing Communist China, this was merely the continuation of a policy of imperialism that equated colonial co-operation with abject subservience. To remind Egypt of her duty, Britain and America duly withdrew the loans that had been promised for the Aswan high dam, but Nasser refused to conform to type, stating that Egypt would pay for the dam out of dues paid to the Canal Company, which he duly nationalized on 26 July. Eden, furious at this show of independence and mindful that 25 per cent of all British exports and imports passed through the waterway,[540] colluded with Israel and France so that, under the Treaty of Sèvres, Israel would attack Egypt, and Britain and France would issue a phoney ultimatum calling for the temporary occupation of the canal to separate the combatants.[541] In the event, the Israelis duly attacked Egyptian positions in the Sinai on 29 October, whereas the Anglo-French force merely managed to chug twenty-five miles down the canal before a cease-fire was announced. The whole endeavour had proved to be a total fiasco. Nasser remained in power with a status greatly enhanced in the Arab world; the canal was obstructed and petrol soon had to be rationed; the Aswan dam was eventually built with Russian aid; Britain's reserves of foreign currency had been drained; and, with supreme irony, the canal quickly returned to capable Egyptian control in 1957. The most significant and far-reaching effect of the whole affair was that Britain could no longer regard herself as a world power. The disgrace of world censure was distressing, the shock at not having been able to defeat the Egyptians enormous, but the recognition that, in the modern age, none but the two superpowers could take independent action on a world scale was, for many, the most humiliating aspect of the entire misadventure. Jimmy Porter's disgust at the country's blinkered self-complacency now acquired a deeper resonance.

The interweaving of old and new theatrical impulses in 1957, impulses increasingly generated by events outside the theatre, is intriguingly documented by Hobson's reviews and social comments. The *Evening Standard* awards for 1956 again reflected the difficulties of the judges in categorizing the new genres of drama that had been emerging since 1955. The choice of the best new play went not to *Look Back in Anger*, but to Peter Ustinov's *Romanoff and Juliet* – Hobson had remained loyal to the French, voting for Anouilh's *The Waltz of the Toreadors*[542] – with a special award for the 'most promising British Playwright of the Year' for Osborne. It seems appropriate that, as with *Waiting for Godot* the previous year, Osborne's work was deemed so innovatory in content that the conventional categories of the awards were unable to cater for it. Conventions were being challenged in front of the proscenium arch, too. Although booing by the audience was not unknown, a new impatience with works that were confusing and melodramatic was now detectable. This sometimes caused pain to a critic as generous as Hobson and he was distressed by what he considered to be the 'murder' of the American musical *The Crystal Heart*, providing an unnerving depiction of audience blood-lust in 'A Protest'[543]:

> I listened to the first performance of this musical by William Archibald in rage and anguish. One of our most sensitive actors, sitting immediately in front of me, buried his face in his hands as the upper circle, the dress circle and the back rows of the stalls cat-called and slow-handclapped the play almost continuously from half-way through the opening act until the end. The audience's worst cruelties were directed

at Gladys Cooper, who responded with magnificent venom; at the close, such victory as there was lay with her, for the tremendous curtsy with which, like a spirited Miranda mockingly kneeling to Caliban, she provocatively challenged the theatre, was decidedly more impressive than the simian howls which greeted it.

The play, not surprisingly, was withdrawn last night. Once again an English first-night audience ... has a murder to its credit. Let it be as proud of it as it can.

Hobson's compassion for Gladys Cooper is provoked by the courage with which she withstood this abuse and it echoes the admiration that the critic felt for the playwright William Douglas Home, when he was similarly vilified after the first night of his play *Ambassador Extraordinary* in 1948.[544] Douglas Home returned in 1957 with *The Iron Duchess*, a work that Hobson arguably claimed provided a bridge between the theatrical values of the past and the future:

William Douglas Home is a bold man, and an optimist. He is ready to affront the class conscious gallery by suggesting that wit, grace, nonchalance, and casual courage are the monopoly of dukes and duchesses ... and to disturb the stalls by arguing that the only sensible way of dealing with recalcitrant cooks and colonies is to give them everything they want as soon as they ask for it.[545]

Hobson's high estimation of Douglas Home's work had begun with *Now Barabbas* ... in 1947 and this further illustrates the importance of loyalty to his criticism. Although (as with Home) occasionally hard to follow, this loyalty helped to create a climate of reassurance for writers whom Hobson was keen to champion and whom he felt might be vulnerable to adverse criticism. The nurturing of theatrical talent was an integral part of his critical vision and, as Michael Billington states, if Hobson was a little over-enthusiastic in his support of Douglas Home, this was acceptable given that 'sticking with Osborne, Pinter, Beckett and Bond was loyalty to a praiseworthy degree'.[546]

During the opening fortnight of April 1957 two eagerly awaited plays, which, in uniquely different ways, focused on the plight of human existence, premièred in London. Deriving part of their impact from the uncertainties of the international situation and Britain's diminishing importance on the world stage, they were both performed at the Royal Court, thereby confirming that the vibrant heart of the London theatre was moving away from the conventional West End of H. M. Tennent-inspired musicals and drawing-room comedies. The first work, Samuel Beckett's *Fin de Partie*, had been published in Britain in February 1957 and eagerly devoured by Hobson, who had predicted in the *Christian Science Monitor* that 'Mr Beckett's admirers will not be disappointed in it, nor will his opponents be converted'.[547] This proved to be an accurate prophesy. Hobson, the chief worshipper at the shrine, was granted extra column space by his sub-editor at *The Sunday Times* to preach the message:

> The reception of Samuel Beckett's new play has been precisely what the admirers of 'Waiting for Godot' would desire. 'Fin de Partie' has outraged the Philistines, earned the contempt of half-wits and filled those who are capable of telling the difference between a theatre and a bawdy-house with a profound and sombre and paradoxical joy. Its presentation is among the greatest services that the English Stage Company has rendered to the British public.[548]

Hobson is rarely as assertive as this in the opening paragraph of a review, normally preferring a contradictory or paradoxical statement which would be resolved later in the article. It is a measure of his delight in Beckett that he commences his analysis in such approbatory terms, and it also testifies to his mischievous desire further to incense the detractors of the playwright, who were capable of such apoplectic reactions when confronted with his work.

The French production of *Waiting for Godot*, more terse and devoid of hope than the English production at the Arts Theatre (and approved by the playwright himself), had persuaded Hobson that his original belief that the work contained a message of Christian optimism had been too definitive, although he was to defend, with characteristic élan, his controversial assertion that the raising of Paul Daneman's hat symbolized Christian hope:

> I have since been assured by the actor who played the role that this was the exact opposite of what he was trying to convey and insofar as I had persuaded Beckett to say anything on the matter, which is a very difficult thing to do, I think that he agrees with the actor rather than with me – nevertheless, the fact that it made an impression on me is the important fact.[549]

His reaction to *Fin de Partie* reveals a more plausible recognition that Beckett's achievement lies in an agnostic approach. Hobson wonders whether Clov and Hamm reside in a place where life is coming to an end and whether the banality of their talk and actions reflects the futility of their existence. He is swift to point out, however, that the apparent simplicity of the work is challengingly deceptive and that the search for concrete meaning is futile:

> Mr Beckett is a poet; and the business of a poet is not to clarify, but to suggest, to imply, to employ words with auras of association, with a reaching towards a vision, a probing down into an emotion, beyond the compass of explicit definition.

As a poet, Beckett 'shows us a mystery outside the grasp of any other dramatist now writing' and creates beauty from the most unpropitious of rhetorical devices:

Mr Beckett is above all the poet of postponement, of avoidance of action and decision. That is why Clov shuffles, for walking would bring him to his objective quicker. That is why he drops his telescope before looking through the window. It delays his action. That is why Mr Beckett is always repetitive.

The point is that by inexhaustible repetition he can almost indefinitely prevent himself from coming to the point. A day will arrive when we shall know even as we are known. Mr Beckett and his characters are mortally afraid of the unveiling of the last dark and terrible secret. He does not believe, he cannot believe, that the secret may be something of joy and light.[550]

As a Christian Scientist, Hobson hopes that Beckett might believe that this secret is the prospect of Christian salvation, but he is objective enough to realize that the play itself offers no conclusive proof either way and that it derives its strength from this very ambiguity. Kenneth Tynan, increasingly preoccupied with the notion of a theatre that reflected ideas of reality and social progress, could not match this brilliantly intuitive assessment of Beckett's style. In the provocatively titled 'A Philosophy of Despair', which appeared in the *Observer* on the same day as Hobson's article, he failed to understand the importance of suggestiveness to Beckett and upbraided him for an offence that the dramatist does not actually commit:

> The play is an allegory about authority; an attempt to dramatise the neurosis that makes men love power. So far, so good. I part company with Beckett only when he insists that the problem is insoluble, that this is a deterministic world.[551]

If Brecht had recently become Hobson's millstone, then, on the evidence of this review, Beckett was about to become Tynan's.

Following on immediately after *Fin de Partie* at the Royal Court was John Osborne's successor to *Look Back in Anger*, *The Entertainer*. It was a significant production not simply because the uncertainties that Hungary and Suez had provoked were implicit within the play, but because it was the first time that a prominent member of the theatrical establishment, its titular head, Sir Laurence Olivier, had joined forces with a representative of the new, acerbic generation of dramatists, John Osborne. That this coming-together took place at the creative home of the new movement, the Royal Court, provided a visual confirmation of the breaking-down of the old order. Hobson had warned Osborne against being unduly influenced by Brecht in his review of *The Good Person of Setzuan* the previous November,[552] and although the playwright claimed, in *A Better Class of Person*, that the seed for the play came not from epic theatre but from a 'shaky fragment of theatrical memory',[553] when his mother related an anti-Semitic music-hall sketch called *Humanity* to him, the structure of *The Entertainer*, with its thirteen numbers creating a montage effect and its songs which offset the action, does bear similarities to Brecht's dramatic approach. John Russell Taylor, in *Anger and After*, claims that Osborne had 'not fully grasped what the epic theatre was about',[554] but the opposite is true. By judiciously utilizing the epic form without placing excessive reliance on didactic thought, Osborne was able to strike a note of poignantly elegiac despair which gave the work its emotional power. Structural considerations were not what caught Hobson's eye, however:

> Coming to the Court Theatre immediately after *Fin de Partie*, Samuel Beckett's bleak and unwavering statement of philosophic despair, John Osborne's new play necessarily appears sentimental.
>
> Like Mr Beckett, Mr Osborne appears not to believe in God, nor in personal relationships, nor in ethics, nor in love of class, nor in self-respect, nor in self-restraint. Mr Beckett would carry this to its logical conclusion of blank negation. Mr Osborne is less tough. His characters are hard, selfish, brutal, gin-swilling, blasphemous wastrels. But, when he has got them into apparently irrecoverable postures of moral contemptibility, Mr Osborne relents.

Hobson recognized that, for all his seediness, Archie Rice's refusal to capitulate to the apathetic audiences before whom he labours and to the dreadful realization that his spiritual life is a sham actually constitute 'a form of heroism'. It did not matter, therefore, that the accumulation of Archie's troubles lacked plausibility, because Osborne demonstrated a tender sympathy towards the entertainer, and Laurence Olivier gave a breathtaking depiction of pride brought low by personal tragedy:

> I do not believe that a man like Archie, with no strength of character, and no positive conviction of any kind could have borne his disasters with such bruised panache. That is why I called Mr Osborne's play sentimental. But its theatrical effect is enormous. Splendid as Sir Laurence is when showing us Archie on the stage, he is even finer when he gets home to his squalid drunken family. There are ten minutes, from the moment when he begins telling his daughter, with a defiant, ashamed admiration, of a negress singing a spiritual in some low night club, to his breakdown on hearing of his son's death, when he touches the extreme limits of pathos. You will not see more magnificent acting than this anywhere in the world.[555]

Hobson's review was by far the most enthusiastic that the play received[556] – the combination of *acteur* at the height of his powers and young writer fulfilling his potential proving to be an irresistible mixture for him. Tynan, although accepting that Osborne had written 'one of the great acting parts of our age',[557] again reflected his concern with social didacticism when he concluded that the author had 'planned a gigantic social mural and carried it out in a colour range too narrow for the job'. It was left to Hobson to describe the sense of occasion that presided over what has passed down into theatrical legend as one of the most memorable nights in twentieth-century British theatre. No wonder Hobson's copy-editor placed his article under the title 'A Magnificent Week'.

The third member of the theatrical triumvirate that Hobson does not mention in 'A Magnificent Week', the director, was by far its youngest. It was only in the immediate post-war years (and particularly after 1956) that the term 'director' had replaced that of 'producer', and before the twentieth century it had not been considered necessary to appoint somebody, independent of the cast, to organize matters on stage. Members of the nineteenth-century stock companies were expected to know their business, and actor-managers, although nominally arranging movements, were usually motivated only by the desire to be positioned to the best advantage. With the demise of the actor-manager system after the First World War, the increasingly more sophisticated technical requirements (particularly lighting) and the popularity of Shaw and Ibsen's new, psychological drama, which necessitated the creation of 'atmosphere',[558] there arose the need for an overall co-ordinator. Basil Dean, Tyrone Guthrie and Michel Saint-Denis emerged as the first generation of talented producers in Britain and during the 1950s they were joined by the leaders of the second, Peter Hall and Peter Brook. Until the Arts production of *Waiting for Godot*, Hobson had paid little attention to the work of the director, concentrating instead on his conception of the actor as an artist, but the need to interpret an Absurdist script enhanced the role of the director and drew the input of Peter Hall to Hobson's notice. It can now be seen that much of the theatrical excitement of the late 1950s and early 1960s in Britain was due to the innovative approach to staging and interpretation of Peter Hall, Peter Brook, Joan Littlewood, George Devine, Tony Richardson and William Gaskill. Although more comfortable discussing matters of subjective interpretation and emotional resonance than theatrical technique, this excitement is partially reflected in several of Hobson's subsequent reviews.

One of Hobson's articles to consider the intentions of a director was 'Helping Shakespeare',[559] where he compared Peter Hall's 1957 Stratford *Cymbeline* to Peter Brook's revived *Titus Andronicus*, starring Laurence Olivier. Hobson considered it fascinating 'to watch the difference in the approach of the brilliant director [Brook], who has faith in his author, and of the director, perhaps equally brilliant, who in this instance has faith only in himself [Hall]', but, frustratingly, he refuses to state which one he prefers. The article nevertheless provoked great interest, with its implication that many of Shakespeare's works were poorer than common reputation would have it, and Brook himself submitted an article in reply, defending the playwright.[560] Any discussion of directorial methodology is absent from Hobson's writing, however, and reveals that he was only able to write perceptively about Shakespeare when the text had been illuminated by a startling individual performance. He inadvertently confirmed this mental block, apparent throughout his career, when he wrote at the end of 1957:

> The reputation of Shakespeare remains (more or less) constant; that of his plays varies with our capacity to act them. Our perception of the riches in them is very dependent on the ability of our players to set them in the brilliant light of personal illumination.[561]

That Hobson is happier writing about actors and modern playwrights, and happiest considering the work of *acteurs*, is undeniable. Robert Bolt's play *Flowering Cherry*, produced at the end of November 1957, provided Ralph Richardson, in the role of Jim Cherry, with a vehicle to demonstrate his vision of life once again:

> The incomparable strength of Richardson ... is his understanding of the goodness and simplicity of spirit of ordinary people. What is not generally realised is that this manifestation of ultimate innocence would be insipid were it not that Sir Ralph is permanently aware that it is not a pearl casually picked up, but one bought with a great price. It is not, in Richardson, the mere absence of evil; it is the consequence of evil vanquished: and the immense sense of the fight won is not the less perceptible because the marks of the struggle have been erased.[562]

This theme is restated in Hobson's brief monograph of the actor which was published the following year.[563]

Professionally, Hobson's career had been on an upward curve in 1957. He was the established critic of the most widely read and influential Sunday newspaper (*The Sunday Times* had celebrated its seven-thousandth issue on 14 July 1957 and possessed a readership of over 750,000); he was a regular contributor to the radio programme *The Critics*; he served as an adjudicator at both the NUS Drama Festival and the *Evening Standard* Drama Awards; and he had been invited to be the castaway on the BBC radio programme *Desert Island Discs* on 14 September. In the British theatre as a whole, 1956 had been the year of breakthrough, 1957 the year of consolidation and 1958 was to prove the year of achievement – and Hobson's own writing mirrored this progression almost exactly.

The new year began with an interesting independent assessment of Hobson's mastery of suspense by a correspondent of the *Western Daily Press*, writing about the NUS Drama Festival at Bristol:

> Mr Hobson's adjudication was itself a performance, for in his comments on the productions of the four finalists he played a cat-and-mouse game with the audience which left the announcement of the result a surprise until the last moment.[564]

H. V. Hodson, the editor of *The Sunday Times*, who presented the trophy to the winning production – Christopher Fry's *A Sleep of Prisoners* performed by University College, Cardiff (chosen because the play contained the one moment when Hobson was 'excited'[565]) – referred to the adjudication as a 'who-dun-it?',[566] and Michael Billington cites further practical evidence of Hobson's sense of the theatrical during the adjudication of the 1960 NUS Festival, a festival in which Billington participated as an undergraduate:

> ... one of his greatest achievements was his summing up of the [festivals]. It was a big job because you would get a week of productions and at the end of it Harold had to make the award. He would do an hour, hour and a quarter speech to everyone and they were absolute masterpieces because he would keep you guessing as to what the winner was. I remember one year, I think it was the year I was an entrant, it came down to something like a choice of a production of *The White Devil* and *The Sport of My Mad Mother* and he praised this production of *The White Devil* in the *highest* terms – he poured encomia on this – and we thought, well that's all sewn up. And then he came to the last sentence and said '*but* in the theatre, what matters more than accomplishment is daring, adventure, risk ... and for that reason I give the prize to *The Sport of My Mad Mother*.' He just had an extraordinary sense of drama and theatre and he used to do that very similar technique every year with that prize giving.[567]

Hobson may have had no practical experience of the stage, but he possessed an intuitive sense of the dramatic which he could convey through speech and prose and which was to be displayed in the review that marked his greatest critical discovery five months later.

At the same festival Hobson had experienced his first encounter with the work of an unknown playwright named Harold Pinter, when the Bristol Old Vic Theatre School and the University Department of Drama performed his short play, *The Room*. It made an immediate impression:

> It was a revelation and the directors of the London Arts Theatre and of the English Stage Company should be after Mr Pinter before they eat their lunch today. It is a brief excursion, in a slum room, into the nightmare world of insecurity and uncertainty. It has touches of Ionesco, and echoes of Beckett: and somewhere not far distant is the disturbing ghost of that Henry James who turned the screw.[568]

As with *Waiting for Godot*, it was the very elusiveness of the play that appealed and appalled:

> What exactly the plot is, where the elusive landlord really lived, who are the unexplained couple seeking lodgings, why the lorry driver husband is so long mute, what is the parentage of the woman who clings so desperately to shabby respectability, are questions that do not admit precise solution. They do not need to. The play makes one stir uneasily in one's shoes, and doubt, for a moment, the comforting solidity of the earth.

This represents the first attempt at defining the Pinteresque style. The occasion stuck in Hobson's mind. Three months later he was to write that the production was 'the best students' performance I have seen'[569] and in May, having been alerted by the uniformly scathing reviews of Pinter's first London production, *The Birthday Party*, Hobson travelled to the Lyric, Hammersmith and made his most notable critical find. He explained the circumstances of his visit in 1960:

> The fate of 'The Birthday Party' will long be remembered ... I saw it at a Thursday matinee when, in a theatre holding 800 people, there were only sixteen present.
>
> There was a little feeble applause at the end of the first act. But everyone – so conspicuous in that relatively vast emptiness – felt self-conscious, and when the curtain came down for the second time there was a dead silence, which was suddenly broken by the voice of one of the players saying, 'This is the most awful drivel I have ever appeared in.' The words rang round the echoing theatre, and we – the whole sixteen of us – shrank back in our seats appalled. I have no doubt now that it was merely embarrassment that caused the incident, but at the time I thought that I personally had never known such an act of betrayal in the history of the theatre. I am glad to say that at the end of the play, if we did not precisely cheer – which is what we ought to have done, for 'The Birthday Party' is as much a thing of triumph as it is of terror – we did at least make as thunderous a noise of approval as sixteen people can.[570]

Hobson's response to this bizarre afternoon was to devise the bravest review that he was ever to write. So convinced was he that he had discovered a masterpiece, so distressed that a young playwright of talent had been crucified by the reviews in the dailies, that he was prepared to stake his critical credibility on his belief that Pinter would become a vital influence on subsequent British drama. The article, 'The Screw Turns Again',[571] is a masterpiece of style, wit and compression. It exemplifies Hobson's ability to convey a sense of occasion without sounding implausible; it demonstrates his passionate commitment to young talent; and it highlights his ability to find stimulating and appropriate analogies to events in a work which both explain uncertainties and stimulate interest. The style of the entire article is dominated by the need 'to put this matter clearly and emphatically'. The deliberate rigidity of the punctuation, the pithy, repetitive construction of the sentences and the breathless, truncated rhythm of the words create the impression that Hobson is battling to contain his enthusiasm within a linguistic straitjacket, such is the importance of his discovery. Hobson told Victor Lazarow in 1976 that: 'if I get the first paragraph right, everything will follow from there',[572] and 'The Screw Turns Again' begins with a suitably intriguing and seemingly irrelevant piece of information which intentionally fails to reveal this state of constantly suppressed excitement. Indeed, it is to be hoped that the information about the hopeless history student would arouse the expectation that Hobson was intending to agree with the earlier damning reviews, since this will increase the effect of the peripeteia: 'One of the actors in Harold Pinter's *"The Birthday Party"* at the Lyric, Hammersmith, announces in the programme that he read history at Oxford, and took his degree with Fourth Class Honours.' The attention of the reader obtained, the critic then reveals the significance of this under-achievement and states at the outset that he has been provoked to mount a crusade on Pinter's behalf:

> Now I am well aware that Mr Pinter's play received extremely bad notices last Tuesday morning. At the moment I write these lines it is uncertain whether the play will still be in the bill by the time they appear, though it is probable it will soon be elsewhere. Deliberately, I am willing to stake whatever reputation I have as a judge of plays by saying that 'The Birthday Party' is not a Fourth, not even a Second, but a First; and that Mr Pinter, on the evidence of this work, possesses the most original, disturbing, and arresting talent in theatrical London.

The courage of this declaration is astounding. In the light of the revulsion of the dailies (typified by W. A. Darlington's disgust at being 'condemned to sit through plays like this'[573]), Hobson was risking complete marginalization by backing such a reviled playwright. But this backing mattered to Hobson:

> I am anxious, for the simple reason that the discovery and encouragement of new dramatists of quality is the present most important task of the British theatre, to put this matter clearly and emphatically. The influence of unfavourable notices on the box office is enormous; but in lasting effect it is nothing. 'Look Back In Anger' and the work of Beckett both received poor notices the morning after production. But that has not prevented those two very different writers, Mr Beckett and Mr Osborne, from being regarded throughout the world as the most important dramatists who now use the English tongue. The early Shaw got bad notices; Ibsen got scandalous notices. Mr Pinter is not merely in good company, he is in the very best company.

This paragraph seeks both to eradicate the damage done to *The Birthday Party*'s chances of survival caused by its slating earlier in the week and to convey the remarkably honest opinion that immediate critical disfavour is not necessarily the disaster that one commonly assumed. It also supplies further proof of Hobson's passion for new writing and his continual belief that high praise of the worthwhile – positive criticism – is more likely to ensure the health of British theatre than constant preoccupation with, and denigration of, the insignificant – negative criticism. This is a belief that he puts most succinctly in *Theatre in Britain*, when he states that twentieth-century British theatre can be divided into two phases: pre-Osborne, in which it concentrated on depicting what seemed good to it; and post-Osborne, on destroying what seemed bad – yet at the heart of *all* twentieth-century drama lies the pursuit of happiness, an activity that should be praised even when it is pursued 'with a worsening temper and a diminishing hope'.[574]

The fourth paragraph of the review contains a restating of Hobson's criteria for a successful play. It 'must entertain; it must hold the attention; it must give pleasure. Unless it does that, it is useless for stage purposes. No amount of intellect, of high moral intent, or of beautiful writing is of the slightest avail if a play is not in itself theatrically interesting' – and there is a beautiful clarity to this that enforces the validity of its message. It is a clarity, too, that will rub off on an appreciation of the play itself, since Hobson then lists with great precision the theatricality of Pinter's work. It is 'absorbing' and 'witty'; it contains characters that fascinate – and here Hobson pertinently summarizes the characteristics of Petey, Meg, Goldberg and McCann; the plot is not just 'first rate' but is described as containing 'echoing explorations of memory and fancy'; and the atmosphere of the play is correctly perceived as being one of 'delicious, impalpable and hair-raising terror'.

Clearly, it is right to hail Hobson for being the only critic to recognize the genius of Pinter immediately, but it is equally important to see that his enthusiasm for a play transcends a need to win recognition for his perspicacity and focuses on the desire to generate an immediate audience for a play. The final three paragraphs, by seeking contemporary analogies to the plot, aim to achieve this by giving the reader an inkling of the startling emotional atmosphere of the work. They also illustrate the degree to which the Cold War had influenced the critic's interpretation:

> Mr Pinter has got hold of a primary fact of existence. We live on the verge of disaster. One sunny afternoon, whilst Peter May is making a century at Lords against Middlesex, and the shadows are creeping along the grass, and the old men are dozing in the Long Room, a hydrogen bomb may explode. That is one sort of threat. But Mr Pinter's is of a subtler sort. It breathes in the air. It cannot be seen, but it enters the room every time the door is opened. There is something in your past – it does not matter what – which will catch up with you. Though you go to the uttermost parts of the earth, and hide yourself in the most obscure lodgings in the least popular of towns, one day there is the possibility that two men will appear. They will be looking for you, and you cannot get away. And someone will be looking for *them*, too. There is terror everywhere. Meanwhile, it is best to make jokes (Mr Pinter's jokes are very good), and to play blind man's buff, and to bang on a toy drum, anything to forget the slow approach of doom. 'The Birthday Party' is a Grand Guignol of the susceptibilities.

The accessibility of Hobson's writing is evident in the way in which he first attempts to convey the unique atmosphere of the work by using a hydrogen bomb being dropped on a cricket match as evidence of the fact that we live 'on the verge of disaster' (the private joke being that Hobson, the devoted cricket supporter, is not sure whether the dropping of the bomb or the truncating of Peter May's innings represents the greater tragedy). He then describes Pinter's refined version of this threat in short, perfectly controlled sentences that mirror the movements of a pursuer and the increasing alarm of the pursued – 'There is something in your past – it does not matter what – which will catch up with you' – until, having addressed the reader directly, he lets slip the most disturbing aspect of the work, that the two pursuers are being followed themselves –'And someone will be looking for *them*, too.' In case the reader is struggling to perceive the atmosphere of *The Birthday Party*, Hobson anchors the review with a literary comparison – the play demonstrates the meticulous suspense of Henry James's ghost story, *The Turn of the Screw* – and he concludes it by making succinct approbatory remarks about the cast and the prophetic comment that 'Mr Pinter and "The Birthday Party" will be heard of again. Make a note of their names.'

There are a number of features of this review that make it representative of Hobson's finest work: it is concise and clear, yet full of information; it conveys an infectious enthusiasm that recommends the play; it is courageous and accurate; it highlights the salient features of the work through appropriate analogies; it aids understanding by means of relevant literary comparison; it takes time to praise fine acting – and, above all, it is right. The review did not manage to save the run at the Lyric, Hammersmith, however, but its true value stems from the fact that it is doubtful that any professional manager would have taken a second look at Pinter had it not been for this piece of writing, and that, as Pinter himself has conceded, it 'gave the play life' and the playwright 'the courage to continue'.[575] Hobson, the devotee of Beckett and Ionesco, could truly claim to have discovered the first British dramatist of the Absurd.

'The strength and vitality of a national theatre ... do not reside in its loyalty to its classic authors, but in its ability to add classics of its own to what has been left to it by previous ages' (1958).[576] Two further accomplished newcomers to be welcomed by Hobson were John Arden and Peter Shaffer. The English Stage Company was praised for having 'discovered another new dramatist'[577] after the production of Arden's *Live Like Pigs*, and Peter Shaffer's *Five Finger Exercise* left Hobson with the feeling that the author 'may easily become a master of the theatre'.[578] If Hobson was unenthusiastic about Arnold Wesker's *Chicken Soup with Barley* – 'Its construction was mechanical, and its writing dull'[579] – he was delighted to welcome the return of Brendan Behan to Stratford East with *The Hostage*, praising it in characteristically subjective terms: 'I do not know whether "The Hostage" is a masterpiece or not. What I do know is that it made on *me* the impression of a masterpiece.'[580] John Osborne made a further entrance with *Epitaph for George Dillon*, written in collaboration with Anthony Creighton, which, though 'badly constructed', provided an 'admirable evening',[581] and Samuel Beckett's *Endgame*, new in translation, promised an even greater 'austerity and rigour'.[582] (Hobson was unable to review the Royal Court production through ill-health.)

This proliferation of new works contributed much to the vibrancy of the theatre in 1958. An even greater diversity was provided, however, by the interweaving of old and new theatrical genres. The passing of the old order was symbolized by Rattigan's most recent work, *Variation on a Theme*, which Hobson felt was ridiculous, since the actresses appeared to be clothes-horses from an earlier era and the script was a pale echo of earlier French plays. After searching for something to praise, and complimenting Margaret Leighton (admirable 'within the limitations imposed on her'), Michael Goodliffe ('a source of welcome rest') and George Pravda ('not bad'), Hobson gave up: 'Everything else, including Sir John Gielgud's direction, is too awful to think about.'[583] Hobson found more to praise in Christopher Fry's translation of Giraudoux – *Duel of Angels*[584] – and T. S. Eliot's *The Elder Statesman*[585] at the Edinburgh Festival, and he even broke with his inveterate hostility towards musicals to delight in *Irma la Douce* (admittedly French)[586] and to share in the general rapture at the phenomenal success of the year, *My Fair Lady*, which 'actually overtopped expectations'.[587] With *West End Story*, however, he most amusingly chose to dissent from the ecstatic reception, defying the admonition of a theatrical legend:

> At the end of 'West Side Story', on Friday Night, I had a brief encounter with the most comprehensive theatrical genius of our time. When the last enraptured audience had left the auditorium, he still remained in his stall, overwhelmed in the vortex of his admiration for the vibrant, tingling, and clever show we had just been cheering. Gripping me firmly by the hand, 'Harold,' he said, with a bitter-sweet smile, 'that was great theatre we've had tonight, wasn't it?'
>
> 'No,' I replied, shaking my head in a manner both wise and sad. He looked at me in astonishment, as if he thought I had got hayfever at the wrong time of the year. Then solicitude for me swept over him. 'Harold,' he exclaimed, 'do be careful; please, please be careful.'
>
> There are not many people whom I would be more loth to disappoint than Mr Noël Coward. So careful I will be.[588]

In October it was announced that the critic who had been most closely associated with the denigration of the old, Kenneth Tynan, was to succeed Wolcott Gibbs as the drama critic of the *New Yorker* for at least a year. One might have expected Hobson to greet the departure of his great rival with a silent satisfaction, but such was his innate generosity that he paid tribute to Tynan's skill in the aptly titled 'London's Loss and New York's Gain':[589]

> ... he is harsh about the theater only because he is passionately devoted to it. He cannot bear to see it doing anything less than its best.

> The slack conventionalism of bourgeois comedy and drama drive him to ecstasies of impatience.
>
> He is a man who has brought excitement and emotion into English drama criticism. He writes about the theater as if it were a vital part of life and not merely a means of passing the evening only one degree less boring than looking at the television ... He kicks the theater hard and accurately, but its well-being matters to him profoundly.

No matter how aggressive the younger man became, Hobson never ceased to regard Tynan with the benevolent gaze of a patron towards his protégé.

Hobson showed less generosity to the renewed interest in the idea of a National Theatre, because he felt that so centralized an institution would militate against the discovery and encouragement of new dramatists of quality. The strength of his feeling can be gauged from the article 'Danger Threatens the Theatre':[590]

> The danger of this country's getting a National Theatre has increased, is increasing, and ought to be diminished. There has been much talk this week about a subsidy of £125,000 a year being necessary to run a National Theatre, the Old Vic, and the Bristol Old Vic as a single organisation. Now, if £125,000 a year would *prevent* the Old Vic from becoming a National Theatre, and keep it in the Waterloo Road, where the harm it can do is limited, I should regard this as a bargain very much in the nation's interests ...

Hobson's fear was that a National Theatre would become obsessed with old classics, particularly Shakespeare, and that British actors, the finest in the world, would lack:

> [the] iron will, and a singularly clear perception of where the true future of the British drama lies, to resist the temptation to abandon the theatre as a living, developing entity in favour of holding a whole audience entranced in beauty with a quiescent smile as you say 'The readiness is all' ...

To his championing of the avant-garde, Hobson was now adding a defence of the New Wave drama, and his belief that the 'new and the living are what the theatre needs' stemmed from his fear that a National Theatre would become a fossilized entity, more concerned with commercial viability than enterprising innovation. His scorn at this idea was deliberately provocative – 'For myself I think that the British theatre has a better destiny than to become a museum for the gratification of culture-starved package tourists' – and the question of subsidized theatre, the development of the New Wave into the Second Wave[591] and the demise of censorship were the chief issues that were to dominate Hobson's writing over the next ten years.

171

Chapter 7

The Dramatists Consolidate: 1959–1967

Whereas a decade ago people came to our theatre to look at our actors, today – though the actors remain practically the same both in personnel and in eminence – they come to look at our plays
Harold Hobson, 'Youth Changes Direction', *ST*, 28 June 1959

The most important theatrical transformation to have been wrought by *Look Back in Anger*, the subsequent New Wave plays and the fascination with Brecht was the reassertion of the dramatist over the actor, and it was to this revolution that Hobson bore witness over the next decade. The last years of the 1950s were characterized by a desire on the part of many to challenge the previously unquestioned orthodoxies of British society – witness the flourishing of the Campaign for Nuclear Disarmament between 1958 and 1962, or the heterodoxical questioning of the monarchy – and playwrights quickly discovered their ability to participate in this reorientation of conventional opinions. Within the space of three years an actors' theatre had become an authors' theatre – a point that was clarified for Hobson in 1960 by reading *Six Thousand and One Nights*, a book by the drama critic of the *Daily Telegraph*, W. A. Darlington:

> An actor's theatre, he says, and he convinces me that he is right, is a theatre in which the plays are written *for* the actor. This is a valuable distinction. Olivier, Richardson, Gielgud, Wolfit, Guinness, Redgrave are great actors, and Scofield, too; but authors do not write plays for them. No thought of Sir Laurence was in Ionesco's mind when he wrote 'Rhinoceros'. Therefore, though we have great actors, we do not have an actors' theatre.[592]

Although until 1955 Hobson preferred allusive drama and works which provided scope for great acting performances, he was nevertheless able to appreciate post-1955 plays that sought to point to a moral, provided that the moral was intrinsic and that the playwright did not sacrifice theatricality in his quest for didacticism. This critical maxim was elaborated in 1963, when he claimed that:

> It is always more effective to demonstrate a thing than to preach about it. The sense of beauty is more vividly aroused when it is beautifully said that there is no beauty, than when it is unbeautifully asserted that beauty is all around us.[593]

He confirmed his consistent belief in the theatrical superiority of the implicit over the explicit by stating that, in a play, the 'hidden persuaders are always the most powerful'. *Waiting for Godot* remained the model to be emulated, even if it had been misunderstood:

> Because ... tramps and urination were noticeable features there has been since a proliferation of plays concerned with layabouts and lavatories. The prospect of the unemployed opening their bowels is not in itself more pleasing than that of ladies and gentlemen coining epigrams ... In other words, the hidden persuaders of 'Waiting for Godot' have been missed. One of them is simply that, like all the well-made plays it superseded, it had suspense: one wanted to know whether Godot would come ... A second hidden persuader is that, in spite of its rags and its freedom of language, it had a splendid and majestic style.[594]

For the rest of his career, Hobson's approval of plays with a moral depended on the extent to which they contained such 'hidden persuaders'.

From the late 1950s, a love of the implicit began to run counter to the mood of a society that was gradually becoming less enclosed and refined and more overt and confrontational. Living standards continued to improve for much of the population. Between 1953 and 1972 seven million houses were built,[595] the proportion of households possessing televisions rose from one in fifteen in 1953 to nine out of ten in 1975, the number of cars rose from 3.5 million (1955) to 11.5 million (1970) and four times more people took holidays abroad in 1970 than in 1951.[596] But it was soon evident that, in spite of this affluence, many people began to feel that this opulence had its drawbacks too. The distrust of the pragmatic (some would argue, pseudo-) socialism of Harold Wilson's Labour government, elected in 1964, was exacerbated by the recognition that over 10 per cent of the population – approximately five million people – still had to endure sub-standard living conditions at the end of the decade.[597] The young, be they increasingly radical university students or mods, rockers and, later, hippies, continued to feel alienated by an Establishment (of which Hobson was now a part) that, in spite of a reappraisal of social values, appeared as class-bound as ever; the politically committed, who felt marginalized by the two-party system, became polarized between those on the extreme right, obsessed with immigration and a 'Soviet threat', and those on the left, eager for the destruction of capitalism and the revolutionary reconstruction of society. The confrontations to which these diffuse positions gave rise came to dominate much of British society in the late 1960s and early 1970s – the final period of Hobson's *Sunday Times* career. His discomfort at dissension and violent change is apparent in much of his writing and made it easy to portray him as a reactionary conservative force clinging to his post long past his shelf-life. That Hobson finally retired from *The Sunday Times* (in 1976, at the age of 72) later than was wise is indisputable, but the complexity of his interests, his undiminished passion for theatre-going and his intelligent and humorous style ensure that this hostile view of his final years as a critic is too simplistic.

Hobson's suspicion of 'the drama that tells us things it is good for us to know'[598] continued to be reinforced by the frequency with which Brecht was performed in the early 1960s. He was scathing about the English Stage Company's 1962 dramatic collage, *Brecht on Brecht*, since he thought it demonstrated the degree to which Brecht was prejudiced and uncharitable: 'Hatred of capitalists is not the same thing as love of the workers. It may on occasion be hatred in a good cause: that is a matter of opinion. But it is still hatred.'[599] He objected to the 'virtual canonisation' of Brecht, after seeing a 1963 performance of *Baal*.[600] The National Theatre's 1965 production of *Mother Courage* reduced the critic to the unusual state of incoherent exasperation: 'There is no disguising the fact that, whatever else may be said about him, he is a gigantic bore. The tedium of the National Theatre production of 'Mother Courage' is beyond description ...',[601] and the Royal Shakespeare Company, with a production of *Squire Puntila* in the same year, convinced Hobson that the playwright had failed in his original intention of mobilizing the masses: 'The tragic paradox of Brecht is that he won the intellectuals and bored the working class.'[602]

Hobson's dislike of Brecht was not inflexible, however, and did not prevent him from honestly acknowledging those moments within his plays which he viewed with enjoyment. He commended the lyricism in *Baal*[603] and called *Happy End* 'the jolliest, gayest, brightest, most amusing, most alive and good-humoured work that Brecht ever wrote'.[604] He was pleased to discover Brecht the poet in 1964, through a production of *The World of Kurt Weill in Song* at the Vaudeville;[605] he hailed the visit of the Berliner Ensemble in 1965 as providing 'Brecht for grown-ups',[606] speculating in his review that the poor translations used in English productions may have led to an unfair perception of the playwright; and he struck a note of genuine enthusiasm after having seen the pivotal thirteenth scene of *Life of Galileo* in 1963:

> Never did I expect that I should have one day to count a production of that old charlatan's a major theatrical experience. Yet this wonder has now occurred ... The conception of Galileo as a man who both illuminated and betrayed reason is dramatically thrilling, and the dexterity with which his recantation is cross-lit by contradictory interpretations is endlessly stimulating.[607]

Hobson's attitude to Brecht over the course of his career is best expressed in his response to the performance by the English Stage Company of *St Joan of the Stockyards* in 1964. Kenneth Tynan had been praised by Penelope Gilliatt in 1959 in *Encore*, the journal of the new theatrical vanguard, for demonstrating a partisan approach to criticism, after Tynan had stated that 'I can't love a play if my side – by which I mean humanism in its widest possible sense – is completely ignored.'[608] Hobson, however, did not consider it part of his function as a critic to argue for social progress and generally attempted to seek merit even in works that did not accord with his own personal tastes. In his assessment of Tony Richardson's production of *St Joan of the Stockyards* he finally manages to explain the source of the irritation and fascination that Brecht represented for him, thereby illustrating the fundamental ecleticism of his critical vision:

> There can be no possible doubt that the final scene of 'St Joan of the Stockyards' ... in which the forlorn, bewildered and disconsolate Joan dies and is canonised before the hypocritical chorus of chanting Chicago business men, is the finest piece of Brechtian writing, the most sustained example of Brechtian production, and the noblest demonstration of Brechtian acting that London has ever experienced.
>
> *It is absolutely necessary that I should say this because the play flouts, derides, and condemns all the things that I respect, and upholds and proselytises those which I oppose and distrust. But it should be possible to recognise the merit and even the grandeur, when they exist, of those who are not on our side.* (My highlights)

This is a critical response of great integrity; Hobson, by reporting honestly on a moment of theatrical effectiveness, is investing his views on Brecht with a greater credibility than they had previously possessed. He has reacted characteristically to a moment of great emotional power and reported this sincerely – even if the dramatic intention behind the scene runs counter to his personal and political view of life. Such fair-mindedness inevitably allows his objections to appear less influenced by Cold War rhetoric than valid dramatic considerations:

> There is a splendour about the Old Guard, even when its charge is against the English. And in this play the accents in which Brecht exposes Christianity as a sham, and preaches violence and ruin, are sometimes the accents of a great dramatist. One repudiates his doctrine, but the doctrine is magnificently presented ... Much of the play is astonishingly naive, suited to the ignorant audiences for which Brecht wrote. Some of it is dull. None of it is fair. All of it is intellectually contemptible. But there are moments when genius blazes.[609]

Hobson's central objection to Brecht remains – 'The propositions he presents are there, not for discussion, but for assent' – but this willingness to concede that Brecht's dramaturgy cannot be dismissed as one-dimensional Cold War propaganda is a much more intelligent reaction than the unappealing and irritable nature of his reviews of Brecht in the 1950s.

The only time that 'drama that tells us things it is good for us to know'[610] was acceptable for Hobson was when the moral was presented in a suitably dynamic and entertaining fashion; when the message imparted possessed a vital and immediate relevance; or when the audience was presented with a genuine choice of interpretations – the true dialectic which Hobson felt that Brecht had avoided. To the first of these categories belonged Joan Littlewood's 1963 production of *Oh, What a Lovely War!* at Stratford East. This satire on the Great War of 1914–18, which utilized Brechtian techniques of projection to highlight the inhumanity of the Allied and German commanders, was the type of didactic show which Hobson was expected to condemn. Penelope Gilliatt had mocked Hobson (in the same 1959 *Encore* article that eulogized Tynan) as a critic who felt 'genuinely unhappy in the presence of mordancy or irreligious jokes',[611] and, if this description were wholly accurate, Hobson was unlikely to enjoy *Oh, What a Lovely War!* Nevertheless, the wily critic greatly enjoyed confounding the gleeful expectations of the management at Stratford East that two specific scenes would drive him 'howling from the theatre':

> Alas, I enjoyed it. The effect of both scenes may be considered blasphemous by the excessively sensitive; but in each case the music's throbbing rhythms are so irresistible, and the singing is so good, that it would be absurd to protest ... despite its injustice – or perhaps because of the sincerity of Miss Littlewood's belief in this injustice – the piece is stamped with originality, with entertainment and pathos, with the true life of the theatre.[612]

This delight in refusing to be pigeon-holed is quintessential Hobson.

Peter Brook's controversial 'Theatre of Fact' production of *US*, an indictment of the involvement of the United States in Vietnam, which featured a scene calling for Hampstead to be napalmed to illustrate the horror of the conflict to a docile British populace, was also praised by Hobson for its theatrical virtue and the relevance of its statement. Hobson was strongly affected by events in Asia in 1966:

> ... to use all the resources of modern science and industry to slaughter a primitive people who could no more invent a napalm bomb of their own than write 'Shall I compare thee to a summer's day?' is something of which I do not trust myself to speak[613]

He is therefore able to suppress his instinctive dislike of the Theatre of Fact, because the message is important and, crucially, it is conveyed in credible dramatic terms: 'It has terror, it has fear, it has bewilderment, it has no hatred.' Such is both Hobson's despair at the conflict in Vietnam and his loyalty to Peter Hall, the embattled director of the financially hard-pressed Royal Shakespeare Company, that he surprisingly defends the RSC production against the 'general assumption that "US" is anti-American'. More convincing is his assertion that *US* is equally no 'justification of American policy in Vietnam; nor of the Viet-Cong':

> ... it assumes no position of superiority. It never suggests that it, in its wisdom, knows any better how to deal with the situation than we do in the audience, nor that it is in any way morally superior to us. It is without self-righteousness. What it does suggest, in a manner and with a power beyond my ability to express, is the inexpugnable sadness of a humanity involved in a tragedy to which it can see no end, and whose end it cannot compass.

Hobson's compassion aroused, he concludes that *US*, which was almost banned by the Lord Chamberlain for being 'beastly, anti-American and left-wing',[614] 'is the noblest and the finest thing done on the English stage in our lifetime'. Hardly the verdict of a sclerotic Tory.

US was an exceptional work, responding to extraordinary events that drew forth a unique reaction from Hobson. The third – and most acceptable – form of drama with a moral for Hobson was that which presented the audience with a genuine choice of interpretation. The moral viewpoint is implicit, even barely discernible and any didacticism is unobtrusive. In 'The Question Master' in July 1963 Hobson explained how he felt that the most theatrically challenging approach was that of stimulating ambiguity, adopted by John Arden in *The Workhouse Donkey*:

> It is absolutely impossible to say, after seeing 'The Workhouse Donkey', whether Mr Arden is on the side of the genially unscrupulous Labour alderman, or on that of the incorruptible Chief of Police.

This skilful balancing of potential interpretations always held more appeal for Hobson, the admirer of the insidiously suggestive, than the directness of Brecht, and the concluding paragraph of this review encapsulates this career-long preference for suggestion over assertion:

> ... the main thing is that Mr Arden sets the audience a real exercise. He leaves them with *his* facts to be tackled by *their* brains. People are always saying that they like authors who make them think. If they really mean this – and not merely that they like authors who make them think that they are thinking – then Mr Arden is their man.[615]

The appeal of Arden over Brecht here was that the British playwright refused to provide simplistic answers, reflecting a recognition that the world was too problematic to be depicted theatrically in terms of cause and effect. In 1961 Hobson had expressed what this now meant for the theatre in terms of plot construction:

> Good plots are usually the mark of oversimplified feeling. The world can no longer be satisfactorily explained in terms of clever curtain lines and neat dénouements. It is too complex, too frightening, too mysterious, too evil, too helpless.[616]

This belief that the complexity of the modern world destroyed the validity as role models for new writing, of the old naturalistic stage practice, rendering futile the attempt to convey simplistic political diagnoses of the ills of society, was to become an important theme in Hobson's writing.

Hobson's position at the beginning of the 1960s – an established, widely read critic, writing for a Tory newspaper, with a love of French theatre and an unfashionable adherence to Christianity – made him an appealing target for parody. The satirical magazine *Private Eye* had commenced publication on 25 October 1961 and the ninth issue, the following April, contained an amusing fictitious interview with Hobson, devised by John Wells, which sought to portray him as an indulgent fool approaching his critical dotage, obsessed with linguistic insignificances, past discoveries, matters French and religious revelation. A short extract from the article, entitled 'Interviews with Myself', conveys the predominant tone:

> *Myself*: (Offering a Gauloise bout filtre) Mr. H*bs*n: the new French play at the Bijou Theatre, Brixton – Ennui Après moi la Douche – has been universally slated by the critics as the most trite, boring and lewd French farce to cross the channel since the original Phloppe of 1912.
>
> *H*bs*n*: (taking a cigarette) Ah, the 1912 production – I remember it well: with Solange Grotesque. A delightfully nostalgic piece, full of dada and pouffe. (Lost in thought for a moment) But this Douche. It is, in my opinion, not only the greatest production of the year, it is also one of the most moving religious plays ever written.
>
> *M*: (With feigned astonishment) Indeed?
>
> *H*: Yes indeed. I am, I hope – that is to say I think, alone in this opinion – a voice crying in the wilderness as it were. But (with a knowing wag of the finger) I *was* right about Pinter, you know.
>
> *M*: You were indeed.
>
> *H*: And all the others were against me: Right and Left, Reactionaries and Bearded Wierdies, but I was right.[617]

It is interesting to note that this comic piece implies that Hobson's writing can be classified as neither right-wing nor left-wing. It also necessarily contains a number of unfairly exaggerated details for comic effect. Hobson's justifiable pride in discovering Pinter is portrayed as hubris, his courage in contradicting received critical opinion is viewed as idiosyncrasy and his appreciation of Christian values in plays is depicted as an exclusive interest in discovering tenuous religious significance. This third point, the most prevalent misconception of Hobson's entire critical output, is the only one that requires urgent redress. That Hobson found delight in a dramatic depiction of Christian theology is undeniable; he was, after all, to state in 1963 that he desired a drama that was both Christian and progressive.[618] But by far the more important element of this prescription was the demand that the British theatre should be progressive, since he firmly believed that, if it ceased to evolve, it would inevitably stagnate. In 'A question of values' (1964)[619] Hobson explained how the changing theatrical context in Britain had resulted in a modification of the role of the critic. Prior to 1955, the task of the theatre critic had been that of a historian: 'In a theatre in which the actor is all, and the contemporary dramatist nothing, the pre-eminent task of the critic is to find words which will preserve for posterity something of the player's performance.' After the appearance of *Waiting for Godot* and *Look Back in Anger*, an additional task was accorded to the critic, that of the crusader (the highlighting is Hobson's):

> These two plays were revolutionary. They changed the face of drama overnight. They could not be judged by the standards of entertainment current at the time. They introduced, suddenly and sharply, new criteria of excitement, stimulus, and delight. In other words they were plays which the ordinary theatre-going public, *having other things to do than to devote the whole of its time to considering the drama*, was likely at first to get wrong.

The critic's task now became to reduce the time that it took the public to recognize the merit of this work:

> Unless he can say in 1954 what the dominating public opinion will be, say, ten years later he is failing in his job. Thus the characteristic triumph of contemporary criticism is not a piece of writing comparable with Hazlitt or Kean, but Kenneth Tynan's fearless defence of 'Look Back in Anger' at a time when nearly everybody else derided it ...

The critic, convinced of the validity of his opinion, should never cease to reiterate his judgement, if this is what is required to ensure the success of the avant-garde:

> Having discerned merit where it has been overlooked, the critic should estimate how valuable the merit is. If he decides that it is very valuable, then in my view it becomes his duty, not merely to say so, but to keep on saying so. In Hazlitt's day the critic was a historian. In ours he is a crusader. It is essential, not that his crusade should be popular, but that it should be right. In other words that it should be popular a decade later.

Inevitably, a critic sometimes makes an erroneous judgement and the possibility of an opposing view should never be discounted – 'Even when he is most certain that he is right he should remember the possibility that he may be wrong. He should never deny that there are other opinions than his own' – but the avant-garde, by the very nature of its ground-breaking purpose, required passionate and vociferous defenders. The latest example of Hobson's willingness to recant a hasty judgement was his regret at describing the first performance of John Arden's *Serjeant Musgrave's Dance* in 1959 as a 'frightful ordeal', since a 1963 performance had convinced him that the play possessed 'great merits which I did not at the time perceive'.[620] For Hobson the Christian Scientist, it was important for a nation to demonstrate an acceptance of Christian theology through the drama it produced. For Hobson the theatre critic, it was *more* important that the theatre was progressive, forward-looking and constantly developing, and the absence or the subversion of Christian values in a play never precluded his appreciation of its merit if it was theatrically effective.

A superficial consideration of Hobson's critical output until the abolition of stage censorship in 1968 might lead one temporarily to doubt whether the term 'crusader-critic' is appropriate to Hobson. As far as the two issues that dominated the British theatre in the 1960s were concerned – the battle to establish the National Theatre and the struggle to abolish the powers of the Lord Chamberlain – Hobson occupied what was perceived to be the reactionary position, initially arguing against the centralizing tendency of a National Theatre and claiming that the prevalence of club theatres, which fell outside the jurisdiction of the censor, guaranteed artistic freedom and obviated the need for liberalizing legislation. He was still suffering, too, from the misconceptions that had been propagated by Penelope Gilliatt's devastating survey of contemporary critics, 'A Consideration of Critics', which had appeared in the November/December 1959 issue of *Encore*. Established in 1956 and appearing bi-monthly until the mid-1960s, *Encore* was the mouthpiece of the new theatrical movement. Writing with verve and pugnacity and counting many of the new practitioners (e.g. Wesker, Tynan and Brook) amongst its contributors, it viewed 'the West End as a citadel in enemy hands'[621] and, with the exception of Kenneth Tynan, it waged a relentless war against the Fleet Street critics, who, it believed, represented a dead hand on the prospect of new invigorating drama. The 'Crisis in Criticism' was a popular topic.

Conceived as a piece of propaganda for the drama critic of the *Observer* (the final portrait begins, 'Tynan is undoubtedly the most brilliant critic we have'), Gilliatt's subjective study is best known for her memorably dismissive claim that: 'It would be unfair to suggest that one of the most characteristic sounds of the English Sunday is the sound of Harold Hobson barking up the wrong tree.'[622] Accompanied by a caricature by James Bucknill of a canine Hobson straining at the leash and yapping at a tree-trunk, this formidable combination of witty cartoon and provocative comment quickly passed into theatrical folklore, with its influence in formulating a view of Hobson's criticism far outstripping its relevance or accuracy. Hobson himself always considered the article to be a compliment (describing it as 'one of the most brilliant things' *Encore* ever published[623]), and an analysis of the entire vignette reveals that there is a sub-text to Gilliatt's accusations that enhances rather than detracts from Hobson's reputation. The opening sentence of her portrait unwittingly confirms that the article is a puff for Tynan which sacrifices objectivity for partisan point-scoring:

> For several years the drowsy melancholy of the English Sunday has been enlivened by the exquisitely unmatched contest between Harold Hobson and Kenneth Tynan, now in suspension until next spring.[624] In fact, their games are not particularly good for each other: Tynan needs a crisper opponent, and Hobson's genuine love of the theatre becomes by comparison almost absurdly sumptuous.

Hobson is suffering here for the magniloquent excesses of his infatuation with the French in 1954 (as well as for writing for a publication that was perceived as being diametrically opposed to *Encore*'s ethos), but hindsight permits one to conclude that it is exactly this 'genuine love of the theatre' which contributed to his longevity and formed the basis of his most courageous critical discoveries – if he had not believed passionately in the importance of *Waiting for Godot*, for example, it is possible that Absurdist drama would never have been able to challenge the predominance of the well-made play in Britain. Gilliatt's second claim, that Hobson is idiosyncratic, is a charge to which an intuitive critic, guided by his own emotional reaction and intelligence of perception, is frequently susceptible:

> It is not that the critic of *The Sunday Times* is over-indulgent: when moved, he can be briskly dismissive; it is merely that he distributes his indulgences in unexpected quarters. Any little thing can set him off. An actor sneezing (especially if the actor is Sir Ralph Richardson) may well initiate half a column on the rare simplicity of so cosmic a sneeze.

Hobson's occasional idiosyncrasy – it is undeniable that his delight in Ralph Richardson sometimes leads to a tiresome over-exuberance which invites parody – is nevertheless counterbalanced by the passion of his beliefs, the enthusiasm that he conveys and the stylish readability of his unpredictable observations. These observations are rarely inconsistent, however, given that, for Hobson, one of the most important criteria for successful drama is theatrical effectiveness. Gilliatt implicitly acknowledges this when she continues: 'To put it more charitably, which is one of the qualities he values, his judgement is that of a lover rather than a critic – enraptured, intuitive, and open to attacks of sudden irrational suspicion.'

It is easy to see why Hobson, who possessed a fervent belief in the institution of marriage, should thrill to this description of his approach as that of a lover, for that is indeed how he perceived his critical philosophy.

Others, however, focused on the charge, forged in the midst of the battle between the two leading – and antithetical – critics, that Hobson's intuitive approach was prone to lead him to self-indulgent excesses, merely highlighting, by contrast, the socially relevant observations of Tynan. The persistence of this erroneous impression can be gauged from the implicit reference to Gilliatt's phrase by Irving Wardle (the theatre critic for *The Times* from 1963 to 1989) in his 1992 work, *Theatre Criticism*, when he states that Hobson 'was famous for dwelling on the profound significance of an upward inflexion, or a sneeze, which then proved to signify nothing whatever'[625] – as if this was the entire sum of Hobson's contribution to criticism.

Contrary to the prophecies of *Encore*, Hobson retained his passionate enthusiasm for the theatre during the 1960s and sought to champion those dramatists, actors and theatre companies of merit, because he believed that the task of the critic had now evolved to help consolidate the breakthrough that had been initiated in the late 1950s. It was not sufficient to seek out new writing talent – subsidized organizations such as the Royal Court, the new regional theatres in Coventry and Nottingham, and the burgeoning Arts Council now actively encouraged new works – but to nurture the dramatists who had made the breakthrough and might reinforce its achievements. Hobson had written, in 'A question of values',[626] that if a critic discovers theatrical merit, 'it becomes his duty, not merely to say so, but to keep on saying so', and thus his notion of the critic-crusader embraced a desire to provide a supportive critical environment to permit the expression of invigorating talent. As Michael Billington pointed out thirty years later, this was a valuable and unusual attitude to adopt: 'What most of us do is say that Mr X's play is not as good as his last one, or what a pity he doesn't write like he used to. Harold, I don't think did that very often.'[627] This concept of loyalty is the most distinctive feature of Hobson's criticism throughout the 1960s.

The playwrights Beckett, Pinter, Osborne, Duras and Douglas Home, the performers Richardson and Feuillère, and the director Peter Hall were all consistently supported by Hobson during this period, even when he had constructively critical points to make. For Feuillère and Richardson, there was never anything less than ecstatic praise, even when they were palpably miscast, a fate suffered by Richardson as Dr Rance in Joe Orton's *What the Butler Saw* – a farce that Hobson felt was 'spoiled by gratuitous obscenity'. It was unable to obscure the talent of Hobson's favourite actor, however, for 'even in "What the Butler Saw" Richardson shows himself to be a very great actor'.[628] More customary was Hobson's reaction to Richardson's performance in Graham Greene's *The Complaisant Lover* – 'Once again Sir Ralph gives us, to our infinite admiration and joy, the superb picture of a perfect love which is ready to offer all, and seeks nothing for itself'[629] – and the tone of Richardson's apotheosis, 'Sir Ralph at his peak', after he had played the waiter in Shaw's *You Never Can Tell*, illustrates the fundamental appeal of the actor for Hobson:

Sir Ralph Richardson can do what no other actor can even attempt: he can make a good man interesting. He can do more than this: he can make him fascinating, exciting, and profoundly moving. Other actors excel in passion, in rage, in jealousy, in fury, in pride, in all the things that make the human race so dubious an experiment. Richardson alone can make affection more thrilling than hate, kindness more penetrating than brutality, a noble simplicity more intriguing than evil. He does this without mawkishness or insipidity.[630]

Edwige Feuillère, too, continued to entrance. Whether viewed in Paris or London, she remained in his eyes 'the greatest actress in the world' on account of 'a radiant tenderness, an all-suffusing glow of affection, and a capacity for self-sacrifice',[631] and Hobson's championing of her was instrumental in his award of the Légion d'honneur by the French government in 1960, for services to the French theatre. Only two other actresses ever approached Feuillère's divine status during Hobson's career, Marlene Dietrich and Jennifer Hilary. On seeing Dietrich in Oxford in 1964, Hobson was sufficiently moved to write an article that attempted to counteract 'the eulogies that have been heaped upon her' but 'convey nothing of her talent', such as 'The world's most glamorous grandmother':

> ... the man who thinks of grandmothers whilst looking at Miss Dietrich is in need of psychiatric examination. A troubling myth, an erotic legend: lovely, philosophic, frightening Miss Dietrich may be; maternal, or grandmaternal, she is not. When she is at her best most grandmothers would, in fact, warn their progeny against her.[632]

The moment of revelation, essential for Hobson's greatest praise, occurred at the Edinburgh Festival the following year, 1965, when he was moved to write of her in terms of the near-divine:

> It is when, as in 'Go away from my window' or 'Déjeuner du matin' or 'Marie, Marie', she takes on herself all the cares of the world, and the pain of its glittering and deceptive sins, that Miss Dietrich passes beyond the sight of criticism into realms of pure acceptance that scarcely any other artist attains. When she ends one of her great wounded ballads she stands utterly still, hurt in alabaster; and her face is marvellous. It is expressive of what, in the ways of a thousand years, men have come to suffer and atone for.[633]

Jennifer Hilary first came to Hobson's attention when she joined the company performing Henry James's *The Wings of the Dove* in 1964. Hobson's observation of her is another example of how he paid close attention to parts that exhibited heart-rending pathos, although the force of his praise is astonishing even for a critic susceptible to feminine delicacy:

> Miss Hilary's accession to the company has received little publicity; but it is an event that could not be overrated by all the trumpets of Joshua thundering together. Yet this phrase is too crude for the fragility, the grace, the patient, enduring affection, the utterly unshakable loyalty of Miss Hilary's exquisitely sad and radiant Milly. No swan has more beautifully sung than does, in Miss Hilary's performance, James's doomed and loving heroine.[634]

This theme was further developed when Hilary appeared in *A Scent of Flowers* by James Saunders (about whose earlier play, *Next Time I'll Sing to You*, Hobson had been equally rapturous[635]). Hilary's performance as a girl on the verge of suicide was described by Hobson as one that 'those who see it will speak of to their children and their children's children',[636] and the actress was 'by far the greatest acquisition of her sex that the English stage has made for many years'.[637] No wonder Alan Ayckbourn feared the reaction of the critic to her next role in his second play, *Relatively Speaking* – as a 'sixties modern girl' who was 'having an affair with a man who was thirty years older than her and was cutting fast and loose'.[638]

If Hobson's loyalty was occasionally hard to follow, as in the case of William Douglas Home, whom Hobson vigorously defended against the charge of anachronism for writing light comedies with an upper-class context, his continued belief in Pinter, Osborne and Beckett and his support of Peter Hall's Royal Shakespeare Company constituted an important contribution to the renewed vigour of twentieth-century British theatre. The battle that Hobson fought for Pinter in 1960 was reminiscent of the crusade that he had waged for Beckett in 1955. At the beginning of the year Hobson rebuked the progressive West End managers for their myopic choice of plays for presentation:

> Some people, when they see a play by Harold Pinter, are worried about its meaning. But what worries me about Mr Pinter is why his plays do not come to the West End. It is a matter of astonishment to me how both the English Stage Company and the Arts Theatre, which can recognise a molehill at 500 yards' distance, have overlooked this mountain.[639]

Hobson had discovered that Pinter had written a new play, *The Caretaker*, and the possibility that he might not be able to find a theatre to stage it had galvanized Hobson into supplying a further testimonial which is both perceptive and accurate: 'Pinter possesses a gift which is valuable in even the most high-brow dramatist, but which too many *avant-garde* writers lack – his plays make the audience wonder what is going to happen next.' He also possesses a view of life, 'an individual world', which Hobson felt that all renowned dramatists displayed: 'His is a world in which it is not advisable to know too much, in which the answers never fully meet the questions, and the effects are disconnected – oh so slightly, but so disturbingly – from the causes.' In his book, *A Sense of Direction*, William Gaskill, who was a director for the Royal Court in the late 1950s before becoming the artistic director from 1965 to 1972, explains that Pinter never became a Royal Court writer in the way that Osborne, N. F. Simpson, Arden and Jellicoe were, because of the article that Hobson had written after the 1958 NUS Drama Festival, actively recommending Pinter to the Court:[640]

> I had shown George [Devine] both [*The Room* and *The Dumb Waiter*] after they were first done in Bristol, but Harold Hobson in his notice in *The Sunday Times* had said that they should be done at the Court and George hated to be told what to do by a critic.[641]

In the light of this, it is ironic that in March 1960, three months after Hobson's second recommendation, the critic should be able to write: 'It is a rare excitement to welcome the strange and compelling talent of Harold Pinter into the West End'[642] – on the stage of the Royal Court, with a double bill of *The Room* and *The Dumb Waiter*. Of greater excitement still was the eventual première of *The Caretaker* in June 1960, which cemented the critic's approval of the Pinter genre:

> Of course the setting of 'The Caretaker' is sordid. Of course nobody in it wears clothes that please the eye. Of course its story – of how a good man shows charity, and then withdraws it – would not look exciting if compressed into a postcard. But I have already seen 'The Caretaker' twice, and I shall see it again at the first opportunity; and after that I shall see it a fourth time, and a fifth.[643]

Hobson's loyalty to Pinter was neither indiscriminate nor undemanding. Having helped to secure his reputation, the critic never feared to express disapproval of aspects of Pinter's subsequent works – for example, he found *The Dwarfs* in 1963 incomprehensible ('I fell off the trolley, and never clambered back again'[644]) and was troubled 'by the complete absence [from *The Homecoming*] of any moral comment whatsoever'[645] in 1965. But by expressing general support in a time of turbulent loyalties, Hobson was providing a valuable artistic counterpart to the much-trumpeted phrase, 'the right to fail', in which supporters of subsidized theatre passionately believed. For Hobson, the attempt to create new drama was always as important as the achievement.

This was particularly true in the case of John Osborne, the British playwright by whom Hobson was most intrigued during his critical career. What impressed Hobson about Osborne was the intensity of his vision, even if Hobson could not identify with it himself. In 1959 he wrote:

> More than any other of the Royal Court dramatists Mr Osborne makes me recognise myself as a Tory: I love rich restaurants, and the romance of rank, and the solemnity of cathedrals, all of which he denounces in 'The World of Paul Slickey'. I even read gossip columnists with delight

and avidity, and am always infuriated that when I enter a theatre the Press photographers look the other way. But, as Helen Gardner says, it is not necessary for an audience to be convinced of the truth of a dramatist's arguments; it is only necessary to be convinced that, with passion and honesty and nobility, the dramatist believes them to be true. And, in this matter, I would sooner doubt the multiplication table than I would doubt Mr Osborne.[646]

With articles like this, it is little wonder that *Encore* had Hobson in its sights.

This admiration for Osborne's presentation of heartfelt opinion was maintained by Hobson throughout the 1960s, irrespective of the shifting sands of critical opinion. He was uncomfortable with the Marxist interpretation of religious history contained within *Luther*, but, unsurprisingly, was the only critic to notice that this play, apparently hostile to religion, concluded by leaving the words of Christ in the audience's mind (a point corroborated by Osborne in his autobiography[647]), which led the critic to commend the playwright for his 'generosity of temperament'.[648] He was stunned and shocked by *Under Plain Cover* in 1962, but praised Osborne by comparing him to Genet;[649] *Inadmissible Evidence* was hailed in 1964 (with a sly reference to Gilliatt) as the best play he had written thus far – 'I do not believe that any language could be too sumptuous to convey the pity and the pathos and the wit and the comprehending compassion of Mr Osborne's work'[650] – whilst the opening of *A Bond Honoured* at the National in 1966 earned the playwright one of Hobson's most munificent soubriquets: 'He is not only our most important dramatist; he is also our chief prophet.'[651] By this time Osborne appeared to have supplanted Beckett as the theatre's most intriguing dramatist in Hobson's view, although Hobson never lost his ability to encapsulate the mood of a Beckett drama, as his comments on the National Theatre's 1964 production of *Play* demonstrate:

> Mr Beckett is a sombre and profound poet, not an inventor of riddles. By associations, by ceremonies, by the stirring of beliefs he has abandoned but not forgotten, he suggests, he creates, he establishes, he fulfils.[652]

In November 1962 Hobson made a public declaration of his critical interests that confirmed both his love of the avant-garde and his belief that a vibrant theatre is an eclectic one:

> My tastes in the theatre are well-known. I am for Beckett, and Pinter, and Osborne, and Wesker, Duras, and Anouilh; for the Aldwych, Theatre Workshop, and the English Stage Company. Without these the theatre would be negligible; but I can see that, without anything else but these, it would be unbalanced. There is room for argument, the angry conscience, and the poetic spirit; but also for frank, free, untroubled laughter.[653]

Tucked in between the more familiar Anouilh and Wesker (whose *Chips With Everything* had been termed 'magnificent' by the critic in 1962[654]) is the name of Marguerite Duras, whose play *The Square* was to be described by Hobson in his autobiography as 'an astonishing *tour de force*'.[655] That such an accolade should be paid to a work which he first encountered in a tiny suburban theatre in Kent is entirely in keeping with the career of a critic who discovered *The Birthday Party* in an audience of sixteen. He had read *The Square* (which is both a novel and a play) in 1962 and atypically revealed in his *Sunday Times* column his eager expectation of the performance by Company 101, led by Robert Eddison, at the Little Theatre, Bromley:

> To suggest that there is even the remotest possibility that at Bromley we shall have an experience comparable with that at the Arts Theatre when 'Waiting for Godot' was first presented would be the maddest optimism.[656]

Yet, for once, expectation matched reality, and the elusive poignancy of the play drew forth not just the comment that it was a 'masterpiece', but further proof that, as with Pinter and Beckett, the undefined, the allusive and the suggestive were the facets of drama that most appealed to Hobson:

> The heart of Marguerite Duras's play is the perception that happiness is something that one does not grasp until it is over: Cowdrey one morning at Lords, all ease and mastery: a long afternoon in the sunshine on the terrace of a great house, with no hurry, no tensions, no anxiety: moments of splendour not realised until they have become memories only.[657]

It is no coincidence that, as with *The Birthday Party*, another much-heralded work, Hobson, a critic whose work is permeated with personal interests, should choose to describe the atmosphere of *The Square* with a cricketing metaphor. Cricket remained an abiding passion.

During the 1960s the rise of subsidized theatres, the struggle for financial support from the state, the creation of the National Theatre and the Royal Shakespeare Company, the interest in new techniques of directing, the investigation of new forms of theatre as diverse as the 'Theatre of Cruelty', the 'Theatre of Fact' and epic theatre, the innovations in theatre design, such as theatre-in-the-round, and the struggle against censorship all meant that new demands were placed upon theatre critics, who had been accustomed to writing about a limited number of star actors performing in the classics or about works by an easily identifiable group of playwrights. Hobson's attitude to the Royal Shakespeare Company during the 1960s illustrates how he was able to make the transition from observer of the theatrical scene to participant, and how his loyalty to Peter Hall was a positive use of his considerable influence. Ever since he had directed *Waiting for Godot*, Hobson had considered

Hall to be one of the most important directors in Britain and he welcomed his appointment to the newly formed Royal Shakespeare Company in 1960. This personal affection did not, however, cloud his critical objectivity. He excoriated Hall's opening show, *The Duchess of Malfi*, at the company's new home, the Aldwych, for having 'no drive, no force, no continuity',[658] and wrote one of his most scathing notices the following week in response to Hall's burlesque version of *Twelfth Night*, which the critic felt was stale and unoriginal:

> There are people who, having once concocted a funny story, think that they can dine out on it for the rest of their lives. They wander from dinner table to dinner table, with a dreadful jollity on their faces. In their sad and frightening absorption in their little anecdote they hardly notice how their friends edge away from them, or what an apprehensive silence falls on the room when they enter.
> Peter Hall seems to be in danger of becoming like one of these terrifying bores.[659]

Against this, he was intrigued by the insight that the 1964 productions of all the histories, from *Richard II* to *Richard III*, gave into the mind of Shakespeare,[660] amusingly relates how, during Peter Weiss's *The Marat/Sade*, he nearly 'died of fright'[661] and mounted a vigorous defence of the artistic worth of *US*.[662] The crucial aspect of Hobson's attitude to the Royal Shakespeare Company was that he felt that, as an innovative, progressive theatre company, it was inevitable that mistakes in the choice of plays and the mounting of productions would be made, but that this was axiomatic if it was to do work of worth and endurance. This belief was most forcefully expressed in 1964, when Hobson defended the company against the charge, made by Emile Littler and Peter Cadbury, that the subsidized RSC was 'killing, or will kill, the profitability of the theatre as a commercial enterprise'[663] – an expression of the discomfort of the old guard at the threat to their income which had been adumbrated by the resignation of Binkie Beaumont from the Stratford board of governors four years earlier, claiming a conflict of interest.[664] Hobson strongly rejected Littler's notion in a polemical article entitled 'The Aldwych Affair':

> The assumption that plays such as the Royal Shakespeare Company puts into its repertory are in general immensely less acceptable to the public than entertainment plays is false. If the theatres are being emptied, it is the so-called entertainment plays that are emptying them.

And he defended the Royal Shakespeare Company's right to have the occasional failure:

> The Royal Shakespeare Company is the most alert and exploratory organisation in Britain. Naturally not every exploration is a success, but that is no reason for giving up exploring. And the percentage of success achieved by Mr Hall, Mr Brook, and the Royal Shakespeare

Company is enviably high ... They are bringing us an international reputation.[665]

This bold defence of an organization that was facing criticism from the commercial theatre for allegedly harming its prospects; from devotees of the National Theatre, who felt that it was duplicating their work; and from the Treasury, ever eager to reduce the arts budget,[666] demonstrates Hobson's approbation of the new in the face of criticism from the old guard and earned him a telegram of thanks from a grateful and embattled Peter Hall: 'Dear Harold Most Grateful For That Strong Support Most Helpful In This Dangerous Situation Ever Peter Hall.'[667] Their friendship strengthened – the two men were later to initiate the custom of an annual lunch together[668] – and Hobson's valuable support in a time of crisis was recognized by Hall when he invited the critic to serve on the board of governors of the National Theatre in 1977.

That Hobson would eventually become one of the men entrusted with overseeing the running of the National Theatre was unthinkable at the end of the 1950s, given his constant disapproval of the nascent scheme. Having articulated his belief, in 'Danger Threatens the Theatre' in 1958,[669] that he could think of 'no greater cultural disaster', fearing that a National Theatre would mount revivals of the classics at the expense of new drama, dissuade actors from experimentation and act as a museum for 'culture-starved package tourists', Hobson continued to maintain a closely argued opposition to the idea in 1959. In a March editorial for *The Sunday Times* (a measure of the public interest in the issue) Hobson claimed that a centralized body would have a detrimental effect on the theatrical activities of the provinces, currently demonstrating renewed vigour – 'The wisdom of spending public money on the arts is not in question; but the provision and maintenance of a central institution in London is not the best way to lay out whatever money may be available.'[670] – but the April visit of the Comédie Française, an example of a successful national company, served as a catalyst for debate and Hobson was forced to concede, in 'Is a National Theater Possible?',[671] that the scheme possessed the enthusiastic backing of young people interested in the arts, the influential, such as Sir Donald Wolfit, and the avant-garde, as represented by *Encore* magazine. Nevertheless, Hobson felt that the emphasis had shifted away from the desirability of the scheme to its practicability. The best actors, such as Wolfit, Richardson, Olivier and Guinness, might occasionally act in the National Theatre for reduced wages, but the critic found it hard to believe that:

> ... in the face of the rival attractions of the commercial theater, the cinema, and television, they would find it possible to give that wholetime devotion without which a national theatre cannot be properly founded.[672]

Its creation, therefore, remained 'unlikely'.[673]

This remained Hobson's view even after Peter Hall, then director of the Shakespeare Memorial Theatre, announced that he would be creating a permanent company, secured on three-year contracts (and including performers of note, such as Dame Peggy Ashcroft, Dorothy Tutin, Peter O'Toole and Eric Porter), that would be housed in the Aldwych Theatre from November 1960. As Hobson recognized, this was a 'revolutionary development' for the British theatre and would test 'whether, in a capitalist society, such an institution as a national theater is possible', though he still felt that economic considerations would militate against success:

> So long as freedom of contract is preserved, players, with exceptions here and there, will naturally enough go where it pays them best. The Comédie Française, even with its centuries of tradition and reputation, found it impossible to retain the services of Pierre Fresnay, Edwige Feuillère, or Marie Bell.[674]

The tide was beginning to run in favour of the scheme's supporters, however, even though the confusing series of official announcements about the proposal in 1961 represented a microcosm of the difficulties that the idea had encountered ever since its original proposal by Effingham Wilson in 1848.[675] Hobson himself, whilst still opposing the scheme, seemed convinced in March 1961 that the Chancellor, Selwyn Lloyd, would give his blessing to the proposal, and urged the National Theatre Committee to devote less time to the design of the complex and more to the consideration of who should run it. The critic provided his own short-list (much to the chagrin of Sir Donald Wolfit, who complained that this was personalizing the issue unnecessarily[676]), which included the names of Peter Hall, Michael Benthall (the director of the Old Vic), Tyrone Guthrie, Peter Brook, John Fernald, Anthony Quayle and John Gielgud.[677] The name of Laurence Olivier did not occur to Hobson until it was announced, a fortnight later, that Olivier had been appointed director of the new Arena Festival Theatre at Chichester.[678]

Even Hobson felt that the decision of the Chancellor of the Exchequer, Selwyn Lloyd, announced on 21 March 1961, to support the Old Vic, the Royal Shakespeare Theatre and the repertory companies to the extent of £500,000 a year, whilst refusing to sanction the building of a National Theatre, represented 'a shock and a surprise', since it had generally been felt that the National's case 'had never been so near succeeding'.[679] He was not alone in his bewilderment. Lord Chandos claimed that the decision was a public insult to the Queen Mother, who had laid the National's foundation-stone ten years earlier, the London County Council, who owned the projected South Bank site, were outraged and the scheme's many supporters were plunged into gloom after eighty, apparently fruitless, years of campaigning.[680] In a *Sunday Times* editorial on 26 March 1961, Hobson demonstrated less a delight in the apparent collapse of the scheme than a reiteration of his unshakeable belief in the importance of new drama:

Not more than half of the increased subvention should be used in furthering the English classical drama or in aiding municipally-supported theatres outside London. The rest of the money should be devoted entirely to creative drama. It is new things, fresh departures, unexpected experiments that are the life-blood of the theatre.[681]

He quickly noticed that the English Stage Company and Theatre Workshop had been overlooked and took to arguing their case in 'That Tempting New Subsidy'.[682]

The scheme was far from defunct, however, and Hobson's articles on the further developments over the next two years read like dispatches from a war zone. In June 1961 he noted the warm support of the theatrical profession for the proposal made by the leader of the London County Council, Sir Isaac Hayward, that the LCC would contribute £1,300,000 to the erection of a complex on the South Bank of the Thames if the government kept its 1949 promise to donate £1,000,000,[683] and he recorded the profession's 'delighted astonishment' at the news in July 1961 that the chancellor had made a quick about-turn and unexpectedly agreed to release these funds.[684] Hobson himself was swift to praise the 'indefatigable and skillful leadership of Lord Chandos', the chairman of the National Theatre Committee, in eliciting the chancellor's graceful capitulation. Having obtained official blessing, matters of organization now came to the fore. The withdrawal of the Royal Shakespeare Company from the scheme in January 1962, coupled with the worsening economic situation in Britain (raising the spectre of grant cuts), appeared as two ominous signs, but the terms of the divorce proved amicable and Hobson was delighted when the financial needs of the Royal Shakespeare Company at both Stratford and Aldwych finally received separate consideration.[685] This guarantee of the continued existence of Peter Hall's company, together with his admiration for Lord Chandos (who was the father of Hobson's future son-in-law, Adrian Lyttleton), permitted Hobson to raise his voice 'in a belated personal cheer' in his *Sunday Times* column at the official sanctioning of the National Theatre in July 1962.[686] This marked a final, pragmatic acceptance of an idea that he had previously strongly opposed but was now keen to see developed along lines that would enhance the nation's theatrical health: the presentation and encouragement of new play-writing talent, the exhibition of accomplished acting and a varied programme that would complement, rather than compete with, the work of the Royal Shakespeare Company.

The inaugural performance of the National Theatre took place on 22 October 1963, with Peter O'Toole playing Hamlet at the Old Vic, and it further improved Hobson's disposition towards the new undertaking. Hobson concluded that Olivier had determined to offer a production 'which will assault the emotions by the sheer force of its acting rather than by its curious titillation of the intellect', an approach shying away from the intellectual, to which the critic could always respond, and he espied a lesson for his colleagues in this:

> There is a common mistake made that a dramatic critic essentially delivers judgements; what he really does is to record feelings, *his* feelings, though these feelings may easily take the form of judgements. Any other sort of theatrical criticism is either self-deception or a fraud.[687]

This stress on an intuitive rather than an intellectual appeal (the production was described as 'Grand Opera' in the *Spectator*[688]) was maintained in the subsequent National productions of *St Joan* – which Hobson felt restored 'the sorcery of the voice'[689] – and *Uncle Vanya* – hailed as 'the supreme achievement of the contemporary English stage'.[690] During the first two months of the National's life, only William Gaskill's direction of *The Recruiting Officer*, which was influenced by the practice of epic theatre, struck Hobson as disconcerting:

> It is inconceivable that 'The Recruiting Officer' should not be a popular success. But I have one doubt about the National Theatre. Brecht looms over it. Brecht was a considerable dramatist whose value lay in the tension between his genius and his theories. It will be sad if at the National Theatre we get the theories without the genius.[691]

Although William Gaskill confirmed, in *A Sense of Direction*, that at this time 'The example of the Berliner Ensemble towered over us',[692] Hobson ironically became an enthusiastic devotee of the National's work during the turbulent years leading up to the abolition of stage censorship in 1968. Once it became clear that another financial crisis threatening the survival of the Royal Shakespeare Company had been averted in 1964 (Hobson, the crusader-critic, contributing a powerful article in the RSC's defence, arguing that there was a need for both of the two largest subsidized companies[693]), Hobson's reviews frequently testify to the high quality of the National productions during this period. He described Olivier's performance as a black Othello in 1965 as 'sensational'[694] (although others felt that the actor's blacking-up was grossly offensive or the performance was simply a technical accomplishment, with Alan Brien of the *Sunday Telegraph* writing: 'Sir Laurence can move every muscle at will – I regret he could not move me'[695]); he hailed Strindberg's *The Dance of Death* in 1967, again starring Olivier, as 'a revelation';[696] termed Franco Zeffirelli's production of *Much Ado About Nothing* as the best 'in my memory England has ever had';[697] was prepared to admit that his belief, that the all-male version of *As You Like It* in 1967 would be a failure, was unjustified – it was 'an outstanding success',[698] and he described the 1967 production of Tom Stoppard's *Rosencrantz and Guildenstern are Dead* as 'the best first London-produced play written by a British author since Harold Pinter's "The Birthday Party"'.[699]

The creation of the National Theatre had one further ramification for the British theatre, in that the appointment of Kenneth Tynan as its literary manager in 1963 deprived Hobson of his weekly sparring partner and theatre criticism in general of one of its most pungent practitioners. Before Tynan's return from New York in 1960 to take up his position as drama critic of the *Observer* once again, Hobson had sought to define their different approaches:

> Mr Tynan thinks the theater ought to make the world better, whereas I think it ought to make it good ... Mr Tynan sees the theater as a means. He enjoys most those dramatists who envisage the theater as a dynamic force, dedicated to bringing about certain social changes which in his opinion will produce a better condition of society. On the other hand, I regard the theater as an end in itself. A good play to me is not an instrument to alter society, but to add to society an absolute good. I think that the theater should provide us with the means of enjoying life now. Mr Tynan thinks it ought to establish the conditions in which to enjoy life later.[700]

In spite of their critical differences, Hobson welcomed Tynan's homecoming with the generosity that characterized his written comments on his younger rival – 'his return to England will enormously increase the pleasure and the excitement of the London theater' – but it soon became clear to the older man that Tynan had come back to a critical environment much altered from that which he had left, writing in October 1960:

> ... after his return to England from his stint on the New Yorker, Mr Tynan has found the pace being set by two younger men who have a range of invective hitherto unrivalled. His clean and clever rapier thrusts are regrettably now in danger of losing some attention, compared with the atomic bombs regularly dropped by Bernard Levin and Robert Muller.[701]

This was an accurate prediction, and there is some regret that Tynan will ironically have suffered from having been copied. Consequently, Hobson expressed genuine enthusiasm in March 1963 at the announcement of Tynan's National Theatre post, the whole project being an enterprise of 'historic importance'[702] and choosing to ignore the view that Olivier had deliberately removed the potentially damaging critic from a position from which he could attack the new venture as he had attacked Olivier's work at Chichester.[703] That Hobson held a life-long affection for the younger critic is demonstrated most poignantly by Hobson's gentle letter to the fatally ill Tynan in 1980: 'The great days when you and I did weekly battle over new plays – generally, indeed almost always ending in your victory – now seem a part of some legendary Homeric past.' Kathleen Tynan relates how Tynan was deeply moved by this, and his reply provided a fitting testimony to their compelling critical disputes of the 1950s: 'I certainly miss our duelling days ... The trouble with our successors is that nothing seems at stake for them.'[704]

One of the rare occasions on which Hobson betrayed any irritation in print with Tynan was when he reviewed Tynan's own production, *Oh! Calcutta!*, in 1970:[705] 'much that is seen in it strikes me as beautiful, and much of what is heard is dreadful'.[706] This combination of nude revue and titillating sketches came at the end of a decade that had seen a progressive relaxation of social standards in society, especially in attitudes to sex, that had been symbolized in the theatre by the vigorous battle to abolish the censoring powers of the Lord Chamberlain. The failure of the Director of Public Prosecutions to secure a conviction against the publishers of D. H. Lawrence's *Lady Chatterley's Lover* in November 1960 marked not just the beginning of an increasing permissiveness, but the feeling that drama should share the same freedom from official restraint as literature. A private member's bill was introduced into the House of Commons by Dingle Foot in December 1962 to make it *optional* to submit a play to the Lord Chamberlain; although it was refused leave to be introduced into the House of Commons by 134 votes to 77, this served to highlight the arbitrariness of the censor's role. Part of the difficulty stemmed from the generalized nature of the only directive guiding the Lord Chamberlain in his duties, contained within a report of a Joint Select Committee in 1909, which had decreed in its third section, 'Proposals with respect to the Licensing of Plays', that the Lord Chamberlain should license a play, unless he considers that it may reasonably be held:

(a) To be indecent;
(b) To contain offensive personalities;
(c) To represent in an invidious manner a living person, or a person recently dead;
(d) To do violence to the sentiment of religious reverence;
(e) To be calculated to conduce to crime or vice;
(f) To be calculated to impair friendly relations with a Foreign Power;
(g) To be calculated to cause a breach of the peace.[707]

In an era in which dramatists, reflecting the increasingly open nature of British society, were demonstrating a desire to investigate sex and sexuality (for example, Joe Orton), satirize conventional social and religious beliefs (Edward Bond), question governmental attitudes (John Arden), and reconsider official versions of events in recent British history (Rolf Hochhuth), these limitations were deemed to be insupportably restrictive and the office of the Lord Chamberlain was considered too inflexible to adapt to this new climate of artistic exploration. The Lord Chamberlain himself, Lord Cobbold, a former governor of the Bank of England and a prominent member of the City of London, appointed from 29 January 1963, was seen to personify the very values which certain dramatists were keen to question, only adding to the sense of frustration caused by the increasingly petty exercise of his powers. This pettiness resulted from the rigidity of his remit, the fact that, once a play had been licensed, any improvisation or departure from the script was illegal, from the anomaly that television was not subject to the same interference and from a suspicion of the spread of permissiveness. It frequently led to over-sensitive decisions which even defenders of the institution, such as Hobson, recognized as absurd. Writing in 1963 about the revue, *See You Inside*, Hobson reported that:

> At the last moment before its first performance, the Lord Chamberlain intervened to prevent the revue 'See You Inside', from presenting a sketch about the Queen and Prince Philip setting out for Australia and becoming shipwrecked in London dock. This sketch had already been seen by 11,000,000 people on BBC-TV, but the censorship deemed it unsuitable for the additional 450 that the Duchess Theater holds.[708]

Throughout Hobson's writing, from the beginning of the 1960s to the Theatres Bill in September 1968, this sense of embarrassment at the anachronistic nature of censorship was to run parallel with a dislike of the excesses that the new licence of speech and broader subject-matter introduced into the theatre. Three articles from 1963 serve to illustrate his varying degrees of discomfort. In 'A trial for the undefiled'[709] the critic, who had always responded to delicate nuances of language, writes intelligently about the threat to linguistic subtlety posed by some forms of new drama:

> I dislike plays which, like Bill Naughton's *All In Good Time* ... have lines such as 'After six weeks of marriage, your little girl is still a virgin.' Writing of this type belongs to the old melodrama; it is about as natural a form of expression as 'Unhand me, villain.' One suspects that generally it is used as an easy way of startling a naïve but would-be sophisticated audience; and it degrades the language of drama and literature by employing words of weight, association, and moment in contexts unworthy of them.
>
> This is a danger of the new licence of speech in the theatre and the novel. When a poster informs us without irony that 'Love is not a dirty word,' one perceives how fast the language is losing its reserves of charged and emotional communication.

This elegant, sincere expression of a conservative view is more convincing than the occasional outburst of exasperated indignation. In 'The Perennial Debate',[710] written for the sanctimonious *Christian Science Monitor*, Hobson prudishly complained about the magazine *Private Eye*:

> A leading member of the British Cabinet has been openly called in the satirical publication 'Private Eye' 'a flabby-faced coward.' The

Headmaster-elect of Eton has in the same publication been subjected to the most outrageous insults. Freedom of expression has in fact, in print, on the stage, and in such (often excellent) BBC-TV programs as 'That Was the Week That Was' gone far beyond rational justification …

It is surely not coincidental that *Private Eye* had parodied Hobson himself the previous year. In a *Sunday Times* article, 'How to kill the London theatre',[711] the critic rails against Frank Harvey's *Norman* as 'a nasty little play' which contained a privy whose chain would not pull, a guardsman accused of improper behaviour in a urinal, a remark about icicles on the udders of a cow and a play on the equivocal use of the word 'balls'. Hobson thundered: 'If this is what the theatre is coming to … then the theatre will die; and, unemployed though I be, I shall dance at its funeral.' And in 'Standards of Daring'[712] Hobson wondered whether any dramatist would have the courage to state, like him, that homosexuality was a sin. Nevertheless, in 1965, the year that the power of the Lord Chamberlain faced its most serious challenge thus far, Hobson started to attempt the formidable task of criticizing the practice of censorship whilst defending its principle.

Between October 1964 and March 1965, out of a total of 441 plays submitted for consideration by the Lord Chamberlain, 378 were licensed without reservation, 45 required one or two verbal changes, 15 required substantial verbal and business changes and 3 required one or more scenes to be omitted.[713] One of the plays that attracted the particular attention of the censor was John Osborne's *A Patriot for Me*, due for presentation at the Royal Court, the theatre in the vanguard of the opposition to censorship. When the substantial list of changes demanded – ranging from linguistic ('the clap' and 'Tears of Christ' had to be excised) to structural (the entire drag ball was banned)[714] – was presented to the Royal Court, the management decided to turn the theatre into a theatre club, to which members of the audience were obliged to belong. This removed the English Stage Society (the name of the club) from the jurisdiction of the Lord Chamberlain, because theatre clubs had always been viewed in law as places of private entertainment. On witnessing the première of the club performance of the play in July 1965, Hobson derided the erratic behaviour of the Lord Chamberlain in refusing a public licence:

> If I did not know it to be untrue, I should think that the Lord Chamberlain was mad. We know that he has licensed a drama that openly displays a lesbian household, a drama in which one lesbian seeks gratification by ordering another to drink her dirty bath water: the whole tricked out with a projection of saliva as disgusting as Jean Genet's most deliberate effort to shock and upset in 'Les Paravents', without Genet's philosophic and poetic justification.
>
> I am not saying that this play ought to have been banned. I am saying that, after giving his sanction to this entertainment, it is ludicrous and

pathetic that the Lord Chamberlain should have refused to allow John Osborne's *A Patriot for Me* to be performed publicly at the Royal Court.

One cannot protest too strongly against that double moral standard which prevails in the government of the English theatre, by which it is permissible to treat a difficult and delicate subject frivolously, but of which any thoughtful consideration is almost automatically penalised.[715]

This is bold and convincing rhetoric, although Hobson still preferred to see censorship as an unfortunate necessity which was presently being misapplied and was merely in need of modification. That modification, if not outright abolition, was needed was patently demonstrated by the prosecution of the various directors of the Royal Court for producing Edward Bond's *Saved* in November 1965 (a première that Hobson did not review as he was in Paris at the time). The derisory punishment of fifty guineas meted out by the magistrate represented a moral victory for the Royal Court, but closed the club performance loophole (since the creation of theatre clubs now ran the risk of genuinely punitive fines[716]). It did, nevertheless, emphasize the draconian nature of the power of the state, more reminiscent of a Communist country than a western democracy.

At the beginning of 1967, the year the Joint Parliamentary Committee on Censorship advocated the abolition of the Theatres Act (1843) which had granted the Lord Chamberlain the responsibility of licensing plays for public performances, Hobson allowed his subjective disgust at a section of a play to come dangerously close to destroying the one credible defence of censorship that he had maintained since his 1932 article, 'Censorship and *The Green Pastures*'[717] – namely, that censorship was acceptable as long as theatre clubs provided a forum for exploratory drama free from official interference. Having seen Colin Spencer's *The Ballad of the False Barman* at the Hampstead Theatre Club, he wrote:

The hero of this piece is a male whore who operates in a sleazy pierhead cafe run by a lesbian barman, who in another metamorphosis, may be a duke. At one point in the second act the whore stands with his back to the audience very close to the front of the stage. He lowers his trousers and shows us a long and complete view of his naked bottom. Now I do not for a moment deny that this sight may be the source of much pleasure to my homosexual friends. I merely say that to me – and I do not care what Freudian interpretations are put on this remark – it is hideous and disgusting and should be stopped. The licence our stage has arrogated to itself goes far beyond any limits which a decent society should permit. There is today a campaign to get the censorship abolished. What in actual fact is needed is that the Lord Chamberlain should exert over theatre clubs as well as theatres the authority which a recent legal decision has shown that he possesses.[718]

In February 1968 Hobson revealed, with some wit, that this desire to see the jurisdiction of the censor extended to theatre clubs had been a hasty reaction to a disturbing play:

> The authority of the Lord Chamberlain to license or to refuse to license plays, modified by the club system of paying no attention to his decisions, is the most perfect protection of the freedom of the drama that has yet been devised anywhere in the world.[719]

As Hobson was aware, however, public and, more importantly, political opinion was running against him. George Strauss's private member's bill, the Theatres Act, which abolished the censorship of drama, attracted all-party support and reached the statute-book in September 1968. Hobson's uncertain approach to censorship and his demand for a more draconian application of the powers of the Lord Chamberlain at a time when it was inevitable that those powers would be abolished meant that his critical career had reached its lowest point since the end of 1954.

Chapter 8

The Grand Old Man of the Theatre: 1968–1988

A curious paradox of stage censorship is that during the last ten years of its operation, a period when it was most stringently attacked by the theatre profession, the British theatre saw a proliferation of new dramatic works. New Wave plays that challenged the conventions of the late 1950s, such as Shelagh Delaney's depiction of motherhood and female sexuality in *A Taste of Honey* (praised by Hobson for being uncensorious [720]), succeeded in eclipsing the appeal of the *ancien régime* (Rattigan's anachronistic 1960 musical, *Joie de Vivre*, was significantly described by Hobson as 'a total disaster' [721]). The Kitchen Sink dramas in turn were followed by a second generation of plays that were stimulated by the greater public appetite for themes that had been previously regarded as inappropriate for the theatre. David Storey's slice-of-life drama about a troubled provincial schoolteacher, *The Restoration of Arnold Middleton* (hailed by Hobson as the best first play to be produced by the English Stage Company since *Look Back in Anger*[722]); Peter Terson's depiction of life on the football terraces in *Zigger-Zagger*;[723] Simon Gray's depiction of transvestism and sexual desire in *Wise Child* (subjects that Gray treated with integrity, in Hobson's view [724]); and Peter Nichols' harrowing play about a severely handicapped child, *A Day in the Death of Joe Egg*, which made the crippled Hobson uncomfortable because it said much about the suffering of the parents and little about the misery of the child,[725] are all examples of significant, first works by dramatists in the vanguard of the second wave, which testified to the continuing vigour of the theatre in the middle of the 1960s. This last play provoked a significant reaction on the part of the critic, in that it brought forward a rare public endorsement of the Christian Science belief in faith-healing. In the play the doctors can suggest nothing for the child, and, Hobson observes:

> the best that the Private Eye caricature of a clergyman can do is to propose the laying on of hands. This is introduced to show what a fool the man is. Of course the laying on of hands is superstition, but if there is absolutely nothing else, why not try it? Million-to-one chances do come off, and apparent miracles do sometimes take place. I have known a doctor, looking at a paralysed boy, say, this child will never be able to earn its own living: and that child to have gone on subsequently to earn about £6,000 a year more than the doctor ever did.

The defensiveness and irritation apparent in this outburst were to become an increasingly familiar feature of Hobson's output for *The Sunday Times* up until 1976. His subjective approach to criticism had been well suited to the 1940s and mid-1950s, when the persona of the critic was a carefully cultivated one of elegance and refinement. There was little public examination of the top theatre critics' *raison d'être*, since their social cachet was considered as important as their social comment, but once the function of the critic became subjected to scrutiny by Tynan, *Encore* and young theatre practitioners frustrated by the sterility of the West End, however, it was impossible to maintain a civilized – and protective – distance. They were required to participate as well as observe, and whilst Hobson had succeeded in achieving this awkward realignment in 1954, it was almost impossible to pull off the same trick in the 1970s, following the two events in 1968 that were to have a profound effect on the direction of the second wave of drama: the formal abolition of stage censorship and the European-wide student unrest of May of that year. For a start, Hobson was separated from many of the new entrants into the British theatre by age (he was 65 in 1969), religious sensibility, orthodox social values and a deep respect for the notion of an Establishment, which was symbolized by his defence of the Lord Chamberlain and recognized by his receipt of a CBE in 1971. Coupled with a sensitive disposition that must have made envious and frustrated attacks on his occupancy of the most significant of critical posts additionally wounding, it is easy to see why many people, friends as well as enemies, regret that Hobson soldiered on too long.

It would be wrong, however, to view Hobson's last eight years at *The Sunday Times* as an entirely disappointing coda to a brilliant career. In April 1968 Edwige Feuillère and Jean-Louis Barrault performed in *Partage de Midi* in London as part of Peter Daubeny's World Theatre Season. For Hobson, Feuillère's performance as Ysé was, as before, the epitome of style and grace – 'I do not think we shall see such a performance as this again in our lifetime'[726] – and Barrault was similarly impressive – 'his incisiveness, grace and clarity of speech have no rivals'.[727] Hobson's review of their performance was published on 5 May 1968. The following week violent demonstrations broke out in Paris against the authoritarianism of de Gaulle, the growth of the consumer society and traditional social creeds. On 15 May 1968 the Odéon Theatre, the home of the Renaud-Barrault company, was occupied by students – the instigators of the protests – who turned it into a forum for debate. Instead of calling the police, Barrault plaintively asked the students why they had been antagonized by him, since he had always sympathized with their views and opposed authority. 'I am an old anarchist myself', he declared, and went on to praise the occupiers as participants in 'a movement of the young who wish to transform society. With all my heart I am with this movement.' Nevertheless, the non-paying audience refused to permit that evening's performance to proceed. The following night, 16 May,

Daniel Cohn-Bendit, a student leader, told the packed audience that the Odéon was now a weapon in the struggle against the bourgeoisie, and the hapless Barrault, although ostensibly condoning the motives of the occupiers – 'Barrault is of no interest, the director of the Théâtre de France no longer exists … Barrault is dead, there remains a living man' – was left with little alternative but to allow his theatre to be used for revolutionary discussion. The squatters were eventually evicted on 14 June.[728] For his tolerance of the students, Barrault was expelled from the theatre by de Gaulle's Minister of Culture, André Malraux, a decision that incensed the mild-mannered Hobson. It so offended his sense of decency, given Barrault's immense service to French theatre, and so provoked his own sense of loyalty that Hobson, the youthful socialist-turned-admirer of rank and privilege, took the most principled decision of his career: he decided to return his much-valued Légion d'honneur, awarded in 1960. A letter to *The Times* on 9 September 1968 explained the reasons for his action. He wished to protest at the dismissal of Jean-Louis Barrault from the management of the Théâtre de France, because Barrault had been instrumental in generating his enthusiasm for French drama in the 1940s:

> This enthusiasm in its turn brought me the award of the Legion of Honour, which I was proud and happy to have. But I am no longer proud and happy to have it. Accordingly I have returned it, as the only concrete action I can take to show my distress and anger at the dishonour that has been done to M. Barrault and, in him, the whole of French culture.[729]

This was a powerful gesture on Hobson's part; as an admirer of French culture and British rank, the honour would have represented a tremendous source of pride. He followed up this action with a rallying article in *The Sunday Times* demanding that concrete action be taken in Britain in support of Barrault and listing the British theatre's indebtedness to the French actor/director – he had cemented the policy of the Edinburgh Festival of inviting distinguished companies from France; he had been responsible for a ground-breaking *Hamlet* in 1951; he had introduced the dramatists Claudel, Salacrou and Feydeau into Britain; and he continued to mount innovative work in Britain, such as his co-operation with Peter Brook at the Roundhouse.[730] Hobson must have taken satisfaction from the fact that, although Barrault was not reinstated, his artistic energies were not impaired by his dismissal. His immediate reply to Malraux was to stage an adaptation of the work of François Rabelais in a Montmartre wrestling-hall, which celebrated freedom from authority and drew large, sympathetic audiences.[731]

The global events of 1968 – the Tet Offensive by the Vietcong, the assassinations of Martin Luther King and Robert Kennedy in the US, the wounding of Rudi Dutschke in West Berlin, the Russian invasion of Czechoslovakia and the student demonstrations and occupations in France that spread throughout universities and colleges in Western Europe – coupled with contentious domestic political events, such as the Race Relations Bill and Enoch Powell's 'rivers of blood speech' – galvanized many members of the theatrical profession. A number of new writers, far to the left of the Labour party, shared the desire to fashion a drama that would act as a catalyst for social and political change, and they recognized the potential of collaborating theatre groups in taking a political message to specific communities. The chief difference between these writers and those of the 1956–60 generation was that, whereas the movement that had been initiated by *Look Back in Anger* was largely centred around two London theatres – the Royal Court and the Theatre Royal (Stratford East) – the new writing was rapidly disseminated throughout the country because of its potential immediacy (it could be presented at short notice to an identifiable audience), its mobility (it no longer relied on conventional theatrical venues and sets, preferring pubs, factories and community centres), its freedom from official restraint in the light of the abolition of censorship, and the general shift in cultural attitudes that now demanded politically challenging drama.[732] However, this movement was motivated less by an optimistic belief in the virtues of political consciousness than by the awareness that the promise of the 'Swinging Sixties' had petered out as the world moved into the 1970s. The impulse for political change would no longer be stimulated from without but needed to be generated from within. To this was added the realization that the Soviet invasion of Czechoslovakia, which removed the last vestiges of credibility for the Communist party as a left-wing alternative in Britain, and the failure of the French uprising in 1968 heralded the very opposite of a revolutionary dawn.[733] This disillusion was compounded for many practitioners of fringe theatre by the unexpected victory of the Conservative party under Edward Heath in the 1970 general election, and gave rise to agitprop theatre groups dedicated to specific interests – feminism, gay rights, black awareness and anti-racism, for example – and a further period of prolific growth in the domestic theatre.

Harold Hobson's attitude to exploratory theatre post-1968 was prefigured by two reviews of the innovative work of Peter Brook during this year of upheaval. Hobson had always championed the earliest experiments of the avant-garde and was constantly intrigued by attempts to extend the boundaries of theatre. Thus, when confronted by Brook's work at the Roundhouse in July 1968, the deliberately convoluted syntax of his review conveys an honest expression of his bewilderment, but also mirrors the sinuous movements of the performers and suggests that present mystification need not preclude future potential:

> Out of the mass of writhing bodies, howls of pain, gibberings of incomprehensibility, and deformed lunatic smiles, which he and his colleagues have, presumably, organised – for surely they cannot just

happen – one feels obscurely, but in the end, hopefully, that something might perhaps sometime, in some as yet unrealised connection, in a place not at the moment to be foreseen, actually emerge.[734]

Against this, a second review in September of Brook's publication, *The Empty Space*, emphasizes Hobson's current position of orthodoxy, his dislike of theory and his suspicion of the director (and, by implication, the newly collaborative approach of theatre groups) as the prime force behind productions: 'He seems unaware that the glories of the contemporary British stage are not any director whatsoever but John Osborne, Harold Pinter and (still) Sir Laurence Olivier.'[735] The critic is also sceptical of Grotowski's intention, widely admired at the Edinburgh Festival of that year, of putting 'the great myths of the past to the *test* of contemporary experience, as if a theatrical production were a verifiable scientific experiment when it is in fact nothing more than the externalisation of subjective conviction'.[736] Much more acceptable was Brook's invigorating experimentation in 1970 with *A Midsummer Night's Dream*, whose technical devices enhanced rather than obscured subjective identification on the part of the audience and which Hobson described as 'the sort of thing one only sees once in a generation, and then only from a man of genius'.[737] In other words, exploratory drama that was theatrically effective would appeal to Hobson, whereas experimental productions that sacrificed entertainment for political didacticism, shock value or the demonstration of the irrelevant novelty of the latest theatrical technique were unlikely to provoke the necessary emotional engagement. Further evidence of a consistent strand to his writing.

On the eve of the new decade Hobson looked ahead to the 1970s and made an accurate prediction: 'Productions which are mainly the product of group invention, and involve improvisation and audience participation, are likely to become increasingly important during the nineteen seventies',[738] but his limited experience of this new form of drama left him undecided as to its lasting significance: 'What we have seen of them up to now leaves the question of whether they will contribute to the theatre still unanswered.' Hobson's disability sometimes restricted his access to some of the more inaccessible fringe venues and even custom-built new theatres could pose a problem. Unusually, he complained about the design of the new theatre at Sussex University in November 1969, describing it as:

> extremely draughty, bitterly cold, furnished with shoddy and prehistorically uncomfortable seats without arm-rests, lacking on its innumerous stairs the handrails that might assist the infirm, totally without food of even the simplest kind and about as cheerful as the inside of a coffin.[739]

In spite of the physical challenge of some venues, his respect for traditional theatre practice and his dislike of dogmatic politics, Hobson did not neglect the new forms of drama in his column in *The Sunday Times* during the 1970s, finding aspects both to praise and to question. An early introduction to audience participation, at a Nash House production of the Black and White Power works, *It Bees Dat Way*, by Ed Bullins and *Arrest* by Vic Corti, proved surprisingly entertaining – even if he appears to have missed the point:

> A well known colleague sent one of the company spinning across the floor with a neat trip after losing his wallet (later restored to him); and when there came a move to throw the audience out, a friend of mine proved unexpectedly and refreshingly belligerent. By the end everybody had forgotten about power in their cheerful and hearty agreement that they had thoroughly enjoyed themselves.[740]

Hobson concluded that drama that demanded audience participation was legitimate if it did not treat the audience itself as 'the enemy, and therefore feels called on to insult, browbeat, and disgust it, by making it as uncomfortable and humiliated as possible'.[741] Hobson similarly enjoyed Charles Marowitz's Open Space production of *Palach*, even given the:

> simultaneous action on four separate stages, the blaring of loudspeakers drowning the voices of the players, the players themselves overlaying each other's speeches – which I have always supposed foredoomed to failure because they would seem incompatible with the single unity that is essential to drama, namely, unity of effect.

He proceeded to offer an intelligent prescription for a successful experimental production:

> I still think that they are dangerous and difficult means, fatal to directors who think that, because they are unfamiliar in the naturalistic theatre, they are therefore new, and of value in themselves. They call for an especially fine quality of mind, an integrity that unerringly perceives where the unusual degenerates into the showy, and a capacity to keep steadily in view a central harmony amid the apparent discord of conflicting cacophonies. These conditions are rarely met: but they are met in this production of Mr Marowitz.[742]

The supple handling of language, the continuing quality of thought, the innate sense of the theatrical and the sense of overview that Hobson reveals in this article is one illustration of how his criticisms still contained much of value after the abolition of censorship.

That Hobson's attitude to experimental theatre was perceived as conservative at the time is undeniable. Kenneth Hurren, the former drama critic of the *Spectator*, claimed in his 1977 book, *Theatre Inside Out*, that: 'In the later years [Hobson] had seemed to strive for a perversity of opinion that made his notices something of a joke in theatrical circles',[743] and Michael Billington thinks that 'there were signs that some of the flair had gone' and that he became too obsessed with minor playwrights such as John Bowen and David Snodin.[744] If posterity has judged that these playwrights have not justified Hobson's great enthusiasm, hindsight also permits one to perceive that many of his apparently reactionary conclusions about experimental theatre have been proved correct. His rare outbursts at the impropriety of the content of experimental productions, such as his discomfort at the Wherehouse La Mama's production at the Open Space of *XXXXX*, appear, on theatrical grounds, to be justified:

> It starts the play by a breathless Ring-a-ring-a-roses, out of which the actor playing God breaks free, strips, using words I do not consider it decent to quote, takes his penis in his hand, and waggles it at the audience – seventeen men and three women the night I was there – who watch in gloomy stupor. Later Jesus is seen to be equipped with an instrument which enables him to squirt water over his companions, as if he were urinating …[745]

His claim in 1972 that experimental theatre with a specifically political purpose had not created the mass audience necessary for the dissemination and successful implementation of its left-wing message is ironically accurate:

> The anti-Establishment theatre was founded on the theory that the drama should appeal, not to a restricted middle-class public, but to a large popular audience. But a great deal has happened since Centre 42, and today this ideal, at least in London, has in practice been abandoned. The contemporary anti-Establishment theatre is wholly élitist. At its best it devotes technical skill, mastery of physical movement, rhythmical changes of pace, and disciplined concerted action to playing to fractional audiences equipped with special information.[746]

And his tackling of the much-discussed notion of relevance in plays, in 1976, is a model of intelligent insight and concise formulation:

> the notion of relevance … is now the fashionable criterion for judging plays. It is a criterion much misunderstood. It cannot too often be said that a play is relevant if it enables us either to solve or to endure our present problems, and not otherwise. Unless the imagination of the dramatist is creatively inspired, no amount of talk about unemployment, military efficiency … collective bargaining, Angola, or devolution will make a play relevant. Nor does the absence of such talk necessarily make it irrelevant.[747]

He was also to demonstrate further perception when commenting on new works both in the main subsidized theatres and in the commercial theatre.

The expected flood of bad language and explicit sex scenes after the removal of the jurisdiction of the Lord Chamberlain did not materialize, and this helped to alleviate Hobson's fear that the new freedom would be misused to the detriment of British drama. He was reassured by *Hair*, the first production to take advantage of this new liberty in September 1968, praising its 'conquering charm, in response to which I very nearly finished up on the stage myself, singing and dancing, being only narrowly beaten to it by Miss Zsa Zsa Gabor',[748] and he even ventured the hope that 'its all-embracing love' might signal a shift of direction away from a portrayal of hatred on the stage.[749] Hobson was similarly unalarmed by subsequent productions that featured exhibitions of nudity (the one identifiable consequence of the abolition of censorship), if they could be justified for aesthetic purposes. Hence, he contrasts the irrelevance of nudity in *Oh! Calcutta!*, which provoked unnecessary overreaction – Hobson believing that a revue which consisted of sketches of *Oh! Calcutta!*'s quality 'would hardly run more than a week unless – an important proviso – it were assisted by the excited protests of officious guardians of public and private morality who lack the elementary common sense to keep their mouths shut'[750] – with Francis Warner's integral use of nudity in *Maquettes* – the two seated, naked figures which open and close the play illustrating that 'We bring nothing with us into the world, and we can take nothing with us out of it.'[751] Warner, one of Hobson's most admired dramatists in the 1970s,[752] is also commended in 1974 for the way in which he employs nudity in *Meeting Ends*: 'principally as a means of creative expression. I have never seen this done before ... absorbingly experimental, forward-looking and brave, as well as, at times, in no unequivocal sense, beautiful.'[753] In this respect, Warner always remained the model to emulate. Hobson's devotion to Warner, an Oxford academic, resulted in some of the most vituperative criticism he was ever to suffer, since it was predicated on the erroneous belief that Hobson was blinded to the failings of anything emerging from his old university. The recent claim by Michael Coveney, the theatre critic of the *Observer*, that Hobson invariably championed 'an overpraised nonentity or Oxonian' represents the nadir of this form of attack.[754]

Hobson occasionally attended productions, such as the National Theatre's production of *Byron – the Naked Peacock* at the Old Vic, which touched the Achilles' heel of his criticism. The references in this play to sodomy provoked an autocratic questioning of the justifiability of spending public money on such a show, in addition to the creation of a delimiting guideline for the acceptable use of permissiveness:

> I cannot formulate any set of rules which would ensure that permissiveness is an asset and not a liability to the theatre. But roughly speaking I should say that its use by men like Mr Hall, Mr Brook, and Mr Robin Phillips (who directed Abélard and Héloïse) is likely to be justified. Yet any use of permissiveness as an end in itself, and not as an instrument for the better accomplishment of the aesthetic aim, makes it progressively more difficult to ensure the viability of such men like them who are the glory of our theatre. It is part of the duty of public authorities to see that they are not put at risk.[755]

That this form of outburst was rare, rarer than one might have expected given the previously pro-censorship views of Hobson, and that it was invariably connected with explicit depictions of homosexuality (the only topic about which Hobson wrote with unappealing prejudice) testifies to the scarcity of controversial productions after 1968. Hobson himself appeared satisfied in 1971 that his fears in the wake of abolition had been unfounded – 'The British stage has, with the abolition of censorship, acquired liberty; but it has not generally given itself over to licence …'[756] – and in the last eight years of his career at *The Sunday Times* he was able to concentrate on his favourite critical preoccupation, the detection of new works of merit.

Between 1968 and 1976 Hobson managed to demonstrate a surprisingly broad taste in new plays that appeared in both the commercial and the subsidized sector, and his writing simultaneously records the diversity of the second wave. The collaboration between a young Royal Court writer, David Storey, and two established actors, Richardson and Gielgud, for the 1970 production of *Home* was reminiscent of Olivier's blessing to the New Wave drama when he agreed to play Archie Rice in John Osborne's *The Entertainer* in 1957. Hobson felt that the encounter between the theatrical knights on stage, the 'perfect embodiments of a vanishing age',[757] was extremely moving:

> Sir John Gielgud is Harry and Sir Ralph Richardson Jack. In the enormous roll of their past triumphs I can find nothing more memorable, more controlled, or more affecting than their performances here[758]

As well as pathos, however, the production provoked frustration that these two actors had not made the acquaintance of the new drama at a much earlier stage of their careers. A year later, whilst reviewing Ronald Hayman's biography of John Gielgud, Hobson places the responsibility for this unfortunate dichotomy with the Establishment's aversion to the New Wave drama of the 1950s and with Gielgud's misguided persuasion of Richardson and Guinness not to appear in the Arts Theatre production of *Waiting for Godot*: 'Sir John's influence and grave misjudgment here robbed the most significant movement in modern drama of some of the best players.'[759] *Home* therefore represented 'a landmark in the theatre', but one that, for Hobson, had regrettably occurred later than necessary.

Peter Barnes's passionate attack on Toryism, hierarchical values and entrenched privilege, *The Ruling Class*, is a good example of a work which might have been expected to alienate Hobson, but whose dramatic presentation and the passion of the playwright's conviction provided a thrilling experience for the critic – once again illustrating that, for Hobson, the display of a heartfelt vision of life was more essential for convincing political satire than a reinforcement of the political beliefs of an audience. After its Nottingham production in November 1968, Hobson, utilizing a line from Macaulay's poem, *How Horatius Kept the Bridge*,[760] asserted that:

Mr Osborne and Mr Mercer, even at their fiercest, were always ready to admit that there are certain aristocratic qualities not unworthy of admiration. Mr Barnes will accept no such thing; his prejudice and unfairness pass reasonable bounds. But he writes with such zest, such fertility of ludicrous invention, such a power of outrageous caricature and extravagant fantastication that one can scarcely forbear to cheer. Whatever else it may be, this shockingly one-sided play is gloriously alive.[761]

This enthusiastic recommendation is reiterated in the introduction to the published work, to which Hobson contributed: 'It mounts a lively and vigorous attack, not only on the upper echelons of society, but also on all of us who rate cruelty higher than compassion, and consider violence more sane than peace.'[762]

One of Hobson's greatest critical attributes is that he can prevent his personal political beliefs, by this stage a gentle Conservatism,[763] from interfering with an appreciation of a theatrically successful drama exhibiting political values with which he disagrees. This had been evident in his admiration of John Osborne's *The Entertainer* and was of particular importance in the 1970s, an era when many playwrights were investigating the possibility of a Marxist reorientation of society. Thus, whilst he does not accept Howard Brenton's attack on Churchill in *The Churchill Play*, he concedes that it is 'a work of great aesthetic and intellectual power'.[764] He lambasts Trevor Griffiths' *The Party* (which marked Olivier's final appearance at the National in 1973) not solely because of its doctrine, but because of the inadequate dramatic presentation of its Marxist call to revolution – 'There will be no revolution in Britain whilst the revolutionary doctrine continues to be preached only by plays like this'[765] – and, conversely, he praises Griffiths' exploration of the subversive potential of comedy, *The Comedians*, for finding the successful formula in being 'sociologically and theatrically ... very exciting'.[766]

Hobson's loyalty to those favoured dramatists whose careers he had followed from their very beginning remained undiminished until he ceased writing entirely in 1988. Christopher Fry's brief reappearance in 1970 with *A Yard of Sun* was an opportunity for rejoicing: 'The distinctive merit of Mr Fry is that he unites a romantic imagination with a classical coolness of temper'.[767] William Douglas Home's *The Secretary Bird* signalled the welcome return of 'upper middle-class comedy',[768] and Terence Rattigan's *Bequest to the Nation* in 1970 drew the surprising claim that 'Rattigan thinks more instinctively in theatrical terms than any of his contemporaries except Jean Anouilh'.[769] One of the rare occasions on which Hobson's intuitive approach was clouded by his loyalty and lapsed into bizarre self-indulgence took place after he had seen Peggy Ashcroft, one of the actresses he most revered, in *Landscape* by Harold Pinter, one of the playwrights he most admired. In his first review of the work in July 1969 Hobson had focused on the 'devoted and ecstatic cry "Oh my true love"' from the character Beth, which, in its affirmation of pure emotion, had struck Hobson forcibly.[770] A second visit to the production in August resulted in the excessive claim that the passion contained within this line ensured that the work was superior to Shakespeare's *Antony and Cleopatra*, since the play conveyed 'the bondage and ecstasy of overwhelming love'.[771] Michael Billington, the biographer of Peggy Ashcroft, relates that the actress was livid at this idiosyncratic interpretation, stating privately that 'if he goes on once more about this ... I'm going to cut the bloody line ...',[772] and the event contains parallels with Hobson's conviction that the raising of Paul Daneman's hat in *Waiting for Godot* signified the presence of God. It was critical ticks such as this that generated much of the hostility towards Hobson in his last years.

In spite of this occasional lapse, Hobson was still able to display shafts of perception in the twilight of his career as a weekly reviewer. Now very much the grand old man of theatre criticism, he had been awarded the CBE in 1971 (an honour announced in *The Sunday Times* on the same day that Hobson was extolling the merits of the 'hysterically funny' *No Sex Please – We're British*[773]), but this recognition of achievement by the Establishment did not prevent him from championing two dramatists who had forged their careers with forceful attacks on official attitudes. John Osborne continued to have an infinite capacity to move Hobson. *The Hotel in Amsterdam* possessed a haunting resonance: 'It is about friendship. It is about goodness. No dramatist of our time is more responsive to goodness.'[774] *Time Present*, and in particular the performance of Jill Bennett, was similarly cathartic and drew forth a rare reference to Elizabeth Hobson – 'I was intensely moved, and my wife wept unrestrainedly'[775] – and *West of Suez* in 1971 possessed the added advantage of featuring Ralph Richardson: 'He has never been more amusing, nor more strangely moving than as Wyatt Gillman.'[776] The only other actor during this period to approach Richardson in Hobson's esteem was Ian McKellen, who made a deep impression on the critic when playing Richard II in 1968: 'No player of similar age has such lustre, such interior excitement, such spiritual grace ... The National Theatre has one great actor, but it needs another. Well, here he is.'[777]

For many critics, *A Sense of Detachment* in 1972 represented the exhaustion of Osborne's play-writing talents, largely because of the allegedly pornographic scene featuring Rachel Kempson, but Hobson loyally supported its inclusion, maintaining that it is 'counterpointed with some of the loveliest writing in the English language'.[778] He similarly defended Osborne's last work before the start of the playwright's long period of exile from the stage in 1975, *The End of Me Old Cigar*, advocating that Osborne's irritation with, and passion for, England made him 'the most patriotic of our playwrights'.[779] In many ways, the wheel had come full circle, with Hobson an isolated voice in defence of a perplexing playwright, in much the same way that he and Tynan had sought to explain *Look Back in Anger* to a bewildered public in 1956. Intriguingly,

Hobson had never been satisfied with his first review of *Look Back in Anger* and by 1968 had come to repent what he termed his own 'arrogance' in writing that Osborne had been a dramatist who had been unaware of what he was doing.[780] Osborne's subsequent stage achievements had caused the critic to reconsider his original view, the hallmark of an open-minded and trustworthy critic.

If the delight of the 1950s in the field of new writing had been the discovery of Beckett, Osborne and Pinter, and the pleasure of the 1960s had been the observation of their progress, the one playwright of the subsidized theatre who commanded a similar loyalty from Hobson during the 1970s was Edward Bond. Hobson had been in Paris and had not seen the original Royal Court production of *Saved* in 1965, the club performance of which at the Royal Court had dealt such a grievous blow to stage censorship, and his first exposure to Bond's work, the controversial *Early Morning*, with its imputations of lesbianism between Queen Victoria and Florence Nightingale, earned the disconcerting rebuke that the play represented 'the complete negation of drama as I know it'.[781] Two events, however, appear to have influenced Hobson in adopting a more favourable attitude towards the Marxist playwright. Firstly, he enjoyed *Narrow Road to the Deep North* and, secondly, he had come to read the text of the earlier *Saved*. Hobson's attitude to *Narrow Road to the Deep North* again illustrates his ability to respond to works that expound a view of life antithetical to his own. It was 'a fine and memorable play':

> ... a play, I should add, which is not reconcilable with formal Christianity. Mr Bond has not shifted his ground since 'Saved', which, after reading it, I am prepared to believe is one of the outstanding plays of our time, though I reserve a definite opinion until I have seen it acted ... Mr Bond offers no alternative to the Christianity and the colonialism which he derides. Nor do I see why he should. No great dramatist has ever felt called on to offer solutions. Shakespeare did not propose a remedy for the misery of Lear, nor John Osborne for that of Bill Maitland. It is the lesser men – the Augiers, the Galsworthys, the Brechts – who are prolific in snap answers. There are some problems, says Mr Bond, to which there are no solutions possible.[782]

Hobson had responded to *Narrow Road to the Deep North* precisely because, as with the work of Beckett and Pinter, it recognized the world as a complex entity that could not be explained within the duration of two hours, if at all. Just as Hobson had welcomed Ionesco in 1955 for creating a drama in which the process was more important than the meaning (this being a truer reflection of life), the critic reacted favourably to Bond's depiction of contradictory emotional and political impulses because it was a sincere view of a society that Bond despised. The Royal Court production of *Narrow Road to the Deep North*, which Hobson reviewed in February 1969, also provided a stark intellectual contrast to

Neil Simon's *Plaza Suite*, an illustration for Hobson of the vacuous drama that he had hoped had been eliminated:

> [*Plaza Suite* is] ... inexpressibly awful ... the triumphant reassertion of everything that the most hopeful movements of the theatre have been fighting against for years: conventional naturalism, superficial smartness, total mindlessness, mechanical feeling and smug materialism[783]

His first review of *Saved*, also in February 1969, argued persuasively that the brutal and exaggerated scenes in Bond are necessary to persuade the audience that society needs rectifying, without convincing them that this is now an impossibly idealistic prospect:

> It is the first both in time and merit of those plays which have exposed the facts of irrational violence in our society, and the cowardice even of good men in the face of it ... we leave the theatre with the consciousness that goodness, though bruised and perpetually despised, is not necessarily defeated.[784]

Even when hope was absent, as in *Bingo*, Hobson could praise the playwright for being 'memorably poetic and mysterious',[785] and it is with palpable regret that he phrased his dislike of *The Fool* in 1975, terming it 'a sad play for Mr Bond's admirers amongst whom I am one of the most devoted'.[786]

Hobson's position as the long-serving critic of an influential newspaper in the early 1970s, championing the Marxist Edward Bond whilst maintaining a suspicion of alternative theatre, admiring Howard Brenton, having received recognition from the Establishment in the form of a CBE (translated to a knighthood in 1977), meant that he was an inviting target for attack by aggrieved members of the theatrical profession. Hobson's response was always generous, but it developed a steely undertone in print that reflected the increasingly fractious atmosphere of the theatre at this time. At the end of the previous decade he had given short shrift to the Royal Court's plan to ban critics:

> The first thing to be said about the Court is that it is manned by people of outstanding brilliance; the second that it is of an emotional instability which disturbs everyone concerned with it ... the time has perhaps come when critics should seriously ask themselves whether, in respect of the Royal Court, the kid gloves should not be taken off and its frequent failures and ineptitudes be trounced with the same vigour that they would be if produced by any other management[787]

In 1972 he explained why drama critics were more exposed now, by stating that drama criticism had become increasingly difficult since the war because 'the criteria are constantly changing ... Agate used to boast that he never let anything second rate get past him. But the test today is to let nothing first-rate get past one.'[788] One playwright whom Hobson felt was producing second-rate work now was Arnold Wesker. Wesker had fought a sustained battle with critics[789] and Hobson thought he was over-sensitive to adverse criticism. Having seen Wesker's *The Old Ones* in 1972, Hobson wrote, with wicked humour, that the playwright 'gives the impression of being in the grip of a nervous terror that everyone is trying to destroy him and his work' and concluded that his sense of well-being was unlikely to be enhanced by this play, which was 'mumbled by the most gloom-inducing lot of bores that I have seen on the stage since I sat through the purgatory of "Pyjama Tops"'.[790] Unsurprisingly, given his readiness to tackle critics over their unfavourable notices of his works, Wesker replied with an open letter in *Drama Quarterly*, entitled 'A Cretinue of Critics', in which he accused Hobson of an 'unethical use of a public review column in a major newspaper for exercising your private revenge' and urged that Hobson should retire forthwith.[791] On being offered the chance to reply by the editor of *Drama Quarterly*, Hobson simply wrote:

> If anything that could be said would calm Mr Wesker's fears, or lessen his misery I would gladly say it. But everything I can do in that way I have already done in my review of his play, 'The Old Ones'; in the circumstances, therefore, the best I can do for him now is to decline the offer of reply which the Editor of 'Drama' has kindly made to me.[792]

Hobson's reticence was diplomatic, although he then wrote an article, 'How to cope with criticism', in October 1972, subtitled 'Harold Hobson underlines the dangers to drama in the vanity of dramatists', which urged artists to seek out a compliment where possible (citing his own reaction to the Gilliatt article) and to shrug one's shoulders at a disapprobatory review if this was impossible, since 'Any other course, as, for example, brooding over it, is artistically speaking the way to self-destruction.'[793] This sensible advice and implicit rebuke (which was prophetic, given the course of Wesker's subsequent career) naturally incensed the playwright further and he retaliated by writing 'How to Cope with Criticism – Arnold Wesker Underlines the Dangers to Drama in the Vanity of Critics'.[794] Hobson chose not to respond.

Throughout his career the only theatrical form that was as likely to cause Hobson to lose his generous good humour as it was to earn his generous praise was the musical. During the 1960s he maintained an unpredictability when assessing the genre that could equally damn a rapturously received production (for example, *Hello, Dolly!*[795]) or eulogize a general critical failure (*Camelot*[796]). During the period following the abolition of censorship two British productions with important Christian dimensions arrived to revitalize the interest of the critic in the genre. Andrew Lloyd Webber and Tim Rice's *Joseph and the Amazing Technicolour Dreamcoat* was described by Hobson as 'one of the most joyous entertainments I have ever seen',[797] and the rock-musical *Godspell* was a revelation, in that it depicted Christianity in terms of rejoicing:

> It has got hold of the primary thing about Christianity, which is that, despite the crucifixion and the betrayal, Christianity is a religion of gladness and joy, which finishes, not with death, but with resurrection.[798]

Hobson consequently described the work as 'magnificent'.

The note of enthusiasm that Hobson strikes here, underpinned by a Christian sensibility, is the predominant tone of his entire critical output – from his earliest days on the *Christian Science Monitor* in 1929 and throughout his career as the drama critic for *The Sunday Times*, which ended on 1 August 1976. The title of his final article, 'The Pursuit of Happiness', and the tone of his review is particularly significant, because Hobson had generally been a positive critic, motivated by an intense love of the theatre, keen to praise where possible, aware of his great responsibility and able to invest his criticisms with an autobiographical fervour that was often revealing, sometimes irritating, yet always stimulating. It is particularly apt, given his passionate support of new talent and his stated intention of providing, in the body of his work, a historical record of what he had witnessed, that he should end his weekly career by being called upon to review the first piece of new writing to be staged by the new South Bank complex of the National Theatre, Howard Brenton's *Weapons of Happiness*. It was 'a great success', Hobson felt, in spite of its commendation of Communism and denigration of Christ, because the episodes featuring the former Czechoslovak Communist minister standing sleeplessly in a London street and his summoning to the presence of Stalin 'are scenes of splendid theatricality', and because the speech about the Grand Inquisitor was a moment of great emotional import which drew Hobson to the work.[799] All the plays that Hobson had most admired contained a riveting theatricality and had revealed themselves to him through a moment of emotional intensity.

Although his principal interest had been weekly reviewing for a newspaper of quality, Hobson's departure from *The Sunday Times* did not represent the termination of his literary output. In December 1976 he succeeded J. W. Lambert as the reviewer for the *Drama Quarterly*, and he continued to submit a brief survey of recent productions, under the inevitable title 'Hobson's Choice', until December 1983. From then on he provided the same magazine with occasional appreciations of theatrical personalities with whom he had been acquainted, including Sir Ralph Richardson, Anthony Quayle, Richard Burton, Sir Michael Redgrave, Billy Danvers, and Jean Anouilh,[800] which testify both to his elegant style as well as his longevity. Hobson also wrote book reviews on drama topics for the *Times Literary Supplement* and *Books and Bookmen*, in addition to the very occasional article for *The Sunday Times* and for the *Christian Science Monitor*, for whom he had ceased to write on a regular basis after his article of 13 September 1974, 'Edinburgh Fest Shows New Pride'. His final published article for the *Christian Science Monitor*, 'George Bernard Shaw: Provoking', appeared on 3 December 1979.[801]

Hobson published three longer works after his retirement from *The Sunday Times*, an autobiography, *Indirect Journey* (1978), an academic study, *French Theatre since 1830*, (1978), and a personal retrospect of twentieth-century British theatre, *Theatre in Britain* (1984). Peter Hall provides a pertinent evaluation of the autobiography in his published diaries:

> It is elliptical, witty, ironic, also vain, and sometimes outrageous – like the man. But I found it sympathetic. Hobson has, after all, a great deal to be vain about. His life proves that men make their own luck. At key moments, when things were bad, he found unbelievable courage, took action and always succeeded.[802]

French Theatre since 1830 confirmed Hobson's reputation as a passionate devotee of the drama of that country, and *Theatre in Britain*, although disappointingly disjointed, with an uninspiring chronological progression and an over-enthusiastic desire to link the theatre with portentous world events, did provide the opportunity for a last reminder of Hobson's favourite literary genre, the allusive, tightly constructed newspaper article, designed to inform, provoke and inspire. Prior to the publication of *Theatre in Britain* in September 1984, Hobson had published the piece, 'Has Our Theatre Lost its Nerve?', an eloquent analysis of the collapse of serious British drama in the mid-1980s, in *The Sunday Times*. Possessing a historical overview (it likens the failure of nerve on the part of serious British dramatists to the cowardice of Auden prior to the Second World War); a passionate belief in new writing as the lifeblood of the theatre; and a clarion call for the rectification of a perceived and depressing trend – 'the prevailing temper of hopelessness and fear' that pervades contemporary drama[803] – the article provides a final confirmation of the deep concern that the critic always held for the theatrical health of the nation. Consistent to the last in this underlying critical approach, Hobson left behind a body of work that both testifies to, and helped to influence, the evolution of twentieth-century British drama.

Notes

1. Harold Hobson, *Indirect Journey* (London, 1978), p. 1.
2. 'Impartial History?', *Christian Science Monitor* (*CSM*), 13/12/1927.
3. Ibid.
4. Harold Hobson, *Interview with D. M. Shellard* (*DMS*), Westhampnett House, Chichester, West Sussex, 2/8/1990.
5. Edwin Emery, *The Press and America* (New Jersey, 1972), p. 567.
6. Ibid.
7. *Report on the British Press* (PEP, London, 1946), p. 140.
8. Erwin Canham, *Commitment to Freedom* (Boston, 1958), p. 75.
9. Ibid.
10. Ibid.
11. Harold Hobson, *Interview with D. M. Shellard*, Westhampnett House, Chichester, West Sussex, 10/7/1991.
12. *Indirect Journey*, p. 166.
13. 'Popular Musical Taste', *CSM*, 30/3/1929.
14. 'Grand Opera in England', *CSM*, 30/7/1929.
15. 'How England Views the Talkies', *CSM*, 19/7/1929.
16. *CSM*, 26/5/1932.
17. 'Fiction and the Public Libraries', *CSM*, 16/9/1929.
18. 'What! No Detective Stories?', *CSM*, 17/4/1929.
19. 'Wordsworth and Browning', *CSM*, 1/5/1929.
20. 'A Poet Laureate's Duties', *CSM*, 13/11/1929.
21. 'The Literary Class List', *CSM*, 12/6/1929.
22. *CSM*, 14/5/1929.
23. 'How England Views the Talkies', *CSM*, 19/7/1929.
24. 'Mr Shaw Also Spoke', *CSM*, 14/12/1929.
25. 'Lazzaro', *CSM*, 30/7/1929.
26. 'Jew Süss', *CSM*, 11/9/1929.
27. *Indirect Journey*, p. 14.
28. Ibid., p. 46.
29. Ibid., p. 18.
30. Ibid., p. 39.
31. Ibid., p. 49.
32. Ibid., p. 51.
33. Mary Baker Eddy, *Manual of the Mother Church*, p. 17, reproduced in *Questions and Answers on Christian Science*, The Christian Science Publishing Society (Boston, 1974), p. 3. This quotation was the motion proposed by Mary Baker Eddy on which the sixteen voted to found the Church.
34. *Matthew* 9: 1–8.
35. Mary Baker Eddy, *Science and Health, With Key to the Scriptures* (Boston, rev. edn. 1910), p. 123.
36. For much of this section on Christian Science, I am indebted to the *Encyclopedia Britannica*, Vol. 5, 1961, pp. 638–9.
37. Baker Eddy, *Science and Health*, p. 472.
38. Ibid., p. 123.

39. *Indirect Journey*, p. 44.
40. Ibid., p. 55.
41. Ibid., p. 71.
42. Ibid., p. 73.
43. Erwin Canham, *Commitment to Freedom* (Boston, 1958), p. 219.
44. 'Current Topics', *Sheffield Daily Telegraph*, 8/1/1923.
45. 'The Call to the Public School Men', *Sheffield Daily Telegraph*, 22/9/1925.
46. Humphrey Carpenter, *O.U.D.S. – A Centenary History of the Oxford University Dramatic Society* (Oxford, 1985), p. 141.
47. *CSM*, 24/9/1931.
48. *CSM*, 7/11/1931.
49. 'Memory Theatre ... Hobson Signs Off', *Plays and Players*, September 1976, pp. 16–17.
50. For the effect that the new media had on the acting profession between 1896 and 1939, see Michael Sanderson, *From Irving to Olivier* (London, 1985), pp. 206–26.
51. Hugh Hunt, Kenneth Richards, John Russell Taylor, *The Revels History of Drama in English*, Vol. 7: *1880 to the Present Day* (London, 1978), p. 41.
52. Christopher Innes, *Modern British Drama 1890–1990* (Cambridge, 1992), p. 242.
53. Ernest Short, *Sixty Years of Theatre* (London, 1951), p. 315.
54. See Peter Roberts, *The Old Vic Story* (London, 1976), pp. 129–34, and George Rowell, *The Old Vic Theatre: A History* (Cambridge, 1993), pp. 121–30, for a brief sketch of this period in the Old Vic's history.
55. Dodie Smith, *Call It a Day* (London, 1936), III, ii, p. 131.
56. Alan Monkhouse, *Cecilia* (London, 1932), II, pp. 33–4.
57. 'Mr Monkhouse Comes to London', *CSM*, 10/4/1933.
58. 'A Test for an Aristocrat', *CSM*, 20/2/1933.
59. *CSM*, 15/9/1934.
60. Hunt *et al.*, *1880 to the Present Day*, p. 41.
61. 'After 2344 Years', *CSM*, 7/1/1933.
62. *CSM*, 23/5/1933.
63. Ibid.
64. 'From the Imp to the Parthenon', *CSM*, 18/1/1934.
65. *CSM*, 23/12/1933.
66. Michael Holroyd, *Bernard Shaw*, Vol. 3: *1918–1950* (London, 1991), p. 337.
67. *CSM*, 23/12/1933.
68. Holroyd, *Bernard Shaw*, p. 334.
69. This sentence encapsulates a firmly held critical maxim and explains the appeal that the première of *Waiting for Godot* in 1955 held for Hobson.
70. 'Intellectual Drama', *CSM*, 6/4/1935.
71. *CSM*, 9/6/1934.
72. 'Wanted, a Pinshaw', *CSM*, 18/10/1938.
73. 'The Aftermath of Shaw', *CSM*, 19/5/1934.
74. *CSM*, 7/9/1934.
75. *CSM*, 20/3/1933.
76. *CSM*, 13/12/1927.
77. Apart from admiring Peter Hall, who directed the first performance of *Waiting for Godot*, Hobson continually undervalued the input of the director.
78. 'The Actor as Artist', *CSM*, 20/3/1933.
79. Irving Wardle, *Theatre Criticism* (London, 1992), p. 13.
80. *Indirect Journey*, p. 76.
81. See, for example, Harold Hobson, *Theatre in Britain* (Oxford, 1984), pp. 10–14; 'Pleasure in the Theater', *CSM*, 15/6/1937; and 'In the Theater', *CSM*, 7/2/1938, when Hobson reveals that the 'strong sweep of excite-

ment caught up in a whirl of emotion' that the last scene of *The Only Way* provokes is used by him as a benchmark against which to judge fine acting. This is an extension of Matthew Arnold's rules for judging poetry, expressed in *The Study of Poetry*, a practice whose adoption Hobson confirms in his career in 'Commentary', *Plays*, November 1984. In this article Hobson explains that his critical touchstones included the poignant questioning of the younger husband by the elder wife as to whether their age-gap mattered to him in Hugh Burden's *The Young and Lovely* (1940); Ralph Richardson being reminded in *The Heiress* (1949) that the wife that he mourned had died long ago; and the Revd George McLeod's Easter Day sermon in the late 1940s, which ended with the triumphant cry: 'The grave is empty; shall we not rejoice?'

82. *CSM*, 16/1/1933.
83. 'The World's Greatest Play', *CSM*, 13/9/1933.
84. 'On Seeing Shakespeare', *CSM*, 15/6/1933.
85. 'Wanted – Poor Plays', *CSM*, 27/2/1933.
86. 'Up for Judgement', *CSM*, 21/8/1933. See also 'The Wandering Jew', *CSM*, 18/9/1933: 'The theater and the drama are not synonymous terms. Bad drama does not necessarily make bad theater. The drama is only an ingredient of the theater. Would not any rational person rather see Irving in "The Bells" than the Puddlehampton Literary and Philosophical Society's presentation of "Hamlet"? In the last resort, it is the actor, more than the author, who is essential to the theater.'
87. *CSM*, 11/2/1933. See also '"The Nightingales" Night Out', *CSM*, 10/2/1934, for Hobson's description of Randle Ayrton in the tiny part of David – 'worth more than a leading actor's monopoly of the stage for an entire evening'.
88. *CSM*, 18/4/1934. See also 'Three Actors', *CSM*, 9/2/1935, for an appreciation of Gielgud, Richardson and Laughton, and 'The Irving Centenary', *CSM*, 18/1/1938, for a later recognition of Laurence Olivier's talents. Hobson often wrote with great insight about Laughton's stage performances. Simon Callow, Laughton's biographer, believes that Hobson's review of Laughton's 1959 Lear found the 'exact image' to describe the actor's intention when the critic wrote: 'That the universe should single out so small a figure for its wrath gives a lurid splendour to the performance, it is as if an ordinary man were called to crucifixion' *The Sunday Times* (*ST*), 'Different Roads To Success', 23/8/1959. For Callow, Hobson was often wayward, but sometimes saw 'clearer than anyone else' – *Charles Laughton: A Difficult Actor* (London, 1987), p. 263.
89. *CSM*, 26/1/1935.
90. *CSM*, 17/1/1935.
91. 'Plays of the London Year', *CSM*, 11/1/1938. Ever the positive critic, he did manage to find eleven works he could commend.
92. 'Economics in the Theater', *CSM*, 24/12/1938, provides a breakdown of the financing of a production.
93. '"Idiot's Delight" in London', *CSM*, 26/4/1938.
94. 'The Theater and the Crisis', *CSM*, 13/5/1939.
95. Quoted in Stephen Constantine, '"Love on the Dole" and its Reception in the 1930s', *Literature and History*, Vol. 8 (2), Autumn 1982, pp. 232–47.
96. Ronald Gow and Walter Greenwood, *Love on the Dole* (London, 1936), I, p. 9.
97. 'Love on the Dole', *CSM*, 9/3/1935.
98. 'The Dance of Death', *CSM*, 22/10/1935.
99. Humphrey Carpenter, *W. H. Auden* (Oxford, 1992), p. 165.
100. Edward Mendelson, *Early Auden* (London, Faber, 1981), p. 269.

101. W. H. Auden and Christopher Isherwood, *Plays*, ed. Edward Mendelson (London, 1989), p. 107.
102. 'The Dance of Death', *CSM*, 22/10/1935.
103. *CSM*, 8/6/1937.
104. 'Fine Writing in the Theater', *CSM*, 2/8/1938.
105. 'Realism Besieged', *CSM*, 4/3/1939.
106. Although the play was not a critical success, 'much of the stir was caused by the final moments when Johnson, carrying umbrella and briefcase, began his ascent to another world. Here Richardson would turn up his collar and walk out into something quite unknown, very huge and very cold. Britten's thrilling music, added to the blue immensity of [Basil] Dean's two cycloramas never failed to bring the house down': Garry O'Connor, *Ralph Richardson: An Actor's Life* (London, 1982), p. 91. The play, and this final moment in particular, was described by Hobson as 'a brief moment of exaltation', in *Theatre in Britain*, p. 111.
107. *The Sunday Times*, 14/5/1939.
108. 'Laughter Rules in British Theaters', *CSM*, 30/12/1939.
109. Esmond Knight, *Seeking the Bubble* (London, 1943), p. 122.
110. Richard Huggett, *Binkie Beaumont: Eminence grise of the West End Theatre 1933–1973* (London, 1989), p. 244.
111. Angus Calder, *The People's War* (London, 1963), p. 103.
112. Sanderson, *From Irving to Olivier*, p. 255.
113. *CSM*, 14/10/1939.
114. *CSM*, 25/11/1939.
115. 'Curtain Up Again', *CSM*, 11/11/1939.
116. '"Wash on the Siegfried Line" Found Tipperary's Successor', *CSM*, 18/11/1939.
117. 'A popular joke of the time suggested that the initials "ENSA" really stood for "Every Night Something Awful"': Huggett, *Binkie Beaumont*, p. 285.
118. 'The Theater Carries On', *CSM*, 16/12/1939.
119. Rex Harrison, *Rex: An Autobiography* (London, 1974), p. 63.
120. *CSM*, 30/12/1939.
121. *CSM*, 4/11/1939.
122. 'Gate Revue – Second Edition', *CSM*, 18/11/1939.
123. 'Laughter Rules in British Theaters', *CSM*, 30/12/1939.
124. *CSM*, 30/12/1939.
125. George Rowell and Anthony Jackson, *The Repertory Movement: A History of Regional Theatre in Britain* (Cambridge, 1984), p. 77.
126. Harold Hobson, *The First Three Years of the War* (London, 1943), p. 25.
127. *Indirect Journey*, pp. 207–9.
128. Hobson, *Interview with D. M. Shellard*, 10/7/1991.
129. 'Book Review: "The Amazing Critic" by James Agate', *CSM*, 6/1/1940.
130. Harold Hobson, *French Theatre Since 1830* (London, 1978).
131. 'The Classics Return', *CSM*, 9/3/1940.
132. John Milton, 'L'Allegro', *Complete English Poems*, ed. Gordon Campbell (London, 1990), p. 35.
133. Harold Hobson, *Ralph Richardson* (London, 1958).
134. 'He is now engaged on a study of Bernard Shaw for a book to be published in the autumn' – *Radio Times*, 12/7/1940.
135. *CSM*, 8/6/1940.
136. '… the things that in the theater make the greatest effect are not, generally speaking, those that look most impressive upon the printed page' – 'In Spite of Macaulay', *CSM*, 24/2/1940.
137. *CSM*, 13/7/1940.
138. *CSM*, 16/1/1943.

139. *CSM*, 20/1/1940.
140. *CSM*, 13/1/1940.
141. 'Exceptions to the Rule', *CSM*, 17/2/1940.
142. 'A Valet and a Plumber', *CSM*, 2/3/1940.
143. John Johnston, *The Lord Chamberlain's Blue Pencil* (London, 1990), p. 153.
144. 'The Light of Heart', *CSM*, 13/4/1940.
145. *CSM*, 11/5/1940.
146. Michael Redgrave, *In My Mind's Eye* (London, 1983), p. 145.
147. 'A New Theater in London', *CSM*, 27/7/1940.
148. 'Long Runs', *CSM*, 28/6/1940.
149. A. J. P. Taylor, *The Second World War, an Illustrated History* (London, 1976), p. 69.
150. *CSM*, 29/6/1940.
151. Ibid.
152. *CSM*, 3/7/1940.
153. John Gielgud, *An Actor and His Time* (London, 1979), p. 146.
154. A view that Hugh Hunt, the first director of the Bristol Old Vic in 1948, corroborates: 'If the theatre suffered much from the effects of war, and was to feel these effects for many years afterwards, it might also be said that its survival and future pattern were largely due to the timely patronage it received from the new organs of public patronage: the state and the BBC': *1880 to the Present Day*, p. 47.
155. *CSM*, 20/7/1940.
156. *CSM*, 3/8/1940.
157. 'The American Complement', *CSM*, 10/8/1940.
158. Taylor, *The Second World War*, p. 70.
159. 'War Shows in London', *CSM*, 14/9/1940.
160. *CSM*, 21/9/1940.
161. *CSM*, 12/10/1940.
162. *CSM*, 4/1/1941.
163. Ibid.
164. Sanderson, *From Irving to Olivier*, p. 265.
165. *CSM*, 8/2/1941.
166. *The Sunday Times*, 9/9/1984.
167. *Theatre in Britain*, p. 118.
168. 'The Nightingale's Year', *CSM*, 1/2/1941.
169. 'Pantomime Carries On In London', *CSM*, 1/3/1941.
170. 'Not in Our Stars …', *CSM*, 15/3/1941.
171. 'An Evening Première Again', *CSM*, 5/4/1941.
172. 'Low Comedy Resumes Grip', *CSM*, 21/6/1941.
173. '"No Time for Comedy" in London', *CSM*, 19/4/1941.
174. 'Has Our Theatre Lost Its Nerve?', *ST*, 9/9/1984.
175. 'Coward as Master of Stage', *CSM*, 16/8/1941.
176. 'Two New Plays by Noël Coward', *CSM*, 22/5/1943.
177. *Theatre in Britain*, p. 126.
178. Kitty Black, *Upper Circle* (London, 1984), p. 57. On pp. 231–8 Black lists the productions of H. M. Tennent Ltd. from 1936–73. Other successful wartime productions by Tennent's included Emlyn Williams's *The Morning Star* (Globe; opened 10/12/1941; 474 performances); Shaw's *The Doctor's Dilemma* (Haymarket; 4/3/1942; 474); Lillian Hellman's *Watch on the Rhine* (Aldwych; 22/4/1942; 673); Rattigan's *Flare Path* (Apollo; 13/8/1942; 670); Congreve's *Love for Love* (Phoenix; 8/4/1943; 471); Rattigan's *While the Sun Shines* (Globe; 24/12/1943; 1,154); Coward's *Private Lives* (Apollo; 1/11/1944; 716); Daphne du Maurier's *The Years Between* (Wyndham's; 10/1/1945; 617).

179. 'Moscow to London', *CSM*, 20/12/1941.
180. 'Double Disenchantment', *CSM*, 25/10/1941.
181. 'Robert Morley, Actor, interviewed', *London Calling*, 1/1/1942.
182. '"Old Acquaintance" in London', *CSM*, 17/1/1942.
183. *CSM*, 31/1/1942.
184. *CSM*, 29/5/1943.
185. 'Mr Priestley Looks at Utopia', *CSM*, 19/6/1943.
186. 'Why We Must Keep Our Mouths Shut', *London Calling*, 21/5/1942.
187. 'Two Plays About the Air War', *CSM*, 29/8/1942.
188. 'War Plays in Wartime', *CSM*, 3/10/1942.
189. Ibid.
190. 'The Princesses Wanted to See the Bodies', *London Calling*, 18/11/1943.
191. 'Masters and Masterpieces', *CSM*, 19/12/1942.
192. Black, *Upper Circle*, p. 46.
193. 'Appreciation of Shakespeare Unparalleled Since Waterloo', *CSM*, 29/11/1944.
194. *CSM*, 18/11/1944.
195. This revoking of an issued licence was a unique event: Johnston, *The Lord Chamberlain's Blue Pencil*, p. 147.
196. Although in an *Interview with D. M. Shellard*, 10/7/1991, Hobson claimed that he was merely reflecting the editorial policy of the newspaper stable.
197. 'As We See It', *Daily Dispatch*, 7/11/1944.
198. Aled Jones, 'The British Press, 1919–1945', in *The Encyclopaedia of the British Press*, ed. Dennis Griffiths (London, 1992), p. 49.
199. Leonard Russell, *The Pearl of Days* (a history of *The Sunday Times*) (London, 1972), p. 329.
200. *The Encyclopaedia of the British Press*, pp. 105–6.
201. James Agate, *Ego 8* (London, 1946), p. 171.
202. Born on 9 September 1877, Agate would actually have been 67 on 19 July 1945.
203. Kathleen Tynan, *The Life of Kenneth Tynan* (London, 1988), p. 46.
204. The extent of Hobson's overwhelming love for his first wife cannot be over-emphasized. The eighth chapter of his autobiography is entitled 'The Shining Marriage' – which is no mere hyperbole but a genuine tribute. During the 1950s it passed into London theatrical folklore that the critic gave warmer reviews if his wife was watching beside him.
205. For the original idea, see 'The Cricketer Without Rival', *Listener*, 9/4/1942: 'A couple of years ago my friend Leonard Russell and I thought it might be amusing to collect some material for a novel set in the period when Napoleon was trying to invade us between 1804 and 1809 and in the memoirs and newspapers of the time we kept coming across the name of Lord Frederick Beauclerk.'
206. Harold Hobson, *The Devil in Woodford Wells* (London, 1946), p. 222.
207. 'Critic on the Hearth', *Listener*, 8/5/1947.
208. *Indirect Journey*, p. 1.
209. James Agate, *The Selective Ego*, ed. Tim Beaumont (London, 1976), p. 260.
210. See James Harding, *Agate* (London, 1986), p. 217. Hobson also confirms this in 'Film Hamlet Assayed, "Must Give Us Pauses"', *CSM*, 24/5/1948, when he stated that the prize that he had gained had been the goal that Dent had failed to achieve, since for years 'he was the secretary to James Agate, who never ceased to regard him as his proper successor, as the most eminent member of his profession'.
211. *Interview with D. M. Shellard*, 10/7/1991.
212. Confirmation of Agate's escape from the brothel comes in *The Pearl of Days*, p. 276.

213. 'Agate was very intimate, of course, with Dent. I don't know whether Dent was a homosexual or not', *Interview with D. M. Shellard*, 10/7/1991.
214. Harding, *Agate*, p. 217.
215. 'Film Hamlet Assayed, "Must Give Us Pauses"', *CSM*, 24/5/1948.
216. *Interview with D. M. Shellard*, 10/7/1991.
217. *Indirect Journey*, p. 212.
218. 'Hazlitt Said No', *ST*, 29/7/1945.
219. *Indirect Journey* (London, 1978), p. 158.
220. According to Richard Jackson, who accompanied Hobson to the theatre in the 1960s whenever his regular companions, his wife Elizabeth and Edward Sutro, were incapacitated and who became his constant theatre companion in the 1970s, daily visits to the theatre had to be meticulously planned to allow easy parking, Hobson always sat at the end of an aisle to facilitate access and he only ever left his seat at the interval to visit the toilet – *Interview with D. M. Shellard*, 59 Knightsbridge, London, 25/3/1992.
221. 'And Now, Thunder', *ST*, 9/3/1947.
222. Harold Hobson, *Theatre 1* (London, 1948), p. 60.
223. 'Long West End Runs', *ST*, 8/7/1945.
224. 'Theatre Boom', *ST*, 18/11/1945.
225. 'Number of Houses Reduced By 12 per Cent Since 1939', *CSM*, 24/11/1945.
226. *ST*, 12/8/1945.
227. *ST*, 5/8/1945.
228. e.g. 'Bevin Resists Pressure In Foreign Office Reform', *CSM*, 16/2/1946.
229. *Theatre 1*, p. 2.
230. 'A Unique Feat', *ST*, 15/9/1946.
231. *Indirect Journey*, p. 109.
232. 'Oh Me, Oh My!', *ST*, 22/9/1946.
233. 'This to me was a revelation, because at that time I was a great admirer of fine writing. I thought there was nobody in the world to compare with Walter Pater': 'A Great Creative Craftsman', *ST*, 1/9/1974. Hobson also took three stylistic tips from Ian Laing: (1) *more* than a thousand and not *over* (2) never begin two consecutive paragraphs with *the* (3) in paragraphing, an occasional very short paragraph leavens the lump – *The Pearl of Days* (London, 1972), p. 220.
234. Alan Dent, 'Royal Lear', *News Chronicle* (27/9/1946); Peter Fleming, 'The Theatre', *Spectator* (27/9/1946); and Philip Hope-Wallace, 'Theatre', *Time and Tide* (5/10/1946) respectively.
235. *ST*, 29/9/1946.
236. *Indirect Journey*, pp. 164–5.
237. 'Mr Olivier's Lear', *ST*, 29/9/1946.
238. W. N. Medlicott, *Contemporary England 1914–1964* (London, 1976), pp. 481–2.
239. *Theatre in Britain*, p. 140.
240. *Indirect Journey*, p. 247.
241. Ibid., p. 248.
242. 'Is This Barabbas?', *ST*, 23/2/1947.
243. Quoted by Hobson in *Indirect Journey*, p. 220. In his eighties Hobson was still able to recite this key passage (Philippians 4: 8) from memory, doing so in *Interview with D. M. Shellard*, 10/7/1991.
244. *Indirect Journey*, p. 220.
245. Ibid., pp. 22–3.
246. Ibid., p. 230.
247. 'Conversation at Luncheon', *CSM*, 16/4/1946.

248. 'Mr Gielgud Wants A New Play', *CSM*, 20/4/1946.
249. *ST*, 6/4/1947.
250. See *ST*, 20/4/1947 and 18/5/1947 for some examples.
251. *Theatre 1*, p. 71.
252. James Agate, *ST*, 25/5/1947.
253. 'James Agate: An Appreciation', *ST*, 8/6/1947.
254. *Indirect Journey*, p. 211.
255. Interview with D. M. Shellard, 10/7/1991.
256. *Theatre 1*, p. xvii.
257. An indication of this is provided by the attendance figures for productions mounted in 1947 by the pre-eminent London management company, H. M. Tennent Ltd. Aside from the phenomenally successful American import, *Oklahoma!* (Drury Lane; opened 3/4/1947; 1,543 performances), only one Tennent play in that year exceeded 300 performances – Noël Coward's *Present Laughter* (Haymarket; 16/4/1947; 328): Black, *Upper Circle*, p. 233.
258. *Indirect Journey*, p. 213.
259. *CSM*, 16/8/1947.
260. 'The West End', *ST*, 28/9/1947.
261. *CSM*, 20/3/1933.
262. Bill Williamson, *The Temper of the Times* (Oxford, 1990), p. 64.
263. 'The New Favourite', *ST*, 5/10/1947.
264. 'And Now Tybalt', *ST*, 12/10/1947.
265. 'The Sun In Spring', *ST*, 7/12/1947.
266. Hobson is referring to Wynyard Browne's *Dark Summer*, discussed in 'Re-Creation', *ST*, 19/10/1947.
267. 'Honors to Mr Shaw', *CSM*, 25/10/1947.
268. 'A Good Week', *ST*, 22/2/1948. *Cockpit* did fail, and Hobson redefines his view of the play, claiming in 'A Moral', *ST*, 11/4/1948, that it was less of a drawback that the play did not provide a solution to post-European problems than that the characters did not appear worth saving.
269. 'Poetic Drama Promoted By E. M. Browne', *CSM*, 29/3/1947.
270. 'Poetic Drama', *ST*, 21/9/1947.
271. 'Well Met by Moonlight', *ST*, 9/2/1947.
272. 'A Phoenix Too Frequent', *ST*, 24/11/1946.
273. 'A Welcome Influence', *ST*, 14/3/1948.
274. Black, *Upper Circle*, p. 233.
275. John Russell Taylor writes that 'If ever a revolution began with one explosion it was this': *Anger and After* (London, 1969), p. 14. The term 'Kitchen Sink' was applied in the London theatre (often pejoratively) to plays that eschewed drawing-room settings for working-class environments following John Osborne's *Look Back in Anger* (1956) and Arnold Wesker's *The Kitchen* (1959). 'New Wave' is a less subjective term to describe the work of the post-1956 generation of British dramatists.
276. 'An Intrusion of Brains', *ST*, 20/7/1947.
277. 'Sartre Resartus', *ST*, 20/6/1948.
278. 'Strange Visitors', *ST*, 4/7/1948.
279. 'A French Actor', *ST*, 12/9/1948.
280. 'French Visitors', *ST*, 17/10/1948.
281. 'A Paris Success', *ST*, 14/11/1948.
282. *ST*, 19/9/1948.
283. *CSM*, 2/10/1948.
284. 'Love', *ST*, 9/3/1952.
285. Terence Rattigan, *The Collected Plays of Terence Rattigan* (London, 1953), II, pp. xi–xii.

286. For a summary of hostile critical reaction (including John Barber and Kenneth Tynan) to Aunt Edna and Rattigan, see Michael Darlow and Gillian Hodson, *Terence Rattigan* (London, 1979), p. 223.
287. Hunt, et al., *1880 to the Present Day*, p. 241.
288. *Indirect Journey*, p. 248.
289. Kenneth Tynan, *Separate Tables*, reprinted in *A View of the English Stage* (London, 1984), pp. 145–7.
290. Peter Roberts, *The Old Vic Story* (London, 1976), p. 136.
291. 'London's Old Vic "Fires" Olivier', *CSM*, 15/12/1948.
292. George Rowell, *The Old Vic Theatre: A History* (Cambridge, 1993), p. 140.
293. *ST*, 16/10/1949.
294. John Elsom and Nicholas Tomalin, *The History of the National Theatre* (London, 1978), p. 91.
295. *ST*, 16/10/1949.
296. See *ST*, 23/10/1949 and 30/10/1949.
297. *Theatre in Britain*, p. 157.
298. 'First Quarto "Hamlet"', *CSM*, 22/1/1949.
299. 'The Oliviers Return', *ST*, 23/1/1949.
300. *ST*, 30/1/1949.
301. Ibid.
302. '*Antigone* was well received in the collaborationist press and was at first assumed to be on the Vichy side': David Bradby, *Modern French Drama 1940–1980* (Cambridge, 1984), pp. 35–6.
303. 'Existentialism', *ST*, 13/2/1949.
304. *French Theatre since 1830*, p. 205.
305. 'Black Magic', *ST*, 13/3/1949.
306. Described by Hobson as 'The most dazzling vaudeville triumph of our age', *Daily Dispatch*, 13/6/1949.
307. 'Mr Millar Amuses', *ST*, 12/6/1949.
308. Harold Hobson, *The Theatre Now* (London, 1954), p. 78.
309. *ST*, 26/6/1949.
310. 'From America', *ST*, 31/7/1949.
311. 'Arthur Miller as Craftsman', *CSM*, 13/8/1949.
312. W. A. Darlington, *Daily Telegraph*, 29/7/1949.
313. 'Williams II', *ST*, 1/8/1948.
314. 'Too Much Wit', *ST*, 16/10/1949.
315. Huggett, *Binkie Beaumont*, p. 418.
316. Anon, 'Aldwych Theatre', *The Times*, 13/10/1949.
317. Anthony Cookman, *Tatler*, 20/10/1949.
318. J. C. Trewin, *Observer*, 16/10/1949.
319. Huggett, *Binkie Beaumont*, p. 420.
320. Quoted in 'State Patronage of Theater', *CSM*, 7/1/1950.
321. *Southwark Cathedral Magazine*, 1949.
322. *Hansard* (London, HMSO, 1949), p. 2086. Following an investigation by a Select Committee of the House of Commons into the practice of managements forming non-profit-distributing subsidiaries in 1950 – convened in the light of *A Streetcar Named Desire* – the practice of the Arts Council forming associations with commercial managements, to permit the latter to avoid entertainment tax, ceased: Hunt *et al.*, *1880 to the Present Day*, p. 50.
323. A quarter of a century later Hobson was to state that the play was of crucial importance to the evolution of twentieth-century drama, in that it introduced 'that social interest, that fascination with the rise and decline of classes that within a few years of its first production was to dominate the drama of the Western world': 'Sick visitors', *ST*, 17/3/1974.

324. *ST*, 13/11/1949.
325. Black, *Upper Circle*, p. 233.
326. *ST*, 28/8/1949.
327. Anon, *The Times*, 23/8/1949.
328. *CSM*, 20/10/1949.
329. *The Theatre Now*, p. 17.
330. 'Fry Again', *ST*, 22/1/1950.
331. *Indirect Journey*, p. 232.
332. 'London Hails Mr Fry, Playwright', *New York Times Magazine*, 12/3/1950.
333. *ST*, 21/5/1950.
334. *CSM*, 9/9/1950.
335. *ST*, 29/10/1950.
336. *ST*, 5/11/1950.
337. *ST*, 12/11/1950.
338. 'No Home', *ST*, 11/2/1951.
339. Henry Pelling, *The Labour Governments 1945–51* (London, 1985), p. 246.
340. Ibid.
341. *CSM*, 4/11/1950.
342. 'Echoes', *ST*, 22/4/1951.
343. 'Sartre: The Same Old Theme', *CSM*, 30/6/1951.
344. 'The Festival Plays', *Comment*, Sept. 1951.
345. 'Success', *ST*, 25/2/1951. Novello was thrilled by this notice, writing to Hobson just before his death: 'My dear H. H. I was moved to tears by your appreciation yesterday – Bless you and thank you. Ivor.' The letter appears in Vol. 18, p. 63, of Hobson's *Scrapbook Collection*.
346. 'Derivations', *ST*, 11/3/1951.
347. 'Of South Pacific', *ST*, 4/11/1951.
348. 'Henry IV', *ST*, 8/4/1951.
349. He was travelling to Scotland overnight and handed his review in three hours after the curtain fell: *The Theatre Now*, p. 130.
350. 'I read all our English dramatic critics say about each new production, wherever they may write. There is no journal so obscure, so ephemeral, that by writing in it, they can escape me': *Theatre*, p. 7.
351. *ST*, 20/5/1951.
352. T. C. Worsley, 'Religious Drama', *New Statesman and Nation*, 26/5/1951.
353. Ivor Brown, 'Guinness and Scotch', *Observer*, 20/5/1951.
354. A. V. Cookman, 'At the Theatre', *Tatler*, 30/5/1951.
355. W. A. Darlington, 'Alec Guinness as Hamlet', *Daily Telegraph*, 18/5/1951.
356. Of course, for some this was open-mindedness and for others indefensible vacillation. The producer, Michael White, praises Hobson's willingness to revisit Leonard Webb's *So What About Love*, about which the critic had been scathing, after the playwright had written requesting reconsideration. 'He then did something unique': Hobson's second review reversed his original opinion – Michael White, *Empty Seats* (London, 1984), p. 47. However, Sheila Hancock, who appeared in the 1969 production, found the about-turn highly embarrassing, since 'to be Hobson's choice in those days was to invite derision from one's fellow actors'. Sheila Hancock, *Ramblings of an Actress* (London, 1987), p. 53.
357. *ST*, 17/6/1951.
358. *ST*, 30/9/1951.
359. 'Partage de Midi', *ST*, 7/10/1951.
360. 'In Paris', *ST*, 23/3/1952.
361. *The Theatre Now*, p. 79.
362. After *Ardèle*, *Ring Round the Moon*, *Point of Departure*, *Antigone*, *Fading Mansions* and *Thieves' Carnival*.

363. 'London Warmly Welcomes Renowned French Players', *CSM*, 6/10/1951.
364. 'Perpetual Rebel', *ST*, 2/12/1951.
365. 'Angry Young Man' is a term applied to the literary and dramatic characters of the New Wave British writers in the 1950s. Jimmy Porter in *Look Back in Anger* is the archetype.
366. *ST*, 30/3/1952.
367. 'Cultural Imports', *ST*, 2/11/1952.
368. Stephen Koss, *The Rise and Fall of the Political Press in Britain* (London, 1984), p. 635.
369. 'London Survey', *ST*, 30/3/1952.
370. 'Taxing British Artists', *CSM*, 13/8/1952.
371. 'The Actor', *ST*, 11/5/1952.
372. *ST*, 15/6/1952.
373. *ST*, 20/7/1952.
374. *Spectator*, 6/2/1953.
375. Harold Hobson, *Verdict at Midnight* (London, 1952), p. 192.
376. Ibid., p. vii.
377. *ST*, 22/3/1953.
378. *ST*, 3/5/1953.
379. *ST*, 29/3/1953.
380. *ST*, 5/4/1953.
381. 'New York Musical', *ST*, 31/5/1953.
382. T. C. Worsley, *New Statesman*, 6/6/1953.
383. Kenneth Tynan, *Evening Standard*, 29/5/1953.
384. *Tatler*, June 1953.
385. John Elsom, *Post-war British Theatre Criticism* (London, 1981), p. 39.
386. It was the excessive concentration on France and not the interest itself that was the problem. William Gaskill, one of the Royal Court directors, freely confesses that French theatre had an important influence on him as a student at Oxford: 'One of the great influences on all of us was *Les Enfants du Paradis* with its panorama of French theatre life, the sexuality of Arletty, the wonderful ham acting of Pierre Brasseur and the mime of Jean-Louis Barrault': *A Sense of Direction* (London, 1988), p. 5.
387. *ST*, 16/5/1954.
388. *ST*, 27/6/1954.
389. 'Marching On', *ST*, 11/4/1954.
390. 'A Leader Lost?', *ST*, 4/10/1953.
391. 'The New Fry', *ST*, 2/5/1954.
392. *ST*, 28/3/1954.
393. 'Fair Play', *ST*, 14/11/1954.
394. Kenneth Tynan, 'West End Apathy', *Observer*, 31/10/1954.
395. John Calder, 'Sir Harold Hobson', *Independent*, 14/3/92.
396. Anonymous, 'Sir Harold Hobson', *Daily Telegraph*, 14/3/92.
397. Michael Billington, 'The Brave Critic Who Waited for Godot', *Guardian*, 14/3/92.
398. Anonymous, 'Sir Harold Hobson', *The Times*, 14/3/92.
399. Alan Ayckbourn, *Interview with D. M. Shellard*, Villiers Park, Oxon, 9/3/1992.
400. Michael Billington, *Interview with D. M. Shellard*, Kew, London, 23/4/1992.
401. Ayckbourn, *Interview with D. M. Shellard*, 9/3/1992.
402. *ST*, 2/1/1955.
403. Penelope Gilliatt, 'A Consideration of Critics', *Encore*, Nov./Dec., 1959.
404. 'Portrait Gallery: Not For Burning', *ST*, 16/1/1955.

405. 'Closed Circle', *ST*, 6/2/1955.
406. 'Revaluations', *ST*, 26/6/1955.
407. 'Richard II', *ST*, 23/1/1955.
408. 'Closed Circle', *ST*, 6/2/1955.
409. This disproves John Russell Taylor's notion that this production of the play was 'a little-noticed curtain-raiser at the Arts': *Anger and After*, p. 17.
410. *ST*, 13/3/1955.
411. Kenneth Tynan, 'Ionesco, Man of Destiny?', *Observer*, 22/6/1958.
412. Eugène Ionesco, 'The Playwright's Role', *Observer*, 29/6/1958. A summary of the Tynan/Ionesco debate can be found in Martin Esslin's *The Theatre of the Absurd* (London, 1982), pp. 128–33. See also Kathleen Tynan's *A Life of Kenneth Tynan*, pp. 143–4.
413. 'Something New', *ST*, 13/3/1955.
414. *CSM*, 28/5/1955.
415. Tynan, 'Ionesco, Man of Destiny?'.
416. 'Avant-Garde Drama in Paris', *CSM*, 28/5/1955.
417. 'London Theaters Face Postwar Challenges', *CSM*, 21/6/1955.
418. Lawrence Graver, *Waiting for Godot* (Cambridge, 1989), p. 13.
419. Peter Bull, *I Know the Face, But …* (London, 1959), pp. 169–70.
420. Milton Shulman, 'Duet for Two Symbols', *Evening Standard*, 4/8/55.
421. 'Stephen Williams at the Theatre', *Evening News*, 4/8/1955.
422. David Lewin, *Daily Express*, 4/8/1955.
423. Colin Wilson, *Daily Mail*, 4/8/1955.
424. W. A. Darlington, *Daily Telegraph*, 4/8/1955.
425. Ibid.
426. Amongst whom Darlington included Christopher Fry, John Whiting, Owen Holder and Denis Cannan.
427. Anon., *The Times*, 4/8/1955.
428. Philip Hope-Wallace, 'Two Evenings with Two Tramps', *Guardian*, 5/8/1955.
429. *Indirect Journey*, p. 42.
430. For an example of Pont's work, see 'The British Character – Absence of the Gift of Conversation', reproduced in *The Art of Laughter*, ed. Lionel Lambourne and Amanda-Jane Doran (Oxford, 1992), p. 21.
431. Samuel Beckett, letter to H. O. White, 10/10/1955, referred to in Deirdre Bair, *Samuel Beckett: A Biography* (London, 1990), p. 480.
432. Kenneth Tynan, 'Waiting for Godot', *Observer*, 7/8/1955.
433. 'Waiting for Godot', *CSM*, 13/8/1955.
434. *ST*, 14/8/1955.
435. Bair, *Samuel Beckett*, p. 497.
436. 'Criticism', *ST*, 18/9/1955.
437. Collie Knox, 'I've been Led by the Nose Long Enough', *Daily Mail*, 17/9/1955.
438. 'Francomania', *ST*, 25/9/1955.
439. Collie Knox, 'This Is Why Garbo Wants to Be Alone', *Daily Mail*, 1/10/1955.
440. *ST*, 12/6/1955.
441. *Indirect Journey*, p. 38.
442. Peter Cunard, a former press officer at the Royal Court Theatre, recalled one such occasion in the late 1960s, in an appreciation of Hobson after his death: *The Times*, 18/3/92.
443. This anecdote is contained in a letter from Beckett to Thomas McGreevy, 17/7/1961, and related in Bair, *Samuel Beckett*, pp. 569–70.
444. A belief to which Richard Jackson and Michael Billington testified in *Interviews with D. M. Shellard*, 25/3/1992 and 23/4/1992 respectively.

Richard Jackson felt that Hobson's dislike of American musicals was in part influenced by Bessie's refusal to go and see them.
445. *Indirect Journey*, p. 39.
446. Ibid., p. 177.
447. Donald Spoto, *Laurence Olivier* (London 1991), p. 221.
448. Olivier revealed in a 1963 interview that this particular facet of the review made a great impression on him: 'It nearly made me support Sunderland instead of Chelsea … In the arts generally, but perhaps especially in the theatre, the mighty are always in danger of falling. It is good to know that there are some people who are not glad about it': 'Olivier – My Life, My Work, My Future', *ST*, 3/11/1963.
449. 'A Modern Play', *ST*, 21/8/1955.
450. Kenneth Tynan, *Observer*, 12/12/1954.
451. Kenneth Tynan, *Observer*, 6/1/1955.
452. Kenneth Tynan, 'Dimmed Debut', *Observer*, 3/7/1955.
453. Kenneth Tynan, 'Some Stars from the East', *Observer*, 26/6/1956.
454. *ST*, 3/7/1955.
455. 'Brecht Drama in Britain', *CSM*, 23/7/1955.
456. Billington, *Interview with D. M. Shellard*, 23/4/1992.
457. 'Mme Feuillère', *ST*, 11/9/1955.
458. 'Letter to the Editor: "Edwige Feuillère"', *ST*, 18/9/1955.
459. 'Criticism', *ST*, 18/9/1955.
460. 'Francomania', *ST*, 25/9/1955.
461. Peter Lewis, *The Fifties – Portrait of a Period* (London, 1989), p. 9.
462. *The Best of Plays and Players*, Vol. 1: *1953–1968*, ed. Peter Roberts (London, 1988), p. 42.
463. 'No Joke in Britain', *CSM*, 24/1/1956.
464. Lewis, *The Fifties*, p. 160.
465. Huggett, *Binkie Beaumont*, pp. 451–2.
466. Ibid., p. 446.
467. Ibid., p. 192.
468. Ibid., p. 436.
469. John Osborne, *Almost a Gentleman* (London, 1991), p. 4.
470. Ibid., p. 20.
471. Huggett, *Binkie Beaumont*, p. 457. Huggett provides a brief history of entertainment tax from its inception in 1916 (in addition to an outline of Binkie's schemes to avoid paying it). See also Charles Landstone's *Off-Stage* (London, 1953), pp. 68–79, and Joseph Macleod's *The Actor's Right to Act* (London, 1981), pp. 115–16.
472. This advertisement, reproduced in Vol. 21, p. 81, of Hobson's *Scrapbook Collection*, is listed as appearing in the programme of the first National Union of Students' Drama Festival at Bristol.
473. 'Caught in the Act', *ST*, 8/1/1956.
474. 'Was Genius Lacking from the Theatre in 1955?', *Evening Standard*, 19/1/1956.
475. *ST*, 1/1/1956.
476. *CSM*, 8/2/1956.
477. *CSM*, 21/3/1956.
478. *CSM*, 4/4/1956.
479. 'Soviet Capital Intrigues Newsman', *CSM*, 10/1/1956.
480. 'Soviets Woo Tourists Who Can Pay', *CSM*, 12/1/1956.
481. 'Soviet Communists Unlike Western Reds', *CSM*, 9/2/1956.
482. 'Red Architecture Accents Size', *CSM*, 2/2/1956.
483. *CSM*, 17/1/1956.
484. 'Stanislavsky Method in Moscow', *CSM*, 4/2/1956.

485. *ST*, 12/2/1956.
486. *CSM*, 23/7/1955.
487. Ronald Hayman, *British Theatre since 1955* (Oxford, 1979), p. 81.
488. *Observer*, 12/2/1956.
489. Quoted on p. 179 of *The Oxford Companion to German Literature*, ed. Henry and Mary Garland (Oxford, 1986).
490. 'On The Stage in Britain', *CSM*, 7/4/1956.
491. Ibid.
492. 'Minority Report', *ST*, 15/4/1956.
493. 'The End Crowns All', *ST*, 8/4/1956.
494. Ibid.
495. 'Carry on up the Zeitgeist – *Look Back in Anger*', BBC Radio 4, broadcast on 3 April 1992.
496. John Osborne, *Look Back in Anger* (London, 1986), Act 1, p. 15.
497. Ibid., p. 20.
498. Ibid., p. 17.
499. Ibid., p. 35.
500. Ibid., Act 3, p. 84.
501. 'Carry on up the Zeitgeist – *Look Back in Anger*'.
502. Patrick Gibbs, 'A Study of an Exhibitionist', *Daily Telegraph*, 9/5/1956.
503. John Barber, 'This Bitter Young Man – Like Thousands', *Daily Express*, 9/5/1956.
504. Colin Wilson, 'This Actor is a Great Writer', *Daily Mail*, 9/5/1956.
505. Milton Shulman, 'Mr Osborne Builds a Wailing Wall', *Evening Standard*, 9/5/1956.
506. Osborne, *Almost a Gentleman*, p. 22.
507. Ibid., p. 11.
508. Osborne, *Look Back in Anger*, Act I, p. 11.
509. Ibid., p. 13.
510. Osborne, *Almost a Gentleman*, p. 22.
511. Ibid., p. 23.
512. John Osborne, *International Theatre Annual No. 2*, ed. Harold Hobson (London, 1957), p. 9.
513. *ST*, 13/5/1956.
514. Hunt *et al.*, *1880 to the Present Day*, p. 54.
515. 'A Revelation', *ST*, 15/7/1956.
516. *ST*, 29/7/1956.
517. 'The Freedom of the Press', *CSM*, 9/4/1929.
518. *CSM*, 7/10/1932.
519. See Lewis, *The Fifties*, p. 47.
520. Huggett, *Binkie Beaumont*, p. 430.
521. *CSM*, 20/8/1956.
522. *ST*, 30/9/1956.
523. 'A Fine Play', *ST*, 14/10/1956.
524. 'Speak Out, Please', *ST*, 2/2/1958.
525. Johnston, *The Lord Chamberlain's Blue Pencil*, p. 171.
526. 'British Theater Censorship Eased', *CSM*, 9/12/1958.
527. *ST*, 9/9/1956.
528. *CSM*, 20/3/1933.
529. *The Theatre Now*, pp. 115–16.
530. Ibid., p. 116.
531. Lazarow, Victor, unpublished thesis, 'The Dramatic Criticism of Sir Harold Hobson: 1947–1976' (University of Georgia, Athens, 1978), p. 37. On page 18 of his doctoral thesis Lazarow refers to one further academic study of Hobson, *Harold Hobson: The Actor's Critic*, by Thomas Cooke that

was written in 1960, but since Lazarow does not footnote this reference and the CD Rom version of *Dissertations Abstract International* contains no mention of the work, it is impossible to trace at the moment.

532. 'The Pinnacle', *ST*, 10/3/1957.
533. 'Edinburgh and London', *Observer*, 9/9/1956.
534. 'Braw and Brecht', *Observer*, 2/9/1956.
535. *ST*, 2/9/1956.
536. *International Theatre Annual No 2*, p. 197.
537. *ST*, 4/11/1956.
538. 'Simple and Complicated', *Observer*, 4/11/1956.
539. 'Avant-Garde', *ST*, 11/11/1956.
540. David Childs, *Britain since 1945* (London, 1979), p. 85.
541. Alan Sked and Chris Cook, *Post-War Britain: A Political History* (London, 1980), p. 149.
542. 'THAT angry young man gets a special award', *Evening Standard*, 3/1/1957.
543. 'A Protest', *ST*, 24/2/1957.
544. 'Strange Visitors', *ST*, 4/7/1948.
545. 'A Good Home', *ST*, 17/3/1957.
546. Billington, *Interview with D. M. Shellard*, 23/4/1992.
547. 'New Beckett Play in Print', *CSM*, 23/2/1957.
548. 'Samuel Beckett's New Play', *ST*, 7/4/1957.
549. Harold Hobson, *Interview with Victor Lazarow*, quoted in his unpublished thesis, 'The Dramatic Criticism of Sir Harold Hobson', p. 199.
550. 'Samuel Beckett's New Play', *ST*, 7/4/1957.
551. 'A Philosophy of Despair', *Observer*, 7/4/1957.
552. 'Bertolt Brecht', *ST*, 4/11/1956.
553. John Osborne, *A Better Class of Person* (London, 1982), p. 27.
554. Taylor, *Anger and After*, p. 47.
555. 'A Magnificent Week', *ST*, 14/4/1957.
556. See the summary of critical notices in Osborne's *Almost a Gentleman*, p. 48.
557. Kenneth Tynan, *A View of the English Stage* (London, 1984), p. 203.
558. Sanderson, *From Irving to Olivier*, p. 184.
559. 'Helping Shakespeare', *ST*, 7/7/1957.
560. Peter Brook, 'As I *Don't* Like It ...', *ST*, 1/9/1957.
561. 'On the Up and Up', *ST*, 29/12/1957.
562. 'Playwright to Watch', *ST*, 24/11/1957.
563. Harold Hobson, *Ralph Richardson* (London, 1958).
564. 'Hobson's Choice is Cardiff', *Western Daily Press*, 3/1/1958.
565. Ibid.
566. Ibid.
567. Billington, *Interview with D. M. Shellard*, 23/4/1992.
568. 'Larger than Life at the Festival', *ST*, 5/1/1958.
569. 'Have We a New Dramatist?', *ST*, 2/3/1958. The dramatist referred to in the title is Gillian Richards and not Harold Pinter.
570. 'Vagaries of the West End', *ST*, 31/1/1960.
571. *ST*, 25/5/1958.
572. Victor Lazarow, *Interview with Harold Hobson*, Ivy Restaurant, London, 1/9/1976, appearing in Lazarow's unpublished thesis, 'The Dramatic Criticism of Harold Hobson', p. 18.
573. 'Mad Meg and Lodger', *Daily Telegraph*, 20/5/1958.
574. *Theatre in Britain*, pp. 21–2.
575. Address at Hobson's Memorial Service, St Paul's Church, Covent Garden, London, 24/11/1992.
576. *International Theatre Annual*, p. 209.

577. 'Firbank, Wilson and Hope', *ST*, 5/10/1958.
578. 'Irma Translated', *ST*, 20/7/1958.
579. 'Repertory at Royal Court', *CSM*, 9/8/1958.
580. 'Triumph at Stratford East', *ST*, 19/10/1958.
581. 'Light From Spain', *ST*, 16/2/1958.
582. 'In the Increasing Cold', *ST*, 17/8/1958.
583. 'Are Things What They Seem?', *ST*, 11/5/1958.
584. 'The Ghost of Tarquin', *ST*, 27/4/1958.
585. 'Pathos and Philosophy', *ST*, 31/8/1958.
586. 'Irma Translated', *ST*, 20/7/1958.
587. 'Better? Yes, Even Better', *ST*, 4/5/1958.
588. 'A Warning from Noël', *ST*, 14/12/1958.
589. 'London's Loss and New York's Gain', *CSM*, 15/10/1958.
590. *ST*, 6/7/1958.
591. The term 'Second Wave' describes the second generation of British playwrights in the 1960s and early 1970s, which followed the breakthrough of the New Wave. It is taken from the title of John Russell Taylor's book, *The Second Wave* (London, 1971).
592. 'The Premier Pessimist', *ST*, 10/7/1960.
593. 'The Hidden Persuaders', *ST*, 20/1/1963.
594. Ibid.
595. François Bédarida, *A Social History of England, 1851–1990* (London, 1991), p. 255.
596. Ibid., p. 256.
597. Ibid., p. 257.
598. 'Knockings at the Door', *ST*, 24/2/1963.
599. 'A Breach with Brecht', *ST*, 16/9/1962.
600. 'Downfall of a Poet', *ST*, 10/2/1963.
601. 'Brecht, the Misunderstood', *ST*, 16/5/1965.
602. 'The paradox of Brecht', *ST*, 18/7/1965.
603. 'Downfall of a Poet', *ST*, 10/2/1963.
604. 'A repellent greatness not to be scorned', *ST*, 14/3/1965.
605. 'A flinching tenderness', *ST*, 16/8/1964.
606. 'Brecht for Grown-ups', *ST*, 15/8/1965.
607. '"Henry" Transformed', *ST*, 21/7/1963.
608. Gilliatt, 'A Consideration of Critics, p. 28.
609. 'Noble in unreason', *ST*, 14/6/1964.
610. 'Knockings at the Door', *ST*, 24/2/1963.
611. Gilliatt, 'A Consideration of Critics', p. 27.
612. 'Business is Business', *ST*, 31/3/1963.
613. 'The impact of fact', *ST*, 16/10/1966.
614. Richard Findlater, *Banned* (London, 1968), p. 55.
615. 'The question-master', *ST*, 14/7/1963.
616. 'Affair of the Committed', *ST*, 24/9/1961.
617. *Private Eye*, Vol. 1, Issue 9, 19/4/1962, p. 4.
618. 'Moral attitudes at the play', *ST*, 18/8/1963.
619. *ST*, 18/10/1964.
620. 'Hardly a Silver Lining', *ST*, 25/10/1959 and 'Secrecy and the Theater', *CSM*, 20/2/1963.
621. Michael Billington, in *New Theatre Voices of the Fifties and the Sixties*, ed. C. Marowitz (London, 1981), pp. 9–12.
622. Gilliatt, 'A Consideration of Critics', p. 27.
623. Hobson describes the article as 'one of the most brilliant things [*Encore*] has ever published', 'Encore and its shock troops', *ST*, 30/5/1965.
624. Tynan had temporarily become the drama critic of the *New Yorker* in 1958.

625. Irving Wardle, *Theatre Criticism* (London, 1992), p. 61.
626. *ST*, 18/10/1964.
627. Billington, *Interview with D. M. Shellard*, 23/4/1992.
628. 'What the dealer saw', *ST*, 9/3/1969.
629. 'The Greatest of These ...', *ST*, 21/6/1959.
630. *ST*, 16/1/1966.
631. 'The Greatest Actress in the World', *CSM*, 7/10/1959.
632. 'The perfections of Dietrich', *ST*, 29/11/1964.
633. 'The world and all its cares', *ST*, 29/8/1965.
634. 'A piece for partisans', *ST*, 24/5/1964.
635. See 'Each man his own island', *ST*, 21/4/1963 – 'I am always ready to take advantage of an excuse – *any* excuse – to pay another visit to James Saunders's "Next Time I'll Sing to You"'. Alan Ayckbourn claims that James Saunders became so embarrassed by Hobson's constant reference to his play, which led people to greet the playwright by saying 'Hiya, Jimmy, how much are you paying him?', that he wrote to Hobson to ask him to cease mentioning it. 'Harold was terribly hurt because he really felt that strongly': *Interview with D. M. Shellard*, 9/3/1992.
636. 'Here's an end to harmony', *ST*, 11/10/1964.
637. 'The Theatre of Love', *ST*, 4/10/1964.
638. Ayckbourn, *Interview with D. M. Shellard*, 9/3/1992.
639. 'Vagaries of the West End', *ST*, 31/1/1960.
640. 'Larger than Life at the Festival', 5/1/1958.
641. Gaskill, *A Sense of Direction*, p. 35.
642. 'Racine's Cold Flame', 13/3/1960.
643. 'Things are Looking Up', *ST*, 5/6/1960.
644. 'The importance of fantasy', *ST*, 22/9/1963.
645. 'Pinter minus the moral', *ST*, 6/6/1965.
646. 'Too Many Targets for Anger', *ST*, 10/5/1959.
647. Osborne, *Almost a Gentleman*, p. 193.
648. 'Sloane Square Surprise', *ST*, 30/7/1961.
649. 'In the Nature of a Miracle', *ST*, 22/7/1962.
650. 'John Osborne's best play', *ST*, 13/9/1964.
651. 'Passion and exaltation', *ST*, 12/6/1966.
652. 'The second time round', *ST*, 12/4/1964.
653. 'A vengeful universe', *ST*, 11/11/1962.
654. 'The Most Deadly of Weapons', *ST*, 6/5/1962.
655. *Indirect Journey*, p. 259.
656. 'Little Ones Not Lost', *ST*, 2/4/1961.
657. 'The Hour of Knowing', *ST*, 16/4/1961.
658. 'The Duchess is Dead', *ST*, 18/12/1960.
659. 'A Travesty of Shakespeare', *ST*, 25/12/1960.
660. 'What Shakespeare believed', *ST*, 19/4/1964.
661. 'Dazzling, purifying, profound', *ST*, 23/8/1964.
662. 'The impact of fact', *ST*, 16/10/1966.
663. 'The Aldwych affair', *ST*, 30/8/1964.
664. Sally Beauman, *The Royal Shakespeare Company* (Oxford, 1982), p. 240.
665. Ibid.
666. Commented on by Hobson in 'The Soldier's Tale' *ST*, 12/12/1965.
667. Telegram, dated 31 August 1964, pasted into Vol. 27, p. 153, of Hobson's *Scrapbook Collection*.
668. Peter Hall, *Peter Hall's Diaries* (London, 1983), p. 68.
669. *ST*, 6/7/1958.
670. Editorial: 'A True National Theatre', *ST*, 15/3/1959.
671. *CSM*, 15/4/1959.

672. Ibid.
673. 'National Theater for Britain?', *CSM*, 28/4/1959.
674. 'British National Theater Near?', *CSM*, 18/10/1960.
675. John Elsom and Nicholas Tomalin, *The History of the National Theatre* (London, 1978), p. 6.
676. Sir Donald Wolfit, 'Letter to the Editor: "A National Theatre Plan"', *ST*, 19/3/1961.
677. 'Choose Your Man Quickly', *ST*, 12/3/1961.
678. 'Olivier Steps in Line to National Theater', *CSM*, 22/3/1961.
679. '£500,000 for Drama', *CSM*, 23/3/1961.
680. Beauman, *The Royal Shakespeare Company*, p. 254.
681. Editorial: 'The State and the Theatre', *ST*, 26/3/1961.
682. *CSM*, 13/4/1961.
683. 'Britain May Get National Theater', *CSM*, 8/6/1961.
684. 'National Theater Gets Lloyd Cue', *CSM*, 27/7/1961.
685. 'Volanakis Releases the God', *ST*, 22/4/1962.
686. 'All Smiles at Chichester', *ST*, 8/7/1962. See also Elsom and Tomalin, *The History of the National Theatre*, p. 125.
687. 'A hand upon the royalty', *ST*, 27/10/1963.
688. David Pryce-Jones, 'Son-et-Lumière', *Spectator*, 1/11/1963.
689. 'The sorcery of words', *ST*, 3/11/1963.
690. 'The peerless "Uncle Vanya"', *ST*, 24/11/1963.
691. 'Farquhar for All Souls', *ST*, 15/12/1963.
692. Gaskill, *A Sense of Direction*, p. 55.
693. 'Why we need both', *ST*, 29/12/1963. See also 'The Aldwych faces its gravest crisis', *ST*, 22/12/1963.
694. 'Black man's burden', *ST*, 26/4/1964.
695. Alan Brien, 'Scenes From Olivier', *Sunday Telegraph*, 26/4/1964.
696. 'Masque of evil, in perspective', *ST*, 26/2/1967.
697. 'It's great after the fiesta', *ST*, 21/2/1965.
698. 'Absorbed in sweet propriety', *ST*, 8/10/1967.
699. 'A fearful summons', *ST*, 16/4/1967.
700. 'Tynan's Return', *CSM*, 14/5/1959.
701. 'Playwrights View With Alarm Prospects of Abuse', *CSM*, 31/10/1960.
702. 'Kenneth Tynan's New Duties', *CSM*, 6/3/1963.
703. A view reflected in Peter Lewis, *The National – A Dream Made Concrete* (London, 1990), p. 4.
704. The extracts from the letters are reproduced in Kathleen Tynan's *The Life of Kenneth Tynan*, p. 399.
705. Hobson was also amazed at Tynan's championing of Rolf Hochhüth's *Soldiers* – 'To say that this adds to Churchill's reputation is intellectual cowardice; it is like stabbing a man in the back, and then claiming you have improved his health': 'Whose crime?', *ST*, 15/12/1968.
706. 'Skin Games', *ST*, 2/8/1970.
707. Johnston, *The Lord Chamberlain's Blue Pencil*, pp. 63–4.
708. 'An Avalanche of Critical Abuse', *CSM*, 16/3/1963.
709. *ST*, 10/3/1963.
710. *CSM*, 8/5/1963.
711. *ST*, 26/5/1963.
712. *ST*, 1/3/1964.
713. J. W. Lambert, 'The Censorship', *ST*, 11/4/1965. The former comptroller, John Johnston, who worked in the office of the Lord Chamberlain from 1964 to 1987, considers that this interview with him provides 'a very good summary of the censorship in 1965': *The Lord Chamberlain's Blue Pencil*, p. 182.

714. The Lord Chamberlain's demands are detailed in Osborne, *Almost a Gentleman*, p. 251.
715. 'The casting out of Lieutenant Redl', *ST*, 4/7/1965.
716. John Sutherland, *Offensive Literature* (London, 1982), p. 84.
717. *CSM*, 7/10/1932.
718. 'Where has all the goodness gone?', *ST*, 1/1/1967.
719. 'Alarms and Excursions', *ST*, 25/2/1968.
720. 'A Born Dramatist', *ST*, 15/2/1959.
721. 'Rattigan at Waterloo', *ST*, 17/7/1960.
722. 'A triumph of uncertainty', *ST*, 9/7/1967.
723. 'Oratorio on the terraces', *ST*, 17/3/1968.
724. 'Pity for the pitiless', *ST*, 15/10/1967.
725. 'No light at Damascus', *ST*, 23/7/1967.
726. 'Roads to Salvation', *ST*, 5/5/1968.
727. Ibid.
728. See *Odéon* entry in John McCormick and David Bradby, *The Cambridge Guide to World Theatre*, ed. Martin Banham (Cambridge, 1990), p. 729.
729. 'Letter to the Editor: An Honour Returned', *The Times*, 9/9/1968.
730. 'How Britain Can Repay Barrault', *ST*, 15/9/1968.
731. David Bradby, *Modern French Drama: 1940–1980* (Cambridge, 1984), p. 169.
732. John Bull, *New British Political Dramatists* (London, 1991), p. 10.
733. Ibid.
734. 'Drama of the unforeseeable', *ST*, 21/7/1968.
735. 'Putting words in their mouths', *ST*, 22/9/1968.
736. Ibid.
737. 'Purification and Perversity', *ST*, 30/8/1970.
738. 'All together now', *ST*, 28/12/1969.
739. 'Digging for defeat', *ST*, 30/11/1969.
740. 'Where the Real Power Lies', *ST*, 18/10/1970.
741. 'Slings and Arrows', *ST*, 8/11/1970. Hobson told Wolfgang Klooss in a 1979 interview that he disliked energetic audience participation because: 'Ich kann daran physisch einfach nicht teilhaben' ('I simply cannot physically take part'): 'Hinter den Kulissen der Kritik, Ein Gespräch mit dem Londoner Theaterkritiker Harold Hobson', *Internationale Beiträge zür Theaterwissenschaft* (Graz, 1981), 27 (2–3), pp. 268–80.
742. 'A noble sacrifice', *ST*, 15/11/1970.
743. Kenneth Hurren, *Theatre Inside Out* (London, 1977), pp. 173–4.
744. Billington, *Interview with D. M. Shellard*, 23/4/1992. In 'Barking up the Right Tree', *Guardian*, 2/8/1976, an article commenting on Hobson's retirement from *The Sunday Times*, Billington wrote that Hobson had possessed three critical eccentricities – his invention of an important new play if one did not exist, an over-eagerness to defend commercial managements and a blindness to the virtues of Broadway professionalism – but that they all stemmed from 'an ungovernable excitement at writing about the theatre'.
745. 'Delight and Disgust', *ST*, 20/12/1970.
746. 'Real and Romantic agony', *ST*, 5/3/1972.
747. 'The things that matter', *ST*, 4/1/1976.
748. 'Flower-powerhouse', *ST*, 29/9/1968.
749. 'The wilder shores of love', *ST*, 6/10/1968.
750. 'Skin Games', *ST*, 2/8/1970.
751. Ibid.
752. See 'Beauties and the Beast', *ST*, 29/8/1971: 'when a man with a sensitivity as delicate as Francis Warner writes a permissive play [*Lying Figures*] ... it

is a thing to be reckoned with ... a surrealist play in language of great subtlety'; and the review of the published *Killing Time* in a 'A new musical star', *ST,* 20/6/1976: 'No other serious dramatist has made such sensationally creative use of eroticism as he ... [His plays] are unique. Possibly the only unique drama of our time.'

753. 'Fringe benefits', *ST,* 28/4/1974.
754. Michael Coveney, *The Aisle is Full of Noises* (London, 1994), p. 16.
755. 'Old Vice & Virtue', *ST,* 10/1/1971.
756. 'Emperor's clothes', *ST,* 19/12/1971.
757. Richard Allen Cave, *New British Drama in Performance on the London Stage 1970–1985* (Gerrards Cross, 1987), p. 163.
758. 'Souls in twilight', *ST,* 21/6/1970.
759. 'The Best Players For The Best Plays', *ST,* 11/7/1971.
760. 'And even the ranks of Tuscany/Could scarce forbear to cheer': 'Horatius', *Lays of Ancient Rome* (London, 1886), ix–x, 60, p. 91. Hobson had edited a selection of Macaulay's prose writing in 1948.
761. 'Visions in a waste land', *ST,* 10/11/1968.
762. 'Introduction', *The Ruling Class* (London, 1969), p. vii.
763. In his published diaries Peter Hall describes Hobson in 1973 as a 'progressive Tory' – *Peter Hall's Diaries*, p. 68.
764. 'Inventing the past', *ST,* 19/5/1974.
765. 'Looking-glass revolution', *ST,* 23/12/1973.
766. 'Against the Tide', *ST,* 1/2/1976.
767. 'The healing power of words', *ST,* 19/7/1970.
768. 'Fresh air through French windows', *ST,* 20/10/1968.
769. 'Love's Blind Eye', *ST,* 27/9/1970.
770. 'Paradise lost', *ST,* 6/7/1969.
771. 'Horror at the Teatable', *ST,* 10/8/1969.
772. Billington, *Interview with D. M. Shellard*, 23/4/1992.
773. 'A Master Magician', *ST,* 13/6/1971.
774. 'Prisoners of Freedom', *ST,* 7/7/1968.
775. 'Drama of the unforseeable', *ST,* 21/7/1968.
776. 'Empire at sunset', *ST,* 10/10/1971.
777. 'A king born to be man', *ST,* 8/12/1968.
778. 'The other Eden', *ST,* 10/12/1972.
779. 'A patriot for me', *ST,* 19/1/1975.
780. 'Echoes of dreamland', *ST,* 3/11/1968. Hobson's original review of *Look Back in Anger* appeared in 'A New Author', *ST,* 13/5/1956.
781. 'Eric Porter's tumultuous Lear', *ST,* 14/4/1968.
782. 'The grandeur of despair', *ST,* 30/6/1968.
783. 'Fizzy Ginger', *ST,* 23/2/1969.
784. 'Shakespeare on the Rocks', *ST,* 9/2/1969.
785. 'Playing for the highest stakes', *ST,* 18/11/1973.
786. 'A sense of happiness', *ST,* 23/11/1975.
787. 'Home truths for Sloane Square', *ST,* 9/11/1969.
788. 'Picking the winner', *ST,* 6/8/1972.
789. Documented in Arnold Wesker's, *Distinctions* (London, 1985), pp. 288–364. The disputatious Wesker has continued his battles with various members of the theatrical profession, long after Hobson ceased to write. See Ruth Picardie's article, 'Feuds Corner: Arnold Wesker v. the Theatre World', *Guardian*, 23/4/92.
790. 'Book learning', *ST,* 13/8/1972.
791. 'A Cretinue of Critics', *Drama Quarterly*, September, 1972.
792. Ibid.
793. *ST,* 1/10/1972.

794. Reproduced in Wesker's, *Distinctions*, pp. 345–50.
795. 'Way down in Tennessee', *ST*, 5/12/1965.
796. 'Dazzling, purifying, profound', *ST*, 23/8/1964.
797. 'Divided devotion', *ST*, 4/3/1973.
798. 'Rejoice, rejoice', *ST*, 21/11/1971.
799. 'The pursuit of happiness', *ST*, 1/8/1976.
800. *DQ*, First Quarter, 1984, *DQ*, Third Quarter, 1984, *DQ*, Fourth Quarter, 1984, *DQ*, Third Quarter, 1985, *DQ*, Second Quarter, 1986, and *DQ*, First Quarter, 1988, respectively.
801. Confirmed as his last article by the librarian of the *Christian Science Monitor*, Mary McGee, in a *Letter to D. M. Shellard*, 20/8/1992.
802. *Peter Hall's Diaries*, p. 368.
803. 'Has Our Theatre Lost Its Nerve?', *ST*, 9/9/1984.

Bibliography

PRIMARY SOURCES (Works by Harold Hobson)

I. Books

Harold Hobson, *The First Three Years of the War* (London, 1943).
The Devil in Woodford Wells (London, 1946).
Thomas Babington, Lord Macaulay. Selected Writings, ed. and introd. by Harold Hobson (London, 1948).
Theatre (London, 1948).
Theatre 2 (London, 1950).
Verdict at Midnight (London, 1952).
The Theatre Now (London, 1954).
The French Theatre of Today. An English View (London, 1953).
International Theatre Annuals: Nos 1–5, ed. Harold Hobson (London, 1956–60).
Ralph Richardson (London, 1958).
Indirect Journey (London, 1978).
French Theatre Since 1830 (London, 1978).
Theatre in Britain (Oxford, 1984).
(with Philip Knightley and Leonard Russell) *The Pearl of Days* (London, 1972).

II. Articles in Books

'George Bernard Shaw', *English Wits*, ed. Leonard Russell (London, 1941), pp. 279–306.
'The Year's Playgoing', *Year's Work in the Theatre 1951*, pp. 10–13.
'Harold Hobson' in 'The Approach to Dramatic Criticism', *An Experience of Critics*, ed. K. Webb (London, 1952), pp .44–6.
'The French Theatre in Britain', *Theatre Programme*, ed. J. C. Trewin (London, 1954), pp. 231–45.
'Introduction', *Measure for Measure*, William Shakespeare (London, 1964).
'The First Night of *Waiting for Godot*', *Beckett at Sixty*, ed. John Calder (London, 1967), pp. 25–8.
'Introduction', *The Ruling Class*, Peter Barnes (London, 1969), pp. v–vii.
'The Warner Requiem', *Francis Warner: Poet and Dramatist*, ed. Tim Prentki (Knotting, 1977), pp.13–24.

III. Newspapers and Periodicals

Articles for the *Christian Science Monitor* from 27 October 1927 to 3 December 1979.
Articles for *The Sunday Times* from 14 May 1939 to 9 September 1984.
'Letters to the Editor', *Sheffield Daily Telegraph*, from 31 October 1922.

'London's Scarcity of Serious Plays', *London Calling – The Overseas Journal of the British Broadcasting Corporation*, 1/1/1942.
'The Cricketer without Rival', *The Listener*, 9/4/1942.
'Conservatism', *Daily Dispatch*, 7/11/1944.
'Critic on the Hearth', *The Listener*, 8/5/1947.
'The Most Astonishing Theatrical Phenomenon of our Time', *Daily Dispatch*, 13/6/1949.
'The Festival Plays', *Comment*, September, 1951.
'Letter to the Editor: An Honour Returned', *The Times*, 9/9/1968.
'Commentary', *Plays*, November, 1984.
Drama Quarterly, First Quarter 1984, Third Quarter 1984, Fourth Quarter 1984, Third Quarter 1985, Second Quarter 1986, First Quarter 1988. For a complete list of Hobson's published work, consult Dominic Shellard, *Harold Hobson: The Complete Catalogue 1922–1988* (Keele University Press, 1995).

IV. Interviews

Interview with D. M. Shellard, Westhampnett House, Chichester, West Sussex, 2/8/1990.
Interview with D. M. Shellard, Westhampnett House, Chichester, West Sussex, 10/7/1991.

SECONDARY SOURCES

I. Books and Articles

James Agate, *Ego 8* (London, 1946).
James Agate, *The Selective Ego*, ed. Tim Beaumont (London, 1976).
The Art of Laughter, ed. Lionel Lambourne and Amanda-Jane Doran (Oxford, 1992).
W. H. Auden and Christopher Isherwood, *Plays*, ed. Edward Mendelson (London, 1989).
Deirdre Bair, *Samuel Beckett: A Biography* (London, 1990).
Mary Baker Eddy, *Science and Health, With Key to the Scriptures* (Boston, rev. edn., 1910).
Sally Beauman, *The Royal Shakespeare Company* (Oxford, 1982).
François Bédarida, *A Social History of Britain, 1851–1990* (London, 1991).
The Best of Plays and Players, Volume 1: 1953–1968, ed. Peter Roberts (London, 1988).
The Best of Players and Players, Volume 2: 1969–1983, ed. Peter Roberts (London, 1989).
C. W. E. Bigsby, *A Critical Introduction to Twentieth Century American Drama* (Cambridge, 1989).
Kitty Black, *Upper Circle* (London, 1984).
David Bradby, *Modern French Drama 1940–1980* (Cambridge, 1984).
John Bull, *New British Political Dramatists* (London, 1991).
Peter Bull, *I Know the Face, But …* (London, 1959)
Angus Calder, *The People's War* (London, 1969).
Simon Callow, *Charles Laughton: A Difficult Actor* (London, 1987).
The Cambridge Guide to World Theatre, ed. Martin Banham (Cambridge, 1990).
Erwin Canham, *Commitment to Freedom* (Boston, 1958).
Humphrey Carpenter, *Early Auden* (Oxford, 1992).

Humphrey Carpenter, *O.U.D.S. – A Centenary of the Oxford University Dramatic Society* (Oxford, 1985).
Richard Allen Cave, *New British Drama in Performance on the London Stage 1970–1985* (Gerrards Cross, 1987).
David Childs, *Britain since 1945* (London, 1979).
Stephen Constantine, '"Love on the Dole" and its Reception in the 1930s', *Literature and History*, Vol. 8 (2), Autumn 1982.
Tony Cottrell, *Evolving Stages* (Bristol, 1991).
Michael Coveney, *The Aisle is Full of Noises* (London, 1994).
Drama Criticism Since Ibsen, ed. Arnold P. Hinchliffe, (London, 1979).
John Elsom, *Post-War British Theatre Criticism* (London, 1981).
John Elsom and Nicholas Tomalin, *The History of the National Theatre* (London, 1978).
Edwin Emery, *The Press and America* (New Jersey, 1972).
Encyclopaedia Britannica, Vol. 5 (1961).
Martin Esslin, *The Theatre of the Absurd* (1962; 3rd edn., London, 1982).
Richard Findlater, *Banned* (London, 1968).
William Gaskill, *A Sense of Direction* (London, 1988).
John Gielgud, *An Actor and His Time* (London, 1979)
Ronald Gow and Walter Greenwood, *Love on the Dole* (London, 1936).
Lawrence Graver, *Waiting for Godot* (Cambridge, 1989).
Frances Gray, *Noël Coward* (London, 1987).
Trevor R. Griffiths and Carole Woddis, *Bloomsbury Theatre Guide* (London, 1989).
Peter Hall, *Peter Hall's Diaries* (London, 1983).
Sheila Hancock, *Ramblings of an Actress* (London, 1987).
Hansard (London, 1949).
James Harding, *Agate* (London, 1986).
Harrap's Book of 1000 Plays, ed. Steve Fletcher and Norman Jopling (London, 1989).
Rex Harrison, *Rex: An Autobiography* (London, 1974).
Ronald Hayman, *British Theatre since 1955* (Oxford, 1979).
Terry Hodgson, *The Batsford Dictionary of Drama* (London, 1988).
Michael Holroyd, *Bernard Shaw*, Vol. 3: *1918–1950* (London, 1991).
Richard Huggett, *Binkie Beaumont: Eminence grise of the West End Theatre 1933–1973* (London, 1989).
Hugh Hunt, Kenneth Richards, John Russell Taylor, *The Revels History of Drama in English*, Vol. 7: *1880 to the Present Day* (London, 1978).
Kenneth Hurren, *Theatre Inside Out* (London, 1977).
Christopher Innes, *Modern British Drama 1890–1990* (Cambridge, 1992).
Catherine Itzin, *Stages in the Revolution* (London, 1980).
John Johnston, *The Lord Chamberlain's Blue Pencil* (London, 1990).
Aled Jones, 'The British Press, 1919–1945', *The Encyclopaedia of the British Press*, ed. Dennis Griffiths (London, 1992).
Esmond Knight, *Seeking the Bubble* (London, 1943).
Stephen Koss, *The Rise and Fall of the Political Press in Britain* (London, 1984).
Charles Landstone, *Offstage* (London, 1953).
Glenda Leeming, *Poetic Drama* (London, 1989).
Peter Lewis, *The Fifties – Portrait of an Age* (London, 1989).
Peter Lewis, *The National – A Dream Made Concrete* (London, 1990).
Joseph Macleod, *The Actor's Right to Act* (London, 1981).
W. N. Medlicott, *Contemporary England 1914–1964* (London, 1976).
Edward Mendelson, *Early Auden* (London, 1981).
Arthur Miller, *Plays One* (London, 1988).
John Milton, 'L'Allegro', *Complete English Poems*, ed. Gordon Campbell (London, 1990).

Allan Monkhouse, *Cecilia* (London, 1932).
New Theatre Voices of the Fifties and Sixties, ed. Charles Marowitz, Tom Milne and Owen Hale (London, 1981).
Garry O'Connor, *Ralph Richardson* (London, 1982).
John Osborne, *Look Back in Anger* (1957; London, 1986).
John Osborne, *A Better Class of Person* (London, 1982).
John Osborne, *Almost a Gentleman* (London, 1991).
The Oxford Companion to German Literature, ed. Henry and Mary Garland (Oxford, 1986).
The Oxford Companion to the Theatre, ed. Phyllis Hartnoll (Oxford, 1990).
Henry Pelling, *The Labour Governments 1945–51* (London, 1985).
PEP, *Report on the British Press* (London, 1946).
Questions and Answers on Christian Science (Boston, 1974).
Terence Rattigan, *Collected Plays* (London, 1953).
Michael Redgrave, *In My Mind's Eye* (London, 1983).
Peter Roberts, *The Old Vic Story* (London, 1976).
George Rowell, *The Old Vic Theatre: A History* (Cambridge, 1993).
George Rowell and Anthony Jackson, *The Repertory Movement: A History of Regional Theatre in Britain* (Cambridge, 1984).
John Russell Taylor, *Anger and After* (London, 1969).
John Russell Taylor, *The Second Wave* (London, 1971).
Michael Sanderson, *From Irving to Olivier* (London, 1985).
Ernest Short, *Sixty Years of Theatre* (London, 1951).
Alan Sked and Chris Cook, *Post War Britain: A Political History* (London, 1980).
Dodie Smith, *Call It a Day* (London, 1936).
Donald Spoto, *Laurence Olivier* (London, 1991).
John Sutherland, *Offensive Literature* (London, 1982).
A. J. P. Taylor, *The Second World War – An Illustrated History* (London, 1976).
Thucydides, *History of the Peloponnesian War* (London, 1991).
Kathleen Tynan, *The Life of Kenneth Tynan* (London, 1988).
Kenneth Tynan, *A View of the English Stage* (London, 1984).
Irving Wardle, *Theatre Criticism* (London, 1992).
Arnold Wesker, *Distinctions* (London, 1985).
Michael White, *Empty Seats* (London, 1984).
Bill Williamson, *The Temper of the Times* (Oxford, 1990).

II. Newspapers and Periodicals (arranged chronologically)

Radio Listings, *Radio Times*, 12/7/1940.
Desmond MacCarthy, 'A New Play', *New Statesman and Nation*, 14/9/1946.
Alan Dent, 'Royal Lear', *News Chronicle*, 27/9/1946.
Peter Fleming, 'The Theatre', *Spectator*, 27/9/1946.
Philip Hope-Wallace, 'Theatre', *Time and Tide*, 5/10/1946.
Southwark Cathedral Magazine, 1949.
W. A. Darlington, 'Paul Muni's Fine Acting', *Daily Telegraph*, 29/7/1949.
L. H., 'The Edinburgh Festival', Manchester *Guardian*, 24/8/1949.
J. C. Trewin, 'Rough Riding', *Observer*, 16/10/1949.
Anthony Cookman, 'At the Theatre', *Tatler*, 20/10/1949.
W. A. Darlington, 'Alec Guinness as Hamlet', *Daily Telegraph*, 18/5/1951.
Ivor Brown, 'Guinness and Scotch', *Observer*, 20/5/1951.
T. C. Worsley, 'Religious Drama', *New Statesman and Nation*, 26/5/1951.
Anthony Cookman, 'At the Theatre', *Tatler*, 30/5/1951.
'Competition', *Spectator*, 6/2/1953.
Anthony Cookman, 'At the Theatre', *Tatler*, 4/6/1953.

T. C. Worsley, 'Guys and Dolls', *New Statesman and Nation*, 6/6/1953.
Kenneth Tynan, 'West End Apathy', *Observer*, 31/10/1954.
Kenneth Tynan, 'Indirections', *Observer*, 12/12/1954.
Kenneth Tynan, 'Big Three', *Observer*, 6/1/1955.
Kenneth Tynan, 'Dimmed Debut', *Observer*, 3/7/1955.
Milton Shulman, 'Duet for Two Symbols', *Evening Standard*, 4/8/1955.
Stephen Williams, 'Stephen Williams at the Theatre', *Evening News*, 4/8/1955.
David Lewin, 'Nothing Happens, it's Awful (it's Life)', *Daily Express*, 4/8/1955.
Colin Wilson, 'The Left Bank Can Keep It', *Daily Mail*, 4/8/1955.
W. A. Darlington, 'An Evening of Funny Obscurity', *Daily Telegraph*, 4/8/1955.
Anon., 'Arts Theatre', *The Times*, 4/8/1955.
Philip Hope-Wallace, 'Two Evenings with Two Tramps', *Guardian*, 5/8/1955.
Kenneth Tynan, 'New Writing', *Observer*, 7/8/1955.
Stephen Bagnall, 'Letter to the Editor: Edwige Feuillère', *The Sunday Times*, 18/9/1955.
Collie Knox, 'I've Been Led by the Nose Long Enough', *Daily Mail*, 17/9/1955.
Collie Knox, 'This Is Why Garbo Wants to Be Alone', *Daily Mail*, 1/10/1955.
Anon., 'Was Genius Lacking from the Theatre in 1955?', *Evening Standard*, 19/1/1956.
Kenneth Tynan, 'Some Stars from the East', *Observer*, 26/6/1956.
Patrick Gibbs, 'A Study of an Exhibitionist', *Daily Mail*, 9/5/1956.
John Barber, 'This Bitter Young Man – Like Thousands', *Daily Express*, 9/5/1956.
Milton Shulman, 'Mr Osborne Builds a Wailing Wall', *Evening Standard*, 9/5/1956.
Kenneth Tynan, 'Braw and Brecht', *Observer*, 2/9/1956.
Kenneth Tynan, 'Simple and Complicated', *Observer*, 4/11/1956.
Anon, 'THAT Angry Young Man Gets a Special Award', *Evening Standard*, 3/1/1957.
Kenneth Tynan, 'A Philosophy of Despair', *Observer*, 7/4/1957.
Peter Brook, 'As I *Don't* Like It …', *The Sunday Times*, 1/9/1957.
Anon, 'Hobson's Choice is Cardiff', *The Western Daily Press*, 3/1/1958.
Kenneth Tynan, 'Ionesco, Man of Destiny?', *Observer*, 22/6/1958.
Eugène Ionesco, 'The Playwright's Role', *Observer*, 29/6/1958.
Penelope Gilliatt, 'A Consideration of Critics', *Encore*, November/ December, 1959.
Donald Wolfit, 'Letter to the Editor: A National Theatre Plan', *The Sunday Times*, 19/3/1961.
John Wells, 'Interviews with Myself', *Private Eye*, Vol. 1, Issue 9, 19/4/1962.
David Pryce-Jones, 'Son-et-Lumière', *Spectator*, 1/11/1963.
Laurence Olivier, 'Olivier – My Life, My Work, My Future', *The Sunday Times*, 3/11/1963.
J. W. Lambert, 'The Censorship', *The Sunday Times*, 11/4/1965.
Benedict Nightingale, 'Osborne in Disintegration', *New Statesman*, 8/12/1972.
Arnold Wesker, 'A Cretinue of Critics', *Drama*, Winter, 1972.
Anon., 'Memory Theatre … Hobson Signs Off', *Plays and Players*, September 1976.
Walter Kooss, 'Hinter den Kulissen der Kritik, Ein Gespräch mit dem Londoner Theaterkritiker Harold Hobson', *Internationale Beiträge zur Theaterwissenschaft*, 27, Graz, 1981.
John Calder, 'Sir Harold Hobson', *Independent*, 14/3/1992.
Anon., 'Sir Harold Hobson', *Daily Telegraph*, 14/3/1992.
Michael Billington, 'The Brave Critic Who Waited for Godot', *Guardian*, 14/3/1992.
Anon., 'Sir Harold Hobson', *The Times*, 14/3/1992.

Peter Cunard, 'Sir Harold Hobson', *The Times*, 18/3/1992.
Ruth Picardie, 'Feuds Corner: Arnold Wesker v. the Theatre World', *Guardian*, 23/4/1992.

III. Theses

Victor Lazarow, unpublished thesis, 'The Dramatic Criticism of Sir Harold Hobson: 1947–1976' (University of Georgia, Athens, Georgia, 1978).

IV. Letters

Ivor Novello, letter to Harold Hobson, *Harold Hobson's Scrapbook Collection*, undated, c. March 1951, Vol. 18, p. 63, formerly in the possession of Bernard Quaritch Ltd., 5–8 Lower John Street, Golden Square, London, W1R 4AU.
Peter Hall, telegram to Harold Hobson, *Harold Hobson's Scrapbook Collection*, 31/8/1964, Vol. 27, p.153.

V. Interviews

Michael Billington, *Interview with D. M. Shellard*, Kew, London, 23/4/1992.
Alan Ayckbourn, *Interview with D. M. Shellard*, Villiers Park, Oxon, 9/3/1992.
Richard Jackson, *Interview with D. M. Shellard*, 59 Knightsbridge, London, 25/3/1992.

VI. Radio Programmes

'Carry on up the Zeitgeist – *Look Back in Anger*', BBC Radio 4, 3/4/1992.

Index

Abbot, Willis J. 11, 17
Abélard and Héloïse 208
Achard, Marcel 92
Acton, Lord 9, 40, 75, 82
Adamov, Arthur 114
Aeschylus 105
Afinogenov, Alexsandr 52
After All 27
Agate, James 8, 38, 41–2, 57–8, 60–1, 63, 64–5, 66, 68, 71–2, 102, 109, 213, 222, 223
Alice, Princess 87
Allen, Arthur 16
Allen, Chesney 51
All In Good Time 196
All's Well That Ends Well 102
Almost a Gentleman 142
Ambassador Extraordinary 78, 159
Amis, Kingsley 134
Anderson, Robert 151
Anger and After 162
Annie Get Your Gun 73, 85, 103
Anouilh, Jean 77, 82, 83, 90, 91, 92, 93, 97, 110, 158, 187, 188, 210, 215
Antigone 82, 83–4, 225, 226
Antony and Cleopatra 92, 102, 104, 211
Archer, William 101
Archibald, William 158
Ardèle 91, 226
Arden, John 169, 178, 181, 186, 195
Ardrey, Robert 45
Armstrong, Anthony 22
Armstrong, Norman 55
Arnold, Matthew 219
Arrest 206
Arsenic and Old Lace 55
Arts Council, The 47
Ascent of F6, The 35, 50
Ashcroft, Peggy 13, 30, 62, 85, 96, 102, 140, 156, 191, 210, 211
As You Like It 193
Attlee, Clement 86, 88
Auden, W. H. 33–5, 49–50, 75, 107, 216

Augier, Emile 212
Austen, Jane 98
Ayckbourn, Alan 107, 108, 185, 233
Ayrton, Randle 219

Baal 175
Bagnall, Stephen 130, 131
Bagnold, Enid 140
Bair, Deirdre 122
Baker Eddy, Mary 14, 15, 25, 217
Balcon, Michael 137
Bald Prima Donna, The 157
Ballad of the False Barman, The 198
Balzac, Honoré de 16
Banks, Leslie 40
Barber, John 142, 225
Bardot, Brigitte 149
Bare Idea, The 45
Barnes, Peter 209
Barrault, Jean-Louis 77, 78–9, 96, 101, 107, 202, 203, 227
Barrie, J. M. 51
Bates, H. E. 38
Batey, Joseph 16
Baudelaire, Charles 154
Baylis, Lilian 20
BBC (British Broadcasting Corporation) 40, 41, 49, 53, 58, 59, 107, 144
Beaton, Cecil 38
Beauclerk, Lord Frederick 41, 59, 222
Beaumont, Hugh 'Binkie' 37, 134–5, 189
Beaverbrook, Lord (Max Aitken) 57
Beckett, Samuel 24, 29, 44, 47, 54, 113, 116, 117, 119, 120, 121, 122, 123–4, 127, 130, 146, 147, 159–61, 162, 165, 167, 169, 170, 183, 187, 188, 212, 228
Behan, Brendan 147–9, 152, 169, 185
Behrman, S. N. 51
Believe It or Not 45
Bell, Marie 191

245

Belle of New York, The 101
Bells, The 30, 74, 96, 219
Bennett, Jill 211
Benthall, Michael 191
Bentley, Eric 155
Bequest to the Nation 210
Berliner Ensemble 128, 139, 155, 175, 193
Better Class of Person, A 161
Bet Your Life 98
Billington, Michael 107, 108, 130, 159, 164–5, 183, 206, 211, 228, 235
Bingo 213
Birthday Party, The 113, 166–9, 188, 193
Birthmark 73
Black, George 39, 51
Black, Kitty 135
Black Chiffon 85
Blackmail 20
Black Velvet 47–8
Bless the Bride 73, 85
Blithe Spirit 50, 51–2, 63
Blue Goose, The 51
Boland, Bridget 75
Bolt, Robert 164
Bond, Edward 159, 195, 198, 212–13
Bond Honoured, A 187
Bonnes, Les 98
Books and Bookmen 215
Boothe, Clare 48
Bost, Pierre 140
Bowen, John 207
Bowers-Broadbent, H. W. 17
Boys in Brown 73
Brasseur, Pierre 227
Braun, Eva 73
Brecht, Bertolt 8, 18, 77, 84, 111, 127–30, 138–40, 152, 155–7, 161, 173, 175, 176, 177, 178, 193, 212
Brecht on Brecht 175
Brenton, Howard 210, 213, 215
Bridie, James 43–4
Brien, Alan 193
Britten, Benjamin 220
Brook, Peter 127, 137, 163, 177, 181, 189, 191, 203, 204–5, 208
Brooke, Rupert 21
Brown, Ivor 96, 100
Browne, E. Martin 76
Browne, Wynyard 224
Browning Version, The 79–80
Buchanan, Jack 19, 124
Bucknill, James 181

Bull, Peter 115
Bullins, Ed 206
Burden, Hugh 54, 219
Burrell, John 81
Burton, Richard 94–5, 99, 215
Burton, Robert 90
Byam Shaw, Glen 17
Byron – the Naked Peacock 208

Cadbury, Peter 189
Caesar and Cleopatra 92, 93
Calcutta in the Morning 73
Calder, John 107
Caligula 84
Call it a Day 21
Call Me Madam 103
Callow, Simon 219
Calvert, Louis 71
Camelot 214
Campbell, Cheryl 138
Campbell, Judy 50
Camrose, Lord (William Berry) 57
Camus, Albert 79, 84, 92
Candida 27
Canham, Erwin 10, 11, 12, 17, 18
Cannan, Denis 140, 228
Captain Brassbound's Conversion 92
Caretaker, The 185–6
Carroll, Sydney 61
Casino Royale 149
Cass, Henry 20
Cat on a Hot Tin Roof 151, 152
Catto, Max 21–2
Caucasian Chalk Circle, The 128, 155
Cavalcade 20
Cecilia 21, 28
CEMA (Council for the Encouragement of Music and the Arts) 40
Chairs, The 112
Chalk Garden, The 140
Chamberlain, Neville 37, 57
Champagne for Delilah 85
Chandos, Lord 191, 192
Chekhov, Anton 22, 101
Cherry Orchard, The 102, 109
Chicken Soup with Barley 169
Chiltern Hundreds, The 74
Chips With Everything 188
Christian Science 14–16, 201
Christian Science Monitor 8, 10–11, 17, 40, 41, 53, 55, 59, 60, 61, 63, 64, 65, 71, 73, 113, 124, 137, 138, 196, 215
Churchill, Winston 47, 57, 98, 210, 234

Churchill Play, The 210
Clarendon, Lord 45
Clark, Kenneth 134
Claudel, Paul 92, 96–7, 154, 203
Clunes, Alec 77, 100
Clurman, Harold 138
Cobb, Lee J. 86
Cobbold, Lord 195
Cochran, C. B. 22, 51
Cockpit 75, 224
Cocktail Party, The 89–90
Cocteau, Jean 64
Cohn-Bendit, Daniel 203
Coleridge, Samuel Taylor 28
Colombe 93
Comedians, The 210
Complaisant Lover, The 183
Confidential Clerk, The 105
Congreve, William 21
Connelly, Marc 149
Cooke, Thomas 230
Cookman, Anthony 87, 96, 104
Cooper, Gladys 159
Copley, Peter 68
Coppel, Alec 45
Cornell, Katherine 27
Corti, Vic 206
Cottage to Let 47
Coupe, Bernice 140
Coveney, Michael 208
Coward, Noël 20, 33, 49–50, 51–2, 76, 78, 79, 170, 221, 224
Cowdrey, Colin 188
Craig, Gordon 27
Cranmer, Thomas 122
Creighton, Anthony 169
Crime Passionnel 77–8
Cripps, Stafford 68
Critics, The 164
Cronin, A. J. 46
Crucible, The 106, 150, 151
Crystal Heart, The 158–9
Cunard, Peter 228
Cup of Happiness, A 31
Cuttell, Colin 87
Cymbeline 163

Daily Dispatch 56
Daily Express 116, 142
Daily Mail 116, 122, 142
Daily Sketch 57
Daily Telegraph 12, 86, 102, 107, 116, 142, 173
Dalton, Hugh 68

Dame aux Camélias, La 130
Dance of Death, The (Auden) 33–4, 50
Dance of Death, The (Strindberg) 193
Daneman, Paul 121, 147, 160, 211
Danger 20
Danvers, Billy 215
Dare, Zena 51
Dark Emmanuel 73
Dark Horizon 26
Dark Is Light Enough, The 105
Dark Summer 224
Darlington, W. A. 86, 96, 116, 167, 173
Daubeny, Peter 202
Daughter Janie 56
Davis, Saville 73
Day by the Sea, A 104
Day in the Death of Joe Egg, A 201
Dean, Basil 38, 163, 220
Dear Brutus 51
Dear Octopus 46
Death of a Salesman 85–6
Deep Blue See, The 80, 98
Delaney, Shelagh 80, 201
Dent, Alan 60–1, 66, 222, 223
Desert Island Discs 164
Deval, Jacques 92
Devine, George 105, 146, 163, 186
Diable et le Bon Dieux, Le 93
Dickens, Charles 29, 95
Dietrich, Marlene 184
Dimbleby, Richard 133
Distant Point 52
Diversion 50
Doctor's Dilemma, The 221
Doll's House, A 27
Donat, Robert 20
Donne, John 76
Dors, Diana 149
Douglas Home, William 24, 68–9, 78, 159, 183, 185, 210
Drama Quarterly 214
Dr Angelus 74
Drummond, Roscoe 124
Duchess of Malfi, The 189
Duel of Angels 170
Dukes, Ashley 13, 42
Dumb Waiter, The 186
Duras, Marguerite 183, 187–8
Dutschke, Rudi 203
Dwarfs, The 186

Eagle Has Two Heads, The 64–5
Early Morning 212

Eddison, Robert 188
Eden, Anthony 157
Edinburgh Festival 78, 130
Edward, My Son 74
Ego 41, 57–8
Elder Statesman, The 170
Eliot, T.S. 45, 50, 75–6, 82, 89, 92, 104, 105, 170
Elizabeth of England 20
Elsom, John 104
Empty Space, The 205
Encore 175, 177, 181, 183, 187, 190, 202, 232
Endgame 170
End of Me Old Cigar, The 211
Enfants du Paradis, Les 227
English Stage Company 68, 137, 140, 143, 145, 160, 165, 169, 175, 185, 187, 192, 201
ENSA (Entertainments National Service Association) 38, 47, 220
Entertainer, The 157, 161–3, 209, 210
Epitaph for George Dillon 169
Equity 46
Escort 55
Esslin, Martin 112
Euclid 111
Eurydice 91
Evans, Edith 93, 109, 140
Evans, Maurice 75
Evening News 116
Evening Standard 90, 104, 115, 137, 142, 158, 164

Fading Mansions 226
Fair Lady, My 170
Farjeon, Herbert 39
Fausses Confidences, Les 96
Felicity Jasmine 56
Fernald, John 137, 191
Feuchtwanger, Lion 13
Feuillère, Edwige 30, 96–7, 107, 130–1, 154, 183, 184, 191, 202
Feydeau, Georges 203
Fin de Partie 159–60, 162
Fish in the Family, A 73
Five Finger Exercise 169
Flanagan, Bud 51
Flare Path 54, 55, 79, 221
Fleming, Ian 149
Fleming, Peter 66
Flowering Cherry 164
Follow My Leader 45
Fool, The 213

Foot, Dingle 195
Forbes-Robertson, Johnston 23
Freeman, E. A. 9
French Without Tears 79
Fresnay, Pierre 191
Froude, J. A. 9
Fry, Christopher 24, 50, 75–7, 78, 89, 90–1, 92, 93, 94, 105, 107, 110, 164, 170, 210, 228
Fuchs, Klaus 133
Furber, Douglas 45

Gabor, Zsa Zsa 208
Galsworthy, John 212
Gardner, Helen 187
Garrick, David 74
Gaskill, William 163, 186, 193, 227
Gaulle, Charles de 202–3
Gay's the Word 93
Genet, Jean 77, 98, 110, 187, 197
Gentlemen Prefer Blondes 92
Ghelderode, Michel de 92
Gibbs, Patrick 142
Gibbs, Wolcott 170
Gide, André 92, 141, 152
Gielgud, John 17, 21, 31, 45, 47, 51, 55, 70, 75, 86, 90, 92, 93, 97, 100, 102, 105, 109, 131, 150, 170, 173, 191, 209, 219
Gilliatt, Penelope 110, 175, 177, 181, 182, 183, 187, 214
Giraudoux, Jean 131, 170
Glass Menagerie, The 86
Godspell 214–15
Goering, Hermann 45
Goetz, Augustus 85
Goetz, Ruth 85
Gold, Jimmy 51
Golding, Louis 33
Goldsmith, Oliver 21
Goodliffe, Michael 170
Good Woman of Setzuan, The 152, 156, 161
Gordon, Bernard 135
Gough, Michael 78
Goulden, Richard 17
Gow, Ronald 32
Grasso, Giovanni 71
Gray, Simon 201
Green Pastures, The 149, 198
Greene, Graham 140, 183
Greenwood, Walter 32
Griffiths, Trevor 210
Grimaldi, Joseph 64

Grock, Charles 64
Grotowski, Jerzy 205
Guardian 57, 60, 107, 108, 116
Guest, E. R. 150
Guinness, Alec 68, 75, 90, 92, 93, 95–6, 102–3, 109, 173, 190, 209
Guthrie, Tyrone 17, 20, 52, 163, 191
Guys and Dolls 103

Hadley, W. H. 57, 59, 60, 61, 72
Hagen, Uta 88
Haigh, Kenneth 140
Hair 207–8
Hall, Glenvil 88
Hall, Peter 111, 115, 140, 163, 177, 183, 185, 188–9, 190, 191, 192, 208, 216, 218, 236
Hamlet 61, 78, 82, 95–6, 101, 137, 192, 203, 219
Hammerstein II, Oscar 77
Hammond, Kay 109
Hancock, Sheila 226
Happy as Larry 73–4
Happy End 175
Hard Times 95
Harris, Robert 75
Harrison, Rex 39
Harvey, Frank 197
Hawkins, Jack 70
Hayes, George 75
Hay Fever 51
Hayman, Ronald 139, 209
Hayward, Isaac 92
Hazlitt, William 29, 61–2, 70, 71, 95, 131, 180
Head on Crash 21
Heath, Edward 204
Hegel, Georg Wilhelm Friedrich 10
Heiress, The 85, 153, 219
Hellman, Lillian 221
Hello, Dolly! 214
Henry IV, Part 1 94
Henry IV, Parts 1 and 2 19, 92
Henry V 64, 92
Henson, Leslie 45, 47, 53, 54, 64
Herlie, Eileen 64–5
He Who Plays the King 90
Heywood, Valentine 65
Hicks, Seymour 49
Hilary, Jennifer 184–5
History of the Peloponnesian War 66
Hitchcock, Alfred 20
Hitler, Adolf 45, 46, 53, 57
Hobson, Elizabeth 8, 35, 78, 124, 211, 223, 229

Hobson, Harold
  accession as drama critic of *The Sunday Times* 72
  assistant literary editor of *The Sunday Times* 58
  belief in Christian Science 15, 16, 161, 181
  childhood 13–16
  CBE 202, 211, 213
  Devil in Woodford Wells, The 59, 124
  disability 7–8, 14, 16, 62, 123–4, 201, 205
  Drama Quarterly reviewer 215
  editorial writer for the *Christian Science Monitor* 11–13
  first *Sunday Times* article 35
  First Three Years of the War, The 38
  French Theatre Since 1830 42, 84, 216
  Indirect Journey 9, 13, 62, 123, 216
  International Theatre Annual 144, 156
  knighthood 213
  Légion d'honneur 79, 184, 203
  London drama critic of the *Christian Science Monitor* 13, 19
  marriage to Elizabeth 35
  obituaries 107
  Oriel, College, Oxford 9, 10, 16–17, 93
  Pearl of Days, The 57, 72
  retirement 216
  support for the Conservative party 56, 98
  support for the Labour party 17, 99
  television critic of *The Listener* 59–60
  Theatre 1 63, 71
  Theatre in Britain 50, 52, 91, 167–8, 216
  Theatre Now, The 97, 153
  training as historian 10
  Verdict at Midnight 101
Hobson, Jacob 13, 14
Hobson, Margaret 35, 59, 78
Hobson, Minnie 13
Hobson, Tom 13–4
Hochhuth, Rolf 195, 234
Hochwälder, Fritz 131
Hodson, H. V. 164
Holder, Owen 228
Holloway, Baliol 71
Holy Isle 44
Home 209
Homecoming, The 186

Hope-Wallace, Philip 66, 116–17
Hostage, The 169
Hotel in Amsterdam, The 211
Houdini, Harry 65
Howard, Sydney 40
Howes, Bobby 45
How Horatius Kept the Bridge 209
Huggett, Richard 135, 136, 229
Huis Clos 110
Hulbert, Jack 45, 54
Humanity 161
Hunt, Hugh 81, 146, 221
Hunter, N. C. 93, 104, 136
Hurren, Kenneth 206
Hurry On Down 134
Hutton, Len 134

Ibsen, Henrik 22, 101, 102, 163, 167
Iceman Cometh, The 90
Idiot's Delight 32
Importance of Being Earnest, The 45, 55
Inadmissible Evidence 187
Independent 107
In Good King Charles's Golden Days 43
Ionesco, Eugène 77, 110–13, 127, 157, 165, 169, 173, 212, 228
Iphigenia in Tauris 22–3
Irma la Douce 135
Iron Duchess, The 159, 170
Irving, Henry 23, 27, 30, 58, 66, 74, 96, 219
Isherwood, Christopher 33–5, 49–50, 75
It Bees Dat Way 206

Jackson, Richard 124, 223, 228, 229
James, Henry 165, 169, 184
Jazz Singer, The 20
Jeans, Ursula 51
Jellicoe, Ann 186
Jerrold, Mary 51
Jew Süss 13
Johnson, Bill 94
Johnson, Samuel 67
Johnson Over Jordan 35, 97
Johnston, John 234
Joie de Vivre 201
Joseph and the Amazing Technicolour Dreamcoat 214
Journey's End 27
Joyce, James 116
Judgement Day 40, 45
Jupiter Laughs 46

Kataev, Valentin 52
Kaye, Danny 85
Kazan, Elia 77, 138
Kean, Edmund 29, 67, 71, 74, 83, 180
Kempson, Rachel 211
Kemsley, Lord (Gomer Berry) 56, 57–8, 61, 72, 85, 98, 99
Kennedy, Robert 203
Kerr, Geoffrey 47
Khrushchev, Nikita 157
Killing Time 236
King-Hall, Stephen 85
King John 52
King Lear 66–8, 81, 98
Kiss and Tell 64
Kiss Me, Kate 93–4, 103
Kitchen, The 224
Klooss, Wolfgang 235
Knox, Collie 122
Knox, Teddy 51
Komisarjevsky, Theodore 20
Korda, Alexander 20
Krapp's Last Tape 123

Lady Chatterley's Lover 195
Lady's Not for Burning, The 75–7, 90, 94
Lady Susan 98
Laing, Ian 223
L'Allegro 42
Lamb, Charles 71
Lambert, J.W. 215
Landor, Walter 21
Landscape 210–11
Lang, Matheson 71
Late Night Final 20
Laughton, Charles 20, 31, 219
Laurie, John 42
Lawrence, D. H. 195
Lazarow, Victor 154, 166, 230, 231
Lazzarro 13
Leçon, La 111
Lehmann, Rosamond 137
Leigh, Vivien 87, 88, 89, 100, 105, 127
Leighton, Margaret 109, 170
Lesson, The 110
L'Etat de Siège 79
Levin, Bernard 194
Lewin, David 116
Libel 109
Lifeline 55
Life of Galileo 175
Life of Kenneth Tynan, The 7

Light of Heart, The 45, 46
L'Invitation au Château 90
Lion Has Wings, The 37
Littler, Emile 189
Littlewood, Joan 110, 127, 128, 129, 147, 163, 177
Live Like Pigs 169
Livesey, Roger 51
Lloyd, Selwyn 191
Lloyd Webber, Andrew 214
London Calling 53
Longmans 59, 90
Lonsdale, Frederick 52
Look Back in Anger 77, 108, 135, 140–6, 149, 156, 158, 161, 167, 173, 180, 201, 204, 211–12, 224, 227, 236
Lord Chamberlain, The 115, 149, 150, 151, 152, 178, 181, 195, 196, 197, 198, 199, 202, 207, 234
Love for Love 221
Love Lottery, The 65
Love of Four Colonels, The 98
Love on the Dole 32–3
Love's Labour's Lost 87
Lucky Jim 134
Lupino, Stanley 45
Luther 187
Luther King, Martin 203
Lying Figures 235
Lynn, Ralph 65
Lynne, Carole 39
Lyttleton, Adrian 192
Lyttleton, Oliver 56

Macaulay, Thomas Babbington 9, 236
Macbeth 20, 99–100, 101, 123, 125–6
McCarthy, Joseph 106
McGee, Mary 237
McGreevy, Thomas 228
Machiavelli, Niccolo 42
McKellen, Ian 211
McLeod, George 219
Macnee, Patrick 63
Macowan, Michael 20
Magnolia Street 33
Major Barbara 25
Malraux, André 203
Man and Superman 92
Mandragola 42
Man with the Flower in his Mouth, The 20
Maquettes 208
Marat/Sade, The 189

Marching Song 105
Margin for Error 48
Marivaux, Pierre 96
Marlborough, Duke of 67
Marlowe, A. 88
Marowitz, Charles 206
Marriage is No Joke 109
Martin, Jean 147
Martin-Harvey, John 15, 29, 74, 96
Maugham, Somerset 24, 31, 143
Mauriac, François 92
Maurier, Daphne du 47, 221
May, Peter 168, 169
Me and My Girl 46
Measures Taken, The 139
Meeting Ends 208
Men Without Shadows 78
Mercer, David 210
Merchant of Venice, The 55
Merry Wives of Windsor, The 19
Michelangelo 28
Midsummer Night's Dream, A 62, 105, 205
Millar, Ronald 85
Miller, Arthur 77, 85, 106, 150, 151–2
Miller, Laurence 21, 24
Milne, A. A. 34
Milton, Ernest 52
Milton, John 28, 42
Miranda 73
Misanthrope, Le 79
Mister Roberts 86
Mommsen, Theodor 9
Monkhouse, Allan 21, 28, 29, 33
Monroe, Marilyn 149, 150
Montgomery, Bernard 57
Morison, Patricia 94
Morley, Robert 53
Morning Star, The 54, 221
Mother Courage 127–8, 130, 139, 155, 175
Much Ado About Nothing 98, 193
Mulberry Bush, The 140
Muller, Robert 194
Muni, Paul 86
Murder in the Cathedral 45, 76
Murry, John Middleton 40
Music at Night 38, 40

Napier, Alan 17
Napoleon, Bonaparte 95, 222
Narrow Road to the Deep North 212
Nasser, Colonel 157–8
National Theatre 81, 171, 181, 188, 190, 191–4, 211, 215

National Union of Students (NUS)
  Drama Festival 12, 137, 164, 165,
  186, 229
Naughton, Bill 196
Naughton, Charlie 51
Nervo, Jimmy 51
Newcastle Journal and North Mail 56
News Chronicle 61, 66
New Yorker 170, 194
Next of Kin 54
Next Time I'll Sing to You 185, 233
Nichols, Peter 201
Nightingale, Florence 212
Nightmare Abbey 98
Night Must Fall 22
Norman 197
No Sex Please – We're British 211
No Time for Comedy 51
Novello, Ivor 22, 93, 226
Now Barabbas ... 68–9, 73, 159
Number 10, Downing Street 85

Observer 8, 58, 87, 100, 106, 108,
  127, 139 142, 143, 155, 161, 181,
  194, 208
O'Casey, Sean 38
Oedipus Rex 29, 66, 67, 81
Oedipus Tyrannus 126
Off the Record 74
Oh! Calcutta! 195, 208
Oh, What a Lovely War! 177
Oklahoma! 73, 77, 85, 88, 101, 103, 224
Old Acquaintance 53
Old Ones, The 214
Oliver, Vic 47
Olivier, Laurence 20, 55, 61, 66–8,
  75, 80–1, 82–4, 87, 90, 92, 93, 97,
  100, 102, 105, 107, 109, 122–3,
  124–6, 127, 130, 131, 152, 161,
  162, 163, 173, 190, 191, 192, 193,
  194, 205, 209, 210, 219, 229
Once a Crook 51
O'Neill, Eugene 27, 90
Only Way, The 29, 74, 96, 219
On the Frontier 35
On the Rocks 25–6
Orton, Joe 183, 195
Osborne, John 24, 77, 135, 141, 142,
  143, 145, 146, 156, 158, 159, 161,
  162, 167, 168, 183, 185, 186–7,
  197, 198, 205, 209, 210, 211–12,
  224
Othello 70–1

O'Toole, Peter 191, 192
Our Town 137

Palach 206
Pal Joey 103
Paradise Lost 28
Paravents, Les 197
Partage de Midi 96–7, 202
Party, The 210
Pater, Walter 223
Patriot for Me, A 197, 198
Pearce, Edward 141
Peer Gynt 81
Phillips, Robin 208
Phillpotts, Eden 31
Phoenix Too Frequent, A 76
Pilgrim Players, The 76
Pilgrim's Progress, The 18
Ping-Pong, Le 114
Pinter, Harold 24, 54, 113, 159,
  165–9, 183, 185–6, 188, 193, 205,
  210, 212, 231
Pirandello, Luigi 13, 20, 22
Play 187
Plays and Players 19, 133
Play's the Thing, The 71
Plaza Suite 213
Point of Departure 226
Pope, Alexander 76
Porgy and Bess 103
Porter, Cole 93
Porter, Eric 191
Portman, Eric 79
Post-War British Theatre Criticism 104
Powell, Dilys 38, 55, 59
Powell, Enoch 204
Power and the Glory, The 140
Pravda, George 170
Present Laughter 52, 74, 79, 224
Priestley, J. B. 20, 35, 38, 40, 42,
  49–50, 54, 74, 141
Private Eye 179, 196–7
Private Life of Henry VIII, The 20
Private Lives 51, 221
Prométhée Enchaîné 105
Public Morality Council 87
Punch Without Judy 45
Pygmalion 18
Pyjama Tops 214

Quare Fellow, The 147–9, 152
Quartermaine, Leon 51
Quayle, Anthony 191, 215
Quéant, Gilles 153
Queen Mary 73–4

Rabelais, François 203
Radio Times 43
Raimbourg, Lucien 147
Rattigan, Terence 45, 54, 78, 79–80, 104, 170, 201, 210, 221, 225
Ravensdale, Baroness 87
Rawlings, Margaret 51
Rebecca 47
Recruiting Officer, The 193
Redgrave, Michael 45, 100, 102, 104, 131, 173, 215
Rees, Llewellyn 81
Reinhardt, Max 27
Relatively Speaking 185
Renaud, Madeleine 96–7
Répétition, La 91
Restoration of Arnold Middleton, The 201
Rhinoceros 173
Rice, Elmer 40, 45
Rice, Tim 214
Richard II 18, 55, 75, 92, 189
Richard III 66, 81, 82–3, 97, 102, 189
Richard of Bordeaux 97
Richards, Gillian 231
Richardson, Clare 15
Richardson, Ralph 21, 30, 31, 35, 37, 42, 75, 80–1, 90, 92, 93, 97, 99–100, 105, 107, 109, 152–3, 154–5, 164, 173, 182, 183–4, 190, 209, 211, 215, 219, 220
Richardson, Tony 163, 176
Ridley Phelps, Lancelot 16
Ring Round the Moon 90–1, 226
Riscoe, Arthur 40
Rivière, Jacques 154
Robeson, Paul 71
Robson, Flora 17, 31
Rodgers, Richard 77
Romanoff and Juliet 158
Romeo and Juliet 75
Room, The 165, 186
Rose, Arthur 46
Rosencrantz and Guildenstern are Dead 193
Royal Shakespeare Company 177, 185, 188, 189, 192, 193
Ruling Class, The 209
Runyan, Damon 103
Russell, Leonard 38, 59, 65, 222
Russell Taylor, John 162, 228

Saint-Denis, Michel 163
St Joan 27, 75, 193
St Joan of the Stockyards 175–6

St Paul 69
Salacrou, Armand 92, 203
Same Sky, The 98
Sarah Simple 34
Sargent, Malcolm 137
Sartre, Jean-Paul 77–8, 93, 110–11
Saturday Book 38, 41
Saunders, James 185, 233
Saved 198, 212, 213
Scarborough, Lord 152
Scent of Flowers, A 185
School for Scandal, The 55, 82
Science and Health, With Key to the Scriptures 15
Scofield, Paul 75, 173
Scott, Clement 102
Scott, Sir Walter 16
Secretary Bird, The 210
See You Inside 196
Sense of Detachment, A 211
Sense of Direction, A 186, 193
Separate Tables 80
September Tide 85
Serjeant Musgrave's Dance 181
Sexual Behaviour in the Human Female 149
Shaffer, Peter 169
Shakespeare, William 21, 23, 24, 27, 43, 70–1, 81, 82, 92, 95, 104, 127, 131, 153, 163, 164, 171, 189, 211, 212
Shaw, George Bernard 13, 19, 21, 22, 23, 24–6, 28, 30, 33, 35, 42, 43–4, 51, 64, 74, 75, 92–3, 101, 102, 131, 163, 167, 183, 220, 221
Sheffield Daily Telegraph 17, 56
Shellard, Dominic (DMS) 10
Shepherd's Pie 47
Sheppey 31
Sherek, Henry 96
Sheridan, Richard Brinsley 21
Sherriff, R. C. 102
Sherry, Gordon 56
Sherwood, Robert 32
Shinwell, Emmanuel 68
Shirer, William 38
Shooting Star 85
Shulman, Milton 115, 137, 142
Silverman, Sydney 148
Simon, Neil 213
Simpson, N. F. 186
Six Characters in Search of an Author 105
Six Thousand and One Nights 173
Skipper Next to God 63

Sleeping Prince, The 104
Sleep of Prisoners, A 93, 164
Smith, Alexander 105
Smith, Dodie 21, 24, 33, 46
Snodin, David 207
Soldiers 234
Sophocles 29
South Pacific 86, 94
So What About Love 226
Spanish Incident 73
Spectator 40, 66, 100, 193, 206
Spencer, Colin 198
Spewack, Sam 93
Sport of My Mad Mother, The 165
Spoto, Donald 125
Square, The 188
Squaring the Circle 52
Squire Puntila 175
Stalin, Josef 137, 215
Stand Up and Sing 124
Stanislavsky, Konstantin 138
Steinbeck, John 38
Stevens, Frank 135
Stoppard, Tom 193
Storey, David 201, 209
Storm, Lesley 26, 85
Strasberg, Lee 77, 138
Strauss, George 199
Streetcar Named Desire, A 86–9, 102, 136, 225
Strindberg, August 193
Study of Poetry, The 219
Sudermann, Hermann 73
Sunday Express 136
Sunday Graphic 57
Sunday Telegraph 193
Sunday Times, The 8, 40, 41, 42, 50, 53, 55, 56, 57–8, 60, 63, 64, 65, 70, 71, 73, 81, 82, 100, 108, 109, 123, 130, 136, 137, 142, 143, 164, 174, 182, 215
Suspense 50
Sutro, Edward 124, 223
Swinburne, Nora 51
Sydenham, Stanley 15
Sylvaine, Vernon

Tale of Two Cities, A 29
Taste of Honey, A 80, 201
Tatler 87, 104
Taylor, Nora 65
Tea and Sympathy 150
Tearle, Godfrey 71, 100
Tempest, Marie 46

Tempest, The 98
Templeton, W. P. 77
Ten Minute Alibi 22
Tennent Plays Ltd. 136
Tennent Productions Ltd. 88, 136
Tennyson, Alfred 73
Terson, Peter 201
That Uncertain Feeling 134
Theatre Criticism 183
Theatre Inside Out 206
Theatre Workshop 110, 137, 147–8, 187, 192
They Came to a City 54
Thieves' Carnival 226
Third Person 98
Thomson, Roy 57
Thorndike, Sybil 93, 105
Threepenny Opera, The 138–9
Three Sisters 55, 93
Thucydides, 66
Thunder Rock 45, 50, 51
Tiger at the Gates 110
Time Present 211
Times, The 87, 89, 107, 116, 120, 123, 183, 203
Times Literary Supplement 215
Timon of Athens 152–3, 154
Titus Andronicus 95, 127, 163
Tomorrow's Eden 63
Traveller Without Luggage 97
Travers, Ben 22
Trewin, J. C. 87
Troilus and Cressida 20
Trumpets and Drums 155
Turn of the Screw, The 169
Tutin, Dorothy 191
Twelfth Night 189
Twice Upon a Time 85
Tynan Kathleen 7, 58, 194
Tynan Kenneth 8, 22, 29, 80, 82, 90, 98, 104, 106, 107, 108, 109, 112, 114, 120–1, 127, 128, 130, 131, 137, 139, 143, 144, 145, 146, 154–5, 156, 157, 161, 162, 170, 171, 175, 177, 180, 181, 182, 183, 194–5, 202, 211, 225, 228, 232, 234

Uncle Vanya 98, 193
Under Plain Cover 187
Unicorn from the Stars, The 44
Up and Doing 47, 53
Ure, Mary 109
US 177–8, 189
Ustinov, Peter 158

254

Vanbrugh, John 221
Van Druten, John 53
Variation on a Theme 80, 170
Venus Observed 90
Versuche 3 139
Vicious Circle 110–11
Victoria, Queen 212
View from the Bridge, A 150
Volpone 100
Vortex, The 51, 98

Wain, John 134
Waiting for Godot 7, 108, 115–22, 123, 126, 127, 131, 137, 144, 146–7, 158, 160, 163, 165, 174, 180, 182, 188, 209, 211, 218
Waller, Louis 71
Walpole, Robert 149
Waltz of the Toreadors, The 158
Wanamaker, Sam 138
Wardle, Irving 183
Warner, Francis 208, 235
Watch on the Rhine 221
Waters of the Moon 93, 136
Way Back, The 85
Weapons of Happiness 215
Webb, Leonard 226
Webster, John 62
Weiss, Peter 189
Wellington, Duke of 95
Wells, John 179
Werth, Alexander 38
Wesker, Arnold 77, 169, 181, 187, 188, 213–14, 224, 236
Western Daily Press 164
West of Suez 211
West Side Story 170
What the Butler Saw 183
When We Are Married 51
While the Sun Shines 79, 221
White, Michael 226
White Carnation, The 102
White Devil, The 62–3, 165

White Horse Inn 20
White Sheep of the Family 98
Whiting, John 105, 113, 114, 115, 228
Wigram, Lord 37
Wilde, Oscar 90, 102
Wilder, Thornton 137
Williams, Emlyn 22, 45, 54, 221
Williams, Harcourt 20
Williams, Stephen 116
Williams, Tennessee 77, 86, 88, 107, 151, 152
Wilson, Angus 140
Wilson, Colin 116, 142
Wilson, Effingham 191
Wilson, Harold 174
Wings of the Dove, The 184
Winslow Boy, The 79
Winter's Tale, The 93
Wise Child 201
Witch, Ray 135
Witches Ride, The 73–4
Wolfit, Donald 13, 21, 102, 131, 173, 190, 191
Women Aren't Angels 48
Women of Twilight 98
Wood, Ronald 51
Workhouse Donkey, The 178
World of Kurt Weill in Song, The 175
World of Paul Slickey, The 186
Worm's Eye View 63
Worsley, T. C. 95, 103
Wyatt, Woodrow 135, 136

Yard of Sun, A 210
Years Between, The 221
Yeats, W. B. 21, 44, 75, 101
You Never Can Tell 183
Young and Lovely, The 54, 219
You, Of All People 45

Zeffirelli, Franco 193
Zigger-Zagger 201

FOR A COMPLETE LIST OF KEELE UNIVERSITY PRESS BOOKS
PLEASE WRITE TO
KEELE UNIVERSITY PRESS
KEELE UNIVERSITY, STAFFORDSHIRE ST5 5BG, ENGLAND